MW01484582

Jakob Otto Wyss

1846–1927

Postmaster in Klau

Letters from California

Edited by Pitt Wyss
In Collaboration with Paul Hugger

Translation from the German
by
H. Dwight Page

PICTON PRESS
ROCKLAND, MAINE

First Printing October 2007

This book is available from:

Picton Press
PO Box 1347
Rockland, ME 04841

Visa/MasterCard orders:
1-207-596-7766
FAX orders: 1-207-596-7767
e-mail: sales@pictonpress.com
Internet secure credit card orders: www.pictonpress.com

Manufactured in the United States of America
Printed on 60# acid-free paper

∞

Table of Contents

When Letters Become Images of an Era

Family records belong to the widely unused sources of our cultural history. In Switzerland they are legion, no one knows their exact number. The Zurich architect Pit Wyss is the spiritual treasurer of a scarcely fathomable store of knowledge pertaining to and preserving the written and iconographical legacy of his widely-branched family. At the same time he is a very dedicated keeper of the genealogical grail: For years, he has been unearthing at regular intervals real treasures which he renders to relatives and friends as handsome private publications upon New Year's. The Series was begun in 1972; in the year 2000 the twentieth book in the series was published. Six of these books are dedicated to Jakob Otto Wyss (1846–1927), specifically letters which the latter and his two wives wrote in the course of their lives. Wyss emigrated as a professional metal-worker to California, where he laboriously built a life for himself and his numerous descendants. It is a troubled life which reveals itself in these writings, a life full of enterprising projects, work, privation and the pioneer spirit, marked by difficult setbacks and reverses. Wyss and his two wives wrote intelligent letters, although they were not "studious" people and were scarcely familiar with literary models. These letters are testimonies of sharp minds and keen observation. In them is reflected everyday experience, first that of the apprentice in Zurich, then that of the trade journeyman on the professional road, in the Neuchâtel Jura, in Paris and in Manchester. Later they become documents from the pioneer era in the "Wild West," a few dozen miles away from Los Angeles, in the days when the mail did not yet run and when the only law and order was the law "of the fist." The letters do however also deal with the continuing development of a modern state and nation, as well as the period's social hierarchy and technical progress. They cover a span of time extending well beyond the First World War. From the letters can also be inferred the meteoric economic growth of this region of California. If at the beginning of the book the California countryside appears economically backward, in terms of technological development inferior to the Swiss hometown of Otelfingen, nonetheless progress comes sweeping over California with giant strides, so that social relationships, too, are soon transformed.

Our texts show first the world in which Otto spent his youth. It is Otelfingen in the canton of Zurich, a small community of farmers. Since as a child Otto naturally wrote no letters to his parents in his own home—with the exception of the customary New Years Greetings—in this first section of the book we find the recollections which his four-year older brother Oskar wrote down later on in life as a professor of medicine in Zurich, recollections about the secondary school time in Regensdorf and the country lane leading to the school, in other words, recollections about an environment with which Otto was familiar. In these pages appears a world of small farmers and tradesmen with its modest opportunities. Otto's own letters begin with his apprenticeship as a metal-worker in Zurich; the long work hours and the distance of 20 kilometers did not allow him to return home to Otelfingen every weekend, and so the letters took the place of oral communication with his family. Then follow the travels of the journeyman, who goes to Solothurn in search of work, then farther on to the Neuchâtel region of the Jura, in the successive employment of various masters of the metalworking trade. Otto describes the working conditions, the lodging and boarding conditions, and notes many observations such as the description of the school system in the Val de Travers. The times were not easy for young craftsmen. Often the masters ran out of work for them, or their salaries were not correctly paid, and so the journeymen had to travel farther on in search of better opportunities. For Otto the French capital Paris is the next destination. He walks a good deal of the way there. It is Paris at the end of the era of Napoleon III with its highly developed commercial and technological culture, but also with social and political tensions and a brutal police force. Otto speaks about all that in his writings, also about the technological achievements, which he admires in the museums and at international exhibitions. His thirst for knowledge is unquenchable. Despite his wonder, however, Otto remains a true Swiss citizen. He becomes a member of the singing group Harmonie, with which he travels to the Swiss national singing festival in Neuchâtel. Above all the letters which Otto directs to his younger siblings are full of details, because he wishes to give them some insight into his newfound way of life as well as a description of life in a foreign country. At the same time this particular group of letters deals with his relationship with his parents as well as the relationships with his brother and his sisters.

Then the Franco-Prussian War breaks out. Whereas most Swiss citizens in Paris clear out of town during the first weeks of hostilities—basically under the pressure of growing anti-German sentiment—Otto perseveres until the last minute, but then he does go back to Switzerland. Scarcely two years later, in March 1872, he is back in Paris again. He finds the city changed, everywhere gape the wounds left by the rebellion of the "Commune." His hopes are directed toward heavily industrialized England. On the first of September of the same year he travels through London to the textile metropolis of Manchester in north England. However, this city also offers no prospects for a solid professional future.

A year later Otto dares to make the leap over the Big Water; he next works on a farm near New York, then travels with an emigrant train farther west, always encouraged by the hope of still finding that land where metal-workers are in demand. At this time Otto's epistolary style becomes, despite increasing disillusionment, more and more vivid and stylistically richer. Thus at night on the long trip through the endless prairies the windows of the train appear to freeze "white and flowery," the mountains are "spherically rounded," and later, in California, the fields extend "as far as the waves of the still ocean permit" and on the western sea "dance the tall ships and steamers." "In the kitchen geese, chickens and young pigs are usually the masters," and the young cowherd knows "nothing about school or religion, only that on Fridays one is not supposed to eat any meat." Later on, on the occasion of a forest fire, he provides a quite epic description: "It was a grandiose sight, to see the unchained element, fanned by a breeze, marching forward, licking, flitting, crackling, across the plain, in order then to blaze up suddenly roaring and bursting into flames in trees and shrubbery along the hills" (November 2nd, 1879).

As one might suspect, California, too, turns out to be no El Dorado for the metal-worker Wyss. He must next eek out a living with various odd jobs, as a milker for 27 cows or as the planter of 400 sacks of potato seedlings. A position as a machine mechanic in a quicksilver mine brings about a decisive change of events. To be sure, the operation does shut down; however, Wyss remains as the grounds keeper, who has to supervise constructions and machines, with the right to use the adjacent land agriculturally.

So now Otto is a farmer. From his childhood he possesses a certain degree of experience in this area. His father—a country doctor—in addition ran a small farm in order to cover the needs of his family. And suddenly she is there: Ottilie, his childhood friend, arrived from Europe, to help Otto with the pioneer work in California. Concerning the "how" of the trip to America and the causes which triggered this transatlantic journey, we know nothing. We don't even learn her family name from the letters. Ottilie becomes an ideal wife for Otto. They have a happy marriage, despite frequent neediness and many privations. The first household furniture which Otto describes is therefore obviously simple and consists mainly of furniture made out of wooden crates. In the winter the couple freezes, because the wind blows unobstructed through the house. A girl, Mimi, is born, and thereupon a veritable idyll is created, so sweet and pleasant do the latter passages sound. Ottilie, who also herself now writes her own letters, notes, for example: "The dear little thing gives us right much joy, she is very glad to be with her dear father; whenever he comes up to her little bed, she stretches out her little arms, and whenever he takes her in his arms, she smiles and nestles against him, although sometimes she does pull a little on his beard" (January 24th, 1870). Only at this point begins that steady stream of letters back home to Switzerland which describe many small details of daily life in California, in a vivid and suggestive manner, for example, how humming-birds hum through the garden and how neighborhood children as young as 8–10 years old ride over the mountains like little Indian boys. Then there is the talk of dangerous individuals, of cattle thieves who roam the region. Above all others, the Mexicans have a reputation for notoriety.

The position of local postmaster falls vacant. Otto applies successfully for it. The position requires not only the dispatch of letters and packages but also the stage-coach. For that reason Otto decides to open a store at the post office.

Business improves slowly. But then there erupts a catastrophe. Of the four children, the three boys die within three days of diphtheria, the most dreaded child illness of the era. Only Mimi, the eldest, survives. The parents' grief is deep and disproves the theory of an indifferent attitude of earlier generations of parents toward the then widespread death of children. The little dead bodies are buried on a hill above the town, flowers and small trees are planted, and the gravesite becomes for Otto one of the main reasons for his decision to remain in Adelaida. Again and again in the text is expressed the pain over this loss: "Many hours a night we cannot sleep despite all our weariness, so we cry together [...] Often when I awake, for a few moments it seems to me as if it has been only a bad dream, that our dear boys have died, yet nonetheless the horrible reality is there once again," writes Ottilie on November 30th, 1885, and even a year later, on November 9th, 1886, because of these events, Otto "often doubts the existence of a benevolent providence." The couple is especially pained by the fact that the three children died shortly before the arrival of the traveling photographer, with the result that they left this world "faceless" without an identity for posterity. Such and similar passages underscore the significance of portrait photography in those days; it often offered the only possibility for correspondents to meet one another visually in life, in the form of the portrait. Another child, Alice, is born and brings some comfort to the distraught parents. But Ottilie herself begins to get sick, her health goes downhill, and she dies on September 9th, 1888.

Otto thereupon falls into a spiritual void. He takes to drink, his household falls apart. At that point brother Oskar in distant Switzerland intervenes. Through a newspaper ad he seeks in Zurich a governess for the motherless household in California, a certain Seline Streuli presents herself. She accepts the challenge, travels without any knowledge of English across the Atlantic and straight across the continent. The corresponding contract is signed—a simple piece of paper, a sheet like one out of a school notebook, an example of how trusting young people were in those days and on what flimsy paper certainties such decisive agreements rested. The young Swiss woman finds—according to her letters—in Adelaida an indescribable amount of neglect, dirtiness, a lack of the slightest comforts, debts. Any other woman would have succumbed, but not Seline. She energetically takes the upper hand, changes the childrens' style of education, struggles against uncleanliness and garbage and against Otto's drunkenness, she tries to pay off the debts and to make the house more liveable. Above all as a pioneer in the temperance movement she demands that the authorities shut down the tavern which Otto has leased to a stranger and which sometimes acts as a trap for his bad drinking habit. And since the neighbors in accordance with the moral code in this land of settlers require that the couple marry or that Seline move on—for concubinage is not tolerated—the young woman even declares herself ready to take this ultimate step. Thus it is that the two marry without the blessing of the father in Otelfingen, out of necessity. Seline and Otto represent no ideal couple; the marriage is not harmonious. There is often quarreling and animosity, although both do see the good qualities in each other. Nonetheless, Otto can become violent, and Seline has a propensity for stinginess. Throughout all the coming years the letters impart views into the couple's conjugal life, in an honest and frank, sometimes also bitter and desperate, manner. If we present them here to our readership, we do so not to resurrect persons long dead or because of a desire for cheap voyeurism, but rather so that the full human scope of these writings from the New World will become well known, and because only in this way will it be possible to participate in the outer and inner destiny of these human beings and to measure their true greatness. Something exemplary presents itself here; it becomes strangely apparent that even out of such unstable marital relationships, which today would likely soon lead to divorce, something new and positive can develop. For Seline and Otto also have their own children—five altogether—and these grow up to become enterprising and responsible citizens, who assimilate themselves into American society through divergent professional routes. Descendants still work the family farm in Adelaida.

The children grow up, marry, reproduce and give birth to offspring; the descendants grow numerous as in Biblical stories. Shortly before the First World War Otto makes known his wish to see the homeland once again. He goes back to Europe, visits with brother Oskar Otelfingen and the sister who lives there, Hanna. The photos show both men in the land of their youth, which has now become foreign to them. They themselves look totally out of place in the simple farming environment. For Otto there is no going back, or rather only going back to the States, to his family and the dead on the hillside. There will his grave be also. Seline, who outlives him by many years, describes his growing old with its infirmities. When she speaks in the letters about the drawn out dying of "dear father," this is not only an obligatory stylistic flourish but rather there stands behind the phrase a certain warmth, the recognition of much which in the long process of living together was also an expression of conjugal affection.

Thus, if read in sequence, these letters form an actual family saga, a dense document of the "life" of two generations of settlers in the New World. In addition, they clarify a piece of history in the western part of the United States and serve as authentic testimonies of not only what was passively experienced and endured by these early western pioneers, but also of the active human coformation of history in the smallest details.

Letters have a special significance for the research and representation of processes of emigration. Swiss emigration history is no exception. Differing from much later prepared reports concerning the emigrant's trip abroad and his reception and situation in his new homeland, letters serve as testimonies which develop out of the immediate situation, out of direct contact and confrontation with the new environment. Since the seminal work of Leo Schelbert, Swiss emigration history has become a richly developed field of academic research. Whereas Schelbert first explored Swiss emigration to America, especially to the United States,[1] since then further specialized directions of research have developed. I mention the studies on Swiss emigration to Russia, which were conducted under the direction of Carsten Goehrke at the University of Zurich, which have a specialized professional orientation; physicians, cheesemakers, ministers and military officers are the protagonists.[2] However, such research and representations invariably rely upon popular direct sources, especially upon the previously mentioned letters. This is not the place to explain the history of emigration research in detail. I would like only briefly to discuss the often criticized subjectivity of personal letters and the related problem of their worth as reliable historical sources. Schelbert deals with this question as follows: "In emigrant letters [...] are revealed [...] not so much reality itself, but rather the multifaceted magical power which newly received impressions exercise over human beings of different origin and different social status."[3] "Letters, therefore, despite their inherently contradictory nature [Schelbert means by this the different reactions to the same new environment], are faithful mirrors of newfound external circumstances and commonly held value judgments. And yet they offer even more. They describe not only the newly encountered realities but also the experiences of the new situations, which on the one hand was rooted in objective relationships, but on the other was also stamped by the individuality of each of the different human characters."[4] I concur. However, the special thing about our letters, in comparison with other published emigrant letters, lies in the fact that these letters deal not only with external realities and circumstances, but rather illuminate as well the intimate domain of the family's private home life and thereby reveal a piece of the spiritual landscape of mankind.

---

[1] Leo Schelbert: *Introduction to the History of Swiss Emigration in the Modern Era*. Zurich 1976. Leo Schelbert/Hedwig Rappolt: *Everything is Completely Different Here. Emigrants' Destinies in Letters from two Centuries*. Olten and Freiburg im Breisgau 1977.
[2] As representative examples let us mention: Gisela Tschudin: *Swiss Cheesemakers in the Empire of the Tsars*. Zurich 1990; Harry Schneider: *Swiss Theologians in the Empire of the Tsars (1700–1917)*. Zurich 1994; Rudolf Mumenthaler: *In the Scholars' Paradise. Swiss Scientists in the Empire of the Tsars (1725–1917)*. Zurich 1996.
[3] *Everything is Completely Different Here*. Loc.cit. 22.
[4] Ibid. p. 30.

In conclusion a few remarks about this edition: as always we have remained faithful to the linguistic form of the manuscripts; the corresponding lavish transcription was prepared by Pit Wyss. Only the punctuation was adjusted for modern understanding in order to facilitate the reading experience. It was also necessary to slightly abbreviate the selected letters. Above all, we have excised the customary greeting and courtesy forms, introductory and concluding texts, which appear regularly with certain variations—expressions of thanks for received letters, announcements of the sender's state of health, etc.–, in order to reserve more space for the, in our opinion, more essential information. Omissions were appropriately noted. In addition, we have added a "title" to many letters in the hope of stimulating the reader's interest. A small thematic index should help the user to locate recurrent topics.

Paul Hugger

A Forward

Human beings are part of a global family. Their character is stamped by this global community, by education, by the social environment. Naturally inherited talents form and influence the human being. These are usually scarcely comprehensible, like the influences of education. For the understanding of many facts and letters, which document a life, knowledge of the family and its ancestry is necessary.

The letters presented here document a troubled life. The most interesting come from America, whither Wyss emigrated in 1873. There are altogether 535 letters, of which 412 were written from the USA.

The authors of the letters are Jakob Otto Wyss, 1846–1927, the brother of my great grandfather, his first wife Ottilie Meyer, 1843–1888, and his second wife Seline Streuli, 1852–1935. The era which is included in the life of these three persons extends from the middle of the nineteenth century until 1935, an impressive era.

In 1847 began in Zurich the age of the railroad, in the houses flickered gas or petroleum light; later electricity, the telephone, the automobile, the radio and the airplane transformed daily life, and when Seline Wyss-Streuli died in 1935, America, despite its immense technological progress, found itself in the midst of a deep economic crisis, and in Europe Germany began to prepare an inferno, although already in 1866, 1870 and 1914 gruesome wars had shaken the world.

In conclusion, allow me to thank those who participated in the preparation of this book. Above all allow me to thank Professor Paul Hugger, who accepted these letters as part of his series of paperback books on folklore and who contributed immense editorial assistance to the project. I would also like to thank Professor Hans Bögli, President of the Swiss Society for Folklore, for his support, and not least of all, my wife Nelly for her great patience and sympathy for my publications "from the family archives."

Destiny is not only what was, is or will come to pass; destiny is also what one does.

Pit Wyss

Concerning the Biography of the Protagonist

Jakob Otto Wyss, known as Otto, was born on November 7th, 1846, on the Steinhof in Otelfingen, canton Zurich, and died on January 2nd, 1927 in Klau near Paso Robles, California, and was buried nearby in Templeton, near Adelaida, California.

The Steinhof in Otelfingen, second half of the nineteenth century.

Otto's father, grandfather, great-grandfather and great-great-grandfather were simple country doctors, and also part-time barbers and surgeons, who learned their trade through practical apprenticeship and later perfected it partly in the hospitals of foreign troops. His father, Johannes Wyss, known as Jean, 1813–1898,[5] married in 1839 Anne Schneebeli, 1817–1871, from the Wylhof near Affoltern on the Albis.[6] In 1834 Jean took over the practice of the prematurely deceased grandfather in Dietikon, moved in 1840 to his hometown of Affoltern am Albis, and in January, 1846, moved his young family to the

---

[5] Since 1972 Pit Wyss has published, in volumes that appear as private publications, materials from his family archives. Volumes 1, 2, 8, 9 and 10 are dedicated to Johannes Wyss.

[6] Anna Schneebeli is described in volumes 8 and 10.

Steinhof in Otelfingen, where besides his extensive practice, he ran a small farm.

The latter was operated by the mother, who had grown up as a farmer's daughter, and by a maid. In addition, the mother took care of the large household in the remote Steinhof as well as looked after the welfare of her seven children. The latter had to assist her with all manner of farm work at an early age, by watching the cattle, by gathering the potatoes and fruit, by gleaning and with the most diverse kinds of housework. His father planted and pruned the trees in the big orchard, but he was kept quite busy by his big medical practice, which extended from the Furttal as far as the Reusstal and required long marches on foot.

His father was a conventional, extraordinarily hard working man. Besides running his practice, he served in Affoltern as a judge for the community, in Otelfingen he was the cofounder of the secondary school and a trustee of the district school, in the military he served as a troop doctor, and later as an inspector in the barracks in Thun. He accomplished a lot, and therefore also required a great deal. He entrusted his thoughts more readily to his diary than to daily chats.

Jean became friends in Otelfingen with the minister Jakob Germann, a tall powerfully built man, who one day as a joke stuck the middle finger of his right hand into a gun-barrel, stretched the gun straight out in front of himself and thereby broke his finger. The doctor luckily happened to be on hand. Pastor Germann became on November 25th, 1846, Otto's godfather, and from him the latter acquired his second name. Luise Wäckerling-Stierlin, the wife of the befriended doctor in Regensdorf, was the godmother.

His grandmother, Barbara Wyss, to whom Otto wrote loving letters again and again, was a member of the Fankhauser family of Trubschachen in the Emmental. After Otto's grandfather had divorced his wife Friederika Stör, Jean's mother, Barbara, came at Lichtmess 1817 to the house to take care of the children. On August 7th, 1821, Otto's grandfather married the young woman, who was born on July 28th, 1795. This second marriage remained childless, and Barbara lived with the family until her death on February 28th, 1886.

Otto had six siblings, who maintained a cordial and brisk correspondence with one another: an elder brother, Johannes Oskar (1840–1918),[7] who likewise became a doctor, then an energetic elder sister Emma (1842–1918), who married her high school teacher Albert Schmid, Anna (1844-75), who died of consumption at a young age, Amalie (1849-65), who died of meningitis at the extremely young age of sixteen, Emilie Susanna (1853–1900), who ran a store in Otelfingen and who devotedly cared for her old father, and finally the youngest, Johanna, born in 1858, who likewise helped in the store and later became the organist in Otelfingen and Regensdorf and died in 1933.

---

[7] Johannes Oskar Wyss speaks in volumes 4, 9 and 10 (and here on pages 1–12).

Otto attended from 1853 until 1859 the "Daily School" in Otelfingen and from 1859 until 1861 the Secondary School in Regensdorf. There are few documents available concerning this school period, various drawings, a few notebooks and the copy of a forgotten letter from later years, in which he wrote down his recollections of his time in secondary school:

"In April 1859 father and I marched before 6 o'clock in the morning from home to Regensdorf to my admission exam for the secondary school. I was lodged in the Hirschen Inn, where Hans Meier, a classmate of the same age as myself, was also lodged. The exam went well and I was admitted.

Hans Meier showed me the stable full of 5 or 6 cows, and a horse, on which I was permitted to ride, when he led it to the trough to drink.

In the evening after dinner Otto's father sat down downstairs at the middle table, with the innkeeper Meier and instructor Grob to his right, and gamekeeper Stäubli and bailiff Bader and a couple of others to his left. There was a conversation, and I heard elementary school instructor Grob say, "Otto is supposed to have gotten a good grade in math." The innkeeper then told father he had also learned to figure numbers, then he stood up and said to father, "Doctor, here is a good test: let's see who of the two boys solves it first; if your son is first, I'll pay the tab for what all men here drink, and if my boy is first, you'll pay." Otto's father agreed.

The assignment was as follows: three men go to the inn and have a tab of 12 francs. The first says, "I pay half, that's six francs," the second says, "I pay a third, that's four francs," and the third says, "I pay a fourth, that's three francs." That adds up to thirteen francs. So they have thirteen francs instead of twelve. How much would each have to pay to add up to twelve francs?

We, Hans and I and Mrs. Meier, sat at the same table, with our backs against the oven wall. Mrs. Meier gave each of us a glass of wine, so that things would go better, and we took paper and pencil. Hans took a sip of wine; I drank mine only after I had solved my problem. I solved the problem and said: I have it! The innkeeper said, "let's wait a little and give Hans some more time."

In the meantime bailiff Bader and farmhand Urech had gone outside and more and more men came inside, until the other table was also full and the gauge bottle [marked bottles made of clear glass] were filled and had to be filled again. This was all new to me, and I also drank with the others. Then Hans explained, "I can't do it."

Then the book was brought out, and my solution was found to be correct. The glasses were raised to me in a toast, and the time passed quickly. My father stood up and said that it was already ten thirty, and he had still a long way to go; so good night, gentlemen.

Hans soon became sleepy, and we went to bed. Many people told me later, it had been a fun evening. But Mr. Meier was angry with me, and I heard him saying in a grumbling low tone, that this fun, by God, had cost him more than 25 francs.

I liked it at the Hirschen, because there there stayed all sorts of lodgers, many of whom had seen a good bit of the world and enjoyed talking about it. I made good progress in school. From time to time there was a wedding at the Hirschen with a dinner and afterwards music and dancing. Thus I learned to dance quickly, because usually there were more girls than boys there. In the winter I helped to split logs, because in the wash house the school principal Meier had a schnapps distillery; and if at first I did not like its taste, later I could "down one" as well as Hans. From time to time we helped to fire the furnace, when the principal could not do it anymore!

In high school we also had students from French-speaking Switzerland. I learned French seriously, which later proved to be useful to me. We often went swimming in the Katzensee, a student from French-speaking Switzerland was a good swimmer, and I learned a lot from him. Then came the last exam with Pastor Pfenninger as the visiting examining professor; I had to recite the "Runner." We, who had just finished the last exam, drank a couple of more bottles of wine and sang once again all our well known and beloved school songs: "Farewell, you beautiful time in high school."

Grades of Otto Wyss, secondary school.

Otto's earliest preserved letter

Excerpt from a letter to the godmother of the eleven year old boy.

Mrs. Dr. Wäckerling in Regensdorf

Otelfingen, January 11th, 1857

Dear Godmother,

I thank you deeply for the beautiful present. Once again, Godmother, you have surprised me with a great gift, which, especially because of the beautiful knife, has given me great joy. I am sorry that I can give you nothing more than my deepest thanks for it. I shall however do my best, through diligence and good behavior, to give you and my parents as much joy as possible.

Many good wishes and greetings to you and your entire family from my dear parents and your obedient and thankful godson
Otto Wyss

I

A Preamble
Oskar Wyss: Recollections of Secondary School

Concerning Otto's childhood in Otelfingen we know only a little; that is to be expected in a child, since in those days, except for brief small letters at New Year, he had scarcely any propensity for writing. The "correspondence" phase of his life first begins during his apprenticeship in the then still distant city of Zurich. On the other hand, his elder brother Johannes Oskar Wyss[8] has left us a very attractive and detailed description of this secondary school time in Regensdorf, which he wrote from the retrospective viewpoint of an adult. Naturally, this text has a different character than letters, which are composed based upon the writer's impression of momentary reality. Oskar's description is, however, in its own right rich in observations of the contemporary daily life in the Zurich Furttal valley and sensitive to the psyche of a young person, so that it has high documentary value. Above all, the description of the way to school shows just how rich in experiences and knowledge such walks could be

---

[8] Johannes Oskar Wyss, later only called Oskar, was born on August 17th, 1840 in Dietikon. He spent his youth mainly at the Steinhof in Otelfingen. In 1858 he completed the cantonal graduation exam and studied in the medical faculty at the University of Zurich from 1858 to 1862. In 1862 he traveled to Breslau, served there as an assistant doctor and was appointed as lecturer in 1867 at the university there. The government of Zurich elected him in 1869 as the director of the outpatients' department of the city's hospital and as a professor with the commission to deliver a course of lectures on children's diseases. On September 23rd, 1869 he married Carolina Kienast (1845–1905). In 1874 he was entrusted with the direction of the children's hospital, in which he was involved for 36 years. For 41 years he was a professor of the University of Zurich, during this period twice dean of the medical faculty, and from 1894 to 1896 the vice-chancellor of the university. Among other achievements, he was cofounder and member of the Swiss Commission on Tuberculosis, cofounder of the World Lung Sanatorium, member of the Board of Health of the canton of Zurich, member of the Zurich Academic Board of Public Works, member of the Public Health Department of the city of Zurich, member of the Commission on Hygiene of the Swiss Society for the Common Good, member of the Board of Administrators of the Swiss Serum Institute in Bern, honorary member of the Society of Physicians of the canton of Zurich, honorary member of the Zurich Society for Scientific Helath Care, etc. In addition, he managed a private practice. He died after a rich life on May 1st, 1918 in Wollishofen-Zurich. Oscar Wyss-Kienast wrote a great deal. For that reason numerous letters, notes and diaries written by him are available. Among these is a little notebook with his recollections of his Regensdorf secondary school years which he recorded when in his fifties.

2 A Preamble

for young people in those days. We have condensed the text into extracts, in the hope that it will essentially agree with the circumstances of the life of Otto, who likewise, four years later, attended the same secondary school in Regensdorf.

I must also recall the road to school, or, as it is also often called, the "school boy's road";[9] for in the life of the schoolboy, it is an important part of that life, if I might be allowed to so express myself. It is not insignificant that a child experiences on the way to school what can under certain circumstances have important consequences for his entire life, both in a good and in a bad sense. Occurring as it does at an early stage in life, it is a recurring activity in which the child is left to himself, where the child encounters situations of the most divine kind, in which the child acts as an independent being, observes and can see either good or bad, and where it, often completely uninfluenced, must decide whether it will do one thing or another, in order to satisfy its urges of curiosity, pleasure or duty. Certainly in these cases the words, the admonitions of the mother play a great role, so that at the moment of decision the child remembers the words of its mother, grandmother or father, and the incessant admonition finally becomes the will of the child.

In early 1852, in the first days of May, as a beginning secondary school student with a leather rucksack on my back, I walked to Regensdorf.[10] The hour of this daily walk was early, at 5:45 AM, in order to get to school on time. I entered the school when it was still held in the house of Colonel Meier,[11] in an excessively small ground floor room with a low ceiling which was poorly lighted from one side and which faced the street. [...] What I found pleasant here from the beginning was the feeling of equality with the other students. There I was no longer a small farmer [a newcomer, not a real citizen of the town], no one asked whether I was a citizen of Otelfingen or not.

At first we were seated according to the beginning letters of our last names, and so I was the last one, seated on the bench at the very front of the room to the left of the outermost bench. But with time began the struggle for seats, because those who did their assignments the best, those who upon examination by the teacher knew what the others did not know, were allowed to sit "above" the latter in a seat of "superiority"; the "highest" seat in the First Class was on the third bench, to the right of the outermost seat. And for this goal, when I had once achieved it, I strove again and again, once I had lost it to a competitor.

---

[9] Compare Familienheft no. 4: The Walk to Regensdorf or Recollections from my Secondary School Years by Johannes Oskar Wyss, 1840–1918.
[10] Regensdorf, in the upper Furttal valley (Zurich lowland), counted at that time about 450 inhabitants. Together with the appertaining hamlets of Adlikon, Watt, Altburg and Oberdorf, there were about 1200 persons who were for the most part active in agriculture.
[11] The house of "Colonel Meier" was in 1973 the run down, large, striking inn "Zur alten Post", a well proportioned baroque structure dating from the 18th century. The "Hirschen," the house "Zum alten Vogt" and the school house dedicated in 1852 are still standing.

And that also invariably occurred every time we did mental arithmetic. If I was normally at the top of the class at the beginning of a lesson on mental arithmetic, I was often at the very bottom by the end of the period. I had never learned it correctly; our good teacher Schlatter in Otelfingen had taught us well the 2 x 2 and slate-board math, but had not been successful in teaching us the complicated mental arithmetic and the related rules of wisdom and lists. As far as slate-baord math was concerned, I had a pretty good grasp of it, as in all the other subjects as well, so I was able to master most academic subjects. Only with calligraphy did I encounter any serious difficulty, and in reference to my sketching, teacher Steffen pointed out to me one day: I was painting and not sketching, so I would have to start over and do it right this time; while my classmates were doing "beautiful" sketches, I had to sketch an axe and other such simple objects designed for beginners. Nonetheless, with time I mastered the latter subjects as well.

The pedagogical methodology of Mr. Steffen was, to be sure, quite different from that in the elementary school. Each student had the feeling that everything was done with body and soul, with joy and desire, and that one's abilities were pushed to the limit; one had the feeling—not that everything had to be done—but rather that both teacher and student liked doing everything. It was an enjoyable, yet serious, mental struggle for perfection. Each of us wanted to be worthy of the love of our teacher, and we all loved him as much as possible. Not by threats or punishments, but rather by inspiring our sense of ambition, by friendly admonitions and encouragement did Mr. Steffen try to animate and to encourage the sluggish slower students. And those who performed poorly were naturally also there. I can still visualize Mr. Steffen,[12] during class when everyone was busy, as he would go back and forth giving directions: travaillez, messieurs, travaillez, or he would say: Oh, you twisted brains, and so on and so forth.

The school was attended almost exclusively by boys and only a few girls; perhaps a ratio of 34 to 6. But the classes were segregated into boys and girls.

Wyss discusses individual schoolmates with whom he competed academically, and praises in retrospect their abilities.

From almost all the communities from which children attended secondary school Affoltern, Watt, Oberdorf, Adlikon, Buchs, Dällikon—the students had to travel from home to Regensdorf in the mornings, and in the afternoons after school was over they had to walk back home. At noon most remained in the school lunchroom and devoured the bread, meat or cheese with wine which they had brought from home. Only a handful ate their lunch at Colonel Meier's or at the Hirschen Inn. The Otelfinger students remained—and I was among

---

[12] Steffen, born in 1821 in Seebach, was elected on December 30th, 1849 by the Regensdorf School Board as the Secondary School Teacher. He died in 1871 in Regensdorf.

these of course—throughout the week in Regensdorf and went home on Saturday afternoon. So every Saturday after lunch I used to travel, sometimes with, sometimes without a classmate, and with my rucksack on my back, from Regensdorf, through Dällikon and Dänikon back home. Occasionally we would make our way from Regensdorf through Riet to Buchs or through Dällikon and Riet—in other words, a route different from the usual one. To be sure, that always had the disadvantage that I got back to Otelfingen at a later hour, and nonetheless I was glad to be back home, where my dear mother and grandmother and brothers and sisters offered me a cordial welcome.

On Saturday evenings or on Sundays in the early morning hours the chores had to be done, on Sundays I had to go to singing class at noon, at 1:30 to Sunday school until 3, and then I was free, provided that I had done my chores. Then I would often help father in the apothecary, or I would search in the house and the barnyard for plants, would look after my tree nursery, and sometimes I would accompany my father on his visits—and all too fast did this beautiful holiday fly by. Only on rare occasions did it occur that I went back to Regenstorf on Sunday evening; sometimes in the middle of winter, with bad roads and snow, it was necessary to do this, because in these cases on Monday morning the path would be too icy and slippery. Otherwise, however, the time of my departure was Monday morning.

Then my dear blessed mother would wake me a little before 5 AM, would make my coffee for me, as well as a piece of buttered bread or French Toast, then I would go to my father, who was sleeping in the apothecary on his hard sofa, would bid him farewell and would depart in a good mood out into the fresh morning air. And in the summer it really was a splendid walk, when the weather was beautiful. First came the splendid green meadows of the Bühl, in those days much wider and bigger than now, since the railroad has truncated the gorgeous meadow; then over the hill, between cornfields, in which would resound the sad quail song "Fear God, fear God" and from which from time to time the lark, chirping its splendid song, would soar heavenward. Then the road dropped, just one more look back: Adieu, dear Steinhof, and with one or more tears in my eyes I would go by the sandpit—notable with its big red field stones and the plants which grew in it: in the summer snapdragon, rose-bay; in the spring March flowers (Tussilago farfara)—on to the Aabach Bridge. Right under the sandpit the footpath leading from the village meets the road, through which the students coming from the village had to walk, if we were to go to school together. If from the hill I saw no one coming from the village, I would keep going and it was useless for any stragglers to try to catch up with me. The Aabach Bridge was in those days much more impressive than nowadays; it was a vaulted arched bridge, on top of which one stood much higher over the water than today over the flat, modern stone slab bridge. The path toward Dänikon led once more through grain fields, whose billowing waves I enjoyed watching so much, as the many stalks of corn spread so gracefully into a billowing mass of steadily flowing waves, never reposing nor resting if there were sufficient wind. The way through Dänikon was the old lower street, which actually only skirts the village; and since in my day no student from this village ever attended secondary school, I met few people I knew here, despite the heavy pedestrian traffic on the path. There were also no dogs there, and I liked that. Beyond Dänikon the road led down a slippery slope past hedges: here were to be found once again a few plants which gave me some pleasure from time to time, when they bloomed: wood-sorrel, orchids, fat-leaves, butter cups (Caltha) in luxuriant bloom, and so forth.

At the top of the hillock the road curved toward the mountains, and one reached two isolated houses, which were still within the town limits of Dällikon. These houses were important for the fact that they marked the half way point on the road to Regensdorf. Moreover, in one of these houses there were supposed to be ghosts; a certain little window was always open: I always paid close attention to whether I ever saw anything weird in this region, but I cannot truthfully say that I ever had the pleasure of meeting a ghost; everything there was just like everywhere else, nothing out of the ordinary. Then the road bends again northward toward the valley, goes uphill a bit, and then one reached the Dällikon field, a beautiful grainfield of a flat character—to the right for some distance blending into the alpine meadows or skirting the forest, to the left sloping downward toward the Riet and toward the middle of the valley—which allowed the eye to sweep uninterrupted as far as Buchs and down the valley toward Otelfingen. Continuing the walk, one came next upon a shabby little house of Dällikon: sect members live in it, students used to whisper to one another with a heavy look, and soon the village was reached. Here the road led by the school house, as it still does today, then a beautiful new structure, then by the church, an old castellated structure with a low tower and a modest appearance. A few more houses, finally the lonely vom Bopp inn, were passed, and then you went over the field to Regensdorf. Although I had to go so many times through Dällikon and although along the way there were five or six houses where classmates from my classes resided, it nonetheless never occurred that we walked to school in corpore. I always passed by the village much earlier than my classmates residing there left home.

After a half hour walk I or we entered Regensdorf, and as a rule I first went "home" and only then to school, after I had picked up what I needed for school and had set aside what I did not need for the day. The house in which I lived lay "on the way to school"; at least with only a small detour. The lower half of the route to school was at any rate the more interesting for me; the upper half offered less for me. Only the Regensdorf brook, which below Regensdorf skirted the street for a stretch, had more interest for me, because on its banks first this and then that water plant bloomed. The last stretch of the walk to my "home" in town led me through the orchard, by a hedge. To be sure, this walk was quite different in the rain or in winter, when everything was covered with snow, when because of the snowfall the entire path had been lost during the night, when I had to work my way through the high wind driven snow drifts;

when I had to pay close attention to the pine trees planted along the walk and overhanging the snow covered path, in order not to miss the right direction, or when thick fog was there, when night and fog covered the region. At such times it might have happened a couple of times that my dear mother gave me a little lantern, which of course my father did not approve of, because one could find one's way much better in the dark; or that I, when I entered Regensdorf and found my boarding house keeper by his morning coffee, before I went to school, drank another cup of coffee with him. In general these walks to school always went quite well, and in the second and especially in the third year I had company more often.

In Regensdorf I stayed with "cousin Konrad," i.e., Fankhauser.[13] The school boys from Otelfingen lived and ate with wealthy farming families. The school girls from Otelfingen stayed with the Schmatzens, a rich family of farmers in the back street at the lower end of the smithy. What it cost to keep me up, I have no idea. My sister Emma lived for only a quite short time at the same place, later however she, like sister Anna and brother Otto, lived with the Hirschen innkeeper Meier.

When I came to Regensdorf, the Fankhauser family consisted of Conrad himself and his two daughters Barbara and Anna; Hans was in an apprenticeship in Pfäffikon. Conrad was a sickly looking old man who walked bent over. He no longer worked at his profession, had two goats and up until I came, a breeding ram, for which he provided fodder and which he cared for. In addition he was the mole catcher of the community, as such made his own traps, set them and then went back to check on them, in order to receive his salary from the farmers and to receive his schnaps. In any event, he loved the latter a great deal, however not to excess; at least I could not accuse him of anything improper in this regard, except that perhaps he once came home tipsy. He liked to take snuff, and his dose of tobacco played a great role in his life. He was thrifty, patient, complained every now and then about how this or that stingy farmer had treated him unfairly, how here and there hunters in the autumn would set off his traps out of mischievousness, would steal his twine and wire, whereby my conscience bothered me, because I once, thoughtlessly following the example of other boys, had perpetrated such misdeeds and thereby thought I had actually done a good deed, because my father had once told me that the mole was a useful animal and it was unjust that the farmers sought to exterminate it; an opinion which cousin Conard obviously did not share, but rather he pointed out the devastation caused by pushing up the piles of earth in the meadow covered with growing grass and pointed out that in fact not only was grass growth partly destroyed by covering with such earth but also mowing was made impossible or at least difficult. Conrad was despite his poverty a quite honest man who certainly would have been incapable of

---

[13] The Fankhausers were related to Otto's "Grandmother" Barbara Fankhauser, the second wife of his grandfather.

embezzling the least amount of money from anyone. He was also moral; he never cursed: in sum, I liked the old man a lot, and he was kind and friendly toward me. He showed true and warm respect for the memory of his dead wife, and he would often begin to cry whenever he spoke of her or his former home, only about 10 minutes away from where he lived. Cousin Conrad died in Zurich when he was in his seventies. He was living at the time with one of his daughters and suffered first from psychological disturbances, then from paralysis: I diagnosed him with a brain tumor. I accompanied him to his final resting place in St. Jakob.

Wyss next presents the three Conrad children, the youngest daughter of these being a year older than he.

My cousin Conrad rented a room with a farmer named Stüssi; he was "at home" there, as they say. In the house he had a little parlor, a kitchen, a chamber and two bedrooms. However, he did not live alone in the house, but also with the sister-in-law of the master of the house with her child Anna Stüssi. Mrs. Stüssi was an already aging woman without any prominent or striking qualities. She liked to gripe about Conrad's children; also special caution was necessary when dealing with her, because upon finding things not belonging to her she was not always in the best mood, but apart from these weaknesses and upon consideration of these weaknesses and through a corresponding prophylaxis, it was actually quite easy to get along with her. She had an elder daughter, who shortly before my arrival in Regenstorf had married a butcher Schmid in Oetwil. The same man was likewise our butcher in Otelfingen, since he had a butcher shop in both Würenlos and in Otelfingen, i.e. he would come every Saturday evening and would sell his meats in the "Metzg," a rented local butcher shop. In those days one had to buy beef on Saturdays for the Sunday midday meal as well as for a second time on Tuesdays, and one had to store it oneself. On the other days there was no meat; eventually we did get pork. [...]

If the room in which we ate, in which I had to do all my homework and learn all my words by heart, was therefore inhabited by quite a few people, I must nonetheless say that as a rule I was able to take care of my necessities in the needed peace and quiet. For during the time from 4 until 7, in which I had mainly to write and to learn, I was alone with Conrad at the upper end of the table; at the lower end, on the other hand, sat Mrs. Stüssi with her Nanni. Although seated at the same table, both households were separated; each had its own light, the old smoking wick oil lamp—almost identical to those ancient lamps excavated in Pompeii, however not made of cast iron but rather of tin plate—each had its own self cooked meal, etc. I had my seat behind the table at the corner of the window; the light fell from the right side of the room, but in floods, for that entire wall was occupied by a row of windows, and along this wall there was a long wall bench, just like a similar one along the windowless inner wall, on which I sat. Only when all 3 seamstresses were there and were sewing and when it was winter, did I lack not only for peace and quiet but also for light, and under those trying circumstances I did have difficulty writing my compositions, solving my math problems or doing my translations.

The board—food—at Conrad's table was very simple. In the mornings the big three legged—at the bottom wide, at the top narrow—coffee urn served as the main piece of furniture dispensing food, and the fact that for the preparation of this coffee the bag itself and chicory were the principally used ingredients, is still very clear in my memory. Of course, I drank milk, because I was so accustomed to it from home, more abundantly than the others. There was not always bread to go with the coffee; there were however frequently roasted potatoes and, if they had become rare, also corn, cooked with water to make a broth, shaped into dumplings and then sauteed with lard. At midday there was soup, very seldom meat—in the spring as a rule goat meat as a delicacy and vegetables and daily potatoes or corn. In the evening around 6 or 6:30 one drank coffee again like in the mornings; at 4, home from school, we received a piece of bread.

Nevertheless, if I even today still think that the food in those days was insufficient for me, at the time I did not have this feeling at all; I was satisfied with it, and if at home in Otelfingen we had more to eat each day, at 4 coffee and nights at 7 soup, the thought never occurred to me that it might be otherwise. In Otelfingen we also had meat only twice a week; therefore I did not miss it. To be sure, my dear beloved mother must have felt this lack, for she often gave me meat to carry back to school, when I walked to Regensdorf on Monday mornings. To drink there was sweet wine in the autumn—earlier than at the Steinhof, where that was seldom served--; I did not partake of wine, and if Conrad also occasionally drank his schnaps to celebrate, that always happened with a spirit of quite festive dignity, and only he alone partook of it, and he had only a tiny thimble sized glass full, so that I neither had the impression that it could do any harm nor that it was improper. And besides, except for him, no one in the family allowed himself this little "pleasure."

The living quarters at Conrad's were cramped. The house was a long farmhouse; it actually consisted of 2 houses built together and their adjoining barns. It also had 3 compartments, for in the houses there were 4 living rooms, which all looked out on the village street and the brook and the adjacent garden. Conrad's living room door opened out onto a hallway; directly across from it was the doorway leading into the living room of the master of the house Mr. Stüssi. Behind both living rooms were the two kitchens, separated from the living quarters by a room, because there was no separation between the hallway and the kitchens. The kitchen received light only from the hallway, which farther back was bounded by walls; to the left one reached from the back part of the hallway via a doorway a room, in which Conrad had a joiner's bench and his carpentry tools; in addition, a lot of lumber; directly across from this was another room, a chamber, in which stood a weaver's loom and where during the winter and also at other times Stüssi wove linen and ticking in order to make use of the spare time which farming left him. The construction of this loom, as well as the manner of its operation, was of great interest to me; the man who was working constantly with both arms and legs, seemed quite interesting, as did the movements in various directions, which followed one another either simultaneously or in rapid succession; the raising, lowering and crossing of the thread of the warp; the striking of the beam weighted down with stones; the back and forth flying motion of the shuttle; and the result, the woven cloth, which was rolled up on the weaver's beam, I saw with delight.—The latrines were located behind the house in small buildings, with the pig sties under the same roof; for each apartment there was a special small building, although Conrad never kept pigs. In the adjacent house constructed in the direction of the mountains from Conrad's living room, there was a single kitchen for both apartments, and there was only one entrance door into that kitchen, so that one came from outside directly into the common kitchen and from there one reached the individual private living rooms of the two families.

Via a wooden staircase one went from the lower hall up to the bedroom, which was located directly over the living room. It was a room with a high ceiling with an aged grayish appearance. It was spacious, adorned with fewer windows than the living room, and during the daytime it was rather dark, because the roof projected far out over it. In this room there were three beds; a large four-poster bed, however without curtains, near the window, in which Conrad and I slept. It was so large that one could in fact sleep well, without one sleeper disturbing the other, and when Hans Fankhauser came to visit, sometimes we all three slept together in this bed, without bothering one another.—In the other half of the room across from the window stood the second big bed, which Conrad's daughters used, while the third bed, against the lower wall of the room, was used by sister Emma when she lived at Conrad's. For me personally such living together presented no problem; I usually went to bed first or with Conrad; and I was already fast asleep when the others came up, and vice versa in the morning.

After school, due to the regular absence of Conrad and his daughters, I was understandably left much to my own devices. To be sure, my homework did take up much of my time; and when in the late evenings an hour was left free, I sometimes went to a classmate's house, for example, to see a fellow Otelfinger at "old Vogt's," to the von Boppelsen house; more rarely I went to see "Regensdorfer" classmates. But there was really no one to whom I became attached, with whom I became close friends, because we had something in common. In my class there was not a single person to whom I became attached. And so in Regenstorf, as earlier in Otelfingen, I came in remarkably little contact with playmates, but rather went my own way. As a result I liked to go back home to Otelfingen, even in the middle of the week. On Wednesday afternoons there was no school, and when I was able to finish my homework early enough or when the weather was not too bad, I left for Otelfingen at 3 or

4 o'clock, often even later; not thinking about the fact that, as a result of my visit, my mother would have to get up early again the following morning. As a result of these Wednesday visits back home, I suffered terribly from homesickness; and this feeling of homesickness would especially overwhelm me just as I had finished my homework, when I could have been out playing games with the other boys. But I lacked suitable companionship, and when, overwhelmed by my homesickness, I could allow myself an opportunity to go for a walk in the country, I went into the orchards up to the hedge and the little forest of linden trees—in order to gaze down at Otelfingen in the valley below. In the winter semesters and at final exam times, Wednesday and Saturday afternoons of course had to be spent until 4 or 5 o'clock at school behind the drawing-board working on our sketches; but despite the longer and longer absence from Otelfingen, my homesickness never left me completely. [...]

When I had my homework done, then I would curl up in a chair behind a library book. The secondary school had a reading library, in which the children's books of Ninita and Körbert could be read. Every Saturday at noon these books were exchanged, and I spent all my free time reading them. And by what light! I still remember quite well how often I would open the window on a summer evening, and would lay the book on the windowsill in front of me, in order to be able to read at that time of night after the ringing of the curfew bells. I seldom went for walks in the country during my spare time, most generally when I had a headache; then it was impossible for me to read; on those occasions I would go through the orchards behind the house as far as their border with the open farmland, which was marked by a thick hawthorn hedge. There I would sometimes cool my throbbing head with wet leaves, I would also search for rare plants or I would follow the path through the grape vines up to the little forest of lindens, a few splendid old trees in a green meadow above the vineyards, near the millpond, a splendid scenic overlook with a friendly appearance.

And on the Katzensee there were the big mussel shells, the peat production, the cranberries in bloom and other plants which did not grow in the vicinity of Otelfingen and which were therefore hard to find. At those times I was always struck by the peculiarities of the landscape, as though one found oneself on a broad plain, with no mountains worth mentioning anywhere to be seen, totally different from Regensdorf or Otelfingen.

In Regensdorf I was further unfamiliar with the Zelg, the big, completely flat farmfield between the valley and the small woods toward Altenburg. I had never seen in Otelfingen such a "boring" monotonous field, almost completely surrounded by additional farmland. And the strict observance of the old provision that all owners of farmland in the Zelg had to grow one year rye, the second year corn and the third year potatoes, had never in Otelfingen struck me so much as here.[14]

---

[14] The old three field economy which had been preserved here—without a fallow period.

And then, if we took a different route home through Adlikon and Buchs, in Adlikon we got the chance to see the new special constructions, the fountains. They were all stone line wells with an approximately two-feet high surrounding wall. The orifice for water was always open. Beside the fountain stood a bucket lifter, at the top a forked tree trunk, in whose fork hung, fastened by a nail, a long pole, which bore a weight on the farther end away from the fountain, on the thin upper end a perpendicular pole or a rope to whose lower end a bucket was fastened. By pushing upward quickly the heavy end of the balancing pole one could lower the bucket down into the fountain, and by means of the attached weight, the water filled bucket was then raised. In those days the people in Adlikon still had to get their water in this manner. These wells have long since vanished[15] and spring water now supplies the village. Watt, another hamlet appertaining to Regensdorf, is supposed to have had in earlier times such fountains; and back in the 1840's there were always outbreaks of typhus there. At the instigation of Dr. Wäckerling, the community had built an aqueduct from pretty far away, i.e. from the heights above the Katzensee, where the next good spring was located. For those times, this costly project proved to be a splendid and wise investment; the typhus disappeared. Mr. Steffen was constantly telling us of this proud achievement and also told us that Dr. Wäckerling had been a great benefactor for this small and poor community. [...]

Wyss now tells us of his impressions of his visit to the market in Weiningen and describes the dedication ceremony for the new school house in Regensdorf in 1852.

Our big first-year class had already by my second year significantly diminished; even more so by the third year. We had very few boys left. What still pleases me today was the strict order which Mr. Steffen required from his students on the way to school. How often did he repeat to the students from other villages that they should conduct themselves in a decent, orderly and friendly manner on the way to school. At every opportunity he checked to see whether the students were greeting people properly and whether they were "tipping their caps" upon greeting other walkers; whether they had damaged anything, and woe unto the student or students who broke these sacred commandments! It was Mr. Steffen's policy to make all secondary school students who took the same route to school responsible for monitoring any misdeed or naughtiness perpetrated by any individual; and thus he awakened unconsciously in us the feeling of solidarity. If we were not willing to tell on those who had committed an offence, then all "Dälliker" or "Watter" or whoever was involved or even the entire class had to expiate "the crime," had

---

[15] They are still to be found in remote Alpine meadows of the Vaud Jura range.

to stay after school on Saturday afternoon or do "punishment" chores or other such unpleasant things.

Mr. Steffen liked to discuss in class any aspects of nature which individuals had observed during their walks to school. Once he discussed peat cutting, the theory of the re-growth of the cut peat. Once someone brought the skeleton head of a huge pike which had been caught in the Katzensee; thereupon Mr. Steffen discussed the question of the origin of very large fish in our lakes, whether these could be dangerous to people, etc. One could easily place one's fist in the mouth of that pike. He also once discussed "snakes," adders, in this manner. On another occasion a student reported that on the Katzensee a tortoise had been found, and thereupon Mr. Steffen vividly discussed the question of whence this sea creature had come; whether it was a stray pet, was lost, or perhaps such a family had lived in the swamp for many years.

Once Mr. Steffen—in the summer of 1854—went on a long hike over the Gotthard Pass down into the canton of Ticino as far as the lake there. How much, how vividly did he report to us about this trip! It was a real pleasure to listen to him describing so beautifully the Reuss and its wild whirlpools in the Schöllenen, the Gotthard, the Devil's Bridge and the Urnerloch, while he recited to us Schiller's classical descriptions. And with what passion did he describe to us the Val Tremola, the Livinental valley, connecting intimately history and natural history with the region's geography; he further recollected the splendid lakes, the chestnut trees, the customary Ticinese care of the vineyards and how that differed from such activities in the canton of Zurich; I still remember even today with joy and pleasure those splendid classes. [...]

II

Otto's Youth and Years as an Apprentice,
Years Spent Traveling in Switzerland

Otto Wyss's selection of a career was not simple, and for further academic training, for example at the Polytechnical Institute of Zurich, the boy was still too young. He wanted to become a machine mechanic and learn to work with fire and iron.

His father placed the young boy in an apprenticeship with the master metal worker Jakob Kunz in Zurich, in conformity with an apprentice contract which ran from October 28th, 1861 until October 28th, 1864. This contract required the master "to teach the boy every aspect of the profession of metal worker in a professional and thorough manner and to do everything possible in order to make a skillful craftsman out of the boy," so that after the period of apprenticeship had expired, the boy's ability to make a living would be assured. Master Kunz also promised to provide the boy with paternal guidance, not to mistreat him, and to supervise his moral conduct. The daily work schedule lasted from 5 in the morning until 7 at night, "can however in an emergency be lengthened according to the discretion of the master and necessity." The father promised to pay an apprentice fee of 300 franks and to support the master in his efforts.

That an apprentice be trained to become a skillful professional, was an essential prerequisite for a future financially certain career. Back then there did not exist the modern style social safety net, with social security and disability benefits. If there were an emergency need for financial assistance, the family of the needy individual provided it, assuming that one met its demands and sufficient funds were available for such charity. In those days, outside the family, the rule was: the bird catches its own food or dies. Otto's later life is clear testimony to this fact.

Otto's grandmother, mother and sisters guaranteed the family bond in the sense of constant epistolary contact. People wrote to one another on family occasions, especially on the name days. This was the most important personal holiday; at least in Otto's family, this tradition was maintained well into the twentieth century. The actual birthday was hardly ever celebrated and came into fashion as a family holiday only much later. Births at home, defective registry of citizenship and the failure to make a notation in the parish register upon baptism of an infant (as a rule on the Sunday after birth) caused uncertainty concerning the actual date of birth; hence the preference for the "name" day.

After Otto had moved to Zurich and thus found himself away from home, he maintained his connection with his family principally through writing. Many short letters accompany the little trunk with the wash, which is kept in order by his mother and sisters. Now Otto can apply the skills of letter writing which he has learned in school and at home and has practiced in composition notebooks. When he is not in Otelfingen over the weekend, he gives the little trunk to the courier, who takes it back home for him.

The shipment of merchandise was, for a long time after the introduction of the national post office and postal stamps, still partly taken care of by official couriers. The lake communities had courier ships, the country communities had their regular couriers, earlier with the back rack, then later with the rack-wagons which were protected by rounded canvas roofs. The couriers placed their wagons in the courtyard of the cathedral or other squares within the city, where it then looked like an emigrant or military camp. They fed and watered their unharnessed horses in a nearby stable and distributed and collected the various items of merchandise. For city boys the courier system represented a small source of income, because they could personally deliver the crates, trunks, wash baskets and packages to the various addresses. These couriers had their permanent schedules and locations, which were published yearly in the Zurich Calendar of David Bürkli. At the time of Otto's apprenticeship with master metal worker Kunz in the Niederdorf, the Otelfinger courier made his stop every Friday at shipmaster Körner's.

At the same time Otto's elder brother Oskar was studying medicine in Zurich and was attending lectures in the south wing of the Polytechnic built by Semper, in which the university was housed. Oskar had his small room at the home of the widow Kienast in the Leuengässchen and thus lived only a few steps from Otto. In the fall of 1862 Oskar left Zurich and spent seven years in Breslau.

The Steinhof, drawing by Otto Wyss, c. 1856.

The Apprentice

From this period we select 20 of 62 letters. They give insight into the life of the apprentice, the working conditions in the workshop, and the living conditions in the Zurich of that era. In addition to the concern about freshly washed clothing, they deal above all with the close bond with the family, which is also expressed in the cordial and respectful correspondence on the name days of the parents. We also learn a great deal, because brother Oskar leaves Zurich during Otto's apprenticeship and begins his career as an assistant doctor in Germany.

Zurich, February 6th, 1862

My Loved Ones!

I'm sending you my wash, as I promised Emma last Monday. Since the New Year two new workers have joined us: Louis Bachstein from Arnheim and Heinrich Rebsamen from Russikon. The latter is an older man, who likes to teach me the trade. Today we constructed a balustrade around a pinnacle on a rather tall house. On Monday night in Hottingen a wine press burned down, however at the house we saw and heard nothing of it.

To Amalie I sincerely wish happiness and all blessings and good progress in school and send her enclosed a sign of the love of a brother. Otherwise I am well. Is dear mother well again? I hope so! I sincerely wish her a swift recovery. So farewell and accept, all of you, a thousand greetings from your
Otto

Zurich, March 20th, 1862

My Beloved!

Last Monday two weeks ago I arrived without incident in Zurich and went immediately to Oskar's, since, although he was not at home at the time, I brought him later after work your presents, good wishes and greetings from home. Mr. Kunz had left on a trip and did not come home until Wednesday.

We had Carnival Monday free. In Aussersihl they reenacted the Battle of Sempach,[16] but because of the great throng of people I was so far away that I could understand nothing.

The Sechseläuten is set for next Monday, because of which we'll probably have another afternoon off. The procession on that day consists of around 200 boys from 8 to 12 years of age.[17] Otherwise everything is fine and a thousand greetings from your

Otto

Enclosed I also send you the waistcoat, which I could really use soon. Is Emma coming to Zurich next Monday?

Concerning the Life of the Foreign Guild Journeymen

Zurich, June 12th, 1862

My Beloved!

I arrived last Tuesday about 9:30 in Zurich.

Two foreign metal-worker journeymen, who were still looking around for work this morning, were hired here. In the afternoon the Württemberger also returned from his trip, that is to say, on Saturday at 2:30 he left the German Union by steamship for Horgen with a crowd of German gymnasts. They traveled farther over Zug, Art and Goldau, until they reached Rigi-Kulm at 4 in the morning, then they went over Rigi-Staffel and Rigi-Scheidegg to Gersau and Luzern, where they spent the night. On Monday they went on to Brunnen, traveled from there to the Grütli, then went on to Seelisberg and its lake, thereafter to Rothenthurm, where they spent a second night, and on Tuesday they finally returned via Einsiedeln to Zurich.

On Wednesday all 3 of these foreign journeymen were working again and the Württemberger still has his little room here. Otherwise everything is going fine. Please accept the warmest greetings from your

Otto

---

[16] Aussersihl developed at this time a special tradition of a festival play. The village, before the gates of Zurich, provided the necessary flat landscape for such an event.

[17] The Zurich Sechseläuten is an old spring festive custom of the guilds. Toward the middle of the nineteenth century developed the new form with the festive and merry parades of the guilds. In 1862 took place the first childrens' parade on Sechseläuten morning, in which at first only boys could participate, after 1867 also girls (Walter Baumann/ Alphonse Niesper: Sechseläuten, Zurich 1976).

Otto during his apprenticeship, confirmation age.

Zurich, June 20th, 1862

Dear Emma!

I am sending my dirty wash and best wishes along with 6 picklocks to dear father on his "name" day. Unfortunately last Saturday a key-bit flew into my eye as I was looking in a keyhole,[18] so that when Oskar took it out on Sunday afternoon (he was not at home that morning), he found some rust in it. For that reason I most close this letter (because today I still have my eye bandaged). Last Monday the Württemberger went away, and so now we have our little room all to ourselves, and also a clean bed.[19]

      To all my warmest greetings and kisses, your
      Otto

Zurich, November 27th, 1862

My Loved Ones!

I am sending you my dirty wash as well as my old Sunday coat and one of Oskar's,[20] which I don't need now. I shall receive confirmation on the last Sunday before Christmas.[21] Therefore please send me my good black suits and

---

[18] Broken off key-bit upon looking in the keyhole.

[19] Apprentices and journeymen lived at the home of the master. In small rooms they often had to share the bed with one another, which also occurred in hostels.

[20] It was customary that younger siblings wore the clothing of the older ones when these had become too small for the latter.

[21] The ceremony of confirmation fell at that time in the Advent season.

(if you have one) a black nightcap for Heinrich, because his ears often are freezing; Emma knows about the rest. In the hope that Emma or someone from the family will come to Zurich (on the preparation day), greets you all your
Otto

Report concerning the Confirmation

Otelfingen, January 4th, 1863
Dear Oskar!

First of all receive my sincerest thanks for the dear letter which you sent me on my name day. Your well intended admonitions, since they came straight from your heart, have made a lasting impression upon my own heart, and will always be unforgettable to me. It is my firm intention to strive to progress with enthusiasm and diligence, so that someday I shall be able to accomplish something in my profession. My dear brother, I especially miss you in Zurich on Sundays, on which day I now go to drawing school from 10–12 o'clock and from 1-3 o'clock and, in the evenings from 5 until 7, to the reading school in the hall of the Fraumünster. Soon after you left, some boiling lead flew into my eye, but after I had put cold poultices on it for a while, it was fine again. Mr. Kunz has now sold his house for the sum of 31,000 franks and is supposed to move next Easter; nevertheless, he has promised me that, if I continue to do a good job, he will see to it that after Easter I shall be able to continue to work as a journeyman here.

Despite the bad weather, Anna also came to the confirmation ceremony, which took place on the Sunday before Christmas. At that time was read the passage of Scripture which goes as follows: 2 Timothy, Chapter 11, Verses 1 and 6: "Now you my son grow strong in the grace, which is in Jesus Christ.—Similarly, if anyone competes as an athlete, he does not receive the victor's crown unless he competes according to the rules."

We received the certificate along with a confirmation gift: "Children, remain steadfast in him," on the holy Christmas Day after the first holy supper. After I had heard the afternoon sermon, in the evening I went to Otelfingen, where I discovered that I had received from the Christ Child Kleist's works, and on the following evening I went back to Zurich. On New Year's Eve I had to play St. Nicholas for the children of Mr. Kunz,[22] and after Mr. Kunz had given me permission to stay at home until Sunday, I went back home early on New Year's Day. In the evening I went to the home of Bopp Wettis, who

---

[22] In certain Protestant regions of German speaking Switzerland, in contrast to Catholic regions, St. Nicholas came as a bearer of gifts at New Year's, comparable to Père Noël in Western Switzerland.

would have liked to send you a Helsweggen,[23] but since it is too far, we could thus only drink to your health and eat the Weggen for you.

On Berchtold Day our three elder sisters went to the parsonage, and I stayed at home with Emilie and Hanneli and made with them Krüsi-müsi,[24] and anything else they wanted to make. Otherwise I can't think of anything else to write about and will therefore close.
Be warmly greeted by your
Otto

Zurich, January 20th, 1863
Dear Father!

Last Sunday I was for the first time in the Technical Drawing School with Mr. Groon, who gave me a simple assignment (inspection of a cube, a pyramid and a cone etc.). He said that I should make sure that I get a drawing board as well as T-squares; if therefore it is still possible, please be good enough to send it to me next Friday. As far as the lock on the shed is concerned, I shall begin it next week after work; just send me the exact measurements of the thickness of the door.

Uncle J. Schneebeli is now a bather in the new hospital, has his own little room with board, although he does have enough to do on Sundays and work days. There is nothing much new here. Farewell and accept, all of you, warm greetings from your
Otto

Zurich, December 3rd, 1863
Beloved Grandmother!

For the third time in my apprenticeship and also probably for the last time, I send you my best wishes on your name day.

May God shower upon you his rich blessings, good health and a long series of content, peaceful and happy years; so that I someday, better than now, can thank you properly for all your noble goodness. As a small token of my gratitude accept this little box with the foot warmer,[25] which you will have already received. Unfortunately I could not do a lot with it, and I had no time for anything else.

Again, accept the warmest best wishes from your thankful
Otto

---

[23] Helsen = present. Egg pastry as New Year's present.
[24] Krüsi-müsi or Chrüsimüsi (mishmash) was a self-made delicacy made from leftovers, mainly nuts crushed in the mortar, hard bread and cookie leftovers, sugar etc. Brother Oskar describes it in detail in his recollections of his own youth.
[25] A small foot basin with a tin container for hot water.

Concerning the Difficulty of Furthering one's Academic Education While Working in a Workshop

Otelfingen, December 26th, 1863

Beloved Brother!

At all events you have been waiting for an answer from me for a long time, but I wanted to wait until I could write you a definite answer. However, I cannot do that, as you wished in your last letter.

If I had tried to go to the lower Industrial School to take courses there in physics and math, I would have wasted too much of master Kunz's time, especially because he is unwell from time to time, so that I must be in the shop. Also, Mr. Kunz will without doubt move next Easter, so that I could no longer attend the upper industrial school during this time.

Thus next Easter I would have finished my apprenticeship, because he has promised to give me as a present the half year which I would still have had to spend learning with him. When he leaves, I also cannot work with another master as a journeyman and at the same time go to the upper industrial school or even to the Polytechnical Institute. To be sure, I do know that, if I had attended the latter school, I could get a good job with a good income in a bigger mechanical workshop; however, it would be difficult for me to be able even to manage any shop on an independent basis. If after Easter I went to work for a while for a skilled mechanic, then afterwards I could go abroad and there get better training by taking courses in physics and mathematics. Later I can begin my own metal working shop and later enlarge this into a larger workshop for machinery mechanics.

As you wrote, Sal. Schlatter still owes you 10 francs, which I was supposed to collect but never received, because I never saw him again. At present I am at home for Christmas and received as a Christmas present Bernoulli's Vademecum of 1862.

I don't have any other news. With warm greetings, your brother
Otto

Zurich, January 21st, 1864

My Beloved!

I finally send you the little brass faucet about which Mr. Kunz had spoken to me. Because it did not close well, I had a new faucet top cast, which J. Schmid adjusted for me. In any event, you must be very careful with the petroleum, because yesterday as I was pouring it into the lamp, the rising vapor suddenly burst into flame, and the flame struck me so quickly in the face that is singed my eyebrows and hair, which however did no further harm when I quickly put it out with my hand.

We were also able to blow out the vapor flame.

Therefore, in any event, you should not come too close to it with an open light. Well, I am freezing and therefore I shall close. I am now more accustomed to the cold (at least in the workshop), although I still have cold feet, and I am so hoarse that I cannot talk at all. Are all of you content and healthy?

Be, all of you, warmly greeted by your
Otto

Zurich, April 14th, 1864

Dear Father!

[...] I met Mr. Künzler on Monday afternoon, a man of medium height and a pale complexion, with a high brow and a black beard and mustache, who in his comportment reminded me very much of Oskar. Unfortunately, he was unable to give me any hope of being able to go to the Polytechnical Institute in the autumn, even if I no longer must use the hammer and ratchet. So, in such a situation, I would do best to wait until the fall and then take the preparatory course. So Wait?! Or what else should I do?

Just a few words concerning the Sechseläuten. Nothing much was noticed the entire day of the festivities, until in the evening around 6 o'clock the Sechseläuten fire was lit and a dummy covered with pitch or Böögg stuck up on a high pole was set on fire and a few rockets, crackers, and flaming serpents streamed up into the sky and three air balloons were sent aloft. Afterwards there took place an illumination of the Polytechnical Institute and the Grossmünster through Bengalese fire (first white, then blue and then red) and another parade of boys with colorful lanterns.

Farewell to you all and be all of you warmly greeted by your
Otto

Expressions of Love and Gratitude

Unterstrass, June 22nd, 1864

Dear Father!

For the third time during my apprenticeship as a metal worker I send you, dear father, my written best wishes on your name day.

I wish and hope to God that he might give you many years in happiness, health and his rich blessings.

I would have very much liked to give you, dear father, something at the end of my apprenticeship as an expression of my love and gratitude, and I very much regret the fact that I also was in no position to do so, because first of all I had no opportunity (because of Egli) and secondly I lacked the time. Now I want to do it later and even better than before. I now know well that it is still not possible for me for a little while yet and that, on the contrary, this time of training will cost you, dear father, much concern, trouble and work, still I want to try and hope to alleviate your trouble and work, through thriftiness and diligence.

Without my knowledge your 25th wedding anniversary went by. Please accept my warm best wishes as also to you, beloved mother, and may your next 25 years fly by even happier and more carefree, since I am now better able to reward you.

Please accept then, dear parents, once again my warmest best wishes and blessings, your grateful

Otto

Unterstrass, June 23rd, 1864

My Beloved!

[...] You will of course already know by now that my apprenticeship is now over, if not my actual work: two centesimal scales are done, now two more can be ready by Wednesday, perhaps by Saturday of next week. Thank God when it is finally over, because Egli (just like Heiri earlier) wants to make my last days and hours as sour as possible. After the end, when I have transported away my belongings (clothing, etc.), I shall probably come back home to Otelfingen, although probably not on Sunday, because I have classes every Sunday and Monday. I would now like to ask Anna to send me in a week about a half ream of ordinary (i.e. cheapest) writing paper.

Also be so kind as to mail me some shoe laces and do not forget the lamp, which our dear father has already prepared. Now you need to send me just one blue shirt, because I shall need none or only a few.

Now farewell and accept, all of you, the warmest greetings and kisses from your

Otto

Zurich, July 15th, 1864

My Beloved!

As we had agreed the day before yesterday, I send you the traveling bag and a loaf of bread. As you all will already partly know, uncle Riffel picked me up at Katzensee and after he had made a brief stop in Katzensee, I drove with him to Zurich, where I arrived at 8 o'clock. After that I went to Mrs. Kienast,[26] where I today had lunch and shall also receive the same in the future.

Farewell and accept, all of you, the warmest greetings and kisses from your

Otto

I wish dear mother and Amalie a good recovery from the bottom of my heart.

---

[26] Brother Oskar had his room at the home of Mrs. Kienast on the Löwengässchen before he moved to Breslau at the end of 1862. In 1869 Oskar married her daughter Caroline.

After the conclusion of his apprenticeship and a year of further education, Otto fails the admissions examination for the first year of the Polytechnical Institute.

Otelfingen, December 31st, 1864

Dear Brother!

I am sure that you expected a few lines from me earlier than this, but because I had little time, I waited until the Christmas holidays to write.

As you already know, I was not, as I had hoped, accepted into the first year of the Polytechnical Institute, and now I want to explain to you why.

I had three days to take the exam, and the first exam was with Professor Christoffel,[27] where I had to solve a few written problems in trigonometry, as well as a cubic equation with one unknown and another cubic equation with several unknowns. On the oral exam I was tested about compound fractions, indefinite equations, combinations, the binominal theorem, analytical geometry and spherical trigonometry. In the afternoon there was an exam in mechanics with Professor Zeuner,[28] but unfortunately I could not take the exam, because I had taken no courses in mechanics.

In representational geometry I had on the second day written and oral examinations with Mr. Th. Reye[29] and in the afternoon I had to write for Professor Keller an essay on the theme: "Thoughts on the Choice of a Profession." On the third day I finally had an exam in physics with Professor Clausius,[30] which first tested me concerning optics, then concerning heat, in both of which subjects I naturally had poor knowledge.

On the following day there was a conference, which was also attended by Mr. Künzler, who shared with me the following concerning this meeting: Professors Zeuner, Christoffel, etc., practically all the professors of the first-year course in the department of mechanics, had been in favor of my acceptance, since my grades in math were good, in representational geometry satisfactory, in German composition average, and likewise in physics. However, it was the opinion of the President of the School Board Mr. Kappeler (formerly a miller at the upper mill bridge in Zurich), that a student coming from the working world, who had hardly attended secondary school, had no general education; if I only had a diploma from an industrial school, I could be accepted, as matters stood, however, he could not give his assent to my admission.

---

[27] Elwin Bruno Christoffel (1829–1900), German mathematician, Professor at the Polytechnical Institute, then in Berlin and in Strasbourg.

[28] Gustav Zeuner (1828–1907), from Chemnitz. Dr.phil., Professor at the Polytechnical Institute for technical mechanics and the science of mechanical engineering.

[29] Theodor Reye (1838–1919), from Hamburg. Dr.phil., University Lecturer for mathematics at the Polytechnical Institute, later in Aachen and Strasbourg.

[30] Rudolf Clausius (1822–1888), from Köslin (Prussia), Dr.phil., Professor at the Polytechnical Institute for mathematical and technical physics.

Mr. Künzler then suggested to me to go into the preparatory course and to tutor a Mr. Liebig from Vienna, who took room and board in his home and was likewise enrolled in the preparatory course, although he was somewhat weak in math, for which he would pay me. After our dear father had spoken about it with Mr. Künzler and had given his approval, I entered the preparatory course and helped Mr. L. von Liebig do his assignments (of which there are many) and explained to him and reviewed with him everything which he had not yet understood.

In math we have lectures with Professor Orelli[31] (earlier a teacher in Mettmenstetten) 12 hours a week, every day from 8–10 o'clock and two hours of review. We have as well in the first week of each month a common assignment to prepare independently, for which purpose each student receives a special sheet of paper and three hours to complete the assignment. Professor Mousson[32] gives lectures on physics, for four hours per week and one hour of review, in which he each time gives a new assignment. We also have three hours a week in French with Professor Rambert, a Frenchman. Unfortunately we have no lectures in German, which I would enjoy.

We have technical drawing for four hours a week, under the guidance of Instructor Fritz;[33] we have no course work in free hand drawing. Professor Pestalozzi[34] lectures on practical geometry, although for only one hour a week. After the New Year Professor von Deschwanden is supposed to begin lecturing on representational geometry. From Professor Orelli we receive daily very many assignments for practice in computation, so we must bring to school every day, worked out and ready to turn in, every mathematical problem on which he has lectured.

From all this you will see that my time is rather occupied, especially because I must share it with my pupil Mr. Liebig. Now we have vacation until the third, I shall therefore go back to Zurich on Berchtold Day. As you know, I was thus far receiving room and board at the home of Mr. Bräm, but he has now moved up to the Hotel Bellevue, and I shall at the New Year move to the home of Aunt S. Ryffel[35] in Seefeld. Well, my paper is running out.

Accept my warmest greetings for the New Year, may it be a blessed one for you, and may God in Heaven give you many, many more. With a warm kiss, your brother   Otto

---

[31] Johannes Orelli (1822–1885), secondary school teacher, later director of the mathematical preparatory course at the Polytechnical Institute.

[32] Albert Mousson (1805–1890), Professor at the Polytechnical Institute for experimental physics.

[33] Hermann Fritz (1830–1893), from Bingen (Rheinland), Professor at the Polytechnical Institute for mathematics and technical drawing.

[34] Heinrich Karl Pestalozzi (1825–1895), Artillery Colonel, Professor at the Polytechnical Institute.

[35] The younger sister of Otto's father Jean, Susanna Wyss, who was married to the merchant Adolf Ryffel and lived from 1815 until 1890.

Seefeld, March 24th, 1865

My Beloved!

Because I have vacation next week (until April 18th), I shall probably come to Otelfingen next Tuesday morning and therefore send the wash and a few books. I probably would have already come home by next Sunday if the Sechseläuten were not taking place on Monday. Perhaps August Favre will also come here next Monday, if he does not have to go to school?

Aunt has written him a little letter herself. In case he comes with the train in the morning, he shouldn't plan to return home that same day, because perhaps that night there will be another fireworks display, a torch procession or something, and we can then leave together for home early the next morning. You'll hear more from my own mouth when I get home. Farewell, with greetings and kisses your
Otto

Concerning August and the later emerging Goumoëns, the following is to be said: in 1864 in a Baden newspaper, a place in a German-speaking home was sought for a fifteen year old boy for learning of the German language, preferably in exchange with a girl. Sister Emma was immediately eager to accept the offer; but since the domestic relationships of this Vaud family were not known, Wyss's father went there to look into the matter himself. In Goumoëns he first met the somewhat shy boy, then the Favre parents, who owned a big farm, and finally instructor Narbel; the agreement was made by the two families without difficulty. August Favre came to the Steinhof, and Emma was well received in Goumoëns. After Amalie's death Emma went back home, and Anna spent a the second year in the Romandie. The success of this arrangement mutually satisfied both families, and it remained a cordial relationship, which was later renewed with Emilie.

Seefeld bei Zurich, May 1st, 1865

Dear Sister Anna!

I was already planning to come home yesterday, but after I had read your dear letter, I decided to wait eight more days.

I spoke with Mr. Künzler on the same day that you were here, and he told me that Mr. von Liebig senior would arrive here in a few days and we could then also speak with him. He actually arrived here a week ago, however on Monday went to Stäfa, and I was able to see him only on Tuesday at noon. Unfortunately it is very difficult to speak with him, because he is hard of hearing and can only understand a few words. He requested that I come at three to the Kronenhalle, where I could meet him with Mr. Künzler. I went there at the determined time and met Mr. Liebig, Mr. Künzler and Mr. Ryffel von Stäfa, director of the institute there (where Mr. Liebig was for two years before he came to Zurich), with whom I likewise conversed. Mr. Künzler now said that he had calculated 7½ francs per day for my salary as a tutor, with which Mr. Liebig senior was satisfied and said that Mr. Künzler would finalize the contract. On Thursday at noon I went to see Mr. Künzler, who gave me 140 francs and said that he had calculated it thus, so 9 francs per week and nothing for Sundays.

I noted that I had always gone to tutor Mr. von Liebig junior on the Sundays before New Year, after New Year, however, I had not been able to continue doing this; whereupon he answered me that I could still make a claim for payment, but I thought it better just to take the 140 francs, especially because Mr. Liebig had already left and I still did not know whether I would have lessons to give.

Now I asked Mr. Künzler whether he still had lessons for me to give and whether Mr. Liebig would be staying here, etc. He then said that Mr. Liebig would still be taking only physics and chemistry at the Polytechnical Institute and had been exempted from the other subjects, and Professor Orelli would now be giving him the necessary instruction in math. He then asked whether I could not attend chemistry classes because Mr. Liebig needed a colleague in this field, but Professor Orelli would not allow me to attend chemistry classes.

So I have no more lessons to give as a tutor, and Mr. Liebig will probably ask a colleague from the first chemistry class to help him with his lessons.

Enclosed I'm sending home only 120 francs, because I must keep some money here to pay this month's rent. Emma can perhaps put it to good use in the store and at the end of the month send 30 francs for the board money. I shall take care of the business you mentioned to me. Next Friday I therefore expect nothing. I can pick up the trousers and shoes on Sunday. (You will see that you will receive them also next Sunday.)

Farewell and greet warmly my dear parents, grandmother and brother and sisters, with greetings and kisses, your brother

Otto

Otelfingen, June 5th, 1865

Dear Brother!

Because I am spending the Whitsunday holidays on the dear Steinhof, I am using these free hours in order to write you a few lines about my situation in Zurich.

There I attend, as you know, the preparatory course of the Polytechnical Institute, in which I am making great progress. Last winter I still had to give lessons to Mr. Liebig from Reichenberg in Bohemia, but I missed a few of them, because Mr. Liebig lived in the Beckenhof, Unterstrass, and I lived with our aunt in Seefeld. After Easter came Mr. Liebig's brother, who would not let him take any more math, because this was not necessary for a chemist. So I had no more lessons to give for the summer, but I did receive compensation of 9 francs per week for those which I had already given during the winter. Mr. Liebig now just attends the lectures in physics and chemistry in the preparatory course. Mr. Liebig now still does receive lessons in math (at 4 francs) from Professor Orelli, and from a soon graduating engineering student of the chemistry department named Lindegger who helps him in chemistry.

In vain I hoped to be able to study chemistry, because this is only permitted to those who want to attend the chemistry course. Throughout the summer we still have math classes, i.e. algebraic analysis, spherical trigonometry, analytical geometry with Professsors Orelli and Reye, technical drawing with the teacher Fritz, map drawing and half a day of land surveying with Professor Pestalozzi, physics with Dr. Mousson, French with Professor Rambert, and especially exercises, calculations and reviews in mathematics.

Will you come back home soon, dear brother?[36] I don't think that you will get ahead there. Today I am going to Zurich again. This morning I was again at the graveside of our good blessed sister Emilie, planting evergreens, forget-me-nots, and roses. Now farewell, with greetings and kisses your brother
Otto

Unwanted Sponsorship

Seefeld, November 22nd, 1865
Dear Father!

Last Monday took place, as you know, the funeral of my blessed guild master J. Kunz. A rather numerous procession followed the hearse; the "Friendship" Club, of which the dead man was a member, increased the size even more.—Perhaps you know that Mr. Kunz had married again in the course of the past three months, to wit, his own housekeeper Sophie Koller von Muri, who has been with him for about two years. Last Sunday a week ago she was delivered of a child, a little daughter, which did not agree with the other children, especially the eldest, Babette.

So today a worker comes to see me (the work in the workshop must naturally still be done despite our grief), and tells me Mr. Kunz had on his deathbed designated his daughter Babette as the child's godmother, so that she will properly love her little newborn sister, and had wished me to be the godfather.

Naturally that came as a surprise to me, but what am I supposed to do? Refuse? No, it was the dying wish of my guild master. There are to be sure some somewhat unpleasant circumstances; the mother is a Catholic and

---

[36] Oskar Wyss at this time was still living in Breslau in Germany.

therefore is pressing for baptism,[37] so that it is supposed to be baptized this coming Saturday, yet naturally it will be raised in the Reformed faith. The baptism will take place Saturday evening in the Prediger Church.—I would have liked to have heard your opinion, dear father, yet I do hope that you will not be against this. Thus I did not refuse and told the worker that I shall come by for the ceremony. My aunt thought there might be some expenses involved and that I should postpone the baptism, etc. I do not wish to do the latter, because I could not postpone the event and then later refuse. Be good enough, dear father, to write me your opinion about this matter, and soon. [...]

Seefeld, December 3rd, 1865

Cherished Grandmother!

Receive on your present name day my sincerest best wishes and blessings. May heaven allow you to experience this day many times more.

Unfortunately I had to recently learn that you, cherished Grandmother, were sick. How gladly I would have come to visit you, to care for you, but that was not permitted me. When I think back, how I was sick four years ago at the beginning of my apprenticeship and you at that time wanted to come to visit me despite the cold weather, I feel myself now under obligation to you for your maternal care. How often, when I think back, how often you have showered care and concern on me as well as on my other brothers and sisters since our earliest childhood. When shall I be able to pay back all that?

In the hope that these lines find you, dear Grandmother, in restored health, greets you and wishes you the best your grateful
Otto

---

[37] Because according to the Catholic teaching of that era, unbaptized dead children went into limbo.

The Departure Abroad: On the Road of the Journeyman

Otto had problems with the preparatory course of the Polytechnical Institute; besides, he was convinced that practical experience in various workshops would be important for his later professional success.

One evening at home in Otelfingen, he stood up and said to his father: "I must work again, and I must do that abroad; doing nothing but studying just does not satisfy me!"

On August 27th, 1866, he bid his family farewell, briefly and hastily, and went on his way abroad.

Looking Around for Work in Solothurn.

Solothurn, September 2nd, 1866

My Beloved!

Of course you are surprised to receive a letter from Solothurn. Now this is how it all happened. I got out in Olten and went to the Central Workshop, but found no work. Then I looked at the exhibition of construction materials, then walked through the little city to Kappel and Fulenbach, where I went to a new workshop of Jäger and Wyss and also received work, but could only begin work three weeks later, when the waterworks on the Aare were complete (one turbine).

Then I had employment in workshops and technical drawing rooms. Of course, I could not continue to do this and traveled farther to Langenthal, where I spent the night in the Bären. I had a clean, good bed and was totally pleased. On the following morning I looked around but could find no work.

The following day I went to Aarwangen, Wangen, Wiedlisbach, Attiswil and under heavy wind and rain to Solothurn. There I first went to see Cully, to whom Weiss in Fulenbach had recommended me, but he had already hired a worker on the previous day. Otherwise, he was very friendly and gave me a few addresses where there might be some work. Thus I came to the home of the machine mechanic Schilt, whom I at first did not find at home. For that reason and because of the weather I stayed in Solothurn, at the White Cross, where I was also lodged again rather well and cheaply. On the following morning I went again to see Mr. Schilt, and he promised me work next Monday, because he is traveling this week. He makes machines for shipment to Berlin and to North Germany and is well known as a skillful and meticulous worker.

Therefore, I decided to stay with him and to take a little trip during the remaining time before my employment.

I therefore went through Kriegstetten, Koppingen and Kirchdorf to Burgdorf and on the same day (Wednesday) to Zollikofen (an hour from Bern). On Thursday I looked around Bern, then went to the Neuenegg monument (a white, single obelisk) and traveled to Freiburg. There I took a look at the suspension bridge, the Jesuit monastery[38] etc. and then traveled by rail to Lausanne. I had forgotten the name of the country estate of Mr. Kubli, for which reason I could not find it and thus paid no visit. Then I walked through hilly Lausanne and went to Goumoëns, where I was well received by our friends. It was Friday, and I had to stay until Sunday, when August drove me to Chavornay.

Then I traveled by train to Solothurn, met here Mr. Schilt, who wanted to hurry to Kriegstetten, where the big, well-known paper factory had burned down. I accompanied him, and the factory is really burned down to its foundations, including significant supplies, which however are insured for three times their worth.

Now farewell, all of you, once again, especially from our friends in Goumoëns. With greetings and kisses your
Otto

"On Friday we often have Stückli and Noodles."

Solothurn, September 23rd, 1866

My Beloved!

Three weeks have already flown by here and I do not yet definitely know whether I shall stay here the winter.

Last Sunday had already past the 14 days, after which you usually receive the first paycheck and after which the salary and a lengthier contract are determined. We have room and board with the master, and also the master did not object to the salary of 5 francs per week which I requested, but he gave me no definite answer concerning a lengthier contract.

With the work (which I am glad to have again), things are going as follows: I am able to do very well things which come by incidentally, repair jobs or smaller things, and there he is quite satisfied with me; less so with the combing machines, where everything must be very exactly and precisely manufactured, especially on the lathe, whose operation I unfortunately still do not know much about. I would like right now to ask the master some questions,

---

[38] This of course does not exist. Supposedly Wyss means the monastery of the Kapuziner, Franciscans, etc.

but he has gone out; nonetheless, I believe to be able to hope that I can stay here.

The master, who is also often with us in the workshop, understands the work very well; thus he is also the manufacturer of a calculating machine, which four years ago won fourth prize at the London World Exhibition; thus I could learn something this winter and would therefore like to stay here.

When I began to work here, there was still here a worker (Karl Meyer von Schliengen, Grand Duchy of Baden), who last Monday went back home, after an absence of 5 years.

Then a day after me began a gentleman from Geneva, Karl Ledermann, who can speak no German, with whom I therefore must speak right much. There is an apprentice boy, Joseph Küfer, from here, who is three-fourth of a the year into his apprenticeship, and the about 16 year old son of the master, who has been in the shop only about six weeks. I get along well with everyone; the man from Geneva especially sticks close to me, because he can speak French with no one else, and I can understand him well.

My room has a window facing the south, is bright, has a chest with two compartments (thus I have my own which I lock), the little table stands right in front of the window, four chairs, a big mirror and a kind of étagère by my bed are its furnishings. It looks out on the street below, upon a little court and the roofs and walls of the neighboring houses. Directly across from it stands an old round fortified tower with a few firing ports, in which grass and shrubbery grow; three linden trees overhang the venerable structure on the right and on the left. The back side of the house opens out onto the entrenchment, a long alley shaded by the hugest lindens.—As far as food is concerned, I am satisfied. In the mornings we have potatoes and bread with the morning coffee at seven o'clock, then at noon soup, meat or bacon, sausages, etc. and vegetables, usually potatoes and beans, turnips, mustard etc. all mixed together. With it dark bread, which always lies on the table.

On Fridays we often have pastry and noodles and potatoes, Lenten fare. In the afternoons at 3:30 there is coffee and a piece of bread in the shop, now and then also wine and bread. Finally at seven o'clock a soup and cheese and bread or apples, pears, etc.

The work runs from the morning at 5 until the evening at 7.

The family of the master, besides the already mentioned workers, consists of the 16 year old Eduard, the 14 year old Viktor, who is now on vacation, a lively 8 year old girl Anna and a 5 or 6 year old Karl. The master's wife (supposedly a Prussian noblewoman) is an educated woman, speaks fluent French like the master and otherwise good German. She has a maid, a woman of Solothurn.[39]

---

[39] Urs Schilt (1822–1880), machine mechanic, living in the Kronengasse in Solothurn, was married to Maria Anna Vogel (1823–1897) from Leimen (Bavaria). The couple had four children. Eduard Victor (*1851), Viktor Emil (*1852), Karl Albert (*1866), Maria Luise (*1869). A daughter Anna is not indicated in the register. Friendly communication from

Last Sunday I wanted to write because of the little chest, but on the Holy Day of Repentance at three o'clock the storm bell rang because there was a fire. I didn't go to see it though because it was too far and I only took a walk along the bank of the Aare.

I had come back home and had had dinner, when to my astonishment the storm bell rang once again, announcing yet another fire which had broken out, this time in Kreuzacker about five minutes from the city or actually a suburb. It was a farmhouse with a straw roof. Luckily there was no wind that night, and about 10:30 I came back home. The master had to stay on the burning site with the firemen until the following morning at seven o'clock. This afternoon I have a mind to go with Eduard the master's son and the man from Geneva up upon the Weissenstein.

Farewell to you all, with cordial greetings and kisses from your
Otto

Looking Around for Work Can also be a Cultural Experience.

Môtiers, October 23rd, 1866

My Beloved!

You have certainly been expecting a letter from me for a long time and, to be sure, from Solothurn, but I left the latter town eight days ago and am now employed here by a mechanic who specializes in making machinery for mills.

I cannot begin work until tomorrow, because the forge is not yet ready, plus the master has just set up shop here.

Now in Solothurn I very quickly collected all my things in good order and also said thank you to everyone for it. I then wanted to settle my accounts with the master; thereby there was a little dispute, and in 14 days I left. Both coworkers had already left, the man from Baden went back home, and the man from Geneva to Zurich.

From Solothurn, on beautiful Sundays in autumn, I had made another excursion up upon the Weissenstein and the Röth, where I had the most beautiful view of the Bernese Oberland, as well as the Valais, Urner and Unterwald ranges. I could also make out in the distance the Uetliberg, but the rock strata remained beyond my viewing range.

The hermitage St. Verena lies in a really romantic spot between high cliffs, which include a chapel and the holy grave, both chiseled out of the cliff. There, there is the Wengistein, a memorial to Niklaus Wengi (who is well known in Swiss history)[40] near which is located a large town square, from which can be

---

Hans Rindlisbacher, Central Library of Solothurn.

[40] Niklaus Wengi, as mayor of the city, in 1533, played a conciliatory role in the religious conflicts in Solothurn (†1549).

seen a pretty view of Solothurn and the environs. So I saw the churches, especially the big church of St. Urs and Victor, the patron saints of Solothurn with 11 altars, pretty paintings, etc. (in the tower 11 bells), then the Jesuit church, which is much older, yet less decorated. In addition, I saw the arsenal, the museum, the grave of the Polish hero Kosinsko[41] in Zuchwil etc.

So, as you can see, I saw pretty much everything in Solothurn; yet now a little about the trip itself. From Solothurn I went through the new village Grenchen and through pretty villages, Lengnau, Pieterlen, Bözingen to the five-hour distant Biel which, surrounded by a large number of friendly country houses, looks quite stately at the end of its lake. Going farther along the Bieler See, I found everything still in the full fall season [grape harvest], I had enough grapes, which here and there were offered by a friendly citizen of Biel. I stayed in Twann and traveled on the following day through Neuenstadt, Landeron, St. Blaise to the city of Neuchâtel. I looked around this beautiful city and went on the following day by train as far as Travers, which to be sure has been largely rebuilt, but still shows many signs of its recent conflagration, for example the mill.[42] In Môtiers I finally found work, to start at the beginning of next week, because the workshop was still new, and no furnace had yet been built.

I further traveled through Fleurier, St. Sulpice as far as Verrières, Switzerland. The following morning I bade farewell to the Swiss homeland, and after my documents had been verified by the French customs agents, I traveled across the border to Pontarlier, where it was just market day and the noisy life of a French commercial city unfolded itself before my eyes. After I had looked around the city a bit, I took the road to Besançon on foot, a distance of 60 kilometers according to the signpost. I walked another 20 kilometers, mainly over wide plains, which were used as fields for cattle, but were otherwise little developed. Tired, I stayed at the inn, the first one I had seen since Pontarlier, and slept quite well in the chaff bed.—On the following day I walked through several villages toward Besançon. The road was better built, and soon at nightfall I saw the Doubs river gleaming in the deep valley before me, and I stepped finally through the gates into the fortress. Yet I must save another time to tell of the city itself. When I found no work there, I took the noon train on Sunday and came back here.

Farewell and be healthy, while I send you my kisses and love your
Otto
My address: Mr. Hofer, Mechanic in Môtiers, (Canton of Neuchâtel)

---

[41] Tadeusz Kosciuszko (1746–1817), leader in the Polish struggle for freedom against Russia and Prussia (1794), who after being wounded and taken prisoner in 1815 came to Solothurn. His corpse was transported in 1818 to Cracow and buried in the cathedral there.
[42] The devastating fire of 1865 had destroyed 101 houses.

"Room and Board in the German Manner" in Môtiers.

Môtiers, November 11th, 1866

My Beloved!

From Solothurn, to which I had written regarding the little trunk, I just received the news that soon after my departure from there a Mr. Vetter had come, however could not imagine who that could be, until Emma's little letter cleared up the matter for me. Naturally it made me angry and all the more so because I had stayed on in the workshop of Mr. Meier, which is only half an hour from Solothurn, and thus would have probably been there to meet him.—Not that I regretted leaving the position with Mr. Schilt in Solothurn, because he changed my board to only two coffee breaks per day, after my coworkers had left and I was alone, and as far as my salary is concerned, I had told him that he should give me what I earn, and finally I was treated like a family member.

Then I just pointed out that during the ten weeks I was in the living room with Eduard only once, and then the ill tempered master asked me what I was doing in his house, whereupon I had to leave the position with the Schilts. What Mr. Schilt would have liked would have been for me to give Eduard lessons in math! Big honor.

Now to my present job. Mr. Hofer is a citizen of Bern, a still young (i.e., 28-30 year old) master, established here for the past three years. NB. He had a workshop, now has however built a beautiful new one, which will soon be ready for occupancy. His wife is the daughter of his guild master, mechanic Hochstrasser in Langenthal, and he therefore gives according to the German custom room and board to his apprentices.

As far as the latter is concerned, I am content, likewise with the room, which is the adjacent room, through which one wall of the oven is heated and is completely paneled and has glass screens to protect us from the heat.—I now have 4 coworkers, among them a carpenter, who is completing the upper part of the building. In the above mentioned room there are beside myself two others, the other two have another little room of their own.

All the workers here, as well as the master and his wife, are from German-speaking Switzerland, so that I seldom hear a French word and will not make much progress in it.

I have no comrade, except when I sometimes go to Fleurier on Sunday, in order to visit Charles Mathey, who was with me and Colonel Meier in Regensdorf in the secondary school there. As far as work is concerned, we now have a transmission for a watch factory in Fleurier, which also must be done in a good and clean manner.

Moreover, the master has especially to make grinders, saws, threshing machines. As far as the salary is concerned, I do not yet know anything definite, there is a lot of piece-work.

Finally as far as my wash is concerned, I bring it on Mondays to the washer woman who lives next door and pick it up on Saturdays or Sundays.

Now farewell, accept, all of you, the warmest greetings and kisses from your   Otto

Dear Emma! Please write down the name of the grammar book which you had and which you always praised so much. Don't send it, because the postage would cost almost more than the little book itself.

"The beds are also good, both straw mattress and feather mattress."

Môtiers, December 2nd, 1866

Beloved Grandmother!

Winter has again begun and brings snow and ice, yet at home on the dear old Steinhof it also brings the intimate family get-togethers; and first of all, the one in honor of your name day, beloved grandmother. May the dear Lord grant you constant good health, so that upon my return I can greet and embrace my good and caring grandmother, in order then to be able to celebrate together many more name days.

May you then say to me: "Yes! God has accompanied you," as you said upon my departure: "May God accompany you!" And now, dear grandmother, I want to tell you something about here. You have certainly wondered and asked how things are going with my wash. Well I can truly say: "Quite good." When I was living in Solothurn the washer woman came every Monday, and then I always gave her the dirty wash and received it back on the following Saturday afternoon. To wash a shirt costs 25 centimes, a blue shirt there 25 centimes, here only 20 centimes. A pair of socks 10 centimes, a handkerchief 5 centimes, etc. Here I must bring the wash to the washer woman and pick it up again, also she does the wash only once every two weeks, therefore I bring it every Monday, because I have little space, because I must share my chest with the others. The washer woman also takes care of whatever needs to be mended.

The beds are good too, both the straw mattress and the feather mattress, only the covers are too short.

The work day lasts from 6 in the morning until 7 at night, so a twelve hour day with an hour break. As I already said, the new workshop is about 600 paces from the house, which is especially annoying in snowy and rainy weather, because you almost always have wet feet. At the beginning of this week the weather was also bad, and since I had to work almost always by the fire, I caught a cold. On Wednesday I became ill, and therefore I spent the afternoon in bed, yet on Thursday I was better again, and since then I have been quite well.

All my coworkers were also not quite well this week, but now we again have right cold weather, and things are better again.

And has the winter begun in Otelfingen? Do you have sledge runs like here? In any event, it will be colder than last year.

Well in three weeks will come Christmas and New Year. While I wish you, dear grandmother, once again happiness and good health on a happy name day, I remain in love your grateful grandson
Otto

"How the children have it here."

Môtiers, December 2nd, 66
My dear Hanneli!

Since you were kind enough to write me such a big letter on my name day, I now want to answer you right away. Your dear little letter just like those of Emilie and Emma, have pleased me a great deal and also the fact that you have written so beautifully.

Then the letter has come to me very quickly, because just think about it, on the same day that it left Otelfingen, it arrived here in the afternoon and I already received it on Sunday morning.

Well I just want to tell you how the children have it here. So in the mornings at nine the school bell rings, announcing that the children must go to school, and then again at noon they can go back home. Because it is sunny, they are however soon back out on the street, until the bell rings at one in the school, and they spend this time outdoors sliding and sledging and also speaking French, which is a joy to see. At three school is out and those who have done their homework go out into the street to sledge, if it is not too cold. – I send you for your album a photograph, and you can write me, whether you recognize it well. In addition, I have enclosed a postcard of the friendly little city of Solothurn, which is also not much bigger than a photograph. I'll send Emma and Anna a photograph later, so that the letter will not be too heavy.

Live happy, healthy and honest, my dear little sister, and be warmly greeted and kissed, like all the rest of you, by your brother
Otto

Môtiers, December 31st, 1866
Dear Parents, Grandmother and Sisters!

The Christmas holidays are past and the New Year is just around the corner. I next want to tell you how I have spent this holiday period. Yesterday it was bright and very cold, as it has been these past ten days. The thermometer sank down to 18 and 21 degrees C, yet here there was little snow, with the exception of the adjacent mountains. I went with a coworker in the afternoon to Couvert, where we talked with one another now about the past and then about the future and so spent the afternoon in a pleasant way.

The following Monday we had much work (as has been the case lately) and therefore worked on the holy Christmas Eve until 12 o'clock. On Christmas morning itself I went to church, where the confirmation was consummated, yet to my great wonderment there was no communion. I could follow very little in the sermon, much more in the prayer, which was spoken more slowly.

In the afternoon I went to Fleurier to see Charles Mathey, and we took a walk together to Buttes, which is completely surrounded by mountains. Once back home I went for a while to the warm shop, where I still found my comrades who later went to the Grütli Union Club.[43] Then I read a little more French and German, until I went to bed at nine o'clock. The following day we still had a lot of work to do, in order to finish the things for a water wheel in Noraigue and on Thursday all we workers went there, to set it up.

On Saturday evening I then went back home to Môtiers, in order until one in the morning to make a number of screws and bolts, with which I then traveled back to Noraigue at five in the morning. There I worked until three with my comrades. After we had returned home, two of the workers calculated their pay with the master, and since they were paid poorly, they left this morning. –Afterwards, I too figured my own pay with him, but he also wanted to pay me six francs less than the promised salary, and so I also announced that I planned to leave.

However, I shall not be without work for long, because for a long time I have had an offer of employment by a local mechanic, who only makes tools for watch makers. This is of course very precise work, and I shall of course at the beginning still receive very little salary, yet I know that I shall learn something by doing this, and this job is not a "promise from the master without actually keeping his word"—as was the case in Solothurn and also partly in the job I just left. I am determined to get the salary I deserve.

The Sylvester Night (which is not celebrated here with the ringing of bells) is over, and yesterday evening I was at the home of the mechanic Mr. Demelais, for whom I can begin working tomorrow. He speaks no German at all and has as a worker only his brother, who is also a good worker. Therefore, for one thing, I shall learn French and, for another, something useful in my trade, which is worth more to me than the best salary. I also hope to be able to remain with persevering diligence and to be able to get ahead in my career. –Thus the New Year has begun at least with high hopes and fresh courage.

---

[43] Founded in 1838 in Geneva by Eastern-Swiss craftsmen, this Association for Self Assistance and Education developed with time into a socially protective workers' union.

And how are things in Otelfingen? May the New Year also bring to you all, my loved ones, much pleasantness, good health and God's blessings. So farewell to all of you with the warmest best wishes for the New Year from your
Otto
Address: Monsieur Demelais, Mechanic in Môtiers

Precision-Lathes for Watchmaking.

Môtiers, March 6th, 1867

My Loved Ones!

If the last two weeks of February tried to bring in the spring, March did not mean for it to be that way and brought with it new ice and snow. Since then there has been the icy northeasterly wind and every day it still snows a little. The sun comes out seldom, so that we could see only a few moments of today's solar eclipse. The first of March was celebrated here in a lively manner as a holiday, and 22 cannon shots from the neighboring hill reminded us of Neuchâtel's admission into the Swiss confederation.[44]—Business here is going badly, and with concern Master Demelais sees that no new orders are coming in. The work which is being done consists especially of smaller and quite small lathes, so called Burinfix, for watchmakers, in order to rotate the individual components of the watches. Then in different kinds of machines for turning or the milling of the teeth of the little watch wheels.

He only makes a few of the small simpler watchmaker tools. Everything must be very precisely manufactured, because the later durability of the watch depends on it.

The fact that he is a skillful worker may be deduced from the fact that he (alone out of ten or eleven local mechanics) manufactured a lathe with nickel silver Burinfix and four machines for the fabrication of casters, for the exposition in Paris. The former is a true masterpiece of the metal worker's art, to which he also devoted special care and attention. These pieces of workmanship were already done when I entered this workshop, with the result that, except for the polishing of a few tiny pieces, I did not help with it.

Since then I have worked on three Burinfixes and four rounding machines. In the meantime, the master made a big harmonica with over 50 double voices, which will be sold for 65 francs. The other worker is away, and the apprentice boy was sick for a little while. Now how do things stand with my salary? Until now (last Sunday) I have received nothing, and from now on finally three francs per week. You can imagine how things look with my money in reserve

[44] On March 1st, 1848 Republican insurgents from La Chaux-de-Fonds seized the castle in Neuchâtel and the Republic was consequently declared.

in the bank. Well, I am content and therefore do not argue with the master, if only more work comes, I shall keep quiet for a little while. [...]

How Emilie, thanks to Otto, finds a Job in French-Speaking Switzerland.

Môtiers, April 14th, 1867

Dear Father!

Emilie finally found for herself the desired position, with the brother of my master's wife, Charles Jeanrenaud.

Three weeks ago I had already found out about a position which pleased me, but which did not want 12-year old girls there, and only last Sunday did I receive a definite refusal. To be sure, I had already asked the master and his wife about it earlier, but since four weeks ago their family was increased by a healthy baby, they of course had other things on their minds.

This week I asked around further about it, but two positions did not please me, until I today went to ask Mr. Jeanrenaud, who lives about a hundred paces from us, near the school. For exchange there is a boy here, who will be 14 years old next Christmas. He himself wants to go to German Switzerland, is of course somewhat nervous, but seems to me to be a lively and clever boy. Naturally, he would attend our secondary school in Regensdorf, whereas Emilie would attend the school here which is voluntary for girls from 14 to 16 (as is the secondary school). As a comrade Emilie would have the 15 year old Anna. Otherwise, there are no more children on the farm. The wife is a lively, skillful housewife, who is trained for everything. The boy is a cadet here and a trumpeter in the school band. I was asked whether he could not take music lessons with us, so that he would not forget what he had learned.

Perhaps in Baden he could. Things could be arranged here within three weeks, and then, dear father, will you come here with Emilie? I am already looking forward to it. In case you can't come, Mr. Jeanrenaud would come to Otelfingen in order to bring Arthur and to pick up Emilie. Mr. Jeanrenaud himself works [I believe now less as a result of illness] as a watchmaker. Moreover he owns a shoe store, which is supposed to be doing well. [...]

Môtiers, April 23rd, 1867

Beloved Father!

Today at home I received your dear lines and was full of joy to know that I shall soon greet you all here in Môtiers. This evening I was also just at the home of Mr. Jeanrenaud, but he thought that you should bring Emilie right away and take back Arthur yourself, so that we would not have to make an extra useless trip, because of course neither Arthur nor Emilie can be allowed to travel alone. This is a good idea, but please allow a week for Arthur's things to be packed, so I'll expect to see you in about a week.—I would be very pleased to have my white ticking trousers, if you can bring those or pack them with Emilie's things. Then I would also like to practice a little shooting and would like to therefore ask you to bring me one of the drawn pistols as well as the bullet mould. It goes without saying that I shall take good care of them.

The weather has turned very unfriendly, and only yesterday it began to snow again, but the snow must soon melt.

Since I shall save the rest for our upcoming reunion, accept, dear father and all my loved ones, kisses and greetings from your
Otto

NB. The road from the Couvet station is a half hour, leads through the middle of the beautiful village of Couvet, then through the trees up to Môtiers. You come into the village and then have on your right the Hôtel de Ville and on your left the great town fountain and the road which leads up to us. Directly to the left is the "Magasin de Chaussure" of Julien Charles Jeanrenaud, whereas our little house is the next to the last house at the top of the village.

I shall try to draw you a sketch.

A First Letter Written in French.

Môtiers, June 21st, 1867

My Cherished Father!

I return for a few hours to my paternal house, to celebrate your holiday. I would love to be in the midst of our family circle, to give you with them my compliments. –Therefore, accept, my father, my cordial congratulations, may the good Lord keep you in good health for many more years, so that I can give you more joy.

It was yesterday and the day before yesterday that they celebrated here the archery competition of Môtiers with a lot of participation by the inhabitants. On Wednesday it was the prize archery contest, especially for the citizens who form an archery club, the object of the competition being to hit a large target called "William Tell," at the distance of 350 paces, the cardboard 3 and a half inches thick. Thursday it was the shooting competition, they shot arrows at the other four targets at the same distance, but the cardboard this time was less than 2 inches thick. There were also five targets for long distance rifles at the great distance of 1020 paces in which there was some fine shooting. Mr. Jeanrenaud had the goodness to give me two shots with his own rifle, but I did not hit anything. They set up beside the shooting range a bowling game and a marbles game, each one with four prizes, worth 16, 11, 6.50 and 5 francs for the best shots. Mr. Jeanrenaud played marbles and the first time he received third prize, a silver spoon worth 6.50 francs, and the second day he received fourth prize, a purse with 5 francs in it, but he also played 45 times (at 10 centimes a time) for the prizes.

A few cabarets. Profit seeking merchants were not lacking, and a carousel had not received permission to be there.—You will also find enclosed our photo and I would like to ask you for yours for me. Giving you once again my congratulations, be embraced by your son

Otto

A gentle Admonition for the nine-year-old youngest Sister.

Môtiers, June 21st, 1867

My dear Hanneli!

On Johannes Day you also celebrate, dear little sister, your name day, on which I wish you from the bottom of my heart happiness and God's blessings.

Always remain healthy and lively, in school honest and diligent and at home cheerful and obedient, so that, when I come home, I shall hear a lot of good things about you, when out of the little Hanneli a big Jeannette has developed. So grow and become big and honest, stay healthy and happy. Last fall, when I was in Solothurn, I took a little trip up on the Weissenstein, which is a mountain somewhat bigger than our Lägern. It was on the first of October, when I arrived at this inn after an hour and a half walk.

After I had had a little "Znuni," I looked at the splendid view. As you can see in the little picture, it has Alps, fields and in the area around the spa hotel it has over a 100 head of cattle, of which the most beautiful have a bell around their necks. As I went back down the mountain, I also found some raspberries and strawberries. In the summer every day a wagon from Solothurn goes up the mountain and back down again, also carrying supplies. Well now for something else.

In your last little letter, which pleased me a great deal, you write to me that you play with Arthur, thus get along well with him, even if you cannot understand him and cannot talk with him. That pleases me a great deal, and I would be very happy if Anna and Emilie got along so well together here. Anna is a little mischievous and fond of teasing and seldom leaves Emilie alone, which is very unpleasant for Emilie. On the other hand, she has in Madame Jeanrenaud a gallant and attentive teacher and housekeeper. I see Emilie every evening (except when I have something else to do) and then I go for walks with her or sing a little song in the living room. Sunday before last we took a walk to Fleurier and Buttes, after we had been in church in the morning in Bovaresse. Well the night watchman has just gone by, with his night call "Peace and quiet, peace and quiet, it has struck midnight, it has struck midnight," and I want to go to sleep.

You, too, sleep well and with cordial greetings and kisses to all, I remain your loving brother

                    Otto

The Master is Sick and is Moaning.

                                        Môtiers, July 23rd, 1867
Beloved Father!

If I am not mistaken, I already noted in an earlier letter that Master Demelais is sick and suffers from consumption. Unfortunately it is getting worse and worse, although he gets up every day, drinks each morning the freshly milked milk and often has a good appetite. His cough persists, his body grows thinner and thinner and for the whole week he is only seen for a few hours in the workshop. Nothing so to speak is happening with the work, because we will soon have a dozen Burinfix in storage and have sold none since Easter.

The machines, which are at the Paris exposition from our shop, have won a bronze medal, but, except for the nickel silver lathe, they have not yet been sold. A few employers from here have visited the exposition.

As far as I am concerned, I am not quite content, because if I say that the master should give me more, he claims he cannot and complains about the bad times, he doesn't have anything himself etc. The workers here are thoroughly taxed, so since New Year I have already paid more than 4 francs and just today came another bill for 2 francs. Well, I don't like to stay this way and I would have preferred this fall to move on to Dijon, where one of the foremen from Môtiers is in a workshop of about 200 workers, which manufactured the machines for the local mills. However, I have no definite promises of work, although there are also other workshops and somewhere something will still turn up. I would like to make the trip on foot, for which purpose I would very much like a flannel shirt.

Right now, however, I lack the main thing, that is, money. I hope to be able to get through, but with Master Demelais there is nothing to be done, and besides, these past few weeks have left me broke. So I turn then to you, beloved father, and hope and think that later on things will go better; if I only remain healthy.

I also want to note that I recently had constipation and from time to time noted small pointy white worms (at this size they are not trichinous) which cause the burning feeling in the intestine. If you had some advice or medicine for that, I would be very grateful.

Emilie thinks that she will receive a package on her name day, and perhaps you could just put the two together and mail them. Also, as far as Emilie is concerned, I note that she is now well assimilated into the household here and the local school, so that, so to speak, I do not note a single trace of remaining homesickness; things are also going well with Anna.

And now farewell and stay healthy, dear father, I want to work and strive to become something good and with God's help eradicate my debt. With warm greetings and kisses your thankful
Otto

Concerning the School System in Môtiers.

Môtiers, August 18th, 1867

Dear Father!

Accept my warm thanks for all the many things which you have sent me, and also especially for the good advice, which I shall follow, which I shall use.

Because of the school in Fleurier, I paid a visit to the family of the deceased Charles Mathey, and today I also met the teacher Mr. H. Meseiller himself, who very obligingly gave me information about everything. The school is of course a secondary school, boys and girls have almost the same classes, at different times of the day. The classes are in the mornings usually from 8–10 o'clock and in the afternoons from one to four or five o'clock with the exception of Saturday afternoons, item, about 31 hours per week. Instruction is given in French grammar, composition, French literature, arithmetic, German language (and to be sure by the German pastor two hours per week), history, geography, physics, botany, (zoology in winter), drawing, calligraphy and singing, at your pleasure, with another teacher. The price for three months is 20 francs and the program has its final exams in May.

Vacation is 14 days in the fall and another few days at the New Year. You can enter at any time, although he would prefer it sooner. If you cannot follow the lectures, you can withdraw after about 14 days. There is rather much homework to do, but you are allowed to omit one subject, for example physics or botany.

Three books are necessary, a grammar, a history book and a physics book, which can be acquired for about 9 francs through the school commission. At the moment there are no other Germans in the school, although there have often been in the past.

Is Mr. Jeanrenaud willing? I think not, because they are very frugal. I would very much appreciate a swift answer, because in about 14 days I plan to travel farther on.

Farewell and stay healthy, I remain with kisses and love your thankful
Otto

Otto and his sister Emilie (b. 1853) in Môtiers.

There is also no staying in Môtiers.

Môtiers, September 9th, 1867

My Beloved!

My bag is finally packed, and I'll soon be leaving, to be sure, eight days later than I had planned. Nothing can be done about the secondary school in Fleurier, because the Jeanrenauds just do not want to. Just last Sunday I debated the matter with Mr. and Mrs. Jeanrenaud, but nothing came of it. At the same time Madame told me that they would bring Arthur back home, and Mr. Jeanrenaud thought he would pay a visit in Zurich to Mr. Nüscheler and then (as a sidetrip) also go to Otelfingen.

I tried futilely to clarify to them the difference between the schools of Môtiers and those of the canton of Zurich. It was their opinion that Arthur was going to school only with the little kids, and such a school was not as good as the one in Môtiers.

I tried futilely to explain to them that the difference between the lectures in the two school systems was very significant, and that the teacher had learned a great deal, even for the teaching of the little ones. The entire week he was very unfriendly, hardly returned my greetings, although at least Emilie was not complaining, whereas Anna was somewhat ill and irritable and could sleep little at night. Mr. and Mrs. Jeanrenaud have written this week, and I still don't know whether the affair will straighten itself out.

Otherwise Emilie looks very well, in any event the change of air has done her a lot of good. Emilie would not want to come home, yet if it is impossible to straighten out the affair with the Jeanrenauds, perhaps something else will work out. Well, we just have to wait and see.

I depart tomorrow after six for France. Emilie accompanies me to St. Sulpice and then I travel from there to Dôle and Dijon.

Farewell for now, with kisses and love, your
Otto

On September 10th, 1867 sister Emilie writes from Môtiers to her brother Oskar in Breslau:

If I was and still am far from my loved ones, at least I was able to celebrate my name day with brother Otto, with whom I have spent up until now many a happy hour and hopefully will spend many more. Yesterday morning he left for Pontarlier etc. first over Dôle, Dijon and so forth, then perhaps on to Paris. I had accompanied him to St. Sulpice, where I took leave of him with tears in my eyes, who knows, for how long.

III
Years of Travel in Europe: Paris

Paris without the Eiffel Tower, without a subway and the youthful style of life, not to mention without the modern buildings. A Paris which had just obtained the wide, long boulevards, which had been laid out since 1852 by Georges Eugène Haussmann.

Then since 1854 the market places with the filigree steel constructions and between 1864 and 1867 the first, newly created green park in the shut down quarries on the formerly bare hills of the Butte Chaumont. In 1857 Garnier began with the construction of the new Opera House; the big city was still surrounded by a closed city wall. It was this Paris which received Otto Wyss in 1867.

The middle of the 19th century was characterized by the formation of national states. Above all, the founding of the German Empire, which was created from a union of 34 sovereign principalities and four free cities, was a stirring event for Europe. The Franco-Prussian War with the abdication of Napoleon III, the siege of Paris, and the proclamation of the French Third Republic culminated in the festive founding of the German Empire on January 18th, 1871, in Versailles.

In the spring of 1871 ensued the rebellion of the Commune in Paris, which was put down in a bloody manner.

The second half of the 19th century brought great economic prosperity for Europe. The Industrial Revolution flourished. Railroad lines were built, important companies founded, and the cities grew enormously. One felt oneself to be at the beginning of a new, better era, and this new enterprising spirit was manifested in expositions.

The social conditions and general circumstances of life, the progressing industrialization, brought political unrest. The setbacks in the trade cycles and the related great economic uncertainties contributed to this.

Whoever was healthy, could work, and had work, came through alright. Social security payments and work contracts in the present-day sense were unknown. And nevertheless life in those days must have been worth living.

Otto Wyss experiences this time of change, of revolution, as a worker in Paris, during the Franco-Prussian War back in Switzerland, and then in Manchester, England, where in 1873 the great workers' strikes broke out.

47

"The Swiss misses the beautiful mountains with their white snowcaps."

Paris, September 22nd, 1867

My Beloved!

This time I am writing these lines a good deal farther from you. Yes, I am in the French capital, and a 14 days trip has once again gone quite well. Emilie (How is she, by the way?) will have told you that she accompanied me as far as Flendrinas, and I was accompanied by a man from Zurich as far as Pontarlier. In the evening he went back home with the train, and I spent the night at an inn after a short walk. On the following day I came on foot almost to Salinas, which is a mainly mountainous highland with pretty and abundant cattle. Toward Salinas (which has perhaps 10,000 inhabitants) the region is very pretty, although the vineyards are very poorly cared for, wine here costs 20 centimes per half liter. The 20 degree mouchard [?] makes it very hot, and because I had sore feet, I took the train to Dôle (for about one Swiss franc). The latter city had a big machinery workshop, but all the jobs there were already taken. After I had looked around this old city with the beautiful theatre and other things and had lodged with an Aargauer, I took the following morning the first train to Dijon (with about 25-50,000 inhabitants). Directly across from the big and beautiful train station I found the machinery workshop of two men from Zurich, Uhler, Bosshart and Company from Altstätten. Here there was likewise no job available, and in the other workshops I found nothing else.

The city of Dijon is nothing less than beautiful, the water however very bad (just like in Dôle), and despite the July heat, the streets were not sprayed with water. I also found here a café, whose innkeeper was a man from Zurich (Hoffmann), and I saw there postcards of all Swiss cities, especially two beautiful views of Zurich. Toward evening I traveled a little farther, on the following day walked to the old Paris road over hills and vales and came in Vittreaux into the new main road, and toward evening I was lodged near the railroad and during the course of the night heard no less than 12 trains whiz by. On Saturday morning on to Noyer (ca. 6-7000 inhabitants), a region where just at that moment an agricultural fair was being held, and I decided to remain for Sunday and to take a closer look at this fair. Prizes were given out, but except for a few mustard plants and big red cabbages and turnips I saw nothing of exhibitions.

Toward evening lively folk games were performed, and finally was there given a large illuminated ball under the green leafy canopy of the festival park, in which contra-dances were danced in a lively and pretty manner by more than 50 persons; the latter represented all kinds of national folk dances and was fascinating to watch. So, in an excellent mood, I traveled on Monday morning to Auxerre and found in the evening good lodgings at the "Guten Winkel." Wine costs only 15 centimes per demi-liter and 20 centimes a bottle. Work was so to speak promised me, but since they kept putting me off with excuses, on

Tuesday I traveled on to Bassou. Here the countryside is, to be sure, also more beautiful, the most beautiful in France, gentle, ondulating hills of vineyards, poplars and acacia woods, long tree shaded alleys and little forests of walnut trees and then wide fruit and stubble fields, then a castle of a marquis, count, the country house of a Parisian and the large farm of a wealthy farmer, but, despite all this French natural beauty, the Swiss still misses the beautiful mountains with their white snowcaps in the distance.

Thus I came to Sens, a pretty, although barbaric, city; I looked around on Thursday morning for work with a half dozen mechanics.

In the evening I was in Monterau, where in the Sogeapuis I met a few mechanics, who gave me little prospect of finding work.

Thus on Friday [I] walked to Melun, a larger city, which has many military installations, an especially beautiful cavalry, then also right much commerce, but very little industry, and I could not find a single small workshop with only 10 workers.

The weather was rainy, so I cleaned up a bit and took on Saturday morning the first train to Paris. Thus I arrived at the Lyon train station, and after I had thanked the individuals who had offered to serve as guides, I looked for more workshops. In the northern and western quarters of the city I had visited about two dozen workshops and in two places I had received instructions that I should come back on Monday morning, and one of these (a manufacturer of all sorts of tools) thought that I should look for a room. Of course, that was easier said than done, because I could not afford the usual stipulations of 10–12 francs per week (always paid in advance). I finally today met this local innkeeper and came to an agreement with him for 5 francs for the next 14 days. There is another in the room, who has a blacksmithing craft, but has already been here a long time. The room has only one small window facing the courtyard, is for that reason a little dark, so that I now have no light and can hardly see to write, yet for the moment and for this price I can find nothing better. The bed has a good mattress, the quilt (as everywhere in France) is more a linen sheet, and a single wool blanket. The bed frame is made of iron, yet everything is at least clean. […]

Paris, September 22ⁿᵈ, 1867

My Beloved!

As far as my meals are concerned, I shall take them near the workshop, because from here it is a 20 minute walk to work. Meals are always cooked in advance, so today for lunch I'm making some coffee. The kitchen is directly to the right, the innkeeper is both cook and waiter at the same time, ladles out a spoonful of meat broth for 5 centimes, bread with it for 10 centimes, and voilà, I have a soup. A piece of beef for 2.5 centimes, cabbage with it for 15 centimes makes a lunch for 65 centimes (but it feeds only one). Today I took a look around the city, but could not find the world exposition (it is about one and a half hours

from here), yet I did go to the Champs Elysées, Hôtel des Invalides, to the beautiful Place de la Concorde, Place de Vendôme, Bastille, etc., saw the churches of Notre Dame, St. Sulpice, Madeleine, etc., so that I had difficulty finding my way back home in the confusion of people and cabs and the crowds in the streets. But another time more about Paris.—I would very much like to know soon how Emilie's affairs stand and shall in any event write to her soon. Accept, all of you, my warm greetings and kisses, your ever faithful
                    Otto
(You will certainly have trouble deciphering this scribble. Pardon, it is dark and I have no other pen.)
My address is therefore: O.W. in care of Mr. N Schlageder, marché de vin, Rue de la Roquette N 115 Paris I

Concerning the Wonders of the World Exposition.

Paris, Novemberf 1st, 1867

Beloved Father!

We have a holiday here today because Paris celebrates such holidays as fall on a weekday, much sooner than Sunday.

For the addresses I say many thanks, yet although I have already looked for all of them, they were all each time absent. A week ago last Sunday I visited the world exposition, but Mr. Maillard was also absent, and the Wegmannschen machines remained covered.

The workshop in which I work makes especially lathes, then parts machines, reamers, and milling machines, etc. The master Mr. Valengin from Morteau (near Switzerland) is a nimble, yet rather meticulous worker, who is up and about from early in the morning until late at night. Madame Valengin likewise works at her husband's shop and, to be sure, in a second workshop. There, where I work, are two other workers, both mannerly married chaps in their twenties, then an apprentice boy.

One of the workers speaks German, but he has a quite Dutch accent, which I cannot at all understand. We work from seven in the morning until noon, and from one until eight o'clock, in other words, twelve hours. We are paid on an hourly basis, and I received 35 centimes per hour and am paid every two weeks. In the mornings I usually get up around or somewhat after 6 o'clock and then have on the way to work a cup of coffee with milk and two rolls, for 25 centimes altogether. At lunchtime we quickly get at 12 o'clock some bread for 13 centimes, and then we go each time to our restaurant, where we pay a special group price of 50 centimes each for a meat broth, a good piece of meat with a vegetable and a quarter of a pint of beer.

In the evenings we usually have a piece of beef with sauce, as the selection might be. The drinking water in Paris is not good, yet at this season of the year it is at least not warm, and mixed with a little bit of wine it quenches the thirst, drunk straight [unmixed], however, it makes you sick. Yet I still want to see a little of the exposition, since it will only last a few more days.

I once again admired to my heart's content all the wonders which this world exposition offers, yet also this time I sought in vain for Mr. Maillard. At any rate, I would have been there very early to speak with him, because precisely he could have pointed out to me this and that worthy of special note. Yet I am pleased with what I have seen, and I had to hurry by many exhibits which I would have liked to study more carefully, yet I do still have an idea of the whole exposition; to see everything you would have had to take weeks instead of days. However, I can no longer begin to tell about the exposition and shall close for today. Farewell, beloved father, and may all my loved ones accept the sincerest greetings and kisses from your distant   Otto

Oskar's address is still: Gartenstrasse N 10, Breslau, right?

Swiss products at the World Exposition.

Paris, November 3rd, 1867

Dear Sister Anna!

My lines arrive at the dear Steinhof a bit later than I had expected, because I had at first planned to change my room, in order to be somewhat closer to the neighborhood where I work. The technical drawing schools, of which there are several in the various quarters of Paris, usually hold their classes from 8 until 10 in the evenings. In the neighborhood where I work, however, there are no such schools; on the other hand, in the Ecole Turgot several courses are offered by a polytechnical company and are even taught free for the workers. Thus on Mondays I attend (from 8:30 –10 PM): English, Wednesdays: Algebra, Thursdays: (Map Drawing and Plotting or Trigonometry), Fridays: French, and Sunday afternoons from 11:30 until 1 PM Applied Mechanics.—Of course, it is a bit late then when I get home at night, so that the downstairs entry door is locked and I must knock. This is of course unpleasant, yet in the heavily frequented neighborhoods where I work, they charge 25-39 francs for a room without a window, so that I shall probably stay here the whole winter. Moreover, I have been alone in this room for some time.

Well we want to make another quick visit to the exposition and go through the Swiss section. Foremost among its attractions is the Swiss Restaurant, which however is completely furnished in the Parisian style and is located beside the Swiss "Watering Hole," which in no way reminds one of the Swiss homeland. Nevertheless, we step inside the palace, and on the outermost edge (because we go from the edge to the center) stand the wines, where I also noted Zurich wines, among others Clevner of J. Hauser in Stadel and Castle Teufener.

Two Vaud wines from Nyon won bronze medals, and the wine from Yvorne received a silver medal. Absinth from Fleurier and Zug cherry-brandy, Alpine honey from the canton of Ticino and the products of Swiss chocolate manufacturers were also on display in this section. Now came the "Tools of the Watch Making Trade," and soon I had discovered the 5 machines from Demelais' workshop; two are already sold. All these pretty machines are however very unfavorably displayed and in a too crowded space

Besides which there are many steel wares, especially files from Bern and Geneva, yet few prizes for them. We pass by the numerous machines of Rieter and Company, which have won two gold and three silver medals, and there we see a few more machines from the telegraph workshops of Bern and Neuchâtel; then we go through the second row, the chemical products of Dr. Cramer in Zurich and the soaps of Steinfels, a few more steps out into a room, whose walls are trimmed in lighter and darker blue. A bed with gorgeous embroidery from Appenzell, then another mass of embroideries and silk fabrics from Basel and Zurich. We soon came to a collection of pretty gold work from Geneva, and now the straw wares of Aargau and the red dye-works of Zurich and the colorful woven materials and printing presses of Glarus and Winterthur. Finally comes something really Swiss, the wood carvings of Brienz and the Bernese Oberland. Further on the watches of Geneva and Neuchâtel, the organs of Ste. Croix and Geneva and pianos from Zurich (silver medal). The Swiss section in the Exposition Palace closes with a collection of architectural drawings by Professors Stadler, Semper, etc., and a pretty model of the Strasbourg Cathedral. I'll save the rest for another time. Accept my warmest greetings and kisses, your brother

Otto

Paris, November 17th, 67

My Dear Sister!

[…] You would perhaps like me to tell you about the things of Paris, of this great capital where there is every day something new. You will receive soon after these pages a little package for the New Year and also a few photographs to place in your album if you still have space (?!! not enough).

They are marked No. 1. This is the July Column (1830). It is placed on the square where earlier was located the prison (the terrible fortress), the Bastille, destroyed in 1789. It is cast in bronze (metal for cannons, quite expensive), and in the interior is located a staircase which you can climb up to the gallery above which still rises the statue of an angel holding the light of liberty in its hand.

This statue is gilded. The column is 143 feet high (the surrounding houses appear small). No. 2. This is the Pantheon or the church "Saint Geneviève." You also see in the photo the following words: "to great men, the grateful homeland." No. 3. The church "Notre Dame" of which you will have already seen drawings. No. 4 and 5 are two Japanese in their native dress. I saw them while they were out walking in the streets of Paris. No. 6 and 7 are two heads and No. 8 are flowers as you can see.

I would really have liked to send you some more photos, but I'll send them later. After that, you have the Almanach of the Flyer which has a lot of beautiful engravings of the exposition. I am not sending you a lot of candy. If you look through the little hole where there is a glass inside, from the rounded side, you will see the panoramic view of the entire exposition and all around it emperors, kings, queens, etc.

Finally a wallet and a machine for threading needles; that is all I am going to send you. The threader is a product of our own workshop, and I have also threaded with it, but it is made for weak eyes, with good eyes you can thread without it. At any rate, we have already sold a few thousand of these (at 2—2.50 francs a piece). This one works for no. 4, 5, 6 needles.

December 22nd. I want to finally finish these lines. It is rather cold again, and I don't know why, but the room is quite cold and damp. It has also snowed a few times, and at the beginning of December the snow lay on the ground for a few days and it is really cold. Are you happy with Mr. and Mrs. Favre? I hope so. What is August doing these days? I'll write to him as well. [...]

Otto

The French has a lot of mistakes, but it is too cold, correct and forgive them.

"Even the voracious prairie wolves and the yellow jackals sleep peacefully side by side."

Paris, January 5th, 1868

My dear Hanneli!

How much I would have liked to have been with you at Christmas and also on New Year's Day and would have discussed with you what the Christ Child would probably bring. Did he actually come? Just think, here they know nothing about the fact that the Christ Child brings people many beautiful things, and I have also not seen a single little Christmas tree.

But now I want to tell you a few things about a walk which I took on a beautiful Sunday in November in the botanical and zoological garden. The latter is located near the Seine, a river which is perhaps a little wider than the Limmat in Zurich. It is of course deep, but nonetheless I don't believe that it has much more water than the Limmat, because it flows slowly and has a yellowish color. Right beside the entrance to the garden is a coffee house, or inn, which, like a Bernese house, is constructed of wood and has the name "Swiss Cottage."

In these gardens there is no entrance fee, and yet one sees animals from all regions of the world and many more beautiful animals than in a menagerie.

They are one, two, or three, or even many more of the same kind beside one another in a garden, around which has been constructed a hedge of iron or wire. These animals range in size from the size of our room (where you sleep) to the size of a half acre. There is the buffalo from America, three splendid Bengal tigers from India, about five or six nimble jaguars from Brazil and two panthers. Further, there are a pair of African lions, Peruvian llamas and a reindeer from Finland, which are all very beautiful animals. These animals are not at all hungry, because even the voracious prairie wolves (five) and the yellow jackals sleep peacefully side by side and beside the pieces of meat which lie by them. Finally there is a big pond with strong posts around it for the hippopotamus, which however at the time of my visit was inside the building. There were also three pairs of bears in a pit, and they attracted with their comical maneuvers many spectators. Now I came to the cages where the birds were being fed. Whereas the condors and eagles chased around after a piece of meat, it was funny to see how in one cage an eagle, an Egyptian vulture and a crow were all living together. Whereas the big eagle sat in its tree with the biggest piece of meat and whereas the vulture likewise tore into its piece in a corner of the cage, the crafty crow hid its own piece between the wire grating and then tried to steal part of their food from the other two birds. Splendid guinea-fowls and gold and silver pheasants with really splendid shimmering colors, the pelicans and stork like birds. There were also the sacred Ibis and the crane, and after a walk through the botanical garden, where beautiful palms and also cotton and coffee plants were to be seen, [I] went back home, but how much more entertaining it would have been, if you had been with me, and we had seen all of this together. But now write me soon and do tell me what the little Christ Child has brought you. Always keep busy and stay happy in the New Year and accept best wishes and kisses from your distant brother

Otto

"No little bell rang in the cold on New Year's Night."

Paris, January 5th, 1868

My Beloved!

Christmas and New Year are over and you have all certainly asked, what on earth is Otto doing now, how does he spend his days? Why didn't he write us at New Year?

On the holy Christmas Day I wrote a little in the morning, but I soon got too cold and I looked for Mr. Heusser, who however was working. After I had attended a Catholic sermon and mass in the St. Bernhard Church, I finally found Mr. Heusser at lunch, and since he intended to work until nightfall, [I] went for a walk on Montmartre, a hill from whose height one has one of the most beautiful views over the city. The temperature was -3°, the weather was bright, but too many chimneys were smoking, so one could not see at all one end of the city. There you saw both towers of Notre Dame, the dome of the Hôtel des Invalides, under which is located the tomb of Napoleon I. Then the new Opera House, the Church of St. Sulpice, the Pantheon and to the east both of the towers, St. Ambroise and the Bastille or July Column. From there I looked for a Swiss brasserie on the Boulevard Magenta and read there a few newspapers such as the NZZ, Bund, Volksfreund, Postheiri.

After that I went to see Mr. Heusser, who had a beautifully heated room, and we talked politics a bit about the political movements in Zurich. How much has happened there so far? Here they do not celebrate a second day of Christmas, which made me happy, because it was growing colder and colder from day to day, and in my room I have no heat, whereas the workshop where we work is wonderfully warm. On New Year's Eve, Mr. Heusser and I went to the Tuileries and took a look at the comings and goings of the respectable world and said to each other at 12 o'clock midnight, "Guet's Neu's Jahr und guet Nacht," but no little bell rang in the cold New Year night, in which the thermometer sank down to -10°. On New Year morning I fled from my cold lodgings to Mr. Heusser's, and after we had looked at his drawings, we went to the Montmartre quarter and had lunch with an Eglisauer. After I had gone to call on the Otelfinger in Paris but had not found them at home, I then went to see a man from Basel, Merian, also to a Swiss brasserie, and then went back home to my lodgings, after I had dined on sauerkraut and bacon. On St. Berchtold's Day [January 2nd], I worked again as usual, i.e. only 8 hours, because the work is going badly. If it were not the worst possible time (because people complain everywhere), then I would have already looked for work elsewhere. Well, perhaps that will still happen this week, when I have finished my two lathes. I would have gladly changed my room today, but I shall pay for the month in advance, and so my address remains the same until the beginning of February.

January 10th. We finally have somewhat milder weather, and if at night it gets down to -5 and -6°, during the day it gets up to from -2 to +5°. Besides we had temperatures here as low as -12 and -13°, and the Seine is frozen over, so that the skaters dare to go out only part way onto her yellow-gray ice. Well last Wednesday I asked around for work in a lot of workshops, without success, on Thursday (yesterday) I was told to come back with certificates, livret, etc., and if these were suitable, I could work. This morning I went there with discharge certificates, etc., and can on Monday morning at seven go to work for Mr. Lecoq, rue Lafayette N. 203 and 205. From my present lodgings it is an hour's walk, and for winter weather that is of course too far, for which reason I shall definitely move out at the end of the month. In the neighborhood of the new workshop I have already looked at another room and also one with a man from Zurich (Glättli von Bonstetten) and shall perhaps then have the new address rue Faubourg St. Martin N. 91. Today at noon I met Mr. Heusser, had lunch with him, and he himself worked for this Mr. Lecoq last spring. He thought that I was lucky to have such a good job, and says that there are a steam machine and 60 workers in the workshop and that they do beautiful work. He himself grows bored with Paris and will move on in the spring, to Belgium, Petersburg or even to India! We are good friends, although he is ten years older than I, and although he has no high school diploma, he still draws rather well and does correct computations. For a while he was with a Baltenschwyler in Aarau, who gives practical instruction in machinery construction. I now attend every evening a drawing school near my present lodgings, because in the school which I previously attended, there is no order, anyone can attend, and when it got cold, all the street people (Auverniers)[45] came inside, because it was warm there, and even if I came a quarter of an hour before the beginning of class, I had to be happy if I found a seat behind the door niche, so I would rather pay the slight fee to go to my new drawing school.

Still, it is curious that on Sunday everything is closed, for example such drawing schools, and likewise during the 14 days over New Year and Christmas. Also zoological and botanical gardens, the Conservatoire des Arts et Métiers and all institutions of the kind where the worker could see and learn something for little or no expense, were closed.

The drawing school which I now attend was founded and is still run by the brothers (monks) and I don't find anything new here, but I do always get practice in drawing. Recently a few people protested that they wanted no Protestants, whereupon however the reasonable brothers explained that, as long as I bothered no one, I should be left in peace. I have just now received the lines from you, because, although they were already in Paris on Monday, they were delayed (the next to the last one came eight days late), because the number 115 had been omitted.

While I thank you all for your best wishes, receive, all of you, my most sincere best wishes and blessings for the upcoming and following year, may every letter always bring me good news from you, thus I am happier and more content abroad. Remain, all of you, happy and healthy and remember from time to time your distant

Otto

"Through my window I see no less than 35 high chimneys."

Paris, February 2nd, 1868

My Beloved!

As I reported in my last letter, so I have now changed my lodgings; through the recommendation of the aforementioned Mr. Glättli, I obtained this little room

---

[45] French immigrants from Auvergne. This region in central France sent large portions of its surplus population to Paris. Compare: Antoine Bonnefoy: *Les Auvergnats à Paris*. Paris 1933.

in a private house, where I live firstly more cheaply and secondly in clean surroundings.

The room is freshly wallpapered and has a big window facing the southeast, thus I have morning and partly afternoon sun. It is on the fourth floor, and through the window you see a very industrialized section of Paris, so I see no fewer than 35 high chimneys. There is nothing very beautiful to see except in the spring, when the four Buttes Chaumont (hilly parks) deck themselves in green. In clear weather you are supposed to be able to see the huge cemetery "Père Lachaise," because there the region is also free of obstructions, but now it is cloudy.

The room itself is furnished with a big, good bed, wardrobe, wall clock, paintings, table and night stand. I pay only 15 francs per month, that is, four weeks. This morning I had to drink coffee with Mr. and Mrs. Bardian (two little old people who are going on 60, but still take care of everything and are very friendly). They are alone, yet almost every day a married daughter is at their house with her two-year old boy. Monsieur is a piano builder and goes to work every day, yet they are certainly not without wealth. I therefore have every reason to be satisfied with my change of lodgings.

And now about the workshop, where I have been working these past three weeks. Altogether, it has around 60 workers and is thus the first bigger workshop in which I have worked. In the beginning they would not leave me alone, once I was supposed to pay the Quantaise (entrance fee) with a few liters of beer for my buddies, and the arrogant Frenchmen tried to intimidate the foreign Swiss guy, to force him to become a comrade.

Now, however, since I would not pay for a single drop of their liquor and would always put an end to their clowning with smiling equanimity, they leave me in peace. Thus far I have not undertaken any projects of much importance, yet pretty pieces of machinery are made, plane machines, presses of all kinds, right now a number of presses with pedals for the manufacture of train tickets. Then soon are supposed to be made machines for the making of gold lace for the weaving and embroidering of shawls. The arrangement in the workshop is very good, nice and good tools and tool machines, which are all driven by a Fargot steam engine with 12 horse-powers. Besides the big central workshop, there are also two warehouses, blacksmithy, office and drawing room, a cabinet-maker and polishing workshop, a sledge, etc.

The light falls through a glass roof into the workshop, and for that reason the latter is very bright and you need no windowpanes. In the evening we are lit by gas. We work from seven in the mornings until 11 AM, and from 12 until six in the evenings, thus ten hours. I am paid 40 centimes an hour, which makes exactly 4 francs per day. This is not much, but you can get by on it here. A few days before me, a man from Zurich, a blacksmith from Winterthur, began in that workshop, yet he was let go last Saturday, I don't know why. Otherwise, the only Swiss working here is a man from Geneva, as my only countryman.

Presently also working here is Jean Meyer, who is looking for work, but something will turn up, because the business is going better and better.

Mr. Heusser has right now a visitor from Russia, who in his youth was in the Escher factory in Zurich, but now has come here from England and would like to work here for a little while.—I am, thank God, healthy and happy and hope that this is also the case on the Steinhof. Emilie has recently written to me, and I shall answer her this evening. Hoping for a prompt answer may you all be greeted and kissed, your

Otto

at the address of Mr. Bardian, rue Canal St. Martin Nr. 15, Paris.

Concerning the Parisian Carnival.

Paris, March 26th, 1868

Beloved Sister Emma!

I finally get around to an answer to your dear lines of February 13th and am ready to answer your questions. As far as my wash is concerned, well part of it is in good condition, other items, on the other hand, are torn. There are enough washer women around here, and while the washing is not expensive, the mending is. A little button costs 20 centimes, a sewn seam 30-60 and a little inserted piece of cloth 70 centimes to 1.20 francs, were the prices asked by the first washer woman to whom I gave items to mend. That was however too much for me to pay, first of all, I could myself fasten things and mend myself a seam with big stitches, and, what was most amazing, even properly insert a piece of cloth. Mending things myself, however, just doesn't work. I already threw on the street a checkered shirt, with 2 white shirts, which are rather torn, because I don't know what else to do with them, and the same is the case with some socks. I have worn very little three white shirts, because since I have my things washed every week, I always put the same ones on. I shall next buy myself a few work shirts, but not yet white dress shirts.

You ask whether I have bought myself any clothing? Nothing yet, except for a pair of trousers and an expensive, plain felt hat for Sunday. Of course, I have already looked around here and there, because you must see to it that you are not deceived here. I have already bought myself four vests and find them very practical for working, but they don't last long. Now advise me what I should do with my old tattered things, keep them or throw them out in the street to the joy of the Parisian rag-pickers? That would probably be the best thing to do, well, write me.

Here things always go the same, both at my lodgings and in the workshop. On Mardi Gras and a week ago at Mitfasten we had the afternoons off, and yesterday took place the funeral of a worker from the workshop. Mr. Lecoq is also supposed to be sick. To be sure, I have no great work, still only subordinate tasks, but I do have great expectations that in the next months I shall be promoted.

And now something about the Carnival and Mitfasten. On Carnival Day a rich butcher here leads around the city two, three, or four fat oxen.[46] This year the first butcher of Paris, Luval, has taken over the procession. The latter owns eight large restaurants and around 20 butcher shops and all of the highest quality; he is supposed to be a millionaire yet he goes himself to the slaughter house, helps to slaughter cattle and sits with his dirty clothes and blood stained apron in his fine carriage.

From a program I saw that the procession would be presented to the Emperor Napoleon III on Mardi Gras, at one in the afternoon, in the Tuileries, and therefore I hurried there, but there were just too many people, and I could see nothing at all of the Imperial couple. The procession itself consisted of four yoked oxen which were bewreathed and bore the names of the oxen. They were beautiful, fat animals, and the biggest was supposed to weigh 1430 kilos, which seems to me incredible. Then came Mr. Duval and his son, processions of riders in historical dress, three floats with people dressed as insects, Frichinen, Bournichons and finally four more floats, which were supposed to represent the four parts of the globe. The procession was small, but considering that it is arranged by a single person, it is still impressive. I personally found little of note in the procession, a few rich costumes; what was nice about this parade was that everything was really diverse and colorful. A week ago took place the carnival of the washer women, or Mitfasten.[47] The Parisian washer women, you see, have their very own holiday, dress up and then parade around on foot and in wagons. A queen is also selected, and I saw her driving around in a carriage in a big blue silk dress with big chignons and a huge bouquet of flowers. Yet there was no orderliness, some drove there, others here, all around the city, until they all sit down together at a big dinner, and finally begins a ball, which lasts until the following morning. Thus is the Carnival of the diligent Parisian washer women.

On Joseph's Day there was also the festival of the carpenters,[48] which involved ribbons and flags and two pretty masterpieces (a Russian church with a wooden dome and a slender tower).[49] Carpenters with leather aprons and

---

[46] In the 19th century Paris celebrated its street carnival. Above all the parade on Shrove Tuesday, the "Mardi Gras," was famous, where, as Wyss describes it, the most beautiful oxen (actually intended for Easter) were led through the city, a custom which was observed in many other French cities (as well as Western Switzerland, where it took place shortly before Easter).

[47] The old carnival, here Mitfasten, was reserved for the pleasure of those simple people who, as servers and hawkers, had no time for such merrymaking on carnival itself.

[48] Joseph, as a carpenter, is the patron of cabinetmakers and carpenters.

[49] They are speaking of pieces of workmanship which a journeyman had to produce in order to be recognized as a true master of his craft.

polished axes were seated in the carriage of their hostel keeper,[50] who each time gets a new silk dress as a present from the guild. They drove to the church to mass and afterwards hold their dinner, which concludes with a ball. And thus will dear spring soon return to us, the days are already longer, yet it is still unpleasantly cool outdoors, and the cold north wind still blows briskly over the Buttes Chaumont. In the streets you see everywhere violets and sometimes a snowdrop, but not the same as at home, which are sold in small bouquets for ten centimes. You often see hyacinths in flower pots. In a few days you, dear sister, will celebrate your name day, for which I wish you God's blessings, happiness and health, and everything good. Warm greetings and kisses to all, may you be especially blessed and kissed by your brother
Otto

Concerning Easter Customs in Paris and Bugs in the Boarding House.

Paris, May 28th, 1868

Dear Sister Emilie!

This time I have made you wait a long time for an answer, yet you will surely receive these lines by Pentecost, and I am pleased that I am once again all well. Since the beginning of this month we have had oppressive heat here, and especially in the workshop you can hardly stand it, because the room has a glass roof and at the same time a steam engine is going in there. Because of this heat you get thirsty quick, and when you drink water, you become even thirstier. Thus twice I became so sick that I had to leave work and go home, where Madame Bardian made me some tea and I soon felt better. Just this week it became hot again, yet it seems to me as though the heat and the water bother me less and the work is going easier. Jean Meier Schmid has been recently experiencing the same thing and thinks that he has overdone it, and I do as well.—As far as the Easter holiday is concerned, we had unfriendly weather here at the time, so that people did not travel far. On Palm Sunday they sold everywhere branches of beech trees and these were stuck on hats, carriages, horses and in our shop on the regulator of the steam engine. In the afternoon I was with Hartmann Schybli and Heusser in the Louvre, in the painting galleries, where we admired the works of Raphael, Sanzio, Rubens, Rembrandt, etc. Also there the guards and the employees had stuck up beech branches and Mr. Heusser commented, "Oh well, the fools have to be marked, too!"

On Good Friday we worked as usual, only at noon, when we went out to eat, all restaurants and tea houses were closed, until we finally got some fish and potatoes from a restaurant keeper. On Easter Sunday I went to a Lutheran

---

[50] The innkeeper of the journeymen's hostel.

Protestant service and in the afternoon went with two Swiss, who eat in the same eating house, to the Faubourg St. Antoine, where a so called gingerbread market takes place from Easter until three weeks later. On Easter Monday we also did not work, but rather I stayed at home and took some notes from a book, which Mr. Heusser had loaned me, and I drew an egg. There were many of the latter for sale around the city, but ten centimes a piece is just too expensive. I did not see any painted eggs, but the confectioners had such made of sugar selling for as high as 400-500 francs (expensive eggs!). I was outside the city twice, specifically in the Bois de Boulogne, where I saw a horse race and last Sunday we went to St. Quen, where we bowled. On Pentecost Sunday I made an appointment with Mr. Heusser to go to the Champs-Elysées, to see there the annual exhibition of French painters, and also perhaps to bathe in the Seine. For Sunday a week from now I have planned with him an excursion to Versailles, in order to see the palace, museum, gardens, etc., and for the following Sunday another excursion to St. Cloud, to see the royal palace, the garden and the great fountains and water works. You see then that I still have a lot to see and plan to use the next few Sundays to do precisely that, provided that the weather is not too bad. In the city there is a completely different life, now that the spring is here, everywhere people are bustling about, people eat and drink in front of the inns in the streets, in the sidewalk cafés. You hear music and singing relatively less, except in the theaters and concert halls.

In general people here are somewhat dissatisfied with the government, although right now it is looking calmer than three weeks ago, at which time you heard people singing in the street "La république," "La marseillaise" and the "Guerre aux Tyrans." Recently nine members of the international workers' union were condemned to three months in prison and 100 francs in fines, because they had given support to the Geneva workers during their strike; the union was dissolved.

I am invited to Mr. Bardian's home once or twice every week, whether it is to drink a cup of coffee or to share a glass of wine with him, and then to chat a bit in the evening. On Ascension Day I helped Mr. Bardian in the cellar, because he had received from relatives in Montpellier a little keg containing 130 liters of wine, which we then drew off into bottles. The wine here is really excellent, but it costs 23½ centimes per liter just to enter the city [road toll]. I meet Mr. Heusser once or twice every week, when I go to the eating house, where he usually eats. Then we often go for walks in the evening in the charming parks of the Buttes Chaumont, the Parisian Switzerland. From the heights of these hills you have a broad vista over the gigantic city, whose boundary is not visible to the eye; only to the north can you see in clear weather beyond the city walls. There we sit and chat for about an hour and then go back home.

With the work in the workshop it almost always goes the same, and I almost always have the same job to do with copy presses of all sizes and formats. Since I deliver these completely done, the work is rather pleasant, but you don't learn much doing it. This week we finished two ticket presses to be sent to Moscow, and we are working a lot on a big weaver's loom for the manufacture of shawls, which is likewise destined for Russia, but it is being specially assembled so that we don't have much chance to see it. When the opportunity presents itself to change jobs without a loss of time, I shall certainly do it. However, I would not want to change lodgings because of my nice landlords, because if my present abode does have bugs, at least it doesn't have too many, because the house and the room are always kept clean, and they say that there is no such thing in all of Paris as a house without bugs (they are supposed to exist even in the Louvre), so if I moved, I could have even more bugs than here.

And how are things now on the dear Steinhof, where of course everything is clothed in beautiful spring flowers and greenery, and the newly planted garden must look quite pretty. Has Emilie come home from Goumoëns? She has probably been expecting from me another letter, which she will receive the next time. In the evenings I would like to get out of this sultry city air and go sit in the grass under the trees back home, but it is too far.

Farewell, dear sister, warm greetings and kisses to all!

Otto

"The new weapons and cannons are not urgently needed."

Paris, June 21st, 1868

Beloved Father!

Today nine months have gone by since I arrived here, and during this time I have seen and learned a great deal; however, there is still a great deal to see and especially to learn. I have seen the larger constructions, of which I heard people talking earlier, and the Museums of the Louvre and of Cluny, the Conservatoire des arts et métiers, etc.

For my particular profession I obviously have a lot to see and to learn in the Arts et Métiers, because there are housed there very rich collections of physical and astronomical apparatuses. The machines and models for mining and foundry works, spinning and weaving looms, steam ships, water wheels and finally chemical instruments and products and agricultural implements (among which for example a beautiful model of a Bernese farm house). All these collections and museums are open free to the public every Sunday.

Now would certainly be the right opportunity to make a profit in the Parisian workshops. In the one where I now work, quite beautiful products are made, presses of all types, gradations and prices and the most diverse purposes, what they are used for, however suitably constructed, they are worthy of note, but now I would prefer to work in a workshop in which are made steam engines or locomotives, or any bigger machines, whose construction would be somewhat complex.

However, right now the time is not favorable for such an enterprise, because since people are no longer talking about war, there is less urgent need of new weapons and cannons, and yesterday in a neighboring workshop they laid off 150 workers, because there were no more orders for the manufacture of the new Chassepat rifles. In our own workshop a few workers were also recently laid off, but now a few more have come to replace them, so that the gaps can be refilled.

Enclosed you receive, dear father, another smaller map of the city of Paris, which was often of service to me, in order to give me orientation. Now I have a bigger map, which however would be too big and too heavy for the envelope. The larger streets and lanes are printed on it, as well as the city's various neighborhoods. My present lodgings are located in a small street, which runs from the "Rue du Faubourg St. Martin" to the canal, the first street south of the intersection of the above mentioned street with the "Rue de Lafayette."

You can get an idea of the city's vast extent when you consider the fact that the length of the fortifications surrounding the city, consisting of a 10 m high wall, has a length of 112 kilometers. It is also curious to note how the Seine bends around Paris both below the city and on its northern side.

On your name day I bring you my most sincere wishes for happiness and my blessings from far away and I go home in my thoughts, in order to see the fresh roses and forget-me-nots, as I once used to bring them home. When shall I be home? May God order that, and may He watch over you and over your distant

Otto

Otto Becomes a Member of the Singing Club Harmonie.

Paris, October 25th, 1868

My Beloved!

You certainly have been waiting for news from me for some time, and I would have written, because I had enough time, just no work. Since Thursday I have been working again in a small workshop of about 12 workers. A new foreman had taken over in the Lecoq workshop; I had a quarrel with him and so left. In the present workshop are made tool machines such as plane- and boring machines, etc., but we have bad tools and the boss is often drunk. At any rate, I can still keep my room at Mr. Bardian's; it is a good quarter of an hour walk to work

Well, how are things at home? Has Oskar come back home? I have often thought so. Schmid Meier was here in Paris on the Napoleon holiday, without bringing me much news except what he brought of Otelfingen village gossip.

Singing association Harmonie Suisse de Paris in 1869. Otto Wyss in the second-lowest row, fourth from left.

You will then have had the visit from Mr. Maag, who came back about ten days ago. Hartmann Schybli brought me a few Otelfingen grapes and greetings from you and told me that there was not much new in Otelfingen. I am supposed to talk with his brother, whom I however have not yet seen.—A month ago I joined the singing club Swiss Harmony, which practices German and French songs on Tuesdays and Fridays. It consists only of Swiss members and presently includes about 30 active members. The entrance fee is 5 francs and the monthly contribution 2 francs, and moreover there exists an open fund to which you contribute 50 centimes per month, from which are paid every two years the travel costs of Harmonie to the Swiss singing festival back home. Last week they took up a collection for Swiss afflicted by the floods, and everyone in the audience gave 1 to 19 francs. Thank God the canton of Zurich has been spared these floods, except for the Sihltal.

Here in Paris business is going badly; thus I was, for example, in 30 different workshops in a single day without receiving any prospect of work.

I'll tell you about the Napoleon festival in my next letter. Hartmann Meier Schmid will probably go home in four or five weeks; I shall also give him a few lines to take to you, and while I await your dear news, I remain with warm greetings and kisses your

Otto

This afternoon I shall watch the gymnastic festival of the local Swiss gymnasts' club, then I'll go to Harmonie, and we shall sing.

"There lives in every Swiss breast an unnameable yearning."

Paris, December 1st, 1868

Beloved Grandmother!

Winter is coming, and certainly, dear grandmother, you have already often asked and wondered whether Otto is being taken care of this winter or whether he is freezing.

Winter is certainly the saddest season of the year for the worker who is living abroad. Yet two winters have come since I have been living abroad, and I am dealing with this one as calmly as if I were at home. I have plenty of clothes, because on workdays I cheerfully wear to work the old light Sunday trousers under my work trousers and a coat over the waistcoat with the warm scarf, and on Sundays I wear my trickled trousers and vest with a coat and the black violet overcoat and little round black hat.

I naturally must pay a little attention to clothes, since I have joined the Swiss Harmony Singing Club, because it has many clerks and tailors who always come clean and well groomed.

I shall soon buy myself a few white shirts and in time also a new hat. I have bought myself blue work trousers as well as woven woolen Parisian socks, which are quite cheap (1.50 francs a pair) but do not last long. I have freshly soled boots and also good slippers.

In the workshop things are going well with the work, for, whereas last week we only worked ten hours, we are now working eleven, specifically from six in the mornings until six in the evenings with an hour break, from 11–12 o'clock. I make 45 centimes per hour, thus four francs 95 per day, which is the average salary in Paris. Mr. Heusser makes the same amount. It is rumored here and there that there will be a mechanics' strike, yet hopefully it will not occur before the spring. I have pretty much filled up my evening hours for this winter, so I go on Wednesdays, Thursdays and Saturdays (from 8 to 10) to a drawing school, and Tuesdays and Fridays from 9–11 to the Harmony Club.

Last Sunday two weeks ago Harmony celebrated its annual banquet, which among others the local Swiss consul Dr. Kern[51] attended. I personally did not attend, am often on Sunday evening at the pub enjoying the friendly evening conversations, where people play the piano, sing and give speeches.

So time flies by abroad, but yet there are moments which pass by slowly and with deep emotion we sing, like back home, the beautiful song: "There lives in every Swiss breast an unspeakable yearning for home."

Well that is all for now and so accept, dearest grandmother, also on your name day, my most sincere wishes for happiness. May God watch over you, bless you, give you good health and fulfill your wishes and accompany your distant grandson. May God command that! With warm kisses I remain your thankful

Otto

A Box of Cacao for Mother at Christmas.

Paris, December 25th, 1868

Dear Parents and Grandmother!

It is Christmas Day, and I sit alone in my little room, because I don't have a Christmas tree. Luckily it is not yet quite cold, so that you do not have to freeze in your room. Toward evening Hartmann Meier Schmid's will come to see me, because he will probably go home next Sunday.

Through him you will receive these lines as well as a package, in which I have packed together a few small items. For you, dear father, the "Guide to Paris," which has already often helped me here, especially with its somewhat detailed map, only the street names are always being changed, so the rue des montagnes, where Mr. Heusser lives, was changed to the rue Bisson, and many more like that. For you, dear mother, I have enclosed a box full of cacao and

---

[51] Johann Conrad Kern (1808–1888), a minister invested with full powers in Paris from 1857–1883, one of the most important diplomats of Switzerland in the nineteenth century.

hope you will like it. I have sent a little coffee to dear grandmother, and it would please me if it is good and you would drink a nice little cup of it. It is not much that I am sending, so take it as a sign of love and gratitude. I would have gladly brought it home myself, but if I were a little bird, then the trip would still cost too much for me on my budget. But we are almost at the end of this year, and I shall spend New Year's Eve in the Harmony Club, which at year's end traditionally provides an evening of musical entertainment. We did so last Sunday as well, and I went there at 8 o'clock, where the pub was already full. This singing company owns its own piano, on which we play and sing. Chorus songs, quartets, solos, recitations followed one another in quick succession, and all too quickly the clock had struck 11:30, at which time the company breaks up and goes home. On New Year's Eve it will probably go on a little longer, because that is a free night.

At the New Year accept then my dear parents and beloved grandmother my sincerest best wishes and blessings from your distant son and grandson
Otto

Wyss gets to know the brutality of the police in Paris.

Paris, July 19th, 1869

Beloved Father!

When I received yesterday the dear little letter from Sister Emma, I was not a little astonished to hear that you had had no news from me for two months. Then what happened to my letters of the 20th and the 21st of last month? One possibility seems to me that the letter in which I talked about the unrest here and had condemned especially the brutality of the police and soldiers, was opened and destroyed by the French authorities. At any rate, I shall tell you again a few things about this and at least explain why I had good reason to condemn the police. When after the 8th and 9th of June the military and the sergeants de ville were making their patrols, they had the order to break up all dissident groups, and they certainly were more than rude in doing this. Thus on the 10th I was going home at 8:30 in the evening down through the Faubourg du Temple toward my lodgings, when a patrol of about 50 sergeants came up and drove before it a mass of people, men, women and children. Some of them shouted: "Vive le Rochefort"[52] and "Vive la république," while the sergeants swang their sabers right and left, hacking their way through the crowd. I quite calmly hugged the houses on the edge of the street, and when the big wave of sergeants came by, I shoved myself into the corner of a house hoping to avoid detection, and indeed most of the police had already gone by when yet another

---

[52] Victor Henri de Rochefort (1830–1913), as a publisher one of the sharpest opponents of Napoleon III.

one came galloping behind them, and gave me a blow on the head with a so called "death stick" (a lead pommel covered with iron wire), but I halted a second blow with my upraised hand and told him he should let me go home, whereupon he let me go. Right next to me there was also a woman who received a blow on the head, whereupon she fell down, yet a sergeant galloping by struck her a second time, so that blood spurted out of her skull and she lay still as though dead. I quickly sought the shelter of my hotel, because already the French cavalry was coming up the street swinging bare sabers. From my room I then saw how the infantry shoved people into doors with their rifle butts. We did not go to Harmony practice a few times, because it was too dangerous to go out into the streets, and even eight and 14 days later the stores and shops were closed at the slightest noise, so terrified was the population of Paris. In recent weeks the workers have been aiding one another financially, in order to help the families whose bread winners are or were prevented from going to work. [...]

If there were a lot of work, I would naturally work in the usual manner, except that we already were laid off from the 1st until the 8th of July a whole week because of the inventory, so that that could be done in two or three days. Last Thursday 14 days ago Mr. Heusser left for Buenos Aires in the Republic of La Plata.[53] If no regular job in his field presents itself there, he then plans to become a farmer in one of the colonies, which consist almost entirely of Swiss colonists. Previously, he had the intention to get a job in Quito, Republic of Ecuador, which however came to naught when he found out what he would be earning there! He had not written any more to Fankhauser in recent weeks, yet I shall probably write to him in the upcoming weeks. [...]

Otto

Paris, July 21st, 1869

My Dear Hanneli!

I would have already answered Emilie's little letter the day before yesterday, because it was Sunday, except there was an excursion of the Harmony Singing Club to St. Denis and since I am now the librarian, it is my job to provide the singers with the Club's notebooks and song books, or rather it is my duty to excuse myself in advance and to explain why I had no more time. The afternoon was somewhat boring, because we were very dispersed, and the various sections of the group came some on foot, some with the train and some in private coaches. St. Denis is a very old little city, and in the last years it has really grown and has besides the old cathedral a beautiful new (non-denominational) church.

Nonetheless, the most interesting thing about the city is the old cathedral, in which all the Kings of France, who died while still on the Throne, are

---

[53] Argentina at that time consisted of loosely unified provinces.

buried. A few grave monuments are very pretty in terms of size and design, yet all are made only of gray sandstone. In the chapels to the side of the central nave are to be found a few pretty paintings, and in the cellars are crowns and scepters of gold from the various kings, etc.

Afterwards we took a walk on the little island and made a boat trip on the Seine, whose waters flow by the city so slowly that one scarcely notices any current. After we had had our dinner together, we went back to Paris with the train at 10 o'clock in the evening.

Dear little sister, have you also perhaps taken a trip this summer, or will you take one? Yesterday I saw three wagons with children on them who had made a little trip.—Further, I must send you best wishes on your name day, since you have not received my first little letter. I am very glad that you like to go to school and especially that you are learning to play the piano. Stay happy, healthy and lively and write to me again, and I remain abroad with kisses and love your brother

Otto

Nostalgic Homesickness for the Cozy Warm Oven.

Paris, December 1st, 1869

Most Precious Grandmother!

Once again we have the long winter evenings, on which I once sat with you, dear grandmother and my brother and sisters, all of us so cozy by the warm oven, while you told us stories. How carefully I listened back then when you told of foreign lands and thought, if I were only grown, I would see for myself the great wide world with my own eyes. Thus it was once—and now, that I am out there in that world, I think back upon those halcyon hours and yearn for a time when I once again can sit with you and tell you of my time spent abroad.

Right now, however, I only want to tell you how things are going with me at present. As you already know, this year I had little luck finding work, yet it seems to me that things are finally looking up for me. From the beginning of August until last week I was always in a small workshop in which I had already worked last February and March. The boss suffered from consumption and in the workshop, where we were first three, then two workers, I finally remained all alone. Last Monday a week ago my boss died, and therefore I feared I would again have a bad winter before me. After the funeral had taken place on the following day, the inventory was taken, and a Mr. Lemoine, for whom we did most of our work recently, bought at invoice price our tools, materials and our already begun work. At the same time, he hired me to work for him, and promised me right away 50 centimes per hour and ten hours of work per day, for as long as I wanted to stay with him. He himself is an engraver and has about 12 workers, among whom there are three mechanics. Thus I once again had a guaranteed job and look forward with confidence to the winter, which yesterday and today is already beginning to make its harsh presence more known to us. [...]

On your name day, dear grandmother, accept my warmest best wishes and blessings; may God keep you healthy, and I remain abroad your faithful grandson

Otto

In the summer of 1870 there is a family reunion back home in Otelfingen. With the Harmony Club Otto travels to the Swiss National Singers Festival in Neuchâtel (July 10/11) and from there farther on to Otelfingen. At the end of July Wyss is again back in Paris. The Franco-Prussian War has broken out, and the news from the front grows worse and worse. The French authorities are speaking about the defense of the capital against the approaching Prussians.

Paris, June 21st, 1870

Dear Father!

Soon it will be time for me to come home for a few days to my dear family home, in order to see all my loved ones.

Time passes quickly and yet slowly, when one looks forward to a happy week or an upcoming reunion, and so one would like to hasten the departure. The latter is set for Friday morning, July 8th, and we shall first arrive in Neuchâtel on Saturday the 9th, because we have to wait about three hours in Pontarlier and Verrières. The 10th and 11th of July are the two holidays in Neuchâtel, during which we shall be housed in private homes. On the 12th most of the clubs will go back home, and since each of the members of our own group will then go his own way, I plan to join up with the Harmony Club from Zurich, especially because that way I shall have the chance to meet Mr. Kienast. Thus I shall be back home on the evening of the 12th or the morning of the 13th on the dear Steinhof.—The time of the return departure for France is still not finalized, i.e. with the train company, but the Harmony Society has set it tentatively for the evening of the 22nd of July or the morning of the 23rd. So I shall have 10 days, in which I shall have many errands to run and many commissions to fulfill, for example, to Eglisau, Töss, Richterswil, etc. Since the Harmony Society receives a 50% discount from the train company, we shall all travel together on both the original and the return trip; the number of traveling singers will be about 15-20, and the number of traveling companions will be about the same. Our treasury is somewhat low, and at any rate each member of the traveling party will only have to pay 15-20 francs for the trip from here to Neuchâtel and return. The teacher, director will also come along, in order to direct himself the French song :"The Peasants," which we are planning to sing at the festival. I shall keep the room which I now share with Heinrich Schlatter, lathe operator. The boss at the workshop said that, if I could, I should come back to work in about a week. [...]

"They say there is a revolution."

Paris, August 8th, 1870

My Beloved!

I have now been back here for two weeks, but they seemed to me longer than the previous days which I spent at home in the dear family home.

As far as the return trip to France is concerned, it went relatively well and quickly. We had to telegraph from Neuchâtel, in order to be transported via Dijon, and could then only on Saturday evening depart from Neuchâtel. It was a beautiful bright Saturday evening when we looked down upon the blue lake toward the Traverstal and saw rising up in the misty blue sky behind the lake the Freiburg Mountains and then the Bernese and Valais Alps. In Pontarlier each of us had to be searched by the customs officials, whereby I however went quickly through the inspection. We arrived in Dijon at midnight, then we ate something, and at 3 o'clock in the morning the train was supposed to move on, yet we had to wait until 3:45, because a regiment of Turcos and a regiment from the line had to also be transported in the same train. We finally sat in the car, and on Sunday afternoon we arrived without further incident at 2 o'clock—only 2½ hours later—in Paris, where Meier, Schlatter, Biedermann, etc. awaited me. There we had to go through customs again to inspect all edibles purchased in Switzerland, and I had to pay a customs tax of 55 centimes for caraway seeds and sausage.

Then the work began again on the following day, yet the first day the time seemed really long to me. Now the work is going worse, and especially as a result of the latest war news, which is unfavorable to the French, we have lost almost all our orders. Already last week our workday was shortened, and now we shall probably only work a half day.

August 10th. Today we worked only 5 hours, and from one day to the next the workshop can be closed. To be sure, I already have my eye on a job in another place, yet it depends on the war news whether it too will be closed. That particular workshop is a good hour from here in Montrouge, a section in the south of Paris. That would be fine with me, because now they are saying that there is a revolution, and then that neighborhood is much quieter.

The young people from 20-30 must all leave, and those from 30-40 are supposed to join the National Guard, in order to protect the walls of Paris against the Prussians, who are believed to be in the vicinity of Paris.

Yesterday I saw the wounded arriving here from the front. I was not up close, but yet I saw the kinds of mutilations and wounds which always make a sad impression. Many Swiss want to leave here, especially because of the revolution, yet for the present I am not yet thinking about that.

Heinrich Schlatter and Jean Meier are also speaking about going home, if they do not have any more work. Right now I think there will be one more bigger battle, and then the other powers will attempt to mediate between France and Prussia, and peace can once again be restored.

Paris Prepares for Defense; Foreigners Leave the Besieged City.

Paris, August 11th, 1870

My Beloved!

6 in the morning. Jean Meier and Heinrich Schlatter have just decided to leave Paris this evening. Well, I would almost go with them, but I first want to see how things go here. Paris is now in a state of siege, and I shall perhaps come home to Switzerland in eight days, especially if the Revolution does indeed break out here. I hope for and expect soon a change with the war conditions, yet we receive few and uncertain reports.

Jean Meier will probably bring home a small package with a torn shirt and 4 or 5 pairs of socks, which you should mend. He will report more to you himself (well I must go).

(Noon) As things now appear, it is still uncertain whether they will leave, because they still must go to the consul and after that to the prefect of police.

They wish to go to Neuchâtel, and Jean from there to Lucerne and then probably home. Henry wants to go to Geneva, where Hartmann Schybli presently works. Both hope to find work, for which I, however, can give them little hope. Naturally, I have neither encouraged nor discouraged their departure, because if I thought I could find work myself, I would also come with them, but still, if more unfavorable war reports come in, I shall follow them. Now entire crowds of Swiss citizens leave the city daily; likewise, citizens of Baden, Württemberg, Prussia attempt to leave, but they are not allowed to go.

If you speak German out loud or French with a bad accent in the street, they right away shout at you here: "Voilà un prussien, beat him up!" Naturally, right many Prussians live and plan to remain here, for they have established businesses in Paris.—The French here are busily occupied barricading the gates leading out of Paris, manning the walls with a few thousand cannon, and in all the barracks and garrison towns the young recruits are practicing with their weapons and are then being transported away to the front, in order to fill in the gaps left by their fallen comrades. In the barracks across from us a regiment often arrives late in the evenings, in order to hasten to the Strasbourg station early in the morning. There I have a friend who is a locomotive engineer, who told me yesterday that he has been taking train cars full of military powder and munitions supplies so close to the enemy that the bullets were flying all around him and many of the train cars were totally riddled with holes. On the way back from the front he carried mainly the wounded, and during the past five days he had to work around the clock with very few hours of rest.

4 in the afternoon. I have just received the dear lines from sister Anna and note that you have been awaiting news for a long time.—With deep regret I've noted that my dear aunt has already died, and yet I did not expect it so quickly. At any rate, I shall still write a few lines to Arnold and also wear the "sorrow,"[54] may she rest in peace.—I have spoken with the boss again this afternoon, and he says that he has a few more orders for engravings, so that we can work for another week, half time, five or six hours a day. I would be willing to work overtime, except that, if one has work, he wants the others to work as well; he doesn't want to show favoritism.

He says, if the Prussians besiege Paris, he, like most other Parisians, will have to join the National Guard in order to defend the walls of Paris and to keep the peace, because once the ministers have fallen from power, the French people wants the Republic.

I shall also probably soon change my room; whether I'll go to Montrouge or to Mr. Bardian, I don't know yet; it is especially important to me to be in a peaceful place where I am recommended or known. The Swiss Harmony Club held their practice last Tuesday, but the membership has dropped to below 20, and if there is bad war news from France, it will perhaps be discontinued. The "Society for Mutual Aid" has likewise discontinued its regular meetings. In brief, the war is having negative effects on everything here.

Perhaps Jean Meier will bring you these lines himself soon, Henry, on the other hand, plans at present to remain in Neuchâtel or wherever he can find work. Thus Adieu my loved ones, once again thank you so much for everything, and don't worry about me, if things get out of hand here, then I shall come home right away.

With warm greetings and kisses from your distant
Otto

"People here speak of treason and have no trust."

Paris, August 28th, 1870
My Beloved!

Daily 2-300 Swiss citizens travel back to their homeland, and thus most of my comrades have left. The bringer of these lines will also leave this afternoon, to

---

[54] i.e. a kind of black ribbon worn on one's jacket as a sign of mourning.

go to Töss. His name is Jakob Leberer and we were at his mother's home when we were in Winterthur and Töss. Mr. Biedermann has likewise gone back home this week and will perhaps visit Otelfingen. Are Schlatter and Meier already home? I don't know when I too shall perhaps come home, yet as long as I have work here and no one tells me to leave, I shall remain. In the workshops things are going very badly, although we only work half time, there are no orders.

It would probably be difficult to find work in Switzerland right now as well, because it is probably like here, even where there is work, there is no money. [...]

As far as my smallpox inoculations are concerned, they had no further effect; moreover, one hears little here about smallpox victims. Here we have not heard a single word from the front for a week; people speak of treason and have no trust.

Now farewell with warm greetings and kisses your thankful
                                            Otto

Otto Wyss in shop clothes, 1871, in Zürich

Return to Switzerland.

Father Jean wrote in his diary:

When the Franco-Prussian War broke out and Otto's boss and the other workers were called to the defense of Paris, Otto as a Swiss citizen had only the duty to keep the workshop in order. Only when all the preparations for the

Prussian bombardment of the city were finalized did his master explain to him that he either had to leave the city before nightfall or enter the ranks of the defenders.

Otto chose the former course, closed the workshop, on August 31st, 1870 placed his writings, drawings, books, clothes, etc. in storage and hastened with light baggage to the train station—just in the nick of time to catch the last train out of Paris.

He came home, unexpected by us, joyfully received, yet he continued to seek work. He no longer felt at home with his family and was ready to accept any work through which he could earn a living.

After unsuitable employment in Frauenfeld, he entered a big machinery workshop in Zurich. From this period originates his photo in working clothes. However, as soon as the German military had pulled out of Paris, Otto tried to go back to his old job in Paris.

On March 23rd, 1872, I accompanied my son Otto via Baden as far as Wildegg.

The father sensed that his second son had become estranged from his parental home, to which he nonetheless remained faithful all his life. The farewell in Wildegg on March 23rd, 1872 was for both final.

Otto's elder brother Oskar came back from Breslau in 1869 and on September 23rd, 1869 married Caroline Kienast. Sister Emma went in the spring of 1870 to Regensdorf, where she ran the local post office, assisted in the management of the inn at the post office there, and got to know secondary teacher Albert Schmid, whom she married on July 3rd, 1873.

On December 3rd, 1871 Otto's mother died at the Steinhof at the age of 54 and on December 7th was buried beside the church.

Return to War-Damaged Paris.

The French capital to which Wyss returned in 1872 presented a sad picture. It had greatly suffered under the Prussian siege and above all during the repression of the "Commune." This revolutionary regime had lasted from March until May 1871 and had resisted the new French government which was assembled in Versailles and which the population of Paris reproached for its bourgeois and above all monarchist tendencies. Anti-social measures had additionally increased the bitterness of the Parisian working class, who had greatly suffered under the siege. The quelling of this rebellion was a bloody affair and led to heavy destruction throughout the city.

Paris, May 3rd, 1872

My Beloved!

I finally get around to writing a few lines, because only the day before yesterday did Schybli and I take the room together and move in and get settled.

Now first of all a few things about my trip. Under incessant rain I arrived in Basel and there looked for a colleague, after I had stored my baggage in the "Ship." I then met one of them, and we took a look at the cathedral, museum, etc.; I then in the evening met two others, Lehmann and Flammer, and thus we chatted together a few more hours. In the morning I bought the train ticket for 33 francs 50 centimes and retrieved my trunk, which was released to me, and soon we were saying "Ade" (farewell) to the Swiss homeland. At 9 o'clock we had a quarter of an hour stop in Mühlhausen, and at 11 we were in Belfort. After half an hour we got on the train again, but then we had to show our tickets and passports, and since I had no visa from the French consul, I, along with a young man from Rapperswil, who also had none, had to go back to Basel. After I had given the tickets to the station master and had spoken with him, to make sure they would be valid for the following day, we looked around the city and the Belfort fortress and traveled on to Basel after 2 o'clock. Having arrived there after 4:30, I tried to hunt down the consul or his secretary, but despite the fact that I chased after porters and commissioners and ran around until 8:30 in the evening, it was of no avail. We soon went back to the hotel to get some rest. On the following morning we had to wait until after 9, until the consulate was open and after 10 we were steaming toward Mühlhausen and changed trains there. After we had looked around the extensive factory city, at 5:30 we traveled on to Belfort and from there after 9 farther on. I got the tickets without any problem, but this time no one else asked about passports or visas, so there were three passengers in the same car who had no visa. The train chugged farther and farther along, only stopping at the large stations, where everything was still and dark. Everyone made themselves comfortable and tried to get a little sleep, but for most it was too cold. The morning dawned early, we got a little water, washed ourselves and yet became even blacker from the coal dust and scrapped together some leftovers for breakfast. At 9 we saw from a distance the forts of Rosney and Aubervilliers, then we came by war damaged houses, new structures, mended roofs, etc. and finally traveled through the spacious freight station between hills of coal, pig iron and construction materials, past endless rows of train cars and finally pulled into the Strasbourg station at 10 o'clock. The trunks had naturally already arrived earlier, and I just left them where they were. I then first went to Scherer, an eating house, where I often ate during my earlier stay in Paris, and was welcomed in a friendly manner. I met a few old colleagues, among others also W. Frey from Regensdorf, who eagerly asked many questions concerning things back home in Switzerland. After lunch I went to see my old friend Mr. Lemoine, who showed me around his workshop in a friendly manner, and told me how he had been condemned to death by the Commune and had had to hide in disguise in another section of the city.—That he was now married and had come back to the business, etc.

May 4th. Business has not been going strong lately, yet all bench-vises are occupied, and if I want to join his business, he will have a new work bench constructed and will buy a vise. I agreed, and I was supposed to begin on Monday. Afterwards, I went to the Hotel Parmentier, and chatted there with the old porter, who said that during the siege they had hungered and suffered, but during the Commune it was even more awful, more than once a bayonet had been thrust into his breast. Then I asked after Schybli in the Hotel St. Maur, where I was told he would come back from work after six. Then I also found an old acquaintance, Schäppi von Horgen, also a mechanic, who however had been without work for three weeks. He complained about how bad it was going, and had decided to go to Amiens at the beginning of next week, whither he has actually gone. Then I looked for the rue canal St. Martin, where I met Madame Bardian and was invited to coffee on the following evening. I have since got back all my old things, and found in order my slippers, my straw hat, etc., only a pair of freshly soled slippers were no more to be found, yet of course I was in no position to make a lot of noise about it. They had almost always someone in the room, and even now a coworker of Mr. Bardian lives there. Tomorrow I am invited again to lunch and shall then hear more about the sad times. Street fighting took place about 300 paces from the house, yet they had fled into the cellar for only a day, on the other hand, there were fires nearby, and for five to six days they saw burning the warehouses of Villette, so that at night it was so bright in the room that you could read. They had enough to eat, but Mr. Bardian received rations for four persons instead of three or two, because he had been able to arrange it.

And now for a walk on the streets and boulevards of Paris. There were a lot of new, repaired and freshly painted houses, the corner houses had been everywhere especially hard hit. A few are still standing, half burned down, damaged by shell fire, with no remaining windowpanes; thus I counted in one square meter of an oaken door of the "magasin réuni" over 50 holes made by rifle shots and three made by cannon shots. The burned out Tuileries Palace stands as a gaunt witness of the war's destruction, the Louvre, with few wooden combustible materials inside, escaped the flames of war, and from outside looks almost undamaged, and of course you cannot go inside. The beautiful gas street lamps, fountains, and statues lie broken here and there on the ground; only the new Opera House stands undamaged, now the most beautiful building of this world capital.

I have worked this entire week and am now once again back into the swing of things. The old colleagues at work are all very friendly, on the other hand there are two new workers who are grumbling about me the newcomer, but it will turn out alright. The room where we now live is bright, roomy, on the fourth floor of the spacious 100 room hotel. I shall close for now. To you all

my loved ones, once again warm thanks for your friendly loving care and gifts and sincere greetings and kisses from your
                                           Otto
Rue St. Maur N. 204; Hôtel St. Maur; Paris
Friendly Greetings from H. Schybli.

Life in Paris Becomes Normal Again.

                                                    Paris, June 23rd, 1872
Beloved Father!

This week I received your dear letter, as well as the one from friend Stamm. From brother Oskar I have likewise this week received news and am pleased that everything is well at home. Also the business here in the workshop in Paris is going in an orderly fashion, we work the entire time, whereas in other, similar workshops they work only half or ¾ of the regular time. The boss again brings me, as he did in earlier days, a great deal of fine work which should be done with taste or chique, and is always friendly and happy. My coworkers, who at the beginning were somewhat coarse and unfriendly, are now very mannerly, part of them courteous with me; there are only two or three, who bother one another and others with their teasing. I could not complain at all because of the workshop. Every Saturday evening after 7 each worker is paid his weekly salary up to the last hour, not a la Locher like in Zurich. For lunch I usually go from noon to 1 PM to a Richterswiler, Scherer, across from the workshop. Several other Swiss people eat there, then the Bund and Bürkli newspapers are there, so that I always feel a little bit at home. Compared to earlier, prices are generally more expensive, so, for example, you used to get wine for 60 centimes per liter, now only for 80 centimes; a piece of roasted meat, once 30 centimes, is now everywhere 40 centimes; a piece of beef, once 25 centimes, now 30 centimes, and when you eat a lot, that adds up quickly. The lodgings are the same; they were previously cheaper, but now some apartments stand empty, which is attributed to the move of the National Assembly to Versailles. Thus we have in this Hotel St. Maur, with over 120 rooms, the Number 36 on the fourth floor, and Schybli and I are quite content, because we have a free view out upon the Buttes Chaumont, Belleville, to the left, and the market place St. Maur, to the right the huge chimney of a bolt and screw factory with 50-60 workers and numerous machines. In the room are one bed for two, one regular table, two armchairs, a big chest of drawers, two racks for hanging up clothes, a night stand etc. This week with the onslaught of the heat, came also the bugs, which let me sleep little, yet now it is a bit better. The landlord is also Swiss, a Chapuis from Lausanne, who rented us the room for a somewhat lower price-24 francs. The Sunday before last I was in the Bois de Boulogne and watched the race, where among other things a prize of 100,000

francs was won. There were 20 horses, but what a gallop!!! Afterwards I went to Suresnes and to Mont-Valerien with its beautiful location. For next Sunday I plan to go to Verssailles, because then the great fountains are supposed to be operating. I find my little trunk just too small, and shall buy a bigger one and send home the old one with the superfluous things. Now I have a request from W. Frey of Regensdorf. Specifically, he would like to receive here a local paper from back home, similar to the Lägernbote or Wehntaler or Dielsdorfer newspaper, and would gladly pay me the downpayment. So I would like to ask you, dear father, to subscribe me to this at the following address: O.W. care of Mr. Scherer, and for a year, and note on the subscription form: 19 Quay Valmy 19, Paris, also how high the postage is. [...]
Otto

The next letter to his younger sister testifies to the era's enthusiasm for technological innovations—we are in the era of industrialization, whihc is also reflected in the matter of exhibitions.

Paris, August 11th, 1872
Dear Little Sister!

Today I want to write you a few more lines, because, if possible, I would like to leave here in two weeks and so put everything soon in order. Today it is more beautiful after a rather rainy week, and in the afternoon I would like to go to the Industrial Palace to see an industrial exhibition, which was opened there two weeks ago. Here every Sunday you can see something new and interesting, and I shall tell you a bit about it.—On the first Sunday, April 28th, I visited the Arts and Métiers. There, machines for machinery workshops, agriculture, etc., are exhibited. Right by the entrance is a hall whose ceiling has an elliptical shape. If you go into a corner and speak only softly, another person standing in the opposite corner can understand you quite clearly, whereas you can hear nothing at all in the middle of the hall. At the same time, there stands in the hall the model of a war steamship, very prettily made in a glass case. It is about 12–14 feet long and 6 feet high. You can see the steam engine quite clearly inside the ship. Beside it there is an older steam engine with a rolling mill. To the left are rooms where all older and new measures and weights, scales, etc. of the various countries are exhibited. Then come optical and astronomical instruments, huge telescopes, splendid clockwork, in glass cases many planets and solar systems with clockwork, then musical boxes, clockworks for pocket watches and wall clocks, small machines for the manufacture of wheels and watch parts, etc. Coming out of the hall to the right are machines for the extraction of metals, steam hammer models of all kinds, then spinning machines and looms, Jacquard and India looms, which look curious enough, farther on the map of the big mine and foundry of Creusot. Wrought iron and foundry products and then a department reserved for agriculture. Upon entering the agricultural exhibit area, the first thing which greets your gaze is a few hundred sorts of apples and pears and other fruit, then mattocks, picks, hoes, rakes, forks and beside them cattle with huge horns, of various colors and races, horses, harnesses, ploughs, windmills, sowing machines, barrels, etc., etc. Still farther and you believe yourself to be almost in a factory, and yet it is the cellar of an old church of the St. Martin cloister, as in general the constructions of this collection are nothing more than the former cloister St. Martin, suppressed since 1790, if I am not mistaken. There is now on one side a steam engine, which drives transmissions, and from this one engine are set in motion lathes, planing machines, boring machines, etc., just so the visitor can see how all the machines function. On the other side is a big water basin and attached to it are pumps of all sorts which pump water into a 12 feet higher trough, farther on a small turbine and a tangent wheel. Thus the viewer has a right nice, comparative overview of the different machines and motors in action. If you climb up a long stairway, you will enter the upper galleries containing collections of physics instruments, machines for sugar and chocolate factories, many models of steam engines, steam ships and sailing ships, wind- and water mills, saws of every kind, locomotives, train cars for American railroads, which contain a kitchen, dining room and billiard room, etc. Still farther on models for bridges and houses and finally collections for lithography, book printing and porcelain and glass.

I made further excursions on Sundays to the Bois de Boulogne, to Surènes, Mont Valerien, St. Cloud and Montarot, the last three hard hit by the last war. St. Mandé, Vincennes with the singing club Swiss Harmony as invited guests; then in Pantin and near St. Gervais, Aubervilliers and St. Denis. I also made another visit to Versailles, with its museums, and the splendid palace, especially its interior. Of course, now a part of the palace has been converted for the meetings of the National Assembly, and other rooms have been closed for repairs. A further excursion to Sèvres, Meudon allowed me to see clearly the effects of the war. In the city I was in the rue Fontenelle in Montmartre, where both generals of the Commune were shot.[55] I also visited the Buttes Chaumont, the Père Lachaise Cemetery, la Roquette, Notre Dame, the prefecture of police, the Pantheon, the Tuileries, and shall, if possible, make another trip through the catacombs. In the Louvre the collections of paintings are still undamaged, and I have also seen the one in the Palais de Luxembourg. The painting exhibition in May and June in the Palace of Industry, twice. Thus you see that, in my free time, I try to see something beautiful and useful.

Well I shall close. You will find "a donkey" to your address, and be warmly kissed by your sincerely loving brother

Otto

---

[55] Claude Martin Lecomte and Clément Thomas. These were generals on the side of the government. Their summary execution on March 18th, 1871 brought an end to the uprising.

New Destination: London.

Paris, August 18th, 1872

Dear Grandmother!

You have certainly recently asked, is Otto already in England? No, not yet, but I soon shall be, in two weeks, thus I would like to depart on September 1st, unless something unexpected occurs. Schybli has already left four weeks ago for London, and I have already received two letters from him, saying that he is doing fine. About London and further relationships he writes little, but no matter, I shall soon see for myself, yet he is growing bored, for he has not yet made friends with anyone. Friend Gretener wrote me that he could not yet return to England and advised me to remain a while in London and then, when I can speak pretty good English, he will see what he can do, in any event, he thinks it would be a good idea for me to introduce myself to Mr. Felber in Manchester, to see if there is an opportunity to enter his office as a technical draftsman. Here everything is going the usual, calm way. Work has not been going strong at all for weeks, so that I could easily take the time to take care of some business for friend Stamm.

With the little trunk I am sending home also some torn and older things, as well as the old coat, if it still can find a place. Looking at one's shirts, one can tell that the Parisian washer women wash them, yet I have worn only 2 white and 3 work shirts and have kept the others in my trunk. Accept, dear grandmother, a small porcelain bouquet as a sign of my gratitude. With kisses and love your thankful grandson
Otto

IV

Manchester

Thus Wyss leaves France in order to find in England more favorable working conditions. He brings with him a rich harvest of professional experiences from Paris. He has consistently used his free time to further educate himself through courses and in the technological museums and exhibits. England, at that time the most industrialized country of Europe, seems to offer him those possibilities for professional development of which he speaks again and again in the letters.

"I have not yet seen the bright sun in the blue sky."

Manchester, September 15th, 1872

Dear Brother!

[…] As I planned, I was able to put my things in order in Paris on September 1st and depart at 4 in the afternoon. I took the route over Amiens and Boulogne, where I arrived at 11 at night. At midnight I boarded the steam ship "Tition," in order to go up the Thames to London. This wheel steamer, about twice as big as one on the Zürichsee, departed at midnight, and steamed by the light houses with their electrical lights and toward the open sea. A fresh sea breeze drove rather strong waves toward the beach, and soon the ship was pitching and tossing on the waves, rising and sinking about 4-5 feet. I was up front at the bow-sprit and looked out upon the open sea. After one in the morning we left the last light houses behind us, the night was starless, yet not dark. The ship's rudder and especially the side wheels created almost silver white waves, which strangely gave off light. I soon became seasick, however, and I went down to the cabins. There on both sides of the ship there were boxes like a rack, and in each of them a mattress and just enough room so that a man could turn around, but all were occupied, so I had to lie down beside others on a mattress on the floor. I could soon sleep a little, and when I awoke at 4:30 in the morning, the sea was calm and soon day broke. I went up on deck, washed myself with the salty sea water and looked around. In the distance one saw a few sails and to the north a dark stripe, which surely had to be the coast of England. After two hours the coast also appeared on the other side, we were at the mouth of the Thames. Coming in our direction were many ships, which

83

were heading toward the open sea propelled by a favorable light wind. From the small fishing boat to the big three-masted ship, they all had sails and presented a quite majestic sight, all sizes and also almost all nations were represented. Soon we met a flotilla of the English navy, which, with gleaming metal orifices, seven steamers at an equal distance from one another, was proudly steering up the Thames.—There were over a hundred passengers on board the ship, but the greatest part Englishmen. Soon we were approaching London. One could see to the right the forest of masts of the Docks, where the ships are loaded and unloaded and also repaired. Soon came a few workshops and then rows of warehouses and depots and shops of all nations and classes which were moored nearby. After 11 our ship finally landed below London Bridge, and I took a cab, loaded my trunk etc. on it and drove to the Hotel Golberger, where I had an address and for 5½ pounds or 7 francs I rented a room for a week.

Then I looked for work; Germans promised to give me something in eight or 14 days, Englishmen thought I could not speak English fluently enough, and then here they take all the new arrivals from Paris for communists. When by Tuesday and Wednesday nothing had turned up, I decided to go on to Manchester, but before leaving, I wanted to see the exhibition in the Crystal Palace and the docks, in general to see whatever was worth seeing. So I ran around there, traveled by train under the Thames and through the city, down the Thames by steam ship, saw the East Indies Company, London docks, etc. I also saw the cathedral of St. Paul, Parliament House, Waterloo Square and Bridge, the Bank of England, the British Museum, Hyde and Regents Parks, ran myself sometimes ragged, yet never ran out of things to do. London is three times bigger than Paris, and you can really get an idea here of what a city should be. London is not beautiful, even if there are many architecturally beautifully built houses here, because most have been aged with time by smoke and fog, and many big beautiful buildings and churchlike train stations are built only of brick.

Life here is rather expensive, you usually have coffee in the morning, 2 soft boiled eggs with toast, at noon 90 centimes worth of roast beef and potatoes, bread and one glass of beer for 1 franc 25 centimes and at night fish or cheese, butter slices and tea for 1 franc. That is thus the cheap, usual thing to do also here in Manchester. However, the workers also eat a lot of bacon, which is not expensive here, 50-90 centimes per pound, yet I have still seen little or none eaten in public inns.

On Sunday, September 8th, accompanied by Schybli, I steamed by train northward toward Manchester, where we arrived at 6 in the evening after a 7 hour trip. We had soon found lodgings, which friend Gretener had recommended to me, and on the following day I looked around for work. At first, prospects seemed rather bad. Only when Mr. Felber, employed with a Zurich-based machinery agency here, made the effort to personally introduce Schybli and me and to recommend us, could we begin to work last Friday. I am now in charge of the assembly of wool, fore- and fine-spinning machines with the Gurthis, Parr and Madely Company, in Chapel Street. It is a workshop of 1400 workers, who only work at this branch. My English is coming slowly, but it will get better. The weather is almost always overcast and rainy, I have never yet seen the sun bright in the blue sky, and the smoke is often blown down into the streets. Factory chimneys are therefore of a height such as I have seen neither in Paris nor anywhere else. The city has little of interest to offer. The one and two story houses are built of brick in almost the entire city, and only in the middle of the city do you find a few three story dwellings, which are of another type.

For now I shall close, from home I received some more letters shortly before my departure from France and shall write home in two weeks, shall occasionally share some news with them, because I shall perhaps change my living quarters, but I do not yet know anything definite. So write me soon with your news, and be, like your wife and dear children, warmly greeted by your faithful brother

Otto

Manchester, which Wyss chose as his next place of employment, was in those days the center of the English cotton spinning industry as well as the embodiment of the modern spirit of profit- seeking entrepreneurship.

"The workers here are not pretentious."

Manchester, September 29th, 1872

My Beloved!

This week I received an answer from brother Oskar that the little trunk has come home safely. I had sent it to Oskar's address, so that it would not remain lying in the Baden train station, but rather would arrive at its destination. Brother Oskar has surely shared with you all promptly something from my last letter to him, because I had to also see here how I would arrange myself and for that reason wanted to wait to write. Now for the beginning I am content. The Gurtis, Parr and Madely workshop has about 1400 workers and is a five story extensive establishment, and in the entire company there is, with the exception of a young Russian, not a single foreign worker.—After we had presented ourselves to Mr. Felber and had been recommended by Gretener, he himself came along, in order to speak with the director Mr. Tompson, as a result of which I got the job in the assembly of machines for wool spinning. My coworkers are, like Englishmen in general, skillful workers; to be sure, the English mechanic serves as an apprentice for seven years, until he can enter another business as a full-fledged worker. Moreover, I do my work quite competently and I likewise get along well with the other workers, who are friendly, decent and try to learn something, and otherwise are not pretentious and keep especially focused on their common interests. The work week is only 54 hours per week, specifically Mondays from 8:30 in the morning until 5:30 in the evening, Saturdays from 6 until 12 noon, and all other weekdays from 6 in the morning until 5:30 in the evening, Fridays until 6. From 8:30 until 9 in the mornings is breakfast and from 1-2 o'clock is lunch. Both of us, Schybli and I, received the complete salary of 30 shillings per week. For room and board we have to pay 15 shillings per week, wash included. For breakfast there is coffee with a little milk, often used here is the condensed Swiss milk, which, if I am not mistaken, is manufactured in Cham.[56] With it buttered toast, often roasted over the fire, and 2 soft boiled eggs. At noon a piece of roast beef and peeled and boiled potatoes and pudding, i.e., some kind of pastry for dessert. In the evening there is tea or coffee with bread or buttered toast and cold roast beef. On Sundays we have the same as during the week, only, in addition, a glass of beer with lunch. The term "room" is here understood almost everywhere to mean bedroom, and in this neighborhood the lodgings are very much in demand. We have here a bedroom on the third floor, but only a bed, little table, little chest, etc. For writing we have available to us at our convenience the upper parlor, where a piano also stands and which is always open to us. We eat in the lower parlor. Our landlords actually have a grocer's shop and a so called dining room or bed and breakfast inn, where, however, drinks are not served. During the week at noon there are rather many people downstairs, upstairs only a few gentlemen. In the evenings no one comes upstairs, and thus we are completely undisturbed. Sunday is very quiet, the stores are closed the entire day, and the inns, which here are not relatively numerous, are open only in the evenings from 6–10. Manchester is really a factory city. In the middle of the city there are only a few exterior house walls made of stone, otherwise one sees everywhere only the one- and two story houses made of red brick, which, when new, have a quite agreeable appearance but, when old and half run down, present a miserable aspect. In the midst of all this, the six, seven and even eight story huge factory buildings rise high above all this with their chimneys overshadowing everything, chimneys which tower much higher than all [which I] have seen so far up into the sky and the mist. The weather here is very unpredictable; this week it rained every day.

Another time more, I have not mentioned anything at all about the trip. Warm greetings and kisses to all of you
Your Otto

---

[56] There is no error. In Cham, in the canton of Zug, the first refineries for condensed milk in Switzerland were operated by the Anglo-Swiss Condensed Milk Company.

Christmas English Style.

Manchester, December 28th, 1872

My Beloved!

Soon another year will come to an end and therefore I want to direct to you a few more lines, so that they may reach you before the next year.

You have certainly already asked during the Christmas holidays, how Otto spends this day? Here Christmas is celebrated for only one day. Thus we worked on Thursday, and besides, this holiday is not celebrated like a high holiday, but rather like a party day. In every parlor, store, etc., green branches are stuck up, for example holly, fir branches, mistletoe, etc., and wherever it looks beautiful, paper flowers and stars, etc. Then at midnight on the street in front of the houses is sung the Christmas hymn, which, if not the same, still reminds me of our well known "Honor to God in the Highest." Then people wish one another a Merry Christmas and Happy New Year. In the morning I was in an English church, where there was a usual service and in the evening I was invited with Schybli to the home of a man from Zurich who is staying here, named Toggweiler, where we had for dinner a stuffed goose. The latter, an older married man, has a commission business, sells especially substances for the hardening of iron and steel.

For the next week I shall work only on Monday and Tuesday and have the rest of the week off, during which time I plan to take a look at a few coal mines near Manchester, also a few museums, etc. in the city. In the business things always go smoothly, although there are always a few there who believe that every obstacle possible must be put in the way of the foreigner, whom they believe to be in England only to cash in on money , but the foreign workers here also have a little patience. Also, recently ships have sunk which were supposed to transport machines from the business to Russia, which now must be newly produced, naturally at the expense of the insurance company. On the other side of the coin, big orders from Russia are supposed to have been cancelled, thus Mr. Felber, instead of sending two mechanics to Russia, has only sent one, who will come back in three or four months. Thus there is naturally little prospect for me to get ahead in the machinery business, because, when you are a foreigner like me, you cannot hope to be sent on business trips by Englishmen. Well, time will tell, in the meanwhile I'll see and learn some things here.

How go things at home on the dear Steinhof? Is sister Emma at home and is Emilie in Regensdorf? Is it also there only rainy like here, or do you have snow and ice? It is always dark here, and we must be happy when we don't have to light the gas again at 9 after breakfast, which we use until 11 o'clock. In the afternoons at 3 or 3:30 we must light the lamps again; I have not seen the sun at all for 3 or 4 weeks, and even then it scarcely peeped out over the houses. In general, however, I am pleased that it is not bright and cold, because in our department there is neither a stove nor a fire.

With my English it is going a little better and better, yet I should learn more words and I should learn how to read. In my lodgings I am no longer quite happy, because I pay a bit too much (naturally foreigners always pay something more) and am also not as completely free and easy as I would like to be, yet I shall in any event wait until some better opportunity presents itself.

Otto

Concerning Fires and Floods.

Manchester, February 18th, 1873

Dear Father!

On St. Berthold's Day I received the dear letters from home and was delighted to learn that all of you were well over the holidays. I had likewise received from brother Oskar on New Year's Day letters and a little calendar and think that also my lines will have reached home during the same time. I already earlier noted, I believe, that I shall change my lodgings, which I then also did in the middle of January, but the food there did not agree with me (it was not clean), and I looked around for something else. Lodgings are very rare in this part of the city, especially those which are in any way tidy, and it is almost too expensive to live alone. Well, on the 2nd of February, at noon, we were going to have lunch, when suddenly someone shouted that upstairs there was smoke in the stairwell, in an upper corner the carpets were already burning, and also the four- poster bed was near the fire. While some people rescued people and carried things out, I searched with two others for ladders and went up on the roof, where the rafters on one side were about to cave in, the nine-inch beams were already burnt through. Soon came the fire department and the danger was shortly past. It turned out that in the fireplace of the neighboring house a few bricks had fallen out, and so the woodwork of the rafters had caught fire and with the cold, sharp north wind the fire had quickly spread. The rooms were naturally a bit flooded, and nonetheless, with the exception of the person who had been made homeless by the fire, the rest of us could move back into our rooms. At this time, however, I misplaced a wallet containing nearly 2 pounds, either lost or stolen? I could find out nothing more about it.

On the following Saturday I moved into these present lodgings, where I presently live, almost at the end of the city. I now have a good quarter of an hour to walk to the workshop, but I take along my breakfast to save time. We are allowed to have coffee or tea at the workshop. At noon I go to a dining room or restaurant and in the evenings I have tea at home and some herring, fish, etc. with it. Thus I have my small bedroom all to myself and a parlor, where I also have a chest of drawers. There is no one else there except two old people (in their sixties), who remind me somewhat of the Bardians in Paris, only not as friendly and affable as they, typical Englishmen, yet tidy and obliging. I have here my own little living room, quiet and all to myself, and this is what I was looking for, in order to spend my free time in here. Schybli, however, rather did not like it, but still that could not hold me back from renting it.

In the workshop I have recently been receiving a greater variety of jobs and get along well with my coworkers. That you have bought a sewing machine pleased me for my dear sisters, and once they have practiced with it, they will learn to treasure it. I am not familiar with the Johnson system, about which you write, isn't it Wheeler and Wilson? […]

Regarding the lubricating oil, I believe that the composition of rapeseed oil and petrol is very much used, yet I have often seen that, especially with transmissions etc., when there is a lot of dust, also pure petrol is applied as a lubricant. Here the most commonly used is only rapeseed, it has no smell of petrol, freezes, that is, it very soon becomes viscous when it is somewhat cold. With the sewing machine I would recommend, especially at the beginning, to lubricate it thoroughly, daily before use, and not to allow the lubricant holes to stop up. […]

I have read about the fire in Otelfingen and the sad end of Bopps in the Friday paper; also Schybli has written some things to me about it. It must have been really windy, for the postmaster's house, between which and the source of the fire lies a wide garden, to catch fire, and when was it, at night? A few details would still interest me. To all my loved ones warm greetings and kisses and in love I remain your grateful son

Otto

Wyss once again changes lodgings, he moves to a neighborhood with new workers' houses. At the moment the situation at work is quite good, because many orders are coming in from Russia and Japan.

A Swollen Knee as a Result of a Bad April Fool's Joke.

Manchester, May 10th, 1873

Dear Father!

[…] On April 1st, which like back home is considered here to be a fools' day, the Englishmen thought they had to make a fool out of me. In the evening upon going home I was pushed and shoved down the stone staircase (there are, namely, a ground floor and six stories, and over 100 workers go up the 14 disjointed staircases to the various floors; I am on the 5th floor). I fell and sprained my right knee. After I was able to limp home, the knee became swollen, so that I had to stay up the entire night. I made poultices with cold water and then with lead water, and on the second day the swelling subsided, but I still could not stretch out my leg. My landlady brought me a doctor, a young man, an Irishman (who was decidedly somewhat tipsy), who thought that I needed 8 more days of rest and rubbing with turpentine and oil. After a few more days I was able to limp around again, and the following weeks I could begin to work again. In the beginning it was a little swollen each day toward evening, and especially because I had big, heavy work. I became very tired, moreover had no appetite and was often miserably sick. After Easter it was somewhat better, but then it was decided we would work only half time. To be sure, they claimed they only had to wait for material, yet one after the other workers were let go, so that I was uncertain about whether I, too, would be laid off.

This week, however, we once again have a full work schedule and plenty to do. My knee is better, I can walk on it quite well, it only hurts going up and down stairs and also especially when I carry something or hit my foot or something.

I am quite happy with my work, on the other hand, less so with the coworker with whom I must do it. Namely, we have the same work on each side of the carding machine. [...]

In the same room also works a son of the director, or rather he is learning the business. He is a tall, somewhat sickly looking 17-year old boy, speaks little, only seldom a few words of French or German to me, since he takes classes in these languages. Further conversation cannot be begun with him, and his conceptions and opinions about world trade and industry are quite English or almost childlike.

His father has not been director (actually boss) for long, but rather since the founder of the company, the ingenious Parr, as they say, died, he, as the cousin or brother-in-law of the present owner, came to hold this position.

Since New Year the firm is known as Gurtis and Sons. One of them, Gurtis, is often at the business and speaks fluent German. The establishment employs 1400 workers here and 700 in Gorton near Manchester and is supposed to be the second largest company in this specialty in all of England.

Scarcely 400 paces from this business is another, J. Hethrington, which likewise employs 700 workers, and specializes in spinning machines, but where a lot of workers are hired and then soon fired, in a highly fluctuating manner. As a rule, businesses do the best here in the spring and summer; things slow down somewhat in the fall and winter. During the week after Pentecost all businesses here close and all kinds of repairs of machinery, buildings, cleaning of the water canals, etc. are performed; in addition, at this time inventories are usually taken, tools labeled, etc.

There are holiday trains departing for all destinations, and they are quite cheap, for entire weeks. Perhaps I shall go to Sheffield or Liverpool, shall just have to see how the weather is and how my finances stand. I now subscribe to

the "Engineer," the well known magazine about mechanics, for 60 centimes per week, and so keep up to date with the latest in mechanics and have just received some information about the mechanical department of the Vienna world's exposition, which especially interests me. To all my beloved warm greetings and with kisses and love I remain your grateful
Otto

Should Wyss Become the Associate of a Tobacco Manufacturer in Winterthur?

Manchester, June 6th, 1873

Dear Father!

Last week I received a letter from friend Berger, in which he suggests to me to become his associate, in order to run the business of his father-in-law. Berger was at our home in Otelfingen New Year before last on a visit, and perhaps you might recall him.—His father-in-law is Mr. Wylenmann, a tobacco manufacturer in Winterthur, and Berger has become his associate since this spring. As it would appear, his father-in-law now wishes to retire because of age considerations, and has himself advised him to seek a young associate. In the last years, due to his advanced age, he has no longer been able to travel, and with the new brisk competitive pace of the business world, he has lost many customers, so that his business has become small and unattractive.

Then he recommended to me to go to Holland and there to learn about tobacco manufacture, especially snuff tobacco manufacture, and also especially, if possible, to try to work in workshops where machines for these purposes are made. He further notes that I had told him earlier that I can make no investment in the company, yet hopes perhaps something would still be possible.

For me his proposal is especially attractive in that it would allow me to be able to found my independent existence in my dear homeland. Of course, my training would there be of only indirect use. Yet tobacco manufacture is a purely mechanical operation, because knowledge of different kinds results from the operation itself, and I would acquire much additional knowledge through a long stay in Holland.

In my profession I shall certainly here in England, as a foreigner, scarcely be able to hope to acquire a better position; in this regard, it would perhaps be easier to find something in the overseas English colonies. I have absolutely no desire to go back to Switzerland and to work at any time as a foreman, and even less desire to go to France or Germany. I saw in Locher's workshop in Zurich that I still have a lot to learn for the position of foreman, and if I have often enough regretted the fact that I did not train in a regular mechanical workshop, so it would now be repugnant to me to oversee a workshop of Swiss,

German and French workers. I also have neither money nor letters of recommendation for a job in Russia, and sister Emma has not answered my request (made at New Year) to receive, if possible, an address for Cabus. She probably forgot it, but it doesn't matter now anyway, because the time for that is now past.

I would like it, dear father, if you yourself could perhaps get some information regarding Berger's proposal and then soon share with me your opinion about it. In the meantime receive warm greetings,

Your Otto

Another Fire.

Manchester, June 21st, 1873

Dear Father!

During Pentecost week I wrote to you and at that time shared with you my friend Berger's proposal. Quite naturally the proposal pleased me, even if I don't accept it, because I am more and more convinced that with the present state of the manufacturing tools available there, manufacturing would not provide an existence at that particular location and, in order to set up a factory, managerial operations and everything, you need money. From earlier correspondence, I know that Berger has available to him a little over 8,000 francs, but with that amount alone, little can be done at the present time. In this regard, moreover, friend Berger might be inclined to overestimate his available funds. At any rate, I would like it very much if you could get some information about this, the sooner the better, and share with me as soon as possible your opinion about it.

In part of our factory building a fire just broke out. We worked until noon as usual, and it will soon be 5 o'clock, I just got home. In that section wood for models was being artificially dried with ovens, and so at about 2 o'clock occurred the fire, which naturally found in the dry wood its welcome nourishment. In the same building are stored a large number of models for machine parts, which was supposed to enormously increase the fire damage and perhaps could cause the work to come to a standstill until the models are remade. The roof and the walls collapsed, but now the high pile of wood is burning all the brighter and with the great heat, they are having difficulty protecting the other structures. Moreover, there is another fire in another machine shop in Newton, near the city; this type of thing has occurred quite often recently. [...]

Otto

The Decision to Make the Leap over the Big Water.

Manchester, August 11th, 1873

Dear Father!

For a long time I had awaited a few lines from you, at least a brief answer with regard to Berger's proposal. Brother Oskar has found out more about it and has recently shared his views with me. If Berger's plan at first somewhat excited me, I have now given it up and have recently sent him an answer in reference to it.

Well, here in Manchester the situation is becoming difficult for me, because this evening it was announced at work that at the end of next week the workshop would be closed for an undetermined amount of time.

Specifically, in a neighboring workshop the workers have gone on strike, in order to receive a salary increase. In response, the other owners now want to close their workshops, and 32 bosses are already supposed to have made the same announcement as our own company. Presumably, the struggle will not be of short duration, because even if people elsewhere were willing to begin working again afterwards, in our own company the employees are speaking about not beginning to work again until the salary increase has been guaranteed. Under such circumstances obviously there is no question of staying on here, and I think it therefore for the best if I leave right away, namely within 14 days, on August 25th, for Liverpool. If I can scrape together a living there for a little while, that is fine, if not, I shall see about somehow finding a ship to go to New York, because I just don't have the money for the prepaid passage.

The strike here can last two to three months and, at any rate, the spirit in our company is very obstinate, because they are generally known as greedy and stingy. There are reserves for such emergency cases, of course, but for the union members themselves only about half of the normal salary will be drawn from these funds, for the others about a third or fourth of the normal salary, and thus a foreigner whenever possible is just put off with a few ugly words. [...]

Hoping in the course of the next week to receive a few more lines from you and the next time to be able to write better news. Be warmly greeted and, as to all my loved ones, warm kisses, your

Otto

On August 28th, 1873, Otto Wyss boards in Liverpool the City *of Paris, a stately English steamer, for the transatlantic crossing to New York.*

V

Bachelor in the California Hinterland

To be able to survive, to achieve something abroad is part of the question of self-identification. To realize an achievement, to search for achievement, the step to the adventurous, to the mystical is sometimes small, but the hard reality requires a certain degree of moderation. And yet the quest for the fantasy world of El Dorado is relentless. The search for work combines with the lust for adventure. The far road to the West perhaps promises success, although the concept "the West" cannot be exactly defined. The conceptions were blurred, were often equated with the concept of the Promised Land. Life was hard, difficult and much more strongly determined by loneliness and monotony than by exciting adventure.

America, a land that we know from stories like The Deerslayer, The Last of the Mohicans, The Pathfinder, Leather Stocking, The Prairies, etc., books which James Fenimore Cooper published beginning in 1823. In 1852 apppeared the work Uncle Tom's Cabin by Harriet Beecher-Stowe.

The Civil War between the North and the South had ended in 1865. On May 10th, 1869 the first complete East-West railway line was opened. In four years was built the 2842 kilometer long stretch of railway from Omaha to Sacramento. California came into the Union in 1850, after it had evolved from a province of Spain annexed to Mexico and had achieved autonomy in 1821 and had acquired independence in 1848 after the war between the Union and Mexico through the Treaty of Guadeloupe.

This Pacific West Coast was settled by Spaniards, Padres, and conquistadores, and in the surroundings where Otto later lived, Spanish names mark the settlements like, for example, San Francisco, San Mateo, San Simeon, San Lucas, San Miguel, Santa Cruz, San Antonio, Paso Robles, Atascadero, Santa Margarita, San Luis Obispo, Santa Barbara, Santa Monica, etc. In 1848 gold was found near Sacramento on the land of Johann August Sutter, the military governor, and the city of San Francisco thereby increased its population through an immense influx of immigrants.

This fourth series of letters from the life of Otto Wyss includes the time between his arrival in New York in September 1873 until his marriage in August 1877. It is for him a hard time; he has to get back on his feet, find work and wages, get settled, acclimate himself and assimilate himself in the broadest sense to American life.

New York offered Wyss no warm welcome; he found no work in his profession and had to hire himself out as a farmhand with a farmer outside the city. So did his gaze direct itself toward the great West, where he hoped to find work. In several stages he thus finally reached the gold land of California.

"I am not at all discouraged."

Raritan (New Jersey), September 21st, 1873
At Mr. A.S. Burr's farm

My Beloved!

As I noted in my last letter, I left Manchester on August 26th, and since nothing turned up in Liverpool, I took passage on August 28th on the "City of Paris," a stately English steamship bound for New York. The first days at sea were stormy, yet the second week was calmer and the end of the trip very beautiful, so that the crossing was over after a quick 11 day trip. On Monday, September 8th, early at 5:30 land came in sight, and at 8 o'clock we entered the harbor of New York. Evening had arrived before we steerage passengers were unloaded, and after I had exchanged my remaining scant English cash for American dollars, I looked for a modest place to spend the night

The following days I was out looking for work in New York, Brooklyn and Jersey City, but nothing was to be found. In the last city I had an address of a foreman who, he himself coming from Manchester, gladly assisted me with advice, yet even he could offer me nothing. He said that now, shortly before the Presidential election (the election is supposed to be in two months), American businesses are standing still, because money is being held back. He advised me to go farther west, to Chicago, Cleveland, St. Louis etc., except that, since I could not do this, I had to take whatever came along.

Instead of a dirty handy-man job in the city, I preferred to go work for a farmer in the country and so I have been here for a week now on a big farm about 10 hours from New York. There is enough work here, and also enough good food to eat, and I feel quite well. Salary 12 dollars = 60 francs per month, at first at least. I thereby have a little time to look around, how and where I might possibly again find work in a machinery workshop. I correspond with two friends out West, one in Ohio, the other in Sacramento, California. The latter guarantees me $3.60 = 18 francs per day, as soon as I come out, but the trip there alone costs $60. Nevertheless, here you must watch for any opportunity, and therefore you need money on hand. Even if I stay here 2-3 months, I shall have only 20 or 30 dollars, which is little money for America, and I shall therefore be happy, if you could send me some money, but soon, because by the end of the second month, i.e. the middle of November, there will perhaps not be so much work here on the farm.

I don't know how much I have in my savings account, but perhaps 150 (?) francs. It would be best to send the money in banknotes and such or in a registered letter. I can exchange Prussian banknotes, dollar bills and also English money with little loss; there is more loss with French or Swiss banknotes. In Zurich you can easily exchange money, if possible get me directly American paper money, yet you must not pay too much for it. A small exchange would of course be more difficultly obtainable, yet that would be the best and the cheapest. At any rate, whatever you do, waste no time!

If I cannot speak at all of any luck until now, I am not at all discouraged; the country and the people please me a great deal and above all, you are not treated as a foreigner, but rather everywhere as a human being-citizen. Everything is expensive; everything must be paid for, but for that reason anyone can live here, and if he is diligent and thrifty, he can earn excellent wages and save something. There are enough swindlers and pickpockets, etc., I have to admit, but if you properly cut off such people and send them on their way, they seek "better business" elsewhere, so they leave me pretty much alone.

More details another time concerning my sea trip and the local farm with its 34 cows (especially milk sales to New York), eight oxen, etc., 21 ducks, about 40 chickens, turkeys, geese, four horses and four mules, then threshing- and fodder-cutting machines, etc., all powered by steam.

Hoping that you are all well, receive warm greetings and kisses from your son, grandson and brother
Otto

Raritan, November 30th, 1873
Dear Grandmother!

Farther than ever from you and all my loved ones, I finally have the chance to send you a few lines on December 4th. To be sure, they will arrive somewhat late, because it is a long way.—The fact that I was unable to find work here in my profession has only shown me that people do not always wait for others here, because in bad times they need less help and employees. For that reason I shall see to it that I am on hand in the good times. It is generally expected that after the current standstill in business, things will pick up all the faster in the spring, and the new questionable gold and silver payments instead of paper money (up to 50 centimes below paper value now) should only accelerate this process. There was also a lot of commotion last week about the "war with Spain over Cuba," but the whole thing is mostly rumor, and so hopefully we'll stay at peace.

For the winter I am now pretty well taken care of, did buy myself this week some more socks and a pair of strong boots, to keep my feet warm, as well as a pair of work gloves and finally a hat, so that I would not look so much like an immigrant with my old beat up hat.—My time here, even on Sundays, is quite occupied, because cleaning the stables and doing odd and sundry small chores takes up the morning, and in the afternoon you have to clean or mend your work clothes. But that is just for a short time, because with more yearning than ever I await the spring and then I shall travel farther west and keep on striving until I can create an existence where I can use what I have learned and experienced. Then, dear grandmother, I shall probably come back home and hope as well to again see you, who have played such a big part in my destiny, and as you wrote in a poem upon my departure from Europe:

Whoever looks up with confidence, does not fear the vicissitudes of life; so shall I strive forward until I reach my goal. […]

"So far I cannot speak in very high terms of America."

Canton (Ohio), December 24th, 1873

My Dear Brother!

We stand on the eve of the holy Christmas holiday, and since I have written no more from Raritan (N.J.), so I choose this place to send you a few words. So last Friday I was paid off in Raritan, because there were too many employees there.

On Saturday I went with my bags to New York, where a lot of workers are unemployed, and so I decided right away to go west. I left New York with the immigrant train and arrived here yesterday. I have here a colleague whom I knew in Manchester, named Paul Zürcher from Teufen (canton Appenzell)—(he has a brother, a medical doctor, in the summer in Interlaken, in the winter in Nizza), who has worked here for about 9 months and who gave me a cordial welcome. There are several big machinery establishments here, but nowhere is there any prospect of employment. Therefore after Christmas I shall travel farther west, and my friend Zürcher advised me to go directly to San Francisco, California. The weather is quite bad, it's the middle of the winter, all businesses are shut down and everything is covered with snow, also there is nothing to do in the country, so I shall head directly for the gold country over Chicago and Omaha.

I was glad that you took care of the money delivery so fast, and I have just received the sum and am right now obviously very happy about it.

So far I cannot speak in very high terms about America, because first of all I arrived here at a quite unfavorable time and then the way of life and the business customs here are quite different from the Old World. The immigrants who fare best here are those who are involved in agriculture and who have sufficient funds for the purchase of the necessary farm tools and equipment. On the other hand, workers, of whatever kind they might be, receive in the summer regular, indeed good pay, whereas in the winter they can work for reduced hours and reduced pay, or some of them cannot work at all, as was the case this winter throughout America. After New Year it is generally expected that business will gradually pick up, and I, especially, hope to soon see the dawn of a better era.

The last days of this year will soon fly by, and I shall probably have to greet the New Year on the wide and snow covered prairie between Omaha and Sacramento, whereas you will greet it in the circle of our loved ones at home. May the New Year bring you and your family the best health as well as happiness and joy. Please send soon a few words regarding my departure from Raritan to my loved ones on the Steinhof and my best wishes for the New Year, as well as to sister Emma and her husband.

Well fare well, beloved brother! The next time more, to be sure, from the most distant West, and with a warm brotherly kiss, your distant brother
Otto

With the Emigrant Train through Prairies and Lonesome Plateaus.

Sacramento, March 19th, 1874

My Beloved!

Last Christmas I had written a few more lines from Canton (Ohio) to brother Oskar, and when I could find no prospect of work there, despite the many machinery workshops in that vicinity, I took the railroad west on New Year's Day. On the morning of January 2nd, I arrived in Chicago, and after a two hour stop, during which time I supplied myself with provisions, we traveled farther over the mighty streams of the Mississippi and Missouri to Omaha, the last big station before the prairies. From there we boarded on Saturday January 3rd the emigrant train of the Pacific Railroad, and at 3 in the afternoon we pulled out of Omaha under steady snow flurries and headed out over the Great Plains. By nightfall the storm had grown more vehement, with not so much snow but with frequent snowdrifts, so that at 10 o'clock that night we remained stuck in the snow for about two hours.

Sunday brought a clear, bright day, and the farther we came, the less snow we saw. The wide, more or less wavy, plains, with little snow and dry, barren sand, were very monotonous, and only on the third and fourth days did the views become hillier, then craggy and mountainous. The weather remained good, and after sun drenched days followed moonlit nights. During the day we often kept the windows open, at night, despite two stoves, we froze until we were blue. The 50-seat train car with wooden seats was well filled by us 47 emigrants (13 freight cars were attached to it), and as you can well imagine, there was no comfort for sleeping. Most of the station stops were only for water and coal, and along the way there were also a few men who worked making repairs, refueling the locomotives and supervising the tracks.

Sometimes nearby, sometimes in the distance, you could see small herds of prairie dogs, prairie chickens and antelopes and higher up on the cliffs a kind of brown wild goat, elk (big stags) and a kind of fox. We saw no trees at all for 4 days, only first through the craggy mountain canyons toward Utah did we see down below a few Scots pines and willow bushes along the brooks and streams. The mountains seldom rise more than 1000-2000 feet above the surrounding plateaus and are more spherically rounded; nowhere are to be seen the long chains like, for example, our Jura mountains. The railroad rises to a height of over 8,000 feet above sea level, and yet there was also there very little snow. In many places, especially at the base of hills, where snowdrifts easily occur, the railway is covered by a protective wood structure. A longer stop is made in Ogden (3 hours), a friendly city lying in a valley bottom, which is surrounded by many spherically shaped mountains at half an hour's distance. While traveling farther, you can see at a few spots between the mountains the Great Salt Lake, and then on we go, now through friendly well watered valleys, now between mountains or through bleak plains and past lakes to the mountainous section of Nevada, where beyond Wadsworth the silver rich mines stretch north and south for miles.

It was on Saturday, January 10th, when, upon leaving Reno, we encountered more snow near California; still, the snow plows had made a way, and so we chugged along between 10–15 foot high walls of snow through dense conifer forests onto the soil of California. (Now the snow there is supposed to be 25 feet high.) Pulled by two locomotives, we had put the highest peak of the Sierra Nevada behind us before daybreak, and a mild breeze was blowing, and the sun shone warmly and brightly. There was soon no more snow to be seen, and through green spruce forests, past the gold mining camps, at 4 o'clock on Sunday afternoon we reached Sacramento, where I placed my trunk and baggage in storage.

Here I immediately asked around in the railroad workshops after an old Paris friend, Bachmann, with whom I had corresponded from Manchester, but discovered that he had unfortunately left. In the various machinery workshops there was nothing to do, and so, once again, I was without any prospects. In three employment agencies they gave me hopes of finding work, yet I soon saw that with the steady rainy weather, we workers were being sought nowhere. After I had spent two weeks in Sacramento, I left my trunks there and with only the barest of necessities in my traveling bag, I marched off toward San Francisco, yet also along the way there no kind of work was to be found, and in San Francisco, hungry, I was about to hire on as a sailor on a ship. Thereupon I took a job as a milker for 27 cows and milked these for three days, as best I could, but my hands became swollen, and so soon another was hired in my place.

Hereupon I turned to the southwest and soon found work again planting potatoes in Lakerville, two hours from San Francisco. There I helped to plant 400 sacks of potatoes in 160 acres of land, i.e., I laid the seeds, loaded the manure, etc. The field stretched as far as the waves of the small ocean would permit, and on Sunday, when I had a little free time, I would go down to the beach and would gaze out at the sailboats and steamships dancing over the waves, or would search for stranded shipwrecks, etc. The people themselves, still young Irishmen, kept the dirtiest, most common house I have ever seen in my life; there was no book or newspaper, no pen or ink in the entire house. In both the parlor and the kitchen mainly geese, chickens, and young pigs served as babysitters and playmates for the three children of one, two, and three years. A 14- year old boy, an orphan, who works as a cowherd there, knows nothing about school or religion, just that on Fridays you are not supposed to eat meat.

Last Monday, after we had finished planting the potatoes, I was paid 20 dollars for five weeks work and did not delay in returning to the big city. A man from Zurich, who has a machinery workshop in San Francisco, promised me work by mid April, but I wanted to see after my luggage in Sacramento, and so I took the steamer up the river. We have now had three days of good weather here, and if it continues, there will soon be work in machinery workshops. A German gunsmith told me today to come back on Monday, but should nothing come of his offer, I shall probably go back to San Francisco, because there, there are very many big workshops. Sacramento is built into regular square blocks and is supposed to have a population of 30,000, of which one fifth to one fourth are Chinese, who live closely together on a small square. Of course, Sacramento is not at all as big or lively as Zurich; except for a few machinery workshops, including the Central Pacific Railroad, with 33 employees, there is no factory, no really big industrial establishment. Right now an iron smelting foundry is supposed to be put into operation. A new, externally pretty building, is the Capitol, the seat of government of California, yet inside it is, in my opinion, very angular and is criticized as being too small. Another time more about this gold country in the Far West, for this time I soon hope to work again with file and hammer, and then I shall allow more lines to follow these. I feel as well as ever and with these warm spring days, when they are already spraying the streets, awakens the hope to see even better days ahead than was the case during the last weeks.

Hoping that these lines find all of you well and happy, be warmly greeted and kissed by your distant grandson, son and brother

Otto

I lodge here in a big hotel or boarding house, which was recommended to me as good and cheap by a German at the station. I pay 5 dollars per week for room and board; my room is very clean.

My address: O.W., machinist, Western Hotel, Sacramento

San Francisco—an ever changing City.

7 St. Charles Place, San Francisco, August 5th, 1874

Dear Father!

A few days ago I received your dear letters and do not wish to delay in answering them. It has pleased me a great deal to hear so much about life back home and especially, since Oskar's last letter concerning dear sister Anna worried me a bit, to hear again that she is doing better, and I hope that she presently will be able to revive new strength and fresh life in one of our beautiful Alpine health resorts. Then I am also pleased that you finally have a spring with running water on the Steinhof and that you are thus spared much trouble and work.

With me a few things have changed, although nothing essential. Specifically, I left Mr. Schinz, where I used to work, at the end of June. The rather monotonous piece work, with which I of course could make 2 to 3 dollars a day, was not always steady, because I often had to wait on material from the foundry, and when he wanted to lower the price, I looked around for another job. I was on several occasions in the bigger workshops, but this summer there is no profusion of work there, and even though in one of the biggest, the Risdon-Iron Works, where mainly ship machinery is built and about 300 men work, I had an acquaintance named Stierlin (he is the brother of Mr. Stierlin, director in Stampfenbach in Zurich), I still could not get a job.

Thereupon I worked in a lock and bolt factory where especially small curtain bolts are made, which was naturally badly paid, and then I left after ten days, because I had my eye on my present job. For the past two weeks I have been working at Will and Fink, locksmiths and cutlers, a workshop of 15 workers, with steam engines. They have two sales stores and are just now opening a third. They import most of their wares, especially from England, and manufacture solely pre-ordered wares. It is the most important business of this kind in San Francisco, and both gentlemen are very skillful and active; both are Germans. Naturally there occurs there very diverse work, besides knives, cutlery, surgical and other instruments, especially electrical bell stops, card-tables, paper cutting machines, construction work, etc.

For the beginning I receive 2¼ dollars per day, but it will soon be increased and, as a rule, good salaries are paid. Most of my coworkers are Germans and almost all have been there from several to eight and ten years.

A lot of building went on in this city this summer, on the site of the former small wood houses now rise beautiful apartment houses made of squared stone and iron, and a beautiful meat and vegetable market hall was built. Then recently a big, wooden exhibition building was erected, in order to display local California agricultural and industrial products.

Likewise, a few churches and big hotels are being built, but the school houses remain quite hidden, one must actively ask: Where are they? Then a grandiose park is being laid out, about 1¼ hours from here, right on the coast, in any event pleasant for those who can drive there. Within the city limits itself, there are merely two small public gardens, and more will probably only be laid out when a few speculators can sell the land for them to the city later on for an enormous price. There are a few gardens for relaxation here, the best known being Woodwards Garden, which is very beautifully arranged and contains a zoo, aquarium, greenhouses, a small painting gallery, a museum of natural history, a pond with over a dozen seals, fountains, etc.

In the City Gardens, which contains beautiful flower beds, gymnastics installations, a bowling alley and rifle range, took place the annual festival of the Swiss Assistance and Charity Union, which I likewise attended on June 14th. There were around 3000 persons present, and there was lively music and dancing. There was no singing at all, although the local Singing Club "Schweizerbund" was there with the flag, plus I missed the fact that there was neither a single speech nor toast. On the other hand, a lottery was not missing, and people betted bravely, just as on the rifle range the marksmen argued virulently about the prices. Nonetheless, 1300 dollars clear was raised, and thus was achieved the main goal of the event, which, among the local festivals, always predominates, specifically to get money out of people; congeniality and the festival spirit are only secondary. I myself am known in the little circle; I have recently subscribed to the "Scientific American," a weekly journal which brings to the reader the newest inventions of business and industry, etc.

I must close. To all my loved ones, warm greetings; with kisses and love your

Otto

I have just received two issues of the Bürkli newspaper, and it pleases me to see and read a well known paper again, warm thanks for it. I shall occasionally send you a local German one.

"How easily have I endured the hardships in America."

San Francisco, August 9th, 1874

Dear Sister Anna!

Your dear lines have pleased me a great deal, especially because I could tell that you again feel somewhat better, and I hope that you will gather new strength again this summer. While you also will enjoy recovery in one of our spas back home, stay a little while, because the golden blessing of health is never too expensive. In fact, how easily have I endured the hardships in America, consistently kept a good attitude and only wish I could have sent you occasionally a part of my healthy appetite. The local fresh sea air has at any rate contributed to it, because in my entire life I have never been as ravenous as here in California. Yet I do see others eating with just as good an appetite, and groceries are really cheap, especially meat. Then I like to have a little glass of wine with my meal, or something else good.

The climate is very beautiful here and since the end of March it has not rained, with the exception of the first days of May, which brought a few rain showers and for that reason were conducive to a very rich fruit harvest. At the end of May came a few hot days, and in the middle of June one week was rather hot, yet the thermometer never climbed over 95°F or about 28°R [Reaumur] in the shade. At noon the sun rays fell so vertically that tall houses cast almost no shadow and the asphalt sidewalks softened.

Around 11 in the morning usually comes a sea wind which becomes stronger toward evening, but toward midnight dies down again. These winds, especially when out of the southwest, very often drive clouds before them, which however first fall on the Sierra Nevada range or farther east as rain, storms or cloudbursts. In the last six weeks we usually had in the mornings beautiful blue sky and in the afternoons it was cloudy and cool, and in the evenings very cool wind. Then it is funny to see how the people here go dressed, some in a light summer dress with a straw hat, whereas others come walking in with an overcoat, or women with fur collars and shawls. In the houses it is very pleasant, and you can sleep at nights because the cool evening wind is not favorable to insects, and especially the biting mosquitoes, which are so numerous in New York and the eastern states, occur here only rarely. The day is not as long, but also not as short as in our country, and if on the longest days the sun still stands high in the sky at a quarter past seven and then sinks into the sea, after a brief twilight the night comes in at 7:30; right now it is already night at 7 o'clock. The air is seldom bright and recently you could see little or nothing at all of the mountain ranges to the east. There it is really beautiful in the dear homeland, where you often see the snow covered giants looking out over the land.

May you now breathe fresh air and strong health near our beautiful mountains and from time to time think about your brother across the wide ocean, who sends you true brotherly greetings and kisses, your brother
                                        Otto

"Wherever you go, you must be on your guard."

                                        San Francisco, August 10th, 1874
Dear Emilie!

[...] I can assure you that every dear letter from home takes me back again to the dear Steinhof, and the yearning for my beloved home grows all the stronger, the farther I am from home. I became accustomed much faster to the country and people in France and England than here in America, but here the surroundings consist not of a single nation in which everyone has the same opinions and schooling, but rather of people from all countries who do not merely behave in an uncivilized manner but also generally behave in a selfish and quarrelsome manner. Wherever you go, you must be on your guard, yet so far I have got along quite well, nothing has yet been stolen from me, and I have in my profession regular success. I have every reason to be satisfied with my lodgings. The landlords are Germans, he is a tailor, called Stuckschutz, and they have five children, two boys of 12 and 14 and three girls of ten, six, and the smallest only three months old, who are all friendly and very attracted to me.

On a little side square or blind alley off the lively Kearny Street, right after where it stops at a steep hill, I have a quiet clean room with a big window. The furniture consists merely of a good bed, a small chest of drawers, a little night stand and armchair.

The master tailor likes to discuss politics and everything possible and is a flower lover, so that the little courtyard is full of flowering pot-plants, from which I keep a bouquet in my room the entire summer.

Flowers grow moreover wild here in California and splendidly in gardens. Rose trellises 30 feet high and fuchsia 10 to 12 feet high overflowing with flowers, then balsamine, colossal cactus, etc. and many which are completely unknown to me.

Fruits flourish beautifully and in profusion; thus at the beginning of May 900 hundredweights of strawberries came into the city daily, red cherries, current, raspberries, gooseberries are over, but there are masses of blackberries, besides grapes, apples, pears, peaches, which are especially abundant; there are few apricots and damson, on the other hand, there are plums as big as peaches, oranges, melons and tomatoes are also pretty cheap, and in general fruits and vegetables are sent east every day in train loads.

Well I must close; to dear grandmother warm greetings, and how it pleases me to know that you are always well; also to your fiancé warm greetings and brotherly greetings and kisses to you, from your distant brother
Otto

An Already Highly Mechanized Agriculture.

St. Helena, December 10th, 1874

Dear Father!

I received somewhat late your dear letter, because I had already left San Francisco and am once again on the road. My work soon came to an end, after I had worked for three weeks doing nothing but stocking supplies, and so at the beginning of November 1 was again without work. There was not the least prospect for professional work, and so for better or worse I had to go out into the country. Over Vallejo and Napa I came here to St. Helena, about 60 miles (20 hours) from San Francisco, where I met a Ruschlikoner named Mr. Trümpler, whom I have since been helping to cut grapes and make wine. There is no prospect of a large salary, but it is a bad season of the year. This year the grape harvest is extraordinarily rich, and many hundreds of bushels still hang on the vines, which must rot because of lack of space or a market. The so-called winter grapes, which often produced a great deal of profit, are everywhere left to stand and rot.

Wheat harvesting with steam tractor in the Sacramento Valley.

As far as the California wheat harvest is concerned, the newspapers do not exaggerate at all about it, and a colossal amount is exported elsewhere; the harvest has gone really well this year. Very large expanses of land are reserved for wheat farming, and in the flood regions of the Sacramento River, etc., there are huge farms, so for example, somewhat above Sacramento, a Bernese Oberlander and two Americans together have a farm where at sowing time (so right now) they move out every morning 48 double plows, each pulled by 4 horses, which plow exactly one furrow per day. Besides that are used steam plows which pull 12 to 14 plowshares behind them.

At harvest time, they have mowing machines, to which are harnessed 8 to 12 horses, and the threshing machines require just as many, but are usually powered by steam, but still there are always 8 to 14 people also actively involved in the harvest process. Threshing is always done in the open field, and since they usually mow off merely the heads of the wheat, almost as much wheat as straw is harvested.

The news and novelties about railroads and the harvest and the autumn have interested me a great deal, as well as the travel reports. Every letter I receive here awakens in me more so than earlier some degree of homesickness, and whereas in the Old World one still always has a regular salary and professional work, here, in the New, they just need people on a part-time basis when there is plenty of work. In the summertime everybody is hired for the harvest, both Whites and Chinese, but in the wintertime there is so much unemployment that you can hire both by the tens of thousands. I know a few dozen machinists, partly Swiss, who have abandoned their trade and are not the worse off for that reason; everywhere all professions are more than strongly enough represented. Under such difficult circumstances it is harder to get ahead than you might believe, but California is only 30 years old, and so, beside the bad luck, you can also expect some good luck. At any rate, I shall not be wanting for anything this winter, however it might turn out! But I shall not be leading a comfortable life. [...]

As a Technical Draftsman in a Quicksilver Mine.

San Francisco, June 18th, 1875

My Beloved!

I have been back in San Francisco for a few days and have received today a postcard from brother Oskar, in which I unfortunately saw that sister Anna is still very sick and also father is doing poorly. How much I would like to come myself and see that things go better, but it is unfortunately too far, yet I do hope that the coming spring will bring better days to all.

As far as I am concerned, you have certainly received my letter from St. Helena and also have read the later one to brother Oskar. So I worked in Manhattan until the end of April and, despite hard and demanding work, always felt healthy and happy there. I would have written earlier from there, but I was still expecting reports from Nevada, because I had been planning for a long time to go there, but the more news I received from there, the more unfavorable it was.

Then came a coincidence which could possibly bring me better times here. In Manhattan I had sketched myself one beautiful Sunday a picture of the mine and then had to make a bigger picture of it for the foreman. At the beginning of April came here a German agent, who was charged with writing a report about the mine, and when he coincidentally saw the drawing, he said: "This man must make a few views and maps with me." So I then made 12 drawings, and when I was finished, I came here, and I shall have to make a few more changes, add some names, etc., and shall have to write out the finalized and perfected report. Then Mr. Knox (one of the owners of the Knox and Osborne Mine) will give me work in the machinery workshop, so that I shall be on hand when he later has to make drawings again.

So I can look forward to the future again with more confidence.

Here I have lodgings again with the same people, who in the meantime have moved here from St. Charles Place. The room is situated rather high, i.e., on the third floor, but the house stands on a hill, so that on one side you can see a large part of the city and, on the other, the bay and the straits of the "Golden Gate" as far as the Pacific Ocean. Although a quarter of an hour from the center of the city, I much prefer it here. The room itself is well lit, not big, simple, but well furnished, and, like the entire house, very clean. Besides myself, there are in the boarding house just two others, who likewise are old German acquaintances.

Businesses are going rather well, but all hotels are overflowing with workers, who are flooding in in droves from everywhere; just tomorrow 21 more train cars will pull into San Francisco with over a 1000 immigrants from the eastern states.—I should really be happy to have someone at hand, in order to receive work. […]

Sister Anna Dies.

San Francisco, June 18th, 1875

Beloved Father!

10 days ago I received the sad news of Sister Anna's early departure from this life.—In vain I have awaited until now other letters and I do not want to delay any longer my reply.

How much had I thought about her recently and could still not always come to terms with the idea that I should never again see sister Anna. So now she already lies in the cool earth, without me being able to see her once again, or to visit her on her sick bed.—So, upon returning home, I shall ask after sister Anna in vain, and I shall be able to send her my quiet tears only on the spot where lie her earthly remains.

Yes, it is hard to find out in a distant country about how a hole has been opened in the circle of your loved ones, and on such occasions, your yearning for the homeland awakens twice as strong. And certainly, dear father, this loss has opened a very deep rift in your soul after the departure of our dear mother, because your deceased daughter had made it precisely her duty to fill the place of our dear, blessed mother in the household. […]

If my first year in California did not go exactly according to my wishes, at least I now do have somewhat better prospects for the future. As far as the travel money (about 600 francs) is concerned, I have it under control, because I have always saved money.

Since I have been back here in San Francisco from the mine, I have spent most of my time drawing, mainly for Mr. Knox and Mr. Osborne, the two owners of the mine. At first about a dozen maps and views of the mine itself, and then maps, cross-sections and pertinent details concerning quicksilver smelting ovens, on which my employers hold the patent. In addition, I had to make several maps for a German agent, Mr. von Jeinsen.

Now there will not be much more to draw, and I really must take off a couple of days and run around to see if there is not something else to supplement, and then I am supposed to go back out in the country next week or the week after next in order to make sketches, etc.

Then, I am supposed to go prospecting with a few workers, i.e., make tunnels and shafts on certain spots in order to see whether there is sufficient quantity and quality of material available in order to open a mine. Whether there is anything to do, and what there is to do, I must just see; at any rate, I shall do my utmost to pursue this beginning.

In any event, I have to be cautious with Mr. von Jeinsen; he really is a speculator and he is always somewhat short of money, so that he can never pay me completely, and always pays me as little as he can, but in this regard I must be patient.

For the present he must know that he can use me, and later on something better will turn up. Mr. Knox and Mr. Osborne will allow me to complete the drawings and further trouble themselves little about it, even if it were possible, but they are real Americans.

Mr. Knox is part owner of a foundry, but since there is little work there for machinists, I must depend more on Mr. von Jeinsen.

In general, business is going very well right now, buildings are going up everywhere, and emigrants from the eastern states arrive daily.

Well I must close. To you, dear father, and to all my loved ones, warm greetings and kisses from your distant
Otto

"No trace of Easter eggs."

San Francisco, June 18th, 1875

Dear Johanna!

Since your last letter of March 3rd, I have spent many hours thinking about our dear home, but even though I knew that Sister Anna was sick, I had no way of knowing that we should lose so quickly our dear sister.

I can well imagine that you on the dear Steinhof must feel a great loss, and hope that you might cheer up our mourning loved ones with your piano playing. Have you always played right much, or do you lack the time?

You also ask me in your letter how I spent Easter. Well, to tell the truth, it was the most boring and most melancholy Easter that I have ever experienced. From morning until night it rained without interruption, a few Danes tried to drown their ill temper about it in brandy, and in the evening there was right much quarreling and noise.

I conversed a little with a couple of Swiss here and a few Germans. No trace of Easter eggs, the only pleasure was a little pipe of tobacco.—Besides, Easter eggs are a custom only among the Germans and the French, thus the family with whom I now live has colored Easter eggs all year long, to the joy of the children, and the children had said this year: "Oh, if Mr. Wyss were here, he would draw them for us again." In general, I am now very happy about my bright, nice lodgings, because I can do some drawing there over the next few days.

From last Sunday until Tuesday we had here right much rain, to people's great astonishment, because here in the summer seldom falls a drop of rain. The harvest has begun almost everywhere here, but, on the average, it is not considered to be very productive, it was too dry.

I enclose for you a small view of the Manhattan mine, for which you can perhaps make a little space in the album. The reddish hill is the main square, which contains much light ore on the surface, around it, and in front the yellow heaps of waste, directly to the right and left in the foreground lodging houses, in the middle the stable, behind it a kitchen with a dining room, the pretty office and warehouse and to the left a house built over a shaft, and to the left at the back the smelting refineries.

Farewell and stay healthy, dear sister, with a warm brotherly kiss
                              your Otto

"I quietly mix my hot tears with the blue waves."

San Francisco, June 18th, 1875
Dear Sister Emily!

When I received Monday before last the sad news of the departure of dear Sister Anna, I could hardly conceive of the idea that I should never again see her. For a long, long time I stared at her dear picture, continued to chat with her in spirit and all my childhood memories were awakened.

Then down on the beach I sought a lonesome little spot, and looking out into the evening twilight at the blue waves, I quietly mixed with them my hot tears.

My thoughts drifted homeward, but unfortunately the time has not yet come where I can once again see the scene of my childhood, the dear Steinhof.

A little while ago I was back at the photographer, in order to send another picture for Sister Anna, showing me as I now look, unfortunately also too late. Your photograph, dear sister, has also pleased me a great deal, and it is certainly an accurate likeness of you as you now are.

Enclosed you will also find one of mine. That you have broken off your relationship with Mr. Diem, I regret, especially because of your disappointment, and only hope that you will not take it too hard. [...]

With kisses and love, your brother

Otto

Moving Farther on with Part-Time Work.

San Francisco, December 5th, 1875

Dear Father!

It has been over three months since I have written you a few lines and already over five months since I have received a few lines from the dear Steinhof.

To be sure, I have learned from brother Oskar, who informed me of the loss of dear Gritli, that everything is fine on the Steinhof.—I have shared with you in the last letter that nothing came of the position which had recently been promised me, and often years go by before trials concerning patents and rights of ownership come to an end. I left San Francisco on August 23rd and went to Nevada,[57] but unfortunately fortune did not smile on me this time either.

Right at the time of my departure occurred the suspension of payment of the California Bank, the most important bank on this coast. The consequences of this event were even more noticeable in Nevada than here in California, and in its wake workers were laid off in many places.

The countryside in Nevada looks barren and desolate, and if the big silver mines, whose shafts go 2200 feet deep into the earth, were not located there, the region would be really sparsely populated.

Virginia City, for example, counts over 15,000 inhabitants, and there everything depends upon the production of the mines. The land is everywhere stony and mountainous, and one seldom sees a little tree or shrub. The closest farms are 10 to 12 miles from the city, and so most provisions must be shipped here from California, for which reason everything is very expensive. The mines are partly very rich; thus a single mine, the Consolidated Virginia Mine, extracts a half million dollars in silver each month. The worker's salary

---

[57] Lying to the southeast of California, this region rich in gold and silver mines was annexed in 1864 as the 36th state of the Union.

amounts on the average to 4 dollars per day, and the miners work 8 hours a day, because they cannot stand it longer because of the great warmth. Work continues without interruption, day and night, the whole year long, because one shift takes over from the other.

I stayed there over three weeks, and when I saw that there were prospects nowhere, I returned to California. At the end of September I came to Sonoma, where I got work making wine, and when we were done after six weeks of work, I came back here to San Francisco. Here I'll be drawing again for a little while, first for Mr. Knox and then for the agent.

Business is going slowly, and especially in the machinery workshops there is very little to do. I had had the opportunity a little while ago (or even now) to buy myself a job in a small bolts and locks business for 100 dollars, but nothing much is happening now, and until the spring there is still time enough for reflection.—I would perhaps be happy to have the rest of my savings account here, because now it could help me, because the Nevada trip has cost me a lot, but more about that next time.

For the New Year, to you, dear father, and to all my loved ones, my warmest best wishes with kisses and love your

Otto

California is Still in Many Ways Underdeveloped.

San Francisco, January 27th, 1876

Dear Father!

Your dear letters of January 6th have been in my hands for a few weeks, and I am pleased to again hear more from the dear Steinhof.

So things are getting really serious about the railroad[58] and really soon, it would appear, also your walking tour of the Toggenburg has interested me, and it is something quite different from the wide grain fields and often barren hills of California. That Aunt Ryffel was in Schwanden, I did not know, does uncle have a position there, and has he sold his house in Wohlen?

I am pleased to learn that brother Oskar has bought a house, because thus he will live more cheaply and better on his own property. I have heard nothing at all for a long time from Regensdorf. Hopefully sister and brother-in-law and little Hans are all well. I am, I fear, in arrears of correspondence, which I shall however soon correct.

Presently I work as a machinist and would have really good and steady work, if I could lathe bigger pieces or if I were quicker at it. Now there is another lathe turner there and 4-5 cabinet-makers, etc. Mainly made are

---

[58] Meant is the national rail line Winterthur—Seebach--Baden

windmills, which here are used very much for the pumping of water on bigger farms, because in the hot summertime the daily returning sea winds regularly set them in motion and so save labor.

For the world exposition in Philadelphia people here generally expected a significant rise in ticket prices back east (the cheapest price is now 300 francs) and many saw in this an opportunity to pay a visit to Europe again, now however it seems that the ticket prices will remain unchanged. At this exposition, California is expected to be represented mainly by its ores, especially gold and silver and quicksilver. California can send very little in the way of industrial products to such an event, because it produces little, and even this in such primitive form that it cannot compete with other countries or states. In machinery alone it hardly manufactures a quarter to a third of its mechanical needs, which are used in the numerous mines, newly built railroads, factories, etc.

The main blame for this lies in the lack of iron works and coal mines, because although in many places in California rather extensive coal fields were found, nonetheless, in terms of quality, they stand way behind the English and Australian coal mines (which are usually used here). In the manufacture of wool, fabrics, beginnings have likewise been made here, but up until now only rougher fabrics. Silk growing may with time likewise become an important branch of this state's industry. Sweeping brooms, for which a good type of tough, yellow-white sedge grass grows here, are manufactured in many places and are exported by the thousands. Finished clothes, shoes, hats, furniture, etc, are, on the other hand, in large measure imported.

Regarding the balance in my Swiss savings account, I would like to have it here in California, not in order to use it, but rather should some opportunity present itself (as occurs more often here than there) for me to participate in a secure business through an investment, then I would have the financial means to do it, as they say, "Slow and steady wins the race."

It is best to send it as a draft, in United States gold (not currency), to the Swiss-American Bank, 527 Clay Street, San Francisco, which has a relationship with the Schweizerische Kreditanstalt in Zurich.—As a precaution, make out two drafts and please send them as soon as possible.

To all my loved one in the dear Steinhof my warmest greetings and kisses, especially to you, dear father, from your distant

Otto

About Swiss as Enthusiastic New-Americans and about "Sons of the Heavenly Empire."

San Francisco, June 18th, 1876

Dear Father!

Both of your last two letters brought me a lot of new and interesting news, and I was really astonished that the railroad was already being completed.[59] Naturally the railroad can only be an advantage for Otelfingen, although I doubt very much whether it will yield a profit. Has the community of Otelfingen subscribed a noteworthy sum to it, have private persons also made contributions, and has the Northeast Railroad taken over its construction and management? Yet I remember that you wrote me that the National Railroad is building toward Regensdorf and Oerlikon, whereas the Northeast Railroad is building toward Bülach and Schaffhausen, so the Winterthur gentlemen still had no complete national railroad. How on earth so many railroads in the same area can make a profit is certainly not yet clear to me.

I did receive both drafts and, after showing my identification, I immediately received the sum of money and deposited it in my savings account in the local German savings bank, where it is available to me at any time.

The bolts and locks business in which I was interested has of course in the meantime been bought by another, and I now work for him, except that for two it is too little work for too little pay, so that I shall probably soon leave this job, since I again have a job drawing for Mr. Knox. Also Mr. von Jeinsen has reiterated to me his promises of last year relative to mines in Southern California, but after the foreseeably early end of the trial, there is still lacking one more thing: the capital for the project's operation. Yet with patience perhaps something good will still come out of it.

The harvest here is in full swing, and from all parts of the state come reports that it will be the richest that California has ever had. Yet despite these prospects of a good harvest, business in general is going slow, which however is to be attributed to local politics. Right now candidates are being selected from all parties and speeches are being made on their behalf on every street corner.

Likewise big preparations are being made to celebrate the 4th of July (100th anniversary of independence). The local Swiss have already collected 500 dollars in order to represent Switzerland with a statue of Lady Helvetia seated

---

[59] They are speaking of the rail lines in the Furttal. In the year 1877, two lines were opened, and one of these was the line of the Swiss National Railroad (SNB) from Winterthur over Seebach, Otelfingen to Lenzburg, by circumnavigating Zurich, and the (competing) line of the Swiss Northeast Railroad (NOB) from Winterthur via Bülach, Otelfingen to Baden. The line of the National Railroad was already forcibly liquidated in 1878 and merged with the Northeast Railroad. The Otelfingen train station lies near the Steinhof.

on a high chair and with 22 children with the coats of arms of the various cantons to be paraded on a wagon throughout the city.

In the rear of the parade the local Swiss clubs, specifically a company of Swiss sharp shooters, the singing club Schweizerbund and the Swiss Mutual Aid Society (health insurance fund), to both of which I also belong. However, I am not counting on any big party, especially if it is a warm day and if a sea breeze comes inland around 11–12 o'clock, we shall look quite powdery.

Four to five weeks ago a ship freshly arrived from China, with 1200 sons of the Heavenly Empire, brought us the Asian smallpox. It is not supposed to be so dangerous, they say, but when in the first week 19 of 26 sick people died, precautionary measures were taken. Last week 21 cases were detected, but most were concealed from the authorities. Thus last week I went to see an acquaintance in order to clean and repair his sewing machine. About 9:30 the man appeared with a large number of pock marks on his face, which was rather red, and asked me if I thought it was smallpox? He had called no doctor for help, because a doctor would have sent him to the hospital. I naturally told him to go to bed and to keep warm and to send for the doctor, if he did not want to suffer lasting damage. […]

Concerning the Genuine Club Life and a Summer Picnic.

San Francisco, June 18th, 1876

My Dear Sisters!

I finally get down to answering your dear letters of May 2nd, which pleased me so much, with the note that "flowers are within." To be sure, violets also bloom here, down in the garden, but they are only the smaller brighter variety.

The small news from home, especially regarding my former schoolmates and friends, will always interest me. As far as your photo is concerned, dear sister Hanneli, it seems I have forgotten to write it in the last letter that I have received it with joy and also have placed it in the album beside the ones of sisters Emma, blessed Anna and Emilie. I find you not so much changed, but you must be rather much taller, soon like Emilie? Do you all still run the store together? For a long time I have not heard a word more about it.

Here in San Francisco I have also belonged for some time to the singing club "Schweizerbund," which has a membership of 50-70, mainly German Swiss, a few Germans and Alsatians. Each club here now has in the spring months a picnic, i.e. an excursion to a neighboring little city or some romantic area or a park. Since one can count on beautiful weather from the beginning of April until the end of September, the clubs usually hire a steamship or make an agreement with the railroad for cheap round trip tickets. Thus our club had its picnic on April 15th, Easter Sunday, about seven miles (about two hours) from here in Oakland in "Zimmermann's Garden."

With music and flags we drove at nine in the morning through the city to the steamship, which trip lasted about a half an hour, then we took the train and finally walked through Oakland on foot to the festival park. The garden was decorated with flags, and we had 600-700 people for the event. A lottery provided numerous gifts, such as a golden watch, cutlery, earrings, etc. Then there was a prize shooting match with little collection boxes and finally a prize bowling game for $20.

In addition, I and another had fabricated a paper air balloon 7 feet high and 4 feet wide, which however caught fire when we filled it up, and thus was wrecked. Song recitals and dances lasted until 6 in the evening. After the lottery drawing and distribution of the gifts, we all went back home, each certainly with the satisfaction of having had a happy day. The club treasury made with the event a net profit of $200 or 1000 francs.

Naturally, much bigger clubs make better returns, and among these the French especially have the most numerous participants.

Recently there were especially a lot of picnics for school children, and now they have come to a halt until the 4th of July is past. In the singing club we sing only German, mostly out of Heim's synodal songbook,[60] but in the winter we also sing operettas. […]

Concerning the Right Hand of the Quarry Supervisor and Concerning a Mangled Left One.

Almaden Cons. Q.S. Mine, November 20th, 1876

Dear Father!

I received your last letters of August 31st somewhat late, because I have left San Francisco. But they brought me much interesting news, both about our dear home as well as about old schoolmates. That Otelfingen has received a new school house pleases me, yet I am surprised that that particular building-site was selected. I deeply regret the loss of Dr. Wäckerling's son Gottlieb, whom I saw several times in '71 and with whom I had chatted for several hours.

Thank you very much for the warning against possible dubious acquaintances, because here I have already met several people from Zurich who have asked me for a lot of money, not to mention money for food and hotels, and who afterwards for thanks tried to disparage me, to mention only a few, a Denzler (son of pastor Denzler in Fluntern), two Cottis and several others. I have also met a Rudolf Meier who has been at Schybli's home in

---

[60] Ignaz Heim (1818–1880), musical director in Zurich and the composer of many beloved folk songs.

Neuhaus and afterwards has been a farm-hand at the home of Colonel Hauptmann, an orderly man who saves money.

I am now here on the job that was promised to me a year back, and because in the meantime it has become something necessary, Mr. von Jeinsen has taken over the position of superintendent. My job is to myself supply the repair shop, the machinist, the smith or the superintendent, when he goes away. In the beginning I understandably had things to do everywhere, because it looked rather run down. Now, however, things are running smoothly and, in addition, it is my job to check measurements and to make drawings, whereby Pressler's "Measurement Hand" (so far my only instrument) provides me with the best service.

I get along well with the superintendent, although he listens too much to anyone who can babble with him, and there are a few older Americans here who can hardly stand the fact that such a young "Dutchman" can give the orders.

Moreover, the mine is not a profitable venture, i.e. the expenditures are larger than the income, and for that reason the company seeks to sell it, so that I cannot depend on being able to stay here a long time, yet the superintendent has already received another offer elsewhere and has informed me that in that case I must come with him.

This region around here, in contrast to many mines, which consist only of a stone field, is planted everywhere with trees, mainly different kinds of oaks and firs and farther down on the brooks the beautifully foliaged sycamore. The ground is covered everywhere with high thin grass and wild oats. Although here we are nearly 400 English miles south of San Francisco, the climate is nonetheless only a little warmer. We are about 1800 feet above and 12 miles east of the Pacific Ocean. Although there are even now still some hot days, they are cooled in the afternoons by the sea wind. The inhabitants are mainly Mexicans, but they are sparsely settled here, and in addition, each month a few emigrate in order to move farther south, where there is more wilderness and where they can lead lazier lives.

Seven weeks ago I had an accident which prevented me from working for a long time. For the explosion of the rock we have here dynamite cartridges, and for lighting these, copper capsules which contain quite a lot of fulminating silver. One of the latter, which I was trying to clean, exploded in my left hand, lacerated the thumb and middle finger of the same and also sent a few small pieces flying into two fingers of my right hand. The superintendent had the horses harnessed, and when after midnight the moon came up, he drove me himself to the doctor in San Luis Obispo 40 miles away, which was naturally great with me and for which I should certainly be grateful to him. Now they are healed again and have healed up better than I had expected, even the nails are growing back.

Dr. W.W. Hays has given me a bill for 100 francs and the pharmacist another for 50 francs (at any rate a lot) which the Swiss Health Insurance Company in San Francisco will pay, since I am a member.

When you receive these lines, Christmas and New Year will be at the door, and these holidays will go by quietly and peacefully at my house, yet I may look back upon this year with satisfaction, because if I now already have an opportunity to put up some savings; this job also gives me the opportunity to get better paid jobs in the future.

At present I earn $45 as a repairman and $5 extra for writing, making entries in books, etc., thus 250 francs per month, room and board free.

Thanks again for your advice about the smallpox, and hoping that Christmas and New Year will be celebrated warmly on the dear Steinhof, I send you and all my loved ones my warmest best wishes for the New Year, with kisses and love

Your Otto

Concerning the Life in a Mining Camp.

Almaden Cons. Mine, November 22nd, 1876

Dear Little Sister Hanneli!

I call you little sister and yet Emilie writes me that you are now as tall as she. It pleases me to learn that you are playing a new piano, and I certainly would like to hear it again, because here you hear neither music nor song.

Now I shall try to tell you a little about the local life in a mine. The mines are usually 5 to 10 hours away from a village or city, because in the flat land and even in the projections and foothills of the mountains it would be extremely difficult to discover a lot of ore and even more difficult to mine it, because in these areas the stony layers of the earth's crust are covered with deep earth. From here to the nearest postal station, Paso Robles, it is 6 hours, and to the next town, Cambria, with about 1500 inhabitants, it is 10 hours. Now a highway is being built there, and soon hopefully a regular postal stage will be operating on it, at least our superintendent will make a petition. In the winter, when the roads are bad, mail is picked up scarcely once a month. Winter begins here only in December, when the rainy season begins, which then often lasts two to three weeks and continues four to five months with interruption. We already had rain for 2 days as a precursor of winter, and now often in the mornings is seen a light frost.

The mines usually all have the same arrangement; so in our camp there is a simple frame house for the whole team with the exception of the firemen, who have a small cabin of their own, where they can sleep undisturbed during the day, because they work half the night. In the main house downstairs is the kitchen, the dining room, where the whole team is fed, and the office, where the superintendent also sleeps and where I am now writing. Upstairs is a room on both sides, and in front bunk bedframes with space for about 20 men. In the middle of the bedroom is an oven, made out of an old steam kettle, in front of it a table and benches on the sides. Beside the window I have an extra bed, beside that the small trunks, as you will be able to see in the sketch below.

Beside the house is a storehouse where we have stored up for the winter the necessary provisions like flour, tea, coffee, sugar, maccaroni, salted pork, fish, sauerkraut, rice, salt, etc. Farther on the blacksmithy, the barn for the cow and 3 horses, 2 cabins where the Chinese live, furnaces with the necessary steam engine and woodshed, etc., ore shed, powder house, etc.

The Manhattan Mine according to a drawing by Otto Wyss.

Those are the buildings, to which soon two more ore sheds are supposed to be added at the end of the tunnel, in order to keep the ore dry. An Artesian well, 35 feet deep, with a crank and bucket, is near the church.

The team here, like in most mines, is composed of various nations; thus there are, for example, four Swiss, three Germans, six Americans, two Mexicans, five Irishmen and Englishmen, one Swede and eight Chinese, who, however, cook for themselves and have no relations with the rest of us, except for work and pay. Two men, a fireman and a machinist, have night watch and so eat their meal at midnight. At 5 in the morning blows the first whistle to get up, and a quarter of an hour later the cook rings on a steel triangle calling everyone to breakfast. At 7 blows the whistle for work to begin, at 11 for the Chinese cook and at noon for lunch. At 12:30 the steam whistle calls people back to work and at 5:30 to dinner. After dinner I usually spend my time writing, discuss things with the superintendent, giving out tobacco or cigars, writing some letters or doing something else, reading something in the newspaper, discussing things, playing another game of checkers, or somebody tells a cock-and-bull story. At 9 we go to bed, and by 10 all lights are supposed to be out.

That is pretty much the daily routine, the camp life, which even on Sundays scarcely changes, when, instead of going to work, the team does its wash, in order to clean and to mend some clothes, washings, shoes, and boots. On Sunday afternoons we take walks, and those who have nothing better to do with their money buy a bottle of schnaps. So far there has been no fighting, yet you do have to watch out, and especially at election times, like recently, occur fights which usually end in a bloody manner.

Our cook is a Swiss, a very practical man who cooks well for us. The menu is about as follows: mornings, beef steaks and pancakes, noon: soup, meat, two vegetables and dessert and evenings: two sorts of meat, cooked fruit, potatoes and some dessert, and always with it bread, butter, preserved pickles, syrup (light), sugar, in the mornings coffee and milk, and in the evenings tea to your heart's content.

November 25th. I was interrupted in my writing by the arrival of the superintendent and an owner of the mine and shall make this letter brief, so that it will be delivered tomorrow morning. The owner, Mr. O'Toole, seemed very satisfied and made me a present of a pair of leather gloves.—I also want to note that, when we arrived, there was nothing alive here except a dog. In the first days I took home two small coal black little cats whom a neighboring boy wanted to drown, and they were and still are my delight when I must be at the machine all night. Now we have other cats, two dogs, three horses, one cow, four dozen chickens, six turkeys, two dozen doves and 12 ducks, two big, and 14 young pigs.

Four more workers have just arrived, and if this keeps up, we'll soon have a big mine here, which I like all the more, because even if there is more work, there are also prospects for more pay.

At Christmas and New Year I would of course like to spend a few intimate hours with family, but here there is nothing. Everything businesslike.

I would have liked to write to Sister Emilie a few lines, but the superintendent is calling me again; for that reason I shall write the next time.

Warm best wishes for the New Year, and when you sit together at Christmas on the cozy Steinhof, so remember your brother in the Far West. To you yourself, my dear grandmother, and to Emilie my warmest greetings, your brother

Otto

The following letter is the first one with a stamped letterhead:

Post Office, Paso Robles Springs, Almaden Consolidated Quicksilver Mining Co. Salinas District, San Luis Obispo Co

Otto Wyss in California at the time of his wedding in 1877.

The First Own Plant Garden.

Almaden, June 20th, 1877

My Dear Sister Emilie!

Answering your dear lines of January 5th, I thank you kindly for your good wishes. I do not doubt that the metric measure will soon become popular,[61] and I wish we had it here, because the 12 inch foot with its eighths, sixteenths, as well as the pound with its ounces, etc., is not convenient.

Of music and song one hears here practically nothing, yet the superintendent of the neighboring mine, who will soon marry, has purchased a piano with his bride's dowry.—You write me that our land is being leased out, how much and to whom? Don't you have any more cows and pigs? Is the pastor's wife still there? You see, I would still like to know a lot.

This spring I have planted a garden here and have organized it rather well. I had a lot of radishes, still have a lot of lettuce. I planted about 300 seedlings, which make beautiful heads of lettuce (unfortunately day before yesterday 2 big pigs came in and they got into the lettuce patch and devoured about a third of them), further about 3000 onions, 280 mustard stalks, white and yellow turnips, parsley (they don't know about chives in California), leek, tomatoes,

---

[61] Reference to the introduction of the metric system in Switzerland, which replaced previous units such as feet and yards.

pumpkins, watermelons and yellow melons, beans and about half an acre of sweet and plain corn. I have about two acres of potatoes, we have new ones today, but they seem to have dried out. A water reservoir, about 50 feet above the garden, with rubber tubes and iron pipes, makes it easy for me to irrigate the garden and to keep it in good condition. There has certainly been plenty of work, because the ground was plowed for the first time this spring and is still full of roots and tree stumps. Last week there was an extraordinary heat wave, and only afterwards did we find out that two forest fires, the one in the northerly, the other in the southerly direction from here, have taken place, the first about 5, the other 11 hours from here, which naturally have caused the hot wind. Since then we had had cooling sea breezes again, especially in the afternoons and at night the cold land winds, which the snowy peaks of the Sierra Nevada send our way and which have caused frosts until the end of May and which damaged our garden.

For a little while I have been studying Spanish again, because there are still a lot of Mexicans around here who are too lazy to learn English, and since in the meanwhile one must do business with them, so one must learn their language.

I shall answer the next time Hanneli's dear lines, write me again soon. Warm greetings to dear grandmother, to Hanneli, to yourself, with kisses and love your brother

Otto

The neighboring mine now has a post office; the mail comes once a week, at any rate better than nothing.

Otto earned a lot of money in the mine and assisted through the improvement of the production to increase the reserves. Thereupon the operation of the mine was under way. With the assumption that the mine would soon open again, he took over a small farm in the vicinity, and the owners of the mine handed over to him for the meantime the supervision of the mine and ceded to him the use of the company's property around the mine.

Otto is now 31 years old. On August 27th, 1877 he marries in San Francisco a 34 year old woman, who has traveled from Switzerland in order to be with him.

VI

Ottilie

Ottilie Meyer (in several pieces of writing also Meier) was born on January 10th, 1843. Her father Rudolf worked as a book printer in Zurich; her mother was a daughter of Pastor Locher in Pfungen. Ottilie had three brothers: Robert (1841–1844), Fritz (1845–1867), and Karl (1846-?).

A woman without a name. In any event, Otto does not mention it and always writes about his dear wife. There are probably missing letters in which he writes more, and yet his reserve could be genuine. We know little about the occurrence of this marriage, which was very happy.

Otto probably got to know his future wife already during his school days in Regensdorf, where he attended secondary school for two years with Ottilie's younger brother, Karl. Then, later back home from Paris, in the winter of 1870-71, he shared a little room with Karl, on the Schipfe in Zurich, and thus renewed and deepened his friendship with Ottilie. From this time on both corresponded with each other. When in 1876 in California, Otto sensed that he would slowly prosper, he had his friend come to join him, or she wanted to come.

Despite the simplest economic situation, despite deprivations, hard work and solitude, both were very happy together. The slow and harmonious growth of the family in their seclusion welded them cordially together; they were there for one another.

Despite all adverse circumstances they created for themselves in their isolation a new homeland, an environment which for them became worth living and worthy of love. They populated their living space with their growing family and everything which appertains to a manysided agricultural operation, like garden, meadows, fields and all kinds of animals.

Beside their farm was built a postal station, unequalled in simplicity. Only the most necessary things were available, as was the case in the main house and the barn. Yet everything animated the spirit, the fantasy, the will power and the daily work of the couple. Despite their immense solitude, they were never completely alone. They had contacts with neighboring settlers and through letters with their old homeland.

Current events, developments in the states and in the wide world and happenings back home in old Europe are recorded, commented upon, but their own family stands in the foreground, fills both lives—including the intrusions,

*catastrophes, puzzling reverses of fortune, which no one could comprehend
and which were difficult to work through.*

*Ottilie wrote her own letters to her husband's family. These writings are
also preserved. Their inclusion in the here presented collection makes possible
something like a stereo vision of the conditions in California and the life of the
emigrants. However, the views do not diverge from one another—quite
different from later on with the second wife Seline--, a testimony to the
harmony which ruled this marriage.*

Ottilie Meyer

Married by the Minister in my own House.

                                    Almaden Cons. Q.S. Mine, February 15th, 1878
Dear Sister Hanneli!

Your dear lines have pleased me a great deal, and I don't want to delay in also
writing you a few lines.

I scarcely thought about writing anything concerning my marriage or
anything else about my dear wife, because I scarcely know myself who belongs
to our family, and I was never at any wedding.—In general, here in this country
people deaden themselves to all family feelings. Each person takes care of
himself as well as possible and lets the dear Lord take care of the rest.

Before and during the wedding things went as follows: On August 15th I came to San Francisco, on the following day I visited the proprietors of the mine in San Francisco, on August 17th I made a trip to Milpitas and Gilroy to see the gentlemen who live on the property. On August 25th I got the legal permission at the County Clerk's Office, on August 26th we went to see Pastor Büchler, and on August 27th the minister came to my house, No. 512 Greenwitch Street (where I had always lived earlier) and performed the marriage ceremony there with Mrs. Mary Lippert and Rudolf Trueb as witnesses. A ham with salad, some cheese, bread and wine and a pie with grapes and fruit provided the entire wedding feast in which only about half a dozen adults participated.

Here in the mine we did not need much at present, the kitchen dishes are of course designed for more people, but we manage. We have furnished as a bedroom a room beside the kitchen, the office serves as our living room, and we also usually eat there. The dining room for 30 people is too big and cold. Should more people come, there are two more small houses here, which through additions could be enlarged and made livable. Snow never falls here and it is therefore much easier to build; rain falls only in the winter months, and thunderstorms are totally unknown here. I always have something to do here, we have a lot of rain, and then ditches must be dug, equipment must be rinsed and the water drained, so that it does no damage to buildings, wood or in the tunnels. Moreover, the buildings are flimsily built, and after strong winds they almost always need repairs.

Enclosed you will find the photograph of my dear wife. I shall write to Emilie the next time; to her, as well as to my dear grandmother, warm greetings, as well as to yourself from my dear wife, from your distant brother
Otto

Really Happy to "have a lifetime partner in this already somewhat lonely region."

Almaden Cons. Q.S. Mine, May 10th, 1878

Dear Sister Emilie!

Answering your dear lines from the beginning of the year, I must confess that I could tell, especially reading your dear lines, how surprised you were by the unexpected announcement of my marriage. Well, we have already been here eight months, and I must confess that in all this time I have never regretted my decision, but rather am very happy to have a partner, in this already somewhat lonely region.

We have purchased little of our own furniture, but everything which is here is available for our temporary use. Kitchen ware, of course bigger than normal because intended for more people, is plentifully available. Beds are also here, but we have our own blankets, and other furniture from the office, which serves as our living room. A few boxes and chests were easily fabricated with hammer, saw and plane, and so we are presently better settled in terms of comfort and cleanliness than I have been since the age of 15. As far as provisions are concerned, we are partly provided with old provisions, and a credit account has been opened for us by the company in the local store next door to buy whatever we need. Further we have a horse (which gave birth to a lovely filly four weeks ago), a goat, 13 pigs, over three dozen chickens, two dozen pigeons and a few ducks and turkeys, which together quite regularly contribute to putting food on our table. You will think that it takes a lot to feed all these animals, but look, it is done quite simply here. The poultry receives daily a couple of pounds of barley or wheat, the pigs go up on the mountain in the mornings and come home in the evenings with bellies full of grass, in order to take a few more handfuls of barley or bran, etc., whereas the horse and goat find green or parched grass almost throughout the entire year.

The area around the mine includes over 200 acres, and the biggest part is covered with good grass, which in some places is 2 to 3 feet high. A big garden, which we plant ourselves, produces corn, cabbage, carrots, turnips, mustard, lettuce, tomatoes, melons, etc., and we already have rather many new potatoes. As you can see, at present we have no needs, and with diligence, thrift and moderation we shall live better here than in the still so dear old fatherland.

Warm greetings and kisses, to Hanneli, to my dear grandmother, as well as to yourself, your brother

Otto

"A Sunday Child, who with her dark blue little eyes, looks out quite merrily at the world."

Almaden Cons. Q.S. Mine, September 10th, 1878

Dear Sister Emilie!

Your dear letters of the end of May have already arrived and I was pleased to receive news again, although not all is very good.

On September 1st a little daughter was born to us, a Sunday child, who cries little, when she is not hungry, and with her dark blue little eyes looks out quite merrily at the world around her. We do not yet have a name for her, but I plan to name her Emilie or Mimi, as it is abbreviated in English. I made a cradle for her the day before yesterday, and her dear mother has made a few little flannel jackets for her. May Heaven keep her healthy!

We live here so isolated that I can report little news. We get the necessities from the store next door, slaughter a sheep or a pig when we need fresh meat, here and there poultry for a change, and also the garden, although somewhat dry, still produces cabbage, from which we shall soon make sauerkraut. We have many ripe melons and tomatoes, and we also had beautiful ears of corn.

Otherwise the hills and fields are dry and yellow, only the green-leaved oaks, which bear a lot of acorns, and the willows and alders along the brook offer any change of scenery. We had hot days this summer, 115°F (37°R) in the shade and even the day before yesterday we had about 35°R.

No rain has fallen since the end of April, and you can well imagine that it looks dry around here.

I have 21 pigs gleaning the ears of corn in the stubble fields. Half of what they gain in weight comes to the owner of the field. Our goat has run away, and I have already looked for it and asked around about it several times, yet until now without success. It has probably already found a willing welcome in our Mexican neighbors' stomachs. Every now and then there is a hare to shoot, also partridges, but we also have beasts of prey such as chicken hawks, wildcats, badgers, etc., and especially they first take from us many pigeons.

We likewise have many squirrels, and our two cats and two dogs hunt them, when they are not too lazy, which makes us happy, because they steal eggs from our hen house, and rats and mice are rare here, however, we do have brown moles, which are highly unwelcome guests in the garden.

About two miles, three-quarters of an hour walk from here, is a so-called camp-meeting. Different preachers preach there. There are cabins and tents there and games and all kinds of amusements, especially a kind of imitation of the Jewish Sukkot festival. About this time every year one is held, and it lasts four to six weeks. I have never been to one and don't ever intend to go, because there is sung Holle-Holle-Hallelujah, temperance is preached, and afterwards schnaps is drunk again.

Instead of our earlier Mexican neighbors, we now have at least American ones, across the road from us, but we still have little more contact with them, except that we can talk with them, but this doesn't happen every week. [...]

Ottilie begins to write letters to the Wyss family in Switzerland as well. These documents are also rich in information about daily life in Almaden.

Almaden

My Dear Sister! [62]

You have given us great joy by surprising us with the beautiful little dress for our dear little child, for which we very warmly thank you. It fits our dear little Mimi so well and I am all the more delighted that you have made it yourself. The cut is really very practical, and I shall during the next few weeks make a shawl of gray llama of the same cut for daily use.

---

[62] Letter to one of Otto's sisters, probably to Emilie.

For the past week our dear little child has unfortunately not been well, it had a lot of diarrhea and therefore became thin and weak, and I was indescribably worried about her dear little life, yet now thank God she is again rather lively and better looking. I always made warm towels for her and often gave her a little chamomile tea. We are uncommonly happy about the little books and medicines which our brother-in-law has sent us, especially the one about child care is for me a highly valuable and dear present, for which I thank dear brother-in-law quite warmly; being so far from a doctor, without these aids we would not have known what to do.

Since we now have a cow, we are far better stocked with milk, which our dear little child loves. I would be very happy if a German woman lived in this region, I am not yet so good at English, therefore I can hardly understand the few American women who live nearby, even less the Mexican women, one of whom came a few weeks ago to see our dear little child, grabbed her sleeping out of the bed, and in order to see her well held her up to the open window, since it was a cool evening, naturally I took the little child away from her right away and laid her again in her little bed. Later the same woman wanted to give us some medicine for the child, but I wouldn't give it to her.

Hoping that this letter finds you and yours all in the best health, your grateful sister greets you all warmly

Ottilie Wyss

Mimi Should Be Baptized.

Almaden, January 24th, 1879

My Dear Sister Emilie!

When your dear letters arrived, I was just then alone with our dear Mimi, dear Otto had left two days earlier for San Francisco. How pleased I am that you, my dear sister, are willing to be the godmother for our little child, I cannot at all express—it is a comforting thought to me that the dear child has a godmother whose example she can someday follow with love and respect. That she should be educated in a fine Christian manner, will constantly be my primary concern. In order to have her baptized, we shall, God willing, travel with her next summer for a few days to San Francisco and then have her photographed, in order to be able to send her little picture to her dear aunt godmother. She is, praise God, now quite lively, has a well nourished little body and eats with a good appetite twice a day a thin gruel out of the feeding bottle; in addition, she drinks daily a bottle of good milk.

The dear little one gives us rather much joy; she is very happy with her dear father, when he comes up to her little bed, she stretches out her little arms, and when he takes her on his arm, she smiles and nuzzles up against him, while pulling a little on his beard. Sometimes she shouts loudly, for example when our big dog (it is one of the biggest there is) comes into the living room. The beautiful little dress from our dear sister-in-law is to be used as a baptismal outfit, since in San Francisco in the summer it is very windy every afternoon, you see there every day at the height of summer ladies with fur coats. For the 2½ years that I have been in California, I have never yet seen snow, yet a few weeks ago it was 8°R below zero. Time goes by very fast here, we always have pretty much work; we live peacefully and therefore also happily. My dear Otto said that he was glad to return from the noisy city again to his quiet small family.

Now may you, my dear sister, like all our loved ones, live happily through the newly begun year and many more to follow. Receive warm greetings and kisses from your faithful sister

Ottilie Wyss

Dear Sister Emilie! To the lines of my dear wife I add my own warm thanks that you are willing to be the godmother of our dear Mimi; we have no godfather, those are rare here; in order to have the baptism performed by a regular minister, we prefer to wait until we go to San Luis or San Francisco, around here there are only Methodists or Baptists, etc., that is, preacher-farmers. The dear little one now weighs 12 pounds and is almost a yard long, is strong, carries her little head straight up and no longer wants to lie, but prefers to sit up, but more about that next time, warm thanks and greetings as well to my dear grandmother; your brother

Otto

The first child, Emilie (Mimi) Wyss, b. 1 September 1878.

Concerning the Fascination of Forest Fires.

Adelaida, November 2nd, 1879

Dear Sister Hanneli!

[…] The local, that is, San Francisco newspaper seldom brings anything about Switzerland, yet I did recently read that the harvest there was below average. Here everything is going great, and I am happy to have around 700 pounds of wheat flour in the house and also further to be rather well supplied. We shall move this week to our own little house, and, even if it is somewhat smaller, it will still seem homier to us.

Regarding your little business, I want to mention that the two Frenchmen (one actually an Alsatian Jew), who began here a quite modest grocery store 2½ years ago, have had an extraordinary commercial success. Since the neighboring mine closed and runs no more store, the gentlemen's nearest competition is 15–16 miles away, or 5 to 6 hours by wagon. They sell the merchandises at a 25–100 percent profit, and when a debtor does not pay within 6 to 9 months, they simply calculate in 1½ to 3% interest per month. To be sure, they are in many ways dependent upon the harvest, and should this be bad, they must also lose.

Just now they transport over 1000 sacks of wheat, each weighing 140 pounds, to the market, must also accept hay, butter, eggs, cattle, etc., as payment, but for which they pay low prices, often not half of the market price in San Francisco.

Their income in the first year amounted to 8000 dollars and they made over 2000 dollars in profit, since then however their income has tripled. One of them recently took an eight- week cure in a spa and had in the meantime appointed a clerk. I shall be careful not to get into their account books too often. It is better to supply myself regularly in the fall, directly from San Luis.

This summer we were often terrified by fire dangers. Hardly two hours from here burned the forest, the dry grass, stubble fields and shrubbery for miles, luckily over a nearly uninhabited area. I was twice called to help put out the flames, the first time, after an hour's ride, we came at noon near the fire; the horses became wild and startled and we had to make a detour, in order to come up to the fire from the wind side. It was an awesome sight, to see the unchained element, borne by a breeze, licking, flitting, crackling and striding forward over the plain, in order then, suddenly roaring and crashing, to burst into flames along the hills in trees and shrubs. We could do little to extinguish the fire, only prevent it from moving close to houses, by removing its fuel and by extinguishing advancing tongues of flame with wet sacks. I shall never forget the sight, when that night toward 10 o'clock I rode back home along over black charred ground, beside burned shrubs were burning the dry branches of four giant oaks like might torches, and wherever a hollow tree was burning, fiery sparks were spewing out of the many upper branch holes like out of a giant chimney. Slowly, shy and exhausted, the horse trotted out of the realm of the fire. On the second occasion, a wide stubble field was in flames, which burned up 100 sacks of wheat and a wagon, yet there was never for us any direct danger, because the fire was borne eastward away from us by the winds.

Many cattle perished, along with stags and deer, and other wildlife, as well as horses and pigs.

The photograph of our dear Mimi is somewhat dark, but it is well reproduced, and shows her sitting still for a moment and listening to the music of a music box. My dear wife wants to add a few things for you. I shall soon write to Sister Emilie and so close for now with warm greetings to my dear grandmother, to Sister Emilie, as well as to you yourself from your brother

Otto

Photos of Small Children—a Difficult Matter.

Adelaida, November 2nd, 1879

My Dear Sister Emilie!

First of all warm thanks for your dear lines and your goodness in thinking about our dear Mimi and for willing to be her dear Aunt Godmother. The dear little child is, thank God, healthy and happy and we are really pleased to finally be able to send you her photograph.

It was really not easy to find someone dependable to watch over everything while we were traveling to San Luis [Obispo], because there is no photographer nearer, and then we received back the photographs only a few weeks later. We wanted to have the dear little child baptized at the same time, but since there is no reformed church in San Luis, we shall just have to wait until we go to San Francisco sometime or until a reformed minister perhaps comes by here. Dear Mimi was uncommonly good and high-spirited on the trip to San Luis and back; on the way back home, she stretched out her little arms toward a field beside the road, where she noticed a single cow which was similar to one of our cows; she shouted at it and actually thought she was seeing her own dear little cow which she enjoys so much and whose milk she likes to drink. The other of our two cows will soon give birth to a calf, just in time that the first cow is giving less and less milk. We also make as much butter as we need for ourselves.

Our dear little one is also a real "meat kitten," she likes to eat meaty soups and meat which she can already chew rather well with her eight little teeth. She is uncommonly attached to her dear daddy, and as soon as she sees him, she always wants to go to him and fawns upon him in all kinds of ways; he also loves her, often carries her around with him in the barnyard and takes her riding with him on his horse, when he does not ride far.

I have also learned to ride a little on our tame horse, yet I still have too little practice to hold our dear little one with me on the horse. When we ask her: What do you send to your dear "Aunt Godmother," she always replies in a gentle tone: "Ah, ah," and she does the same thing when we show her your photo.

She likes to be washed and take baths; she walks quite well, holding on a little to the armchairs or walls, almost too fast, but when not holding on to something, she does not yet feel confident about walking, yet she did manage recently to stand up on the floor for a little while without holding on to anything. As far as the photo is concerned, it is too dark, her little eyes in fact have not been so dark for a long time, and her actually quite white skin is likewise much darker in the little picture; in addition, she is holding her left arm somewhat higher than her right, whereby she looks lop-sided; to tell you the truth, in the studio she kept looking around, scratching herself and fidgeting, and only when the photographer started playing a music box, did she calm down and sit motionless, attentively listening to the music. Then the photographer snapped the photo, although he should have put her left arm at the same height as the other one. Otherwise the little picture is completely accurate. […]

Ottilie

[…] We have also enclosed one of the locks of hair of our dear Mimi, the back of her head is quite full of them.

Concerning Splendid Fruits, Big Birds and Christmas Trees for German Immigrants.

My Dear Sister-in-law!

The dear little letter from you pleased me a great deal and I thank you warmly for it; it has now been six months since we have received your dear letters. We had a lot to do this past spring re-sowing and re-planting our garden, because the birds scratched up and pecked up many seeds and young small plants. Now, however, everything has already grown back, and this year we are again expecting rather many melons, tomatoes, corn and pumpkins. Last year we had a great many melons and various sorts; we often said, if we could only have our loved ones in the homeland come to see these splendid fruits.

My dear Otto has shot many of the harmful birds and squirrels, and he also shoots almost every day hares and partridges, the last of which often come in flocks quite near the house. He shot many chicken hawks, night owls and a big eagle, which he has stuffed, as well as a big night owl, a chicken hawk and a big jay; from various glass buttons which he found in my sewing box, he made for each stuffed animal natural eyes.

Your dear little children would certainly be delighted to see the glistening humming birds which fly about in our garden, and to ride on our tame horse; yet I do know that this is not easily possible, since we live quite too far away. Here the children of the neighboring farmers start riding at the age of four, and children 9–10 years of age ride around on a horse in the mountains in order to drive the cows home to be milked. Our cow comes home herself every night, and she usually stays over night in the big, grass covered barnyard. [...]

My dear Otto drives around a little here and there with us. That is always a big pleasure for our dear little one; she almost constantly stretches out her little hands towards the horses, and does not cry when the carriage jolts so much on these rather uneven mountain roads. I wish that you could just once enjoy this beautiful view, it is like a panorama, when one looks down from our nearby hill over the ravines, the fields and the lower lying hills, all around you see the most beautiful flowers, which grow unplanted by the hand of man and smell so sweet. You wanted to know whether there are also fir trees here? Yes, there are many fir trees and other evergreens which make excellent Christmas trees; our dear little one was still too little last year, but next Christmas, God willing, she will also have a Christmas tree

In American families no Christmas trees are displayed, only among German families is that customary here, that is, in the city.

Now we hope that these letters find you and my dear brother-in-law as well as your dear little children healthy and happy, and we shall be pleased, hopefully not after too much time, to receive more good news from you. I warmly greet you and all our loved ones, your faithful sister-in-law

Ottilie

Dear little Mimi also sends her dear uncle and dear aunt and her dear cousins Hansli and Oskar and dear Cousin Alma many kisses. As I am writing these last lines, she is sitting on my lap, is nudging me and is trying to take the pen out of my hands; she would like just now to go back outside.

A New School House which Serves many Purposes.

Adelaida, P.Q. May 30th, 1880

Dear Sister Hanneli!

[...] Since the beginning of the year we have had as our neighbor a German, M. von Heine, who has bought a plot of 80 acres, which borders on mine. A bachelor, in his forties, and a completely unpractical man in whatever he tackles, but he is rather well-schooled, gave earlier private lessons, math, German, etc., subscribes to three or four newspapers, plays chess regularly. He receives a pension of eight dollars per month and reckons that he could almost live on that, if he only raises a few chickens and hogs and a little fodder for them.

Since last New Year we have a new school house quite nearby, almost on my property, which in addition serves as a church, village hall for elections, and as a dance hall, etc. School is held there for about six to seven months, and in two or three weeks will come summer vacation, about which I am happy, because the pupils come to school on horses, which sometimes come too close to my hedge and my wheat.

I have a lot of work everywhere, because not only is the hay harvesting season just around the corner, but everywhere there are cattle, horses and pigs which discover here and there a gap in the fence around the grain field and try to break in.

I shall write to Sister Emilie a little later after the harvest and for right now close with warm greetings and kisses from your brother
Otto

"A warm, good and friendly little boy."

Adelaida, May 30th, 1880

My Dear Sister Emilie!

Your dear lines have once again overjoyed us and after I report to you that we all are, thank God, healthy and happy, I want to first answer what you asked me about in your last dear letter.

I always bake the bread myself, usually with potato yeast, for whose preparation a German woman gave me the recipe a few years ago. It is quite easy to make: after three or four smaller potatoes are quite softly boiled with about two glasses of water, one takes a handful of flour, a spoonful of sugar and the same amount of salt, stirs this into a smooth, thin puree, then adds to this mixture some fermented yeast, which one has scooped up from time to time from the freshly made yeast and held over.

Each year we pickle a small barrel of sauerkraut, we also again have rather many cabbages and turnips in the garden. Our fruit trees have not yet borne any fruit, we can expect them only next year. We often drink acorn coffeee, but also have regular coffee. I have melted down about 50 pounds of lard, and we have the smokehouse quite full of smoked ham and goat meat, of which we can sell a little here and there.

You will perhaps already know, dear sister, that we now also have a dear little boy. How much joy does her little brother give to dear Mimi. She always tries to feed him with bread and meat, and lays her playthings and everything she can reach on his little bed, when the latter on hot days stands for a few hours in the shady hall in front of the house. Since there are no other small children for miles around, dear Mimi has no suitable playmates, therefore she entertains herself all the more with our dogs and cats and chickens; we also have 22 more young chicks.

The garden is rather big, but a lot of weeds still grow in it, because it was little cared for by the previous owner. We have planted yellow turnips, lettuce, corn, melons, tomatoes, onions, some potatoes, cabbages and turnips. Also many sunflowers, whose seeds besides wheat and barley seeds make very good fodder for chickens.

Right now my dear little boy is calling me and would like to have his nine-o'clock milk, dear Mimi is also coming inside, to see whether there is anything to eat, she is rather grown up and can already easily peep over the edge of the table. The dear little baby smiles as soon as you come up to his bed, he is a warm, good, friendly little boy. He was also as a newborn baby already rather big, he could not at all wear the little shirts which dear Mimi had worn for the first two months of her life.

Now I hope that these lines find you in quite a good mood and healthy and well; dear Mimi also sends warm greetings to her dear Aunt Godmother, she has a whole mouthful of teeth which recently appeared together or right after one another. Every morning around four Mimi crawls into her father's bed for about an hour; in the evenings she brings him his slippers because she knows that, when he has taken off his boots and has put on his slippers, he will take her on his knee and play rocking horse or show her pictures. […]

Ottilie

A Dangerous Cattle Thief in the Neighborhood.

Adelaida, August 8th, 1880

My dear sister-in-law!

[…] ten days ago one of our two cows gave birth again to a calf, and so we have continuously enough milk to make butter for our needs. There are several springs on our property, the nearest of which is about 100 paces from the house; our dear Mimi slips away there as soon as she is left unattended for a few minutes.

It is really true, what you wrote in your dear little letter, that the dear little children need so much more than we adults; their care and supervision require that we constantly devote ourselves to them; which however every mother gladly does for the dear little creatures and feels happy if they are only healthy and develop well.

As far as clothing is concerned, in this sparsely populated region one does not need many changes of clothes, and thus with the help of my good sewing machine I can make the necessary clothes for all of us.

This year we have raised 50 young chicks, which will be of good use to us next year. Our fruit trees have not yet produced any fruit. In general our little farm is satisfactory, although it was very neglected and gave us rather much work, especially for my dear husband, until he had repaired the many big holes in the fence, where entire herds of strange cattle and pigs used to come in and eat from our crops.

About a mile from our family lives a very dangerous Mexican, who stole one of our young oxen, which we wanted to slaughter at the beginning of the winter, and since in this region it is very difficult to get witnesses, we could do nothing at all about it, the same man also stole other people's cattle, and one of these days they are going to catch him for good. [...]

Ottilie Wyss

The Trip to San Francisco.

Adelaida, November 28th, 1880

Dear Sister Hanneli!

[...] At the beginning of September I had to go to San Francisco and, even though it was only a business trip, it also turned out to be a holiday trip, and I want to tell you a few things about it. On September 6th I left early in the morning on horseback for San Simeon, which is 28 miles away. M. von Heine, my German neighbor, accompanied me and after a rather hard ride, by noon we had put 23 miles behind us; we fed the horses and then I let him go back home and take my horse with him, while I walked the rest of the way to San Simeon. There toward evening arrived the big steamer; several barrels and crates with butter and eggs, bales of hides and poultry in big cages, etc. were loaded, and it was already dark when the ship set sail. A sharp north wind was blowing against us and the white foamy waves from time to time crashed high over the bow of the ship. I could not stand it for long on deck and went downstairs, where I soon stretched out in my cabin and despite feeling a little giddy, I soon fell asleep. The commands of the officers in charge awakened me early in the morning, and soon the ship came to a halt. I went up on deck and saw almost nothing in the dense fog which enveloped us, yet by and by dawn broke, the ship ploughed ahead slowly under constant bells and whistles until toward 8 the fog had lifted and we found ourselves near the Monterey station, a little old city located on the bay of the same name.

In the background arose forests of firs, dark, uniform in appearance, while the coast looked dry, sandy and desolate at this season of the year. Here and there white cliffs, against which the surf crashed and foamed upward, or isolated boulders rearing up out of the water. After a second landing in Santa Cruz, a lively little coastal city, 80 miles from San Francisco with a bay surrounded by limestone cliffs, numerous limestone kilns, solid and well built houses, the ship again headed northward, and when toward 4 o'clock in the afternoon another fresh southwesterly wind sprang up, a few more sails were quickly unfurled and with doubled speed the beautiful steamer now danced, even flew over the great expanse of water, while the seagulls circled overhead and followed the vessel—and fell back. Soon appeared the Ocean View House (behind which I had once 6 years earlier planted potatoes), then the Cliff House high up on the cliff and opposite it Lobos Point Observatory, Light House and Foghorn. Then the sails were furled up, and we sailed in between the cliffs of the Golden Gate, at whose feet the sea lions were frolicking by the hundreds, into the beautiful smooth bay of San Francisco. Then we sailed past a proudly three-masted ship with mainly English colors flying on the mast pole, which was waiting for a load of wheat, also past the threatening cannon mouths of the fortress of Alcatraz, and by nightfall the steamer had docked at the wharf.

One of the first off the ship, I was trying to escape the hordes of the coachmen, who are so pushy, when suddenly someone called out my name. Why, Otto Lippert, how much you have grown, I must say, and we hasten to the old boarding house, to the home of the neat German people where I had always lived in earlier years. Talking and asking questions, the time passed quickly, my business took me two days. I spent the third buying things like 60 pounds of coffee, 20 gallons of petroleum, 1 case of soap, material for making shirts and clothing and in general a lot of good and necessary items.—I went back home by train (the steamer was away, it only travels once a week) and by wagon conveyance from Soledad ,and going the rest of the 30-35 miles on foot over bad roads and poorly developed terrain, I came home. Happy to be back home and finding everything well, I now had to spend several days chasing down my horse, which was finally found. However, foxes and chicken hawks had taken advantage of my absence and had unmercifully ransacked our chicken coop.—Also, the pigs had got into the hay, yet on the whole I was content that things were not worse. Well I must close, dear sister, "Mimi want write too," she says and chats almost the whole time, and already says rather much quite correctly. Warm greetings and best wishes for New Year's, to dear Aunt Ryffel, to you, to our dear grandmother, to all of you from your distant dear brother

Otto

Concerning the Damage which Foxes and Neighborhood Pigs Do.

Adelaida, November 29th, 1880

Dear Sister Hanneli!

[…] For several weeks the nights have been very cold, always below freezing, and since the houses here are not built to withstand such cold, we put our iron cooking oven out of the kitchen into the living room, whereby the dear little children have it much warmer at night, if I, before going to bed, stick another thick piece of wood in it. In the mornings the dear sun shines quite early on our little house, and it is quite warm for the entire day.

This summer we had already partly raised 50 young chicks, of which unfortunately more than half were devoured by chicken hawks and foxes. A neighbor's pigs also often came over and ate up our young chicks and a lot of wheat while dear Otto was in San Francisco. You can certainly imagine that we were very happy when he came home again. Yet the trip was absolutely necessary because of business which he had to take care of with a gentleman in the city. Then he brought back to us along with many other necessary and useful items a whole piece of Indienne-pattern fabric, out of which I made bed coverlets, little clothes for our dear little children and also a house dress for myself.

We would also like to enclose for you a photo of our dear Mimi; should the letter however be too heavy, we shall have to wait and send it the next time. Our dear little boy is now already as big and fat as dear Mimi was when she was photographed, he wears the very same little dress, and it will soon be too little for him, he weights 20 pounds and is very lovely, has quite light blond hair. [...]

Ottilie

Application for the Position of Postmaster to the General Post Office in Washington.

Adelaida, November 29th, 1880

Dear Emilie!

Usually the first rain comes here at the beginning of October, yet this year it seems to be extraordinarily late, yet even if it has been dry so far, now at least it looks like rain. There is always work for me to do, I still have more land to fence in, a hen house and small smithy , pig pen, etc. to build and an extra garden with hot beds, flowers, etc. to plant, and in fact, the last should be done first.—Yet that still does not give me enough work, which brings me to the fact that the two neighbors, Frenchmen, who run the store next door, are planning to give it up, as well as the post office. I live here almost in the middle of this district, and so I made the effort to get the post master job for myself, filled out a job application to the general post office in Washington (the national capital) and obtained around 100 signatures from residents of the local area. In order to obtain these, I had to ride around every day for nearly a week, wear out each of my three horses riding them (not to mention myself), until I had obtained the signatures and met each of the residents in an area of about a three-hour ride in all directions, and the roads were bad.

I do of course have a competitor for the position of post master, and it wouldn't make any difference to me if he got the job if he lived around here, but the way it stands, if he were hired, the mail in that case would no longer go by here, but rather we would have to ride two- or two-and-a-half hours (eight miles) to get it.

I now already care for the postal horses, feed and clean them, and if I do receive the job as postmaster, then the two jobs would go hand in hand, and grant me at least a guaranteed, if small, income. [...]
Otto

Request for Flower Seeds.

Adelaida, November 29th, 1880

Dear Sister Emilie!

A rather long time has again gone by since we received your last letter, which pleased us so much and for which we thank you kindly. We are, praise God, all healthy and happy and time passes so uncommonly fast that we must wonder that we are again almost at year's end, yet we are happy and content that throughout the year we could do all our work without others' help.

Our dear Mimi would already like to make herself useful, she brings shavings to the kitchen, goes with me to the hen house to feed the chickens, and in the barnyard she stretches out her little hands full of wheat and corn kernels, and she is very pleased when she finds eggs in the nests, which she usually carries undamaged to the kitchen.

A few weeks ago dear Otto built a little shed onto the back side of the kitchen, which we now have full of wood for the rainy season, but, of course, it has not yet rained much. A windmill, which we bought during the harvest season, gave little Mimi a lot of joy, just as a little mill which is used to grind the kernels for young chicks often gives her entertainment. [...]

In the course of the upcoming weeks we shall pickle a little sauerkraut, because we still have only about a dozen beautiful heads of cabbage. The pigs, of which we have 36, came into the garden and devoured a lot in one single night. If only pork had a better price here, animals are much cheaper to feed here than in the dear old homeland; most of the time they stay outdoors and find rather many acorns to eat. [...]

Dear Emilie, since you have written us that you have mignonettes in your garden, I would like to ask you for a few seeds from them. I love mignonettes a lot, and there are none to be seen in this region. In our flower garden we have, with the exception of a few rose trees and lilies and several "Strassburger" flowers, only a little bed of summer flowers in various colors, from which I stored up some seeds. [...]
Ottilie

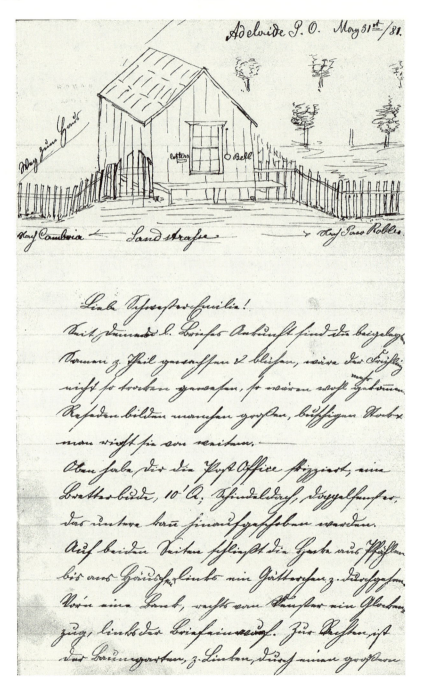

Letter with sketch of the simple post office.

Life and Work at a Country Post Office.

Adelaida P.O. May 31ˢᵗ, 1881

Dear Sister Emilie!

Since the arrival of your dear letter, the enclosed seeds have partly grown and are now blooming; if the spring had not been so dry, then more would have bloomed. Mignonettes make big, bushy trees, and you can smell them from far away.

Above I have sketched the Post Office for you, a cabin 10 by 10 feet in size; it has a shingle roof, a double window the lower half of which can be pushed up. The picket fence encloses the little house on both sides, and to the left there is a little gate you can go through. Out in front there is a bench, to the right of the window a bell rope, to the left the slot for the deposit of mail. To the right is the orchard, to the left, through a bigger gate, leads the way up to the house, barn, etc.

The postal coach, a light vehicle drawn by two horses, comes six times a week, Mondays, Wednesdays and Fridays from San Simeon around one o'clock and every Tuesday, Thursday and Saturday from Paso Robles at nine o'clock. The leather padlocked postal bag is usually filled on Tuesdays and Saturdays, my dear wife helps me with the sorting, and Adelaida usually receives mainly newspapers. Cambria's mail goes only partly through here. San Simeon has a lighthouse and telegraph station. The postal horses are changed right in front of the post office, and by the time they are hitched up again, I am usually ready with the postal bag. […]

I must stamp every letter deposited here with the name of the post office and the date and cancel the stamp. Every thus cancelled stamp must be recorded, for example 1,2,3,4, each such and such, etc. Every day the total amount of that day's revenue and the date are recorded, and 60% of that amount is my daily salary, which always is the best on Monday.

To receive stamps, post cards and postal envelopes, I just write to the postal department, and then they are delivered, as well as blank forms and twine and packing paper. At the end of every quarter, the number and value of the stamps and envelopes, etc., before and after the quarter, must be verified, further those received during the particular quarter must be counted, and thus the sum of the sold stamps, the income, must be determined.—The daily log of the cancelled stamps produces the post master's commission, and the surplus of the income is sent to the U.S. Treasurer in San Francisco; but a report is sent to Washington to the third Assistant Postmaster General.

In the office itself, I have a stamp, scales for weighing mail, a desk, and file folders from A to Z marked for letters, and bigger files for newspapers; I bought them from my predecessor for $15. We still need to set up some holders for blanks on the upper parts of the walls; it is too easy for Mimi and little Otto to rummage around in the lower desk drawers. I don't leave money and valuables overnight in the office, the door and window are well locked when I go home, but somebody could raise open the window without us noticing it, even if the dog would start barking if there were an intruder.

People come at any time to get their mail, but Saturday is our busiest day; we have the fewest customers on Sunday afternoons and Mondays. Of course I can often plan my work accordingly; often my dear wife must spring into action, especially now in the harvest season. The people are in general friendly and obliging and seem to be happy with me, and if there are those who think there should certainly be mail for them when there is actually nothing and I can't help them, these people are usually the ones who receive the least mail. Most of the mail is received by school teachers (four receive their mail here), ministers, and Americans; the Mexicans and Portuguese receive the least amount of mail. To register a letter costs 10 cents extra, that is, to stick on the stamps, and a half dozen per month is the average number. Money-orders cannot be sent from here.

Well I'll close for now, more another time. Warm greetings to dear grandmother, to Hanneli, to Aunt Ryffel, your brother

Otto

Concerning the Comings and Goings of the Settlers.

Adelaida, December 4th, 1881

Dear Sister Hanneli!

Your dear letters from Churwalden put us in a worried frame of mind, and we wondered if it wouldn't be a good idea if Hanneli came to visit us. The warm, dry climate, the mild winter here would doubtless do you good, and the trip—well people today travel quickly—would cost no more than two such cure stays in Churwalden. Now, thank God, your lines of September 30th bring better news again, and hopefully you will be able to fully heal at home.

Concerning us all here, I can say that we are, thank God, healthy, although every now and then little Otto does cough at night, but otherwise he is happy, and the children are delighted with the little Christmas tree, for which Ottilie and I also have a rocking horse in the works. For rainy days I also have to get our Bernese buggy in good shape and I have to paint it, my old reaping-machine also needs repairs, but I do have the tools to fix it mending it myself. I finally have improved my "vine shears" for work in my vineyard, which, if they work well, should actually be patented. A young man here has invented a new harrow, and 3000 dollars was offered to him by the state of California for the patent.

By next spring we shall be milking five cows and hopefully shall then be able to make rather much butter; I have ordered a butter churn with a thermometer. The store owned by the two Frenchmen has closed down, the two associates couldn't make any money off it, plus they were very selfish neighbors. They gave a lot of credit and sold merchandise at a big profit, and so customers who actually paid them in a responsible manner had to cover their losses from other pursuits, but still they made quite a lot of money in four years.

This summer several people, mostly elderly, from 60 to 75 years old, have died around here, and many have left, including many Americans, who are happy nowhere; they settle down for a few years someplace, and then when things no longer go the way they want, they pack up, sell their property and move to another state of this big Union, where there is more and better government land, and I'm talking about old, gray-haired people as well as young people. My last neighbor, a Mr. Bunch, came here about three years ago, settled on ¼ section (160 acres) of government land around an old shabby cabin which he had found, fixed it up without windows or a floor. He lived there with his wife, who was already from the beginning sick with consumption, and this spring she was bed-ridden, until she died this fall.—Mr. Bunch then grumbled a lot about the doctors and pharmacists, quickly sold his property for 75 dollars (naturally still government land) and moved down south. I am not sure, but I heard that doctors, pharmacists and even carpenters lost what he owed them.

Other neighbors, of course, go to other counties to make a preliminary check and come back with the observation that things look better elsewhere, but it costs money, a lot of money, to buy land.—Once our little herd of cattle is a little bigger, the orchard full of fruit, then our dear children will be a little bigger and can even early in life, help out, and thus we shall certainly have an ample income.

I have already occasionally taken dear Mimi and also Otto riding around with me, and each of them finds this fun, provided we go at a fast gallop.

We have every prospect of a green Christmas, here and there the grass is growing finger-long and the ground looks green, mignonettes are blooming despite occasional frost, and the new seedlings, etc., look fresh and green. Well I'll close, dear sister, with warm greetings from the dear children and myself, your

Otto

Adelaida, December 4th, 1881

Dear Grandmother!

Today is your name day, which of course was always celebrated on the dear Steinhof, and I am also with you in thought, just want to offer you my best wishes and also show you the dear children. I also certainly know that you think of me, of us here in the Far West.

It always pleases me to hear from you through letters that you are, thank God, healthy for your age and that, even if you do suffer from rheumatism and other elderly complaints, you are at least spared the more difficult illnesses. If it only were not so far, I really would like to visit you or have you come see us, let the dear children dance around you and call grandmother "has come", but it is of course just too far. We are sending you a little lock of little Otto's hair. You had kept the locks of my own hair so long that I can still remember how you showed them to me in a shingle box; they were still bright and curly.

Mimi is now over three years old, quite sensible and lively; Otto is shyer, but fat and strong, and he is beginning to repeat the words of his older sister.

Little Oskar is somewhat slimmer than his brother, has a quieter, calmer personality, but he is attentive and, when I come home at night from work, he stretches out his little hands to me, while Mimi and Otto come jumping out and clutch onto me, shouting "Good Evening" and "Dad is here," and then I must have them, and only be careful beside the horses, because the children are very daring, and even though the horses are tame, caution is always necessary and yet so hard to make the dear little ones understand. […]

                                                        Otto

                                        Adelaida, December 4th, 1881
Dear Sister Emilie!

[…] The dear little ones are, thank God, quite happy, but they do make a lot of noise in the house, and since the dear little Christ Child has not yet been able to bring them their playthings, they bring into the house a big pile of hardware from their dear father's smithy and rattle it around as much as they can. Despite all that, dear little Oskar sleeps like a marmot.

We have three geese (among which one gander) and four ducks with a "duckling," which, since you can pluck soft feathers from them every summer (without killing them), give us better pillows than chicken feathers. In this country, feathers have a much lower price than in the dear old homeland, because few people sleep in feather beds, everyone prefers wool blankets and cotton sheets. We still have eight pigs; dear Otto sold 25 of our pigs last fall.

                                                        Ottilie

Concerning the State of the Cultivations.

                                        Adelaida, Pentecost, 1882
Dear Sister Emilie!

Your last letters with the seeds and the letter from Heinrich Kofel and the nice little pictures for Mimi (upon whose receipt she was so possessive that I had to give the picture of grandfather to little Otto in order to keep the peace) have given us all pleasure for a long time. I have planted the seeds from Heinrich Kofel, but they have not come up yet, on the other hand white forget-me-nots are blooming and pansies and soon maggies as well, sweet-smelling morning glories, mignonettes; we have never yet been able to get asters to bud, impatiens do not tolerate the heat, and finally we have around our house yellow clay for soil, which, despite fertilizing and mixing with sand, remains inhospitable to flowers and vegetables. The small yellow kind of immortelles also grows wild here, while we have bigger brown and red ones in our little garden. Seeded roses are partly two yards high, but they still have no flowers, also there are no bluebells yet.

We have four cows, one of which I don't milk, while the other three give beautiful milk, of which we give away a daily portion to the teacher. In San Francisco butter costs around 1 franc 25 centimes per pound, but with the deduction of freight charges and commission, etc., one hardly gets 75 to 80 centimes per pound for it in San Luis.

Oxen or fatted calves bring in $20 to $30 for the former and $6 to $10 for the latter, but since I still have only a few cattle, I usually keep the calves until I have good, young fat cattle for slaughter. I only have a few pigs left, because some were always stolen from us. I have three young horses, besides the two old ones, and a three-year old young horse is now supposed to learn to work, yet it still behaves pretty wild, recently shook loose its saddle and threw me to the ground and broke the bridle. [...]

Because of the late frost there will probably be little fruit such as peaches, plums, almonds and pears, which had bloomed beautifully. For vegetables we have mainly peas and beets and corn, whereas the chickens have mischievously picked to pieces our lettuce and cabbage, even the neighbor's chickens came over and ate up all our beets and onions.

Wild animals, such as foxes and badgers, are often in the neighborhood, and I recently shot a lynx (California coon) out of a tree. Squirrels and ground hogs and moles also seem to be extraordinarily active and come in great numbers into the neighborhood, and we have only one good cat and a young sluggish good-for-nothing cat. Of the two dogs, one is a pretty good watch dog and is respected by the boys because of his sharp barking, while the young one shows signs of being good for herding cattle and both together can chase off strange cattle and protect our property and save me a lot of walking, plus they eat like young dogs and have insatiable appetites, but let's hope they turn out well. Swallows have built several nests around the house, one quite low near the ground, so that I must prevent our children and the neighborhood boys from destroying it, which the latter have partially done anyway.

To dear grandmother and Aunt Ryffel best greetings, with kisses and love to you and to Hanneli from all of us, your brother

Otto

Christmas like Back Home.

                                                    Adelaida, Whit Sunday, 1882
My Dear Sister Hanneli!

[…] So you would like to know, dear Hanneli, how the Christ child came to
our house at Christmas; well just a few days before Christmas we keep the
presents and the little tree in the little room we added to the house, where the
children don't often go, and we set up everything there, so that on Christmas
Eve at first dark I can quickly carry everything into the parlor and can light the
candles on the tree, while dear father entertains our dear children in the little
post office. Afterwards I give the signal with the little bell, whereupon dear
father quickly brings the dear little ones up to the house, the surprise and joy
were quite delightful every time we did this.

Now however the playthings we bought (which were quite cheap), even the
elephant, have been broken for a long time, because our children are rough
with their toys; only the rocking horse which father made himself is still
undamaged, despite the extensive use it has had.

We had this spring eight young geese, which unfortunately died in the big
cold spell, because the goose which had hatched them coaxed them one night
outdoors, and the following morning most were frozen to death. Now we have
two hens each sitting on five goose eggs, one of them will soon have hatched
her eggs, and we now hope, since it is warm, to be able to take better care of
this brood.

Next time, God willing, more. In the meantime be warmly greeted by us
all and by your faithful
                                        Ottilie

The First Name of the Godfather for the New-born Baby.

                                                  Adelaida, September 4th, 1882
Dear Sister Hanneli!

We have been talking this whole past month about writing you, but I had to go
to Cayutos and then also to San Luis, in order to bring home our winter
provisions on time. Also materials for winter dresses, for shirts and sheets are
there, and that gives Ottilie rather much work with her sewing machine.

Right now we are still having hot days which compete with the hottest we
have had this summer, because the heat is stagnant and the cooling sea breezes
only reach us every now and then.

Our family increased on July 29th with the birth of a healthy little boy.
Mother recovered very fast with the warm weather, and the dear little one is
getting stronger, because he has already tried to raise his little head. My dear

wife and I would like to request that you be his godmother. I have asked Heinrich Kofel to be his godfather and we would like to name him Heinrich or better Henry or Harry. Should we also give him the name Hans? Please write to us about this, we would so much like to know your opinion, and who knows, he may even come home to go to school.

The harvest was small, but the corn did make beautiful cobs, and we are just about to shell the cobs and put them in the corncrib, where several dozen basketfuls are already drying. We use it as excellent chicken and geese fodder, and it also puts more fat on hogs than anything else. The five- to ten-foot high stalks with the long leaves make good fodder for cattle. We finally have a lot of ripe melons.—Potatoes don't do well at all here, every other year there are some early potatoes, if the spring is not too frosty, but later on for example in July, the roots make, instead of potato bulbs, only four- to six-foot long roots, obviously a result of the heat. I bought five hundredweights over on the coast, where they grow better, but with freight charges etc. they often are more expensive than cornmeal, so that people around here just don't use them much. We have many cabbages and beet plants, but few onions, the school teacher has helped himself to our onions.—The school teacher, by the way, is an impudent, shameless guy and will probably not stay here long!

You already hear a lot about the upcoming elections, which will take place at the beginning of November, and as usual, there are a lot of candidates for the good paying jobs. [...]

"Don't I have a brave wife?"

Adelaida, December 6th, 1882

Dear Sister Emilie!

Thank you for your dear letter, which brought diverse news from old acquaintances, which of course always interests me.—Mimi is standing beside me and is saying: "We want to write a letter to Godmother, too, and about the Christmas tree and the picture." The Christmas tree is of course now the main thing with the children, and what they especially want for Christmas, a wagon, a doll, which also gives Otto a lot of joy, and a few other playthings.

We shall also have a Christmas tree in the nearby school house for both young and old.—This fall we have lost a lot of chickens through chicken hawks, which were bolder than ever. My dear wife hit one on the head with a stone and killed it. She grabbed another one by the leg, as it was about to fly away with a big chicken, and despite the fact that it struck at her with its beak and wings, she held on to it and hit it with a piece of iron, until it was glad to get away. Don't I have a brave wife?

Since then I have shot down a dozen or more and wounded a few more, so things are going noticeably better.—I am almost finished with sowing and have loaned out the horses for a short time. I have sold all the young horses, because Otto once got too close to one, and the animal hit him under the arms, luckily without any serious damage.—Right now we are milking just one cow, but soon after New Year there will be two more which bring calves. I still have to make myself a milk house, almost totally underground. I have dug about ten square feet and shall put a small store room on top of it, to keep it cold. Next spring I shall milk 10 or 11 cows and hope to make a few churns of butter.

Planting a few more trees, fixing old fences and making new ones will give me rather much to do. […]
                                                                        Otto

The Mexicans—"lazy, thievish and very old-fashioned."

Adelaida, February 16th, 1883

Dear Sister Hanneli!

Your dear letters came today, after the "samples with no commercial value" had arrived in good condition the day before yesterday. We enjoyed everything with the children, and Mimi wanted to go to school right away, so that she may have the handkerchief.

You ask how we celebrated Christmas? Although in the neighborhood school house on Christmas Eve a Christmas tree was lit, we still made a small one at home for our dear children. Mimi received a big doll (now it has only one eye, the other one is inside the hollow body), Otto a wagon and a small harmonica, little Oscar a sled with two horses, magnetic fishes, and Henry got a big kick out of all the little lights on the tree. Henry is a very good, patient child, he sleeps almost the entire night, yet he is lively and so friendly and weighs about 18 pounds, he puts on weight fast and is strong, he can soon go back out in the warm sun in the big wagon which I have made for the children, ¾ of a yard wide and 1½ yards long; it gets used.

Emilie writes: Isabell Besserer-Kienast is said to be on a farm in Mexico. I have no idea what farms in Mexico are like, there are lots of Mexicans around here, they're always going to Mexico and coming back here or they are writing for money so they will be able to come back. They are mostly lazy, dirty, thievish and very old fashioned, any odd tool will do.—In which state, near the capital of Mexico? How big is the farm, I would be interested in learning more.

The railroad is supposed to soon come this way, within 16 miles of my place, about a 5-6 hour drive, which is as close as it will get for some time, yet close enough for all our practical needs, like freight delivery, eggs, butter, etc., to San Francisco or any market for that matter.

We had snow on February 4th and 5th, four inches and it remained three to four days on the northern slopes.—We had three inches of rain this week and four inches on New Year's Eve and New Year's Day, so that both these days went by quite peacefully, and on New Year's Eve we two sat reading a few Bürkli newspapers from the homeland thinking about our distant loved ones and making plans for the future.

Now farewell, many greetings to Sister Emilie, to dear grandmother and to Aunt Ryffel, with a brotherly kiss

Otto

Concerning the Work and Salary of a Country Postmaster.

Adelaida, April 13th, 1883

Dear Sister Emilie!

[...] Small packages do go through,[63] but others come to the customs office and are not opened but rather according to postal law, the postmaster of the addressee is advised of the amount of any customs duty, and when the concerned party pays the customs duty to the postmaster, then the package is sent on, otherwise however it is kept at the customs office. Naturally costs and customs duties quickly rise higher than the worth of such a package. My sincere thanks.

At the post office there are significant changes this summer and fall.

From October 1st on letters are supposed to go for 2 instead of 3 cents, yet in order not to hurt postmasters in small offices, postmasters who cancel less than $50 worth of stamps per quarter will be allowed to keep the entire amount as salary, instead of the previous 60%.

Total cancelled this past quarter $41. My 60% thus $24.60.

Or let's take an average day:

30 letters at 3 ct.	90 ct. October 30 letters at 2 ct. 60 ct.
3 ct, 2 ct, and 5 ct.	10 ct. one 10 ct. 10 ct.
Cancelled	$1.00 stamped or cancelled 70 ct.
My pay for the day 60 ct.	My pay 70 ct.

So I end up better off, in addition, more was written.

Many people request that I put in an application to do money orders, it costs me more insurance money, stamps, but it does bring in a lot of cash, perhaps I'll try it next winter. Again many people wish that I would open a small store beside the post office, to sell tobacco and a few groceries, and it would be really annoying if somebody else began such a store and then took the post office away from me when it was making $150-200 a year, after I had worried with it when it was hardly making 40-50 dollars.—Now I make about $100 a year, and should the railroad come, things will get even better.

---

[63] Otto is referring to a small package containing a scarf which he had received without any problems.

Well, we'll just have to see. Warm greetings and many thanks, to you and to Sister Hanneli from us all, your brother
Otto

The "Laterna Magica" in the "Wild West."

Adelaida, April 14th, 1883

Dear Sister Hanneli!

[…] A few weeks ago the son of a farmer in our postal district brought a magic lantern from Philadelphia, by means of which he can magically project pretty moving pictures on a wall in the dark. Recently he gave a demonstration of it in the school house. He did not have strong enough light to give sufficient reflection to his apparatus in such a big room. We still have a big lamp from our earlier furnishings, which however burns too much petroleum for our use, for which reason we use a smaller one; the man borrowed this big lamp and therefore allowed us to come to the demonstration with our dear little children.

The teacher of our school had his piano brought over to the school house for this evening and played a few pieces. I wish, dear Hanneli, you could have seen how our dear children all listened to the music so attentively and excitedly.

When he stopped playing, they looked somewhat shyly toward the piano and at the teacher, and if she had thought it would do any good, Mimi would undoubtedly have run up to him and would have begged him to play some more. Some time afterward a traveling comedian gave a performance in a school house, he fed his two horses at our house, and therefore we also went to his performance, his wife played the guitar, and he fiddled during the breaks between his artistic performances. However, Mimi said later that the school teacher had played more beautiful music.

Well here comes dear little Henry, he has slept well and now wants to have his glass of milk. Warmly greets and kisses you, your
Ottilie

National Holiday.

Adelaida, July 4th, 1883

My Dear Sister-in-law!

Today is the fourth of July, which every year is celebrated in the United States in remembrance of the nation's independence. Also about three miles from our place is a festival square. Dear father went there this morning on horseback with dear Mimi, to let her see the children dressed in white who, wearing scarves and flags, are supposed to represent the 50 states of the Union. There will also be a little music to hear, which is always a great job for dear Mimi, because she loves music so much. Since today is not Sunday, we cannot close the post office before evening, and so I stayed at home with the dear boys, at first they did cry, but now they are calmed down and consoled with the hope of next time; right now dear Otto and dear little Oskar are tumbling on the big haystack near the house, and dear little Henry has fallen asleep, whereby I received a few quiet moments for writing, because today not many people are coming to the post office.

The last dear letter, which we received from dear Mr. Brother-in-law soon after New Year, had put us in a rather sad mood; yet we hope that those periods of illness will soon be over for you all and especially that dear Mr. Brother-in-law will not have to suffer much more. Has your faithful maid got well again, and is she back at your house? Right this minute dear little Oskar is coming back inside, he has found a small little red beetle, which however flew away when he laid it on his little hand to show it to me. The dear little naturalist is always finding something interesting, now a rare little stone, now a piece of colored glass on the spot where the store used to stand; then here and there a gleaming little animal which he can catch. On January 15th he went alone up on the hill and brought down the first little spring flowers. […]

Ottilie

Request Advice for Running a Store.

Adelaida, November 22nd, 1883

Dear Sister Emilie!

Your description of the national exposition in Zurich has interested me, but, of course, I would have preferred to see it myself. I have not yet seen in the new world a good exposition, in which beautiful, tastefully arranged exhibits make such a good impression. There is an annual exhibition in San Francisco, but there a certain stall is given to a predetermined exhibitor (usually a business or manufacturer), who takes advantage of this opportunity to advertise and, if possible, to sell his products and merchandise. At these events imported merchandise is often displayed as manufactured products, and it looks like a street with many shop windows.—In recent letters you have mentioned little about your store, but since I now intend to open my own store beside the post office, I would like to request some information from you. I shall have to determine the prices and quality of my merchandise from the local demand, yet your experience could be of use to me in one way or another.—So, for example, if when you weigh 100 pounds of coffee, you come out somewhat too short, how much if two to four pounds is given to the customer? Sugar dries out (especially here), as well as spices, tobacco and others. What are the items on which you earn more? Here merchants earn little on sugar, a lot on tobacco, and so forth.—Does this or that item spoil faster (spices) or does it lose its attractive appearance or taste? What is the profit on dry goods in comparison to groceries?—Then bookkeeping; are the daily journal, the ledger and the cash record book sufficient? Should you take inventory annually? How do you force debtors to pay the balance they owe? Etc. You will say that those are too many questions for one letter! However, this is the main thing which occupies my attention right now, and since I know that your experience could give me many good suggestions, I do not doubt that you will willingly share it with me. Even though the people, circumstances and the country are different, much will be an advantage to know.—This winter I don't expect many customers, most have stored up their winter supplies, and I don't plan to order over 3 to 400 dollars worth of merchandise. I shall not sell dry goods in the beginning, later on probably. The store (as der Laden is called in English) is built, and tomorrow the roof will be nearly finished. Mimi goes to school now, spells a couple of short words and scribbles something like letters, and the main thing is, she understands most of the English spoken by the teacher and the other children. Mimi's certificate of baptism will arrive with this letter.—Warm greetings and kisses from the dear children and your brother

Otto

Baptismal Trip with the Children to the Wonderful City of San Francisco.

Adelaida, November 23rd, 1883

Dear Sister Hanneli!

Your dear letter of September 26th has pleased us and, upon reading, it I would have wished to have been there on September 20th at least with written best wishes.—Concerning the exposition in Zurich, I learn this and that through the old well known and constantly welcome Bürkli paper, which has already gladdened our hearts for many an hour and which certainly takes us back every week to the dear old homeland. As soon as the children go to sleep, the material in the Friday paper from time to time serves to stimulate not only reading out loud, but even more conversation and the revival of our memories about this and that in dear Zurich.—The long winter evenings are here, and the German pharmacist, Mr. Manderscheid in Cayucos, has once again provided us with reading materials, and then I read out loud in front of the open fire in the hearth, while mama sews and mends clothes.

On this past September 11th, I had to go to San Francisco on land business and, in order to have Mimi and Otto baptized, I took them along. On September 6th we traveled with an acquaintance to Cayucos, stayed there with Mr. Manderscheid and on the 7th took the steamer to San Francisco. The children looked out on the wide sea (a lot of water) with astonished and wondering eyes,

The port town of Cayucos, from where Otto and his children left for San Francisco.

a fresh wind had made the sea turbulent, and soon the children were seasick, threw up, but without screaming they went to sleep for the entire night; Otto remained asleep also for most of the time the next day. The next morning Mimi came up on deck with me, but whatever she ate or drank came back up. At 5 in the evening on the 8th we again stepped on dry land, and the children got back their appetites. I went to the Hotel Rhein, went shopping with the children, naturally the going was slow, because there was so much to see. On Sunday we went to Pastor Büehler's for the baptism and to the homes of some old acquaintances, as well as to the home of a Mr Deucher, once a shoemaker in Wettingen, who now is going on 80 and who remembered dear father. On Monday we went to Woodwards Garden with its menagerie, lion pit, green house, stuffed animals, birds, etc. The children looked around to their hearts' content until they were worn out, and on the way back they fell asleep in the street car. On Tuesday I went to the Land Office, where I spent almost the entire day, on Wednesday and Thursday we went shopping again until dinner time, and it was the toy store which especially appealed to the children, "look at this and look at that!" On Friday we saw a fire with steam driven fire engines and firemen at work, and then we went by train (new surprise) to San José,

where I went to see the owners of the mine (earlier employers). I received the best welcome and was able to arrange things so well that I could start on the way home on Monday, September 17th, with a good mare and a light two wheeled wagon. After a journey of five days we had traveled more than 170 miles and were all happy to be back home in the new house. [...]
                                    Otto

"With a favorable west wind we hear the waves of the sea thundering onto the shore."

                                                    Adelaida, December 1st, 1884
Dear Sister Emilie!

Your dear letter with its travel description of the Rheinfall and Schaffhausen took me back to the time when I still lived in the beautiful fatherland and gazed at the blue waters of the Rhine and the Limmat. Here, on the contrary, in the summer you see a big wide sandy riverbed, almost dry or only here and there a little water of yellowish color, like the sand over which it flows. Still I have little free time and can hardly get away from here and the business to go to San Luis, which is necessary right now. To be sure, 200 miles directly east of here lie the snow covered mountains of the Sierra Nevada, which send down sparkling streams full of melting snow. These streams irrigate the wide plains and make garden land, sugar and cotton fields, where earlier there was nothing except barren plains.

To the west we have the wide sea, whose waves we hear thundering on the shore when there is a favorable west wind, as though it were just half an hour away. Now I have a lot to do everywhere, and though I leave the plowing and fence making to others, I still have to ride around after this or that cattle or hunt down debtors who owe me money, in short, there is a lot to do around here. But I should be happy about it, because the man—even one with family—is poor who must waste his time looking for work. If we keep our health, and we keep making progress, we also may hope to be able to come back home some day and pay a visit to our loved ones, and perhaps put our children in a good school in Switzerland.—The store business is going well, the store is filling up more and more with merchandise, the cattle are multiplying, and we must have more room for our growing place.—To be sure, I could often use more hands, but dear Mimi already helps mama a lot, plus Otto brings in the wood and water, and even if we promise them something every now and then, they are nevertheless accustomed to doing something useful and helping us. Just a few more years, and they'll be riding around, driving home and milking the cows and looking after the cattle.—Of course, I must write everything at night. Orders, payments, claims, bills, ledger, etc., everything is crowded into the space from one evening to the next, and I am happy about our hearth fire, which always has an awakening effect, whenever you are somewhat sleepy.

Well it's past midnight. At year's end our best wishes to dear grandmother, Hanneli, to you and to all, your brother
Otto

When the Neighbor Bangs on his Piano.

Adelaida, December 2nd, 1884

Dear Sister Hanneli!

The mail coach is not here yet, and I want to write you a few more lines. Yesterday I was at the home of our neighbor, Mr. Stocker. He bought not long ago a piano, a good Weber one, but since the beautiful instrument is badly tuned, it gives you a headache. He fancies himself to be musically inclined, and bangs and beats around on the poor piano as though it were an old tin can. No trace of a chord, but he does beat time with 2 big boots. His children had received a few lessons from our school mistress, but she herself could only play a little.—I hope Mimi will be able someday to take lessons from you, dear Sister, she already often speaks of piano playing and sings the little songs which she hears in school, she also sings quite nicely "Be Happy about Life" and "With the Arrow to the Bow," and tries to teach it to Buebi (Otto). The mail is coming, next time I'll write more if possible, to dear grandmother belatedly best wishes on her name day and to all warm best wishes at year's end. Henry is screaming and screeching, he had boiled eggs and wanted to crack them. Your brother
Otto

The Catastrophe: The Death of the Three Boys.

Adelaida, October 13th, 1885

Dear Sisters! All our Loved Ones!

Have you all received the few lines which I sent to you 4 weeks ago in the charge of dear father? Oh, it is the saddest thing I ever had to write in my life. As a child I lost a good father and a tender loving mother, but back then I could not feel the sharp pain as deeply as it gnaws at us now about the loss of our dear good three little boys. Oh, we would think that only we ourselves had seen so much good in them, if every person who knew them did not tell us that we had the most splendid children far and wide.

Last May, when dear father was in San Luis with two of the dear four, he made an appointment for the photographer to come out to take pictures of all our dear children and also the business portion of our property; similar to a photograph, made by the same photographer, which we had already seen; he promised to come out in the course of the same month, but since he did not come, we reminded him about it in writing. He again promised quite definitely to come in July, except he didn't do it, we waited for him every day; the dear little ones were all ready in lovely simple little clothes and looked so rosy cheeked and healthy that no one would have imagined what misfortune would befall us before the month was out.

Oh why did that demonic woman with her clothes full of fungus from that awful illness have to come over, just after dear Henry, may he rest in peace, had wounded two of his little fingers on the previous day when he had squeezed them in a door.—The second doctor, whom dear father called on that day when I wrote you all, asked whether one of the dear children had had any kind of wound, even the tiniest scratch, at the time when they were around that woman. Then he explained to us that those lacerated little fingers had most likely absorbed the spores of this awful illness directly from the clothes of that person and had then infected the others, without us having any idea of what was going on. We saw that the little fingers were getting worse on the first evening of the day that person was at our house, but we had no idea that diphtheria could be in them. Four days later dear little Oskar, may he rest in peace, complained that it hurt him to swallow; dear father sent right away for the doctor, then came this bad guy, because the real doctor, who then saved dear Mimi, was away. A few days later, after they were all buried, the photographer came by and said he could photograph the property, but by then we had nothing more for him to do. As soon as dear Mimi can be taken without danger to San Luis, we shall gladly send you a little picture of the dear child. Dear father will write to you about everything else. With warm greetings and kisses; to all of you, my love

Ottilie

On September 9ᵗʰ, 1885, died Oscar, 4 years, 6 months and 12 days old, on September 10ᵗʰ Henry at the age of 3 years, 1 month and 12 days old, and on September 11ᵗʰ died also Otto, 5 years, 6 months and 7 days old, all of diptheria. [64]

"We cry together many hours a night."

Adelaida, November 30ᵗʰ, 1885

Dear Brother-in-law and Dear Sister-in-law!

You have given us a great deal of comfort in our deep mourning through your little letter, and I thank you warmly for it. Dear Mimi is, praise God, as was

---

[64] Diptheria was at the end of the 19ᵗʰ century the angel of death for small children. A third of child mortalities among three- to five-year-olds was attributed to this disease. Iris Ritzmann: *Child Diseases and Child Mortality*, in: Paul Hugger (Hg.): *Being a Child in Switzerland*. Zurich 1998 (in German), p. 307 ff.

your kind wish and your so confident certainty, again quite recovered and already as strong as she was before the illness. Dear father took her along a few weeks ago to San Luis, to be photographed; however, it has really distressed me that the little picture is not better made. In it the poor child looks as if she were deformed, because the stand for her little arm was too high. Well, we won't fret about that; oh, if we only also had pictures of our dear blessed little boys.

How could it be otherwise than that we must still cry a lot over the irreplaceable loss of all our dear splendid little boys. Many hours a night, despite our fatigue, we cannot sleep, so we cry together—(dear Mimi sleeps well), oh but dear father and poor mama just cannot get over it. Often, when I awake, for a few moments it is as though it has only been a bad dream that our dear little boys have died, but right away the horrible truth comes back to me.—Oh, we are often like cripples; how delighted we were when our ever active, eager boys rolled a lot of big stones down from the hill, to build a wall around the garden, so that the cattle could not get in, or when they stuck pipes together to make a waterline to the store, and dear blessed Otto really knew how to put together some of the pipes and could pipe the water nearer. Our dear children were never seen idle, they were always busy with something. I have filled several small boxes with rare little rocks, which I have found among the playthings of our dear blessed little angels, which our sweet, dear little Oskar had collected and carefully preserved. Oh how now should I not keep such little boxes as holy shrines to the memory of our dear little Oskar. The big, beautiful cow, which today has given birth to a snow white calf, was the darling of our sweet Henry, and he also seemed to be her darling; the extremely tame animal looked at him in a friendly manner, whenever he came close to her, she would stand in the right place when he wanted to milk her, and would not move; naturally he couldn't really milk her, but he was glad when he was able to squeeze a little milk out of her, dear father would often set the dear little one on her back, and she would walk around a little with him in her slow, calm way. Oh, we see in every object reminders of the dear little children.—My dear sister-in-law! I would like to send you special warm thanks for the comforting "children's greetings from over there." These truly beautiful verses full of faith were already known to me in my dear homeland, as they are to be found in the splendid book of poetry: "Peace in God" (by Julius Hammer [65]), yet now so transformed into real greetings and words of comfort from our dear little angels in heaven, they made an indescribably comforting impression upon us. We already sang the "O please don't cry" a few times, dear Mimmi listens attentively and has also already learned it pretty well. Mimi believes that our dear little angels have certainly found her dear little Cousin Alice in heaven; or she wonders whether dear Alice has fetched her dear little cousins; o how precious is the innocent childlike mind.—Nothing else is possible than that the

---

[65] Lyrical-didactical poet, the author of much sensitive, religiously motivated epigrammatic poetry. Born 1810 in Dresden, died 1862 in Pillnitz.

loss of our three dear children will still pain us for a long time, yet we shall try with God's help to obey your well intentioned, kind admonitions and obey the will of the Almighty with humble resignation.—Pray for us all, our beloved, because our pain will still often overwhelm us to such an extent that we shall not be capable of recognizing the ways of the Lord. Oh, you need to have a deeply pious mind, to be able to say with a sincere heart: "The Lord hath given, the Lord hath taken away, praised be the name of the Lord." May the almighty Father in Heaven give us this pure, pious frame of mind. When our loved ones were separated from us, in a state of the greatest distress, I opened up the Bible to the book of Job; dear Otto and I read for a while in it, as we were crying, then dear father said: "After all, things went well for Job, afterwards he had many more children." Oh how our dear Otto loved his children, still he could not have loved them more than I. How deplorable it is when dear Mimi sees us crying. She says in a soft, sad voice, while she clings to us: "We shouldn't cry any more." We are glad that a family with four children has moved into the mine house, they are pretty decent people, the children come over every day to play with Mimi, and Mimi often goes over to play with them, there are two girls of eight and ten and two boys of four and six.

It is late, and tomorrow we shall not have time to write, and tomorrow the mail coach takes the letters back east. May it be God's will that this letter finds you all in good health. May the new year bring you much happiness and many blessings, and may almighty God protect you all with your dear little children from further misfortune. Please kiss the dear children and may they all be warmly greeted and kissed. Your deeply bereaved

Ottilie Wyss

"About Photography."

Dear Brother,

It is late, but tomorrow morning I have to take my horse and hunt for cattle. We had a lot of storms and rain, and now during the day I must check on all the damage. It is cold. We wanted to have a picture of Mimi when she lost her little brothers, and there she is.—She is smiling a little too much, but apart from the fact that her right shoulder appears too high, you see her as she really is in life, good-natured, good-hearted, friendly and pleasant, as she always has been from birth—a real Sunday child. The fact that the one pantalet did not come down properly, shows that mother was not with her at the photographer's. But the main thing, face and head, is rather good, I think.

Give one to Sister Emma, and the other is for you, your brother

Otto

Otto as Justice of the Peace in Indian Affairs.

Adelaida, June 7th, 1886

Dear Sisters!

How much we had intended that these letters would reach you, our loved ones, by dear grandfather's name day, but there is always something which prevents us from writing; thus, for example, about two weeks ago, as we were sitting down to write to you again, an Indian came into the store and he stayed there about two hours; he bought a few things, tobacco and a pipe, a silk handkerchief and red woolen material, paid for it, and at the same time wanted to do a small lawsuit against a previous employer who had not paid him; the employer likewise an Indian. Since both however understand almost no English, a neighbor, who presently lives in the mine house and is half Indian himself, had to be called to serve as translator and simultaneously as lawyer, and he then so intimidated the superstitious Indian in his language that the latter soon gave a 20 dollar gold piece to his accuser and paid for the judge's costs as well.

Dear loved ones, I have written you this to give you some idea of how things often go here; many funny things occur in the office of the justice of the peace which dear Otto holds. Usually in the evenings one or several men come from various parts of the region to seek advice from dear Otto about some matter. Yesterday evening the old cattle doctor Harris was there again for a few hours. He is a very experienced man and has already given us much good advice concerning our horses and cattle. There seldom passes an hour of the day when some stranger is not here; not always to buy something; rather the people, who have ridden several hours to come here to pick up and to bring their mail, take a rest break in the store, others sit down in the cool store to see what comes and what is bought, and if we do not pay close attention, also occasionally to steal something. Well enough of this. Right now a group of women and children is coming in; I don't know when I can finish this letter.

It is 11 o'clock at night, dear father and dear Mimi are sleeping; I am not very sleepy yet, because we have been so determined that these letters should leave with the mail which is going east tomorrow; now it is quiet, and there is no one else to wait on. The day before yesterday, as we were going to bed, two more strangers came, they wanted to have dinner and stay over night; at 4 in the morning they wanted to have breakfast, and before sunrise they had already left. We lead a rather agitated life, and there is a lot of work to do. Your

Ottilie

The Boys' Final Resting Place.

Adelaida, June 8th, 1886

Dear Sister Emilie!

I do know that we are late writing, but several times when I wanted to write, I had to lay down the pen from my trembling hand and rub my tired eyes, and so the writing was saved for another time. So you rather like your goddaughter, whom I took to San Luis last fall to have her picture made, with her somewhat smiling little face, her right arm a bit too high, but in general she looks in the photo like she is in real life.—Mimi especially misses her little brothers in the evenings, and then she sings impromptu, as I have written down on the enclosed paper. Throughout the day she has school mates and the neighborhood children who are of course not really the most desirable playmates, but nothing can be done about it. Of course, we do try to keep her at home and keep her busy, but we don't always have something new which can keep the lively child's attention. We often wish we had a jigsaw puzzle, like we used to have, a picture with lines which I could paste on thin wood and then cut out.—She has also begun to crochet and could soon begin to embroider small pieces of cloth, and perhaps you might have some idea how we could occupy the good child, cultivate in her a love for the home and keep her at home. If so, please send us a letter and write to us about it. It is so hard for us all to have to miss everybody, the dear boys, and also to give up all the plans I had to transform our home and our property into the most beautiful home in the region, naturally with the help of the dear boys. Also, considering that my property is their final resting place, it should be improved and beautified, and the little round hill on whose highest point our loved ones rest, once bare and dry, how has 200 grapevines growing around it and a mulberry-, a peach-, an almond- and a chestnut tree, which all seem to be growing rather well and in a few years will shade their final resting place.

We shall receive more pictures of Mimi and then send one to you, dear sister, to Aunt Ryffel and to Heinrich Kofel, because she is now our only, our last child.—We have very good prospects for an excellent harvest around here, wheat and cattle more moderate, but after much winter rain came a cool spring and now constantly warm summer weather. Friendly greetings to Aunt Ryffel and to the Kofels, I shall write to them and to you, dear sisters, greetings and kisses, your distant brother

Otto

"Often we doubt the existence of a good Providence."

Adelaida, November 9th, 1886

Dear Aunt Ryffel!

It certainly seems ungrateful to delay so long an answer to your kind letter with its gift of ten dollars for dear Mimi.—The sum has been deposited in the dear child's special savings account.—Our sincerest thanks. Early this morning, however, the dear child got another surprise, because Mrs. Walker (the midwife) brought into the world a little sister, with whom Mimi is totally delighted and from whom we could hardly drag her away to school; the baby is big and strong, and the mother is also well.—It will help us infinitely to get over the gnawing pain which still overwhelms us whenever we think about our three dear sweet boys who were snatched away from us last year, who 15 months ago were still our pride, our strength and our joy. Never to see them again, never again to have them around us, the good gentle sweet little Oscar, the lively, happy Heireli, the smallest, who could find so many things when our memories failed us, the big, strong, sensible Otto, who could already help Mama so much, when father was away. When, after years of patient and hard work, we saw growing up a little daughter and three little boys, each one mentally and physically well developed, all of whom justified our most beautiful hopes, we often would say that we had not lived in vain, because we had children who would help us, who already did help us so much, with their presence, joy and encouragement.—Yet it was not to be, and although we often doubt the existence of a good Providence, nonetheless the beautiful Christian faith teaches us not to despair, but rather to hope for, to believe in, a reunion in heaven. We have gone down financially this past year. Bad people always profit from others' misfortune, but yet with the dear little one new joy will bloom in our lives, so we hope, if it is allowed us, to see it grow up, to move forward and to strive for a better future.

People are coming, time is getting short, and the mail will soon come. Warm greetings and kisses to all our loved ones and much thanks and warm greetings from Ottilie and your nephew

Otto

The Office of Justice of the Peace Has its Disadvantages.

Adelaida, December 9ᵗʰ, 1886

Dear Sisters Emilie and Hanneli!

We finally get around to writing you a couple of lines, and thank God, the arrival of a dear little daughter who looks out into the world so quietly, kindly and contentedly, makes even us again more content with our destiny.—What should we name the little child? Alice, Mama says, that was the name of Oskar's last child, and that may well be the name we give it—Alice—will we get to keep her? That is our constant fear and concern.—When Mimi heard that Mrs. Walker (the midwife) was here, she could hardly sleep, and when she later awoke and heard something screaming, then she would not leave Mrs. Walker's side until she finally could hold her little sister for a while.—Mimi is growing, and she is feeling better again since the cooler weather began and the school is closed for about three to four months.—Right now her attention is divided between her dear little sister and five young dogs, which she wants to teach to eat, besides she sweeps the store, harnesses the dogs, looks for and brings in a couple of eggs, and especially in the evenings she takes the slate and the pencil and writes or reads in school or picture books. In school she was placed beside pupils three years older than her in the same class, one of whom was still in school Friday a week ago, got sick there, and died on Saturday night at 11 o'clock and—was only three months older than Mimi.

Alice Wyss, the second child of Ottilie who survived, born 9 November 1886.

The office of justice of the peace is becoming a burden to me and I am planning to give it up. People here are just too bad. One, who was accused of theft and whom I sent to prison in San Luis, swore vengeance—later I found two cows dead and the tame cow with the bell shot through the chest, but she is getting over it.—But what can I do against such shamelessness? I cannot prove these crimes.—In the store business we see how little it matters to people who can pay, to steal, and those who don't have any money just laugh in your face or deny it when they're accused of doing it.—Of course even if we are just novices in this business and it is a curse for us, we need the money and so we'll just have to put up with it.—The railroad will bring in more immigrants, here and there people will sell their property and thus eventually bring in a better class of people.—Recently I was awakened at one in the morning, there were two men there who were making an accusation against a man in San Miguel for disturbance of the peace, etc. at night.—It was three o'clock in the morning before I finished writing down their statements, and the two were snoring in front of the fireplace. I slept myself then for an hour, then had to make coffee for them, and they left. Two days later I went to San Miguel, where I held court, heard the witnesses and sentenced the accused to 30 dollars or 30 days in jail.—He did not pay—for this I received 3 dollars and 2 dollars extra for expenses.—There I spent the night with a man from Zurich, a Mr. Kunz from

Wädenswil; 12–14 years ago he had bought some land there and had established a homestead, etc., so that he now has 480 acres.—In the old adobe cabin before the hearth fire he told how he fed and housed there 18-20 sheep shearers twice a year. (Kunz has earned a lot with sheep earlier.)—Now the railway station is hardly a stone's throw from his place, so he has given 60 acres to the railroad company, and he has invested some of his land in town-lots, of which $20,000 worth of property has already been sold—so he became a rich man. In 18 months he will have cleared a big profit and then he wants to go back to Switzerland. He is about 45 and still unmarried.

Last September there was a Swiss festival in San Luis Obispo, and since I had been appointed to a committee, I was there; I got to meet many Swiss, most of whom were from Ticino, but Aargau, Zurich, Bern, Basel, etc. were also represented.—There were there—the postmaster of San Luis Mr. Simmler, Collattor from the harbor and the big landowner and the big family Schiefferly,—the bank cashier Mr. Brunner, brewery owners,—many dairy owners, innkeepers, beer brewers, merchants and 200 altogether in the parade.—The things for dear Mimi have all arrived fine, and while she still is very restless, she did try them on now and then.—Winter is here, and even if so far there has been little rain, the evenings are long and cold, and the tic-tac-toe must again be brought out, but unfortunately there is not always someone to play it with. Yet Mimi is always in a good mood, rummages around in her little valuables, and we are of course happy just to have her at home where we can keep an eye on her. Things are now going better with her little sister, but everything helps us to keep her busy, and so thank you so much for your gift.—Although the pain over the loss of those little spirits who have gone to heaven often moistens our eyes with tears, our thoughts about Mimi and the dear newly born Alice will revive our spirits, and we shall learn to adapt ourselves to the phrase "It should not have happened." A good, dear little child is Alice, her little eyes look at you clearly and earnestly, and right now she is quietly watching me as I write.

One more question—when should I teach Mimi to write some German? She understands high German, not just Züridütsch. To good Aunt Ryffel warm greetings and New Year's wishes and also to both of my dear sisters warm greetings and kisses for the coming year, best blessings from
Otto, Mimi and Mama

The Trip to the Photographer.

Adelaida, August 9ᵗʰ, 1887

Dear Sisters Emilie and Hanneli!

Each time we had intended to definitely write letters to you all, my loved ones, especially on Sundays, we were prevented from doing so again and again. Then we finally received the opportunity to travel all together to Cambria. On a Sunday at the end of June there were no important postal matters to attend to, and so we got up early in the morning in order to go and have made the long desired photo of our dear little Alice. At 5 in the morning the dear little child was taken out of her little bed, put straight into the wagon and slept for about an hour on the road, so that we feared that she would look sleepy in the picture, but on the contrary she looked quite lively, because a music box which dear father played and held up in the air, helped to keep the dear child awake, and right after the picture was taken, she fell soundly asleep, and an hour later we were already again on the road home. It was the first time since the three dear boys died that I was away from home, the trip was beautiful, and, praise God, without accident we arrived back home on the same evening at 8 o'clock and found everything just as we had left it. The dear children were naturally very tired and the dear little ones sunburned, so that they looked like they were burning, but I spread some sweet cream on them, and soon it got better. The picture of dear Alice turned out better than we had expected. Dear Mimi is nearly always away from home, a Ticino family is now living in the mine house, they have a lot of children, and there Mimi finds companionship, sometimes more than we would like, because she is usually not here when you need her to do something. The two vacation months will soon be over, and I'll be happy when school starts again. Dear father has conducted the water from a big spring on the hill down through a pipe, where it now flows into a trough across from the store, which also pleases our many calves. We have over 40 small calves, the smallest must still be fed with milk. At present, not much is bought in our store, because several new stores have been built in the new railroad stations Templeton and San Miguel, yet we hear that a few of them are already about to close down and have no more credit. In the meantime, we allowed most of our things to run out. That gives to many people less opportunity to sit around so long, yet it is precisely the ones who buy and pay the least who take up the most time. The melon season is back, if you, dear loved ones, only had a portion of the many melons which people always bring to us and think that we should sell them for them; yesterday a woman brought another wagon full, and since we would not accept them, she still left half of them here, just so she would not have to take them home again.

August 11th

Everything here has a very low price this year, yet people have no money, hopefully things will soon get better. At the end of last week the air was full of smoke for many miles around, and we discovered that it came from a big fire, whereby much fodder and grain were burned up, and yesterday the house of one of our customers burned down, while no one was at home. We wanted to send the letters at the beginning of the week; but as always, we can seldom spend an hour writing. Tomorrow dear father must go to San Luis Obispo to

the mill, to help a neighbor as a witness in his land affairs. Next month we shall be busy with building, most houses here are made entirely of wood, are put up pretty quickly, are built of inexpensive materials, however, through the long heat and dryness, they become practically unusable for winter, when they are about 10 years old; therefore we, too, now need to build a new bedroom and a new post office. […]
Ottilie Wyss

Farm of the Wyss family. In the foreground, the road with post office and store.

The Traveling Photographer Makes it Possible.

Adelaida, Calilfornia, November 28th, 1887
To All My Loved Ones in the dear Homeland!

We are really delighted to be able to finally send you a photo of our place. To be sure, it is so small (it was taken from too great a distance) that you, dear loved ones, will hardly recognize many things. It was still pretty hot when a traveling photographer came by, without us knowing anything about it in advance. The cows and calves, which usually spend the night and the morning in the barnyard, were already back out in the meadow. We would have liked to have a few of them in the picture; on the other hand, the old Jack, our faithful workhorse, and a few other horses did get in the picture. We have now altered and enlarged the store and post office; everything is not yet ready, for example, racks, windows, porch, etc. Dear Otto had to be away so much, yesterday and day before yesterday in Cajucos and tomorrow back again to San Luis to discuss land affairs.

School photo 1887 of Adelaida, not yet named Klau.

That same photographer also took a picture of Mimi's class at the school a few weeks ago; we knew nothing about it, otherwise dear father or I would have gone over to watch, so it happened that dear Mimi has such an awful hairdo in the picture, because one of the school children wanted to fix her hair prettier than it normally is. The teacher is a very decent, educated woman, it's such a shame that she looks so bad in this picture, probably because she is standing right in front of the open school house door.

I now want to add a few more lines and, to start, request that you distribute the 4 photos of our home, one each to brother Oscar, Sister Emma, Aunt Ryffel and Heinrich Kofel.—Tomorrow I must go to San Luis, but upon my return I shall write to all, so that you will definitely hear from me at New Year.

The cattle give me more work than earlier, there is more sickness, and I lost 9 calves out of 30, and now there is an eye disease going around, and our good old cow is almost blind.—It's getting late, so please write us soon, and when you celebrate a merry Christmas in the intimate family circle, then think

about us in this distant country, who send you all our best wishes, also for the coming new year, with kisses and love your brother
Otto

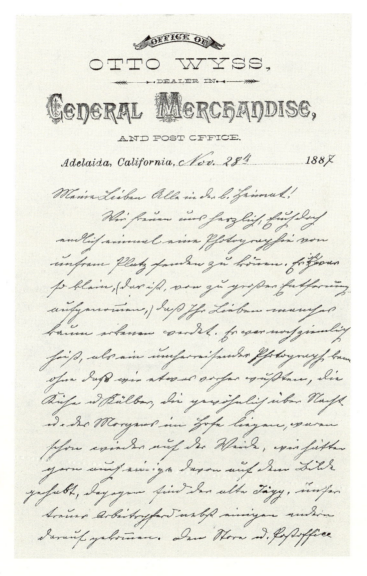

One of the letterheads that Otto had printed.

Concerning Mimi, who is not at all Obedient, and the Negative Influence of Schoolmates.

Adelaida, December 10th, 1887

My dear Sister-in-law!

Dear Mimi was not quite well last week, she had a headache and no appetite. I am really very worried when something goes wrong with one of our dear little ones, especially since the frightful loss of our beloved little boys; Mimi had a head cold and then caught a cold, while she was running around for several hours on the damp hill. The two-month-long school vacation has begun again, and the children of the Ticinese neighbor come over all the time to get dear Mimi. If you get these letters, have you seen the photograph of the school? We recently sent it to dear father. Thus you will be able to get some idea of our school children here and our dear Mimi's schoolmates, who partly consist of half-breed Indians, who certainly do not exercise the best influence on our dear children, because they use rough and shameless expressions and do not obey and know very little; but dear Mimi is beginning to realize this herself, and if she herself also sometimes is not inclined to obey, she usually soon realizes that we only have her best interest at heart. [...]

Our big good cow, who already allowed herself to be milked a little by dear blessed Heireli, went completely blind a few weeks ago, and it was sad to see the good faithful animal bumping into things and groping its way to the barnyard and the stable, where her beautiful little calf is, but now she can see again, we had to throw salt in her eyes every day, she gives very good milk, and dear Alice likes her milk. The picture of our little farm is on the whole well done, but it was taken from too great a distance; the house looks so black, because the roof of the porch (platform in front of the house) threw shadows on the doors and windows. Everything looks so small in it, we hope later perhaps to receive a better picture of the farm. The fruit trees, especially the apple and pear trees in our garden, were this year so full of fruit that several big branches broke, although many supports were constructed, we have put up 3 barrels of apples, if we could only send some of them to you, but it is just too far, oh 7000 English miles really is a long way. [...]

Ottilie's Loss of Strength.

Adelaida, California, June 4th, 1888

Dear Father!

It has already been a rather long time since I wrote, and unfortunately I could not say that we are all well, and therefore writing is hard for me. At Christmas I had an accident, two horses and a wagon went over me. But in a couple of days I was well again. Then my wife had rheumatism again, but this time it was quite different from last year, and she was sicker. At the beginning of February we had here Dr. Norton from San Luis, who diagnosed her illness as organic heart disease, which he had conjectured from my letters. He gave her several kinds of medicine, especially also tonic, to help her digestion and nourishment, and recommended a lot of fresh meat.

In the beginning my dear wife had attacks of brief and painful shortness of breath, a few times even causing her to lose consciousness, which worried me. By mid March however no more. Mid April was very warm, the rheumatism then left her almost completely, but there was still no return of her strength. Three weeks back she was in San Luis and seemed somewhat better, but the tonic she was drinking seemed and still seems not to agree with her stomach. Right now she is dragging herself around and tried to do and to cook what she can, but on her right side beneath the stomach her body is swollen, also her feet and legs are somewhat swollen, more so in the evening. Tomorrow I'm sending again to Dr. Norton for medicine. He is a short, cautious man, who has a good name as a doctor, and my dear wife has confidence in his prescriptions.

Both children are, praise God, healthy, as am I. Mimi helps already a lot, if she also does like to play and jump around, little Alice is developing in a lively, talkative and always active manner. She is good on her legs and always runs toward the water, where she gets wet and cold. –Cattle are doing pretty well, but no buyers and low prices, harvests are average, below average for California.

I just wanted to write something on your name day, dear father, and send our best greetings and kisses with our best wishes, your

Otto

On September 9th, 1888 Ottilie Wyss-Meyer dies. In memory of "our dear blessed Ottilie Wyss," Otto Wyss wrote the following poem:

Now at long last have been shed the last mournful tears,
Yet fidelity remains in the quiet night,
Now at long last is stilled the yearning for past years,
Extinguished by now is pain's hotly glowing light.

Hard was her dear life, full of cares without number,
Life's hard battle is over, all has now been said,
So peaceful, like the tired old man's gentle slumber,
In the so cool dark room is the sleep of the dead.

In the cool damp dark earth lie her fragile still bones,
Safe from life's many worries and pain's piercing dart,   .
Under sweet fragrant flowers and not cold tombstones,
The blessed lady finds peace for her gentle heart.
Some day we too shall ascend to the heavenly light,
Like the budding seed in the earth which does not abate,
On the golden wings of the angels we shall take flight,
And with the blessed departed share their sublime fate.

VII

Seline

Contract between Miss Seline Streuli von Horgen and Dr. Oskar Wyss in Riesbach:

Miss Seline Sträuli hereby contractually promises to travel to Adelaida, San Luis Obispo, California, United States, in order to accept the position of housekeeper in the home of Mr. Otto Wyss. She hereby promises to keep this position for the period of three years at the salary upon which we have agreed today.

In return for the said services, Professor Oskar Wyss of Riesbach, as brother of the above mentioned Mr. Otto Wyss, promises and covenants to pay:
1. The costs of the trip to Adelaida.
2. He guarantees her from the day of her arrival in Adelaida a monthly salary of 75 francs and gives her the choice to be paid the said salary either in Adelaida by Mr. Otto Wyss or here in Zurich by himself in quarterly installments. Upon payment in Zurich proof must be given that the salary has not already been paid in America.

Sig. Prof. Oskar Wyss   sig. Seline Streuli
Riesbach, November 29th, 1888

After the death of the three boys and his deeply loved wife Ottilie, Otto was left alone, completely alone with the remaining two girls to take care of by himself. American neighborhood wives tried to help out some in his house, but without any real success.

At this time of depression, Otto began to take to the bottle. He probably described his problems to his brother in unpreserved letters and expressed the wish to have a Swiss woman to help him in his California home.

Oskar found such a woman who was willing to take upon herself this trip into the unknown. He signed a contract with her. After an exhausting trip half way around the world, Seline Streuli found in the isolation of Adelaida difficult circumstances. Her courage is all the more to be admired in that she scarcely understood a word of English.

171

She was accustomed to bad roads and to the simplest lodgings, but the disorder, the loving, but loosely educated girls, and a broken man who sometimes drank and then became aggressive and unpredictable, disillusioned the woman soon after her arrival. Seline, obviously an energetic person, tried to bring order into the situation, with the household, the operation of the farm, post office, store and the local tavern. That did not occur without friction between the two. The puritanical attitude of the neighbors demanded a marriage. Single people were not supposed to live together under the same roof. More children were born, and the couple, Seline and Otto, was often overwhelmed with the demands of family life.

Yet after a quarrel the two did not split up; the family, the children and of course the lack of money held both together. Where would they have gone? A return to Europe would have been a hard trip into the unknown. So slowly they created for themselves a new homeland in California, where children and grandchildren grew up and prospered.

Staying together, building a common family despite frustrations, disappointments and divergent points of view, all that was not easy. The two were hard on one another, just as the circumstances were not prim and proper; but they both stayed together until their deaths.

Is it any wonder then that both sought a vent for their frustrations, and that was the purpose of the letters to the old homeland, to relatives whom they sought to win as allies in their conjugal disputes. From this point in time information begins to gush in increasing amounts back to Europe. One letter follows another, and many domestic quarrels are shared with the reader in detail.

From this wealth of observations only a small portion could be transcribed in the present work.

Another Type of Education.

Adelaida, Calilfornia, January 20th, 1889

Dear Aunt Ryffel!

Seline Streuli has arrived and said that you, dear Aunt, had especially urged her to always be good with the dear little ones.

She is good to them, but she said repeatedly, "well, they better not spoil it." How could it have been otherwise than that I had spoiled a lot the dear little ones, but Miss Streuli sees things as though she were back home in Europe and tells me and has told me from the beginning nothing except the truth.

Mimi, who has an open, merry and adaptable mind and personality, gets along with her quite well, but she certainly rightly scolds her. Whenever Mimi begins something, she should also finish it and not run off, as she often unfortunately does, so she also forgets the small chickens and lost 3 in one day this week.

Seline Streuli of Horgen, Canton of Zürich

The dear little one has a hard and stubborn little head. She acts right, gives Seline her hand and also a kiss, then she cleans off her mouth—like an adult. She is good with Seline, but she also knows that she has more freedom with daddy, and today she came up behind me with the umbrella (Mama's), wanted to ride "Billy" the horse, between whose legs she often runs. Little Alice fears nothing at all, goes in the water like the geese (of which the foxes have caught six) but does not come out of it so clean.

Earlier she came to see me every night, but since Seline Streuli has arrived, she sleeps better and only crawls over to Mimi when she can wake her up.—Which is not easy to do.

The old chessboard and figures which Seline brought from Switzerland looked to me like old friends, dear Aunt, and please me a great deal. Right now I have no fellow chess players, however, I have already played many games around here and have also won a set of chess pieces, which is perhaps now no longer complete, because the dear children also play with it.

Enough for tonight, accept, dear Aunt, my warm thanks and my sincere wish to see you again someday with the dear children back home on the dear Steinhof, your nephew

Otto

"How on earth can a person adapt himself to such a gypsy life!"

Adelaida, January 20th, 1889

Very honorable Dr. Wyss and Daughters!

Finally, after a three week stay here, I take the time to share with you some things about my state of health. I beg you to excuse my long silence, because I have, as you can well imagine, found so much work here that I even must use Sundays to do it. I have found your son and brother as well as the dear children in the best of health, and they feel quite comfy and happy to hear once again the true Züridütsch. Especially Mimi awaited with yearning the announced presents, which I unfortunately could not yet unpack for them, because my trunk had stayed behind on the route from New York to San Francisco, and I had to travel on without it.

On this past Saturday, the 12th, Mr. Wyss picked it up in Paso Robles, the next train station from here, about 12 miles away. The trunk had more bad luck on the trip than I, because it was broken and had to be mended. This opportunity was moreover used to steal my silk things and my travel umbrella and to ransack everything else. I myself traveled rather well across America on the trip here from Europe; each time I thought I was about to get into an embarrassing situation, I found another German speaking person, to whom I could inquire about the most urgent necessities. These people were angels of mercy for me, because I was constantly worried.

From Paso Robles an old man (Appenzeller) droved me here, and about 3 minutes from the house our vehicle got stuck in the mud, because as a result of the rainy weather roads here are very bad, so far I have seen no good roads in all of America, and then Mr. Wyss got stuck in the same spot with the trunk. On the same evening of my arrival we decorated the Christmas tree. The children were delighted with all the beautiful things I had brought from Switzerland, the Dirggeli [Zurich honey pastry] were something new for them, one cannot get them here, Mimi especially liked the big doll from Madame Professor, also little Alice, the often wild little pig- head, was pleased. Their father was no less delighted by all this, and I believe that he felt a little homesickness for all his anxious loved ones, especially when he examined the photo of his nephew, then he wanted to see his old homeland once again.

I have kept for the children a couple of pieces of the dried fruit which you gave me on the trip. This really helped me out, especially during my 4 day seasickness. I still have the nest egg which you, honorable doctor, gave me for the journey. I think that it can be put to the best use here, even if not exactly for myself. Mr. Wyss has planted the little shoots of red-currant in the garden. I do hope that they will grow well, so that we shall have evergreen plants on the graves. I have often said to Mr. Wyss since I have been here, that it would be wonderful if we had only half the house of your father, because we just have a cabin with four walls and a roof. At first I could just not get used to it, but now that I have finally cleared out the mountains of boxes, paper and dirt in the store (which is also our living room), it is easier for me to live with, but I shall never really like it, and on the very first day I had to tell your son and brother: "How can a person, who has grown up and been raised in such circumstances as yourself, adapt himself to such a gypsy life, I just wish that your family could see this mess." You perhaps find this phrase too strong, however, if you could see how this household has been run, you would certainly agree with me. To enumerate everything here and now would take up far too much space, for which you will excuse me, because I plan to write more extensively tomorrow to the professors about the situation here, as I promised them upon my departure, and you will then learn about everything from them (the letter to them is going out with this one). You will find out about a lot of things you are not going to like, and briefly note that I pity your son and brother.

You should not be surprised to learn that in the beginning I suffered from strong homesickness, and as you can well imagine, it will last for a long time yet, although it now is getting somewhat better. When, in the evening, I often tell many beautiful stories about Zurich, father and Mimi always listen to me with great interest and pleasure. Mimi is pretty intelligent for a child of her age, still she does need in every respect good education and guidance, she is, especially, not accustomed to the rules of an orderly household, which you will certainly perceive from my descriptions to the professors. The little baby is very gifted, but spoiled, her father is too good to her. He cannot punish her, and several times I have had to fight a little with him.

Yet I cannot complain about his treatment of me. He is friendly, good to me, and very concerned to make my new homeland pleasant for me, which makes all the work easier for me.

Well I shall close for now. It will soon be 10 o'clock. I am sitting by the fire with my writing table and I'm still freezing, because we don't have any oven. Throughout the day we always have splendid sunshine, but at night it is cold.

Mr. Wyss is still reading the Bürkli newspaper. It pleases me a great deal that you send it to us. To you honorable Dr. Wyss and to your worthy daughters warm greetings from your son and his children and from your grateful

Seline Streuli

The Old Yearning to Go Home.

Adelaida, California, January 22nd, 1889

Dear Sister Hanneli!

I have been meaning to write for so long, and if this letter is not long, that is probably better. Seline Streuli has been here now for three weeks, and she is a housekeeper in the fullest sense of the word, about whose acquisition I can only be pleased. At first I was afraid it would only be so-and-so, as it could have been, but I find myself pleasantly disappointed.

When the "selling" season begins in our store, the language barrier will of course present some difficulties, but then I am hoping for and also waiting for brother-in-law Karl Meier who has already lived in America for eight years. He has a second wife, also a woman from Zurich, and a 15-year-old boy—four children also already in the grave.

Thus this year I am looking forward to the future with fresher courage, but I must say one thing: all the dear letters, everything from the dear homeland which came here to us at Christmas, then Seline Streuli (either Miss or Fräulein does sound quite right), and finally the dear beautiful presents, pictures and everything from dear home, they all stirred up again in my soul the old yearning, the old homesickness, and although the graves of several loved ones bind me to this place, I wish and shall think about coming back home, coming home with the dear children, whom you will teach to play; dear Mimi always likes to talk about the piano, and dear Alice has a good clear voice and sings together with Mimi, which is often a true joy,.

To be sure, it will take a couple of more years of good, hard work, wise expenditure of funds and wise savings, in order to make a beginning again, to pay off the old debts and to create a good new credit record. Then hopefully will again come the time when land can be sold advantageously. […]

Your Otto

Adelaida, January 30th, 1889

Dear Sister Emilie!

It has already been a week since my last lines were mailed, and I want first of all to thank you for the dear lines which found us all on the day after Christmas in the best of moods, because at Christmas we had received brother Oskar's and Caroline's letters. Seline Sreuli has now been here for almost four weeks, and even if everything is not yet clean and in order, the store and the living areas already do have a completely different appearance, and everyone congratulates me.

I myself am outside every day, plowing and sowing, because I have little in the store and the roads are still bad, and they have been worse this winter than ever. I myself am sleeping and eating again, the children are well cared for and by and by things will be put in order; yet at the beginning Miss Streuli had shaken her head in disbelief and said: "With so much stuff one cannot manage and keep things clean, it's all mixed-up, and if the women already took away what they liked, they were right."

You see, I had had two neighborhood women helping out and cleaning up before Miss Sträuli arrived, but in reality they just turned the whole house upside down and took back home whatever they liked.

And earlier, a Swiss woman, Mrs. Graves, previously Mrs. Hössli, was here twice for four to five days in July and August, but despite all her overestimation of the worth of her own work, it looked to me almost comic how she wanted to organize everything. There were also two neighbors' wives who wanted to help and had earlier brought us a pound of tea or coffee and some sugar and were even ready to do night watch duty, but unfortunately I would not let them clean up, which ticked them off and caused them to leave.

I had over a dozen offers to make clothes for the children, to wash and otherwise to help out—but Seline says there is more than enough help here already, and she herself is making a couple of dress patterns herself.

Mimi must learn to finish what she starts, while little Alice has already learned that "Sine" does not want to see her always covered with dirt. [...]
Otto

The Financial Situation—Not Rosy.

Adelaida, February 18th, 1889

Dear Father!

Several times I have planned to give you some explanation of my financial situation, but, on the one hand, my books were not yet in order, on the other hand, I could not mix such details with a letter with regular news, and so now I come with my figures and numbers, and in order to make my adjacent land here clearer to you, I have made a special sketch [lost] of it. There are also the 80 acres [32 ha] which as government land I acquired under the Purchase Rights Act of 1883. Also the 160 acres [64 ha] of homestead land, where I usually live and for which I shall receive the complete paperwork for a resale, etc., only in 1¼ to 1½ years.

I bought last summer the 89 acres, around the old quicksilver mine, in which I worked from 1876 to 79, and the main reason for this was that there is a big spring there—30 to 40 liters of water per minute in the driest season of the year, which I have brought in pipes to a trough in front of my house. To be sure, that cost money and came at a bad time. Besides this I also have 160 acres, about a one hour's ride away, good pastureland and water, for which $1000 are offered me, but I'm asking for $2000.– , shall probably sell it this summer.[66]—Thus I shall now put together for you below the present market value and mortgages and liabilities:

North Property (N) ½ and Northwest (NW) ¼ sec. 34
    80 acres, mortgage value $300—and 15% interest = $45.–
    per year. Present market value $15. –per acre   = $1200.–

---

[66] Wyss owned therefore altogether 195.6 hectar of which he wants to sell 64 hectar because they are located an hour away.

- lots 1, 2 and 4 Southeast (SE) ¼ sec. 33
  89 acres, mortgage value $600—and 9% interest = $54.– per year
  Present market value with house and cellar   = $1100.–
- Northeast (NE) ¼ of sec. 33—Homestead free—
  Was already offered: = $3000.–
- Northeast (NE) ¼ of sec. 17
  160 acres, mortgage value $500.– and 10% interest = $50.—per year
  For this land $100.– offered; ask: = $1200.–

Value of my land without Homestead   = $3500.–
Borrowed on mortgage $1400.—with a yearly interest of $149.–
Liabilities in San Luis, San Francisco, etc.
Add up to over $800   = $850.–
Interest   = $150.–
    = $1000

The $500.– for the last mortgage should resolve in May the
$300.– mortgage on the 80 acres. With interest etc. $375.–
there remains   = $125.–
Credit $250.—in notes, worth $150.–
Credit $800.—is scarcely worth $400.–
Rent on House on Lot 1 $60.–   = $735.–

So I am over $300.– in debt for this year, because the expected income from the store is now equal to zero and last year I had to sell more cattle than I would have liked, and since the previous winter was cold, it brought some snow and only late fodder, so that ⅓ of the young cattle were lost. So now I don't have enough cattle and must see if I can sell weaned calves in May or June for $6-8 a head.

The worth of the land is evaluated according to how similar land around here was sold, while it is expected that, if the railroad is once built, the worth will double, of course that will only happen after the land is more used and built up. Interest is too high, and just keeping cattle, as I do now, unfortunately does not make any money, if one must still pay for all the work. […]

                             Otto

Marriage Plans.

                        Adelaida, California, February 20th, 1889

Dear Father!

I would like to enclose a few lines on special paper.—I had spoken with Ottilie in case of her death, and as I also supported her hope for recovery, she advised me herself that it would be best for me and the children to remarry, in that case.

Ottilie had some savings and a small inheritance of $300-400, and I promised her to save that for the dear children. As you can see, I still have some property, but it does not make much profit, especially under the present circumstances. I plan to manage the land, cattle, etc. separately—but to hire Karl Meier to be my associate in the store and wherever possible also in the post office. I especially don't like to do all the writing, and when I'm doing so much of it, an important matter is often neglected.

Concerning marriage I see in Miss Streuli a good, honest, hardworking woman. She is neat, accustomed to keeping the house in order and is high spirited.

She likes the children, and even if she does see their faults, I see that she enjoys their company. She still is somewhat homesick and will not so easily become accustomed to life here, but rather she wishes to return in a couple of years to beautiful Zurich or the Zurich region.

Were she not here and I were to marry an American (!), my homecoming would certainly be postponed for a very long time.

She has no external obligations in Europe, and as far as her inclination for marriage is concerned, I fear neither, to acquire it or to reciprocate it. Mutual creative work, order and cleanliness are the foundations of respect and also of the family and love.—Thus is it ordained by God.

Dear father, I await an answer, before I do anything decisive, and also hope for better days, because I need them. Warm greetings and kisses, your thankful son,

Otto

February 22nd, 1889

There has been a long period of inactivity; yet the letters must be posted. Miss Seline's trunk had been broken on the trip from New York to San Francisco, umbrellas and a few small valuables had been removed from it, but otherwise it got through safely.—From the beginning our house seemed chilly to her, and she was freezing, whereas the rest of us felt quite comfortable. I immediately relinquished to her my job caring for the dear children and directed my attention to the earlier post office. She thought that meat three times a day was unnecessary for meals and reduced it to two. There was and still is a lot of washing to do, but she is enterprising, and she does everything to perfection

In the store I still have many things, but the most-wanted articles as well as groceries are lacking, and with the bad roads profitable transportation is unthinkable; another problem is that Seline has still learned little English, because the children speak with pleasure "Zuridütsch."

I am now expecting here in a week Karl Meier—a death announcement addressed to Karl Meier, opened by Rudolf Frei im Hard as guardian of Karl's 15 year old son Henry, brought me Karl Meier's address, and Karl was soon ready to come here, has already sold his 80 acre place in Missouri and will soon be on the way here. He has a second wife, also a woman from Zurich, the 15-year-old boy and a wife, and four children in the grave.—Unfortunately we have similar destinies.

Where he was before, the winters are cold. He was afflicted by rheumatism and therefore is seeking a warmer climate. We were together in the secondary school for two years, lived in 1870 and '71 on the Schipfe in the same roon, and I don't doubt that he will make the best associate in the store whom I could have found. Then I hope to get the store going, like it was earlier—because, just as at times here you can move forward faster, you can move backwards even faster—downhill.

To be sure, I must be more careful about giving credit, but I have now the advantage of knowing the customers here; I just have to see how I shall deal with this and that. When Karl Meier comes, he will not bring much capital with him, but he will bring enough to buy his own place. Rudolf Frei manages 9000 francs for his son Henry; which Karl of course should be able to obtain, and which he will be able to do after the recent decision of the Swiss Supreme Court, despite the resistance of the local authorities. […]

                                                                Otto

"I have truly seen no city and no town which equals Zurich."

                                    Adelaida, California, February 24th, 1889

My Dear Nephew Hans!

Your many beautiful and dear photos have really pleased me, and while I greeted the cathedral, city hall, the Schipfe and Lindenhof as old acquaintances, both lions and their surroundings were partly strange to me, until Miss Streuli explained to me the renowned beautifications of Zurich as well as their location at the end of the Bahnhofstrasse.

17 years ago the Bahnhofstrasse did not go all the way to the lake. - Papa's and all your little houses are quite first rate, well photographed, with your explanation I can almost always imagine the interior furnishings.

The picture which shows you with sister and brother, Pascha, and Meersäuli is likewise good. You yourself look tall and strong, likewise in the bicycle clothes, Oscar also looks muscular, and Alma makes a friendly face.—The picture of Pascha is similar to our watch dog, ours is somewhat shorter and not so fat (says Seline), he is a Newfoundlander, and Alice often rides him. In addition, we have a small black sheep-dog who is good for cattle herding.

All these photos excite my desire to come home again and to see the beautifications of Zurich, because the region lacks nothing in natural beauty, and I have not yet seen any city or town on earth which can equal it, on my long trip around the world.

Write to me again, dear nephew, greet your sister Alma and brother Oscar for me—for whom I shall enclose a couple of lines if there is still time—and you yourself be greeted by your uncle in the far, far West.

Otto Wyss

"I have already stopped him from drinking liquor"—but the Debts!

Adelaida, March 22nd, 1889

Very Honorable Dr. Wyss!

Out of concern and embarrassment I must take pen in hand, in order unfortunately to trouble you with a request, because your son is not willing to do it, so I must do it, because otherwise I don't know what to do. Mr. Wyss, you see, is presently in great financial trouble. The day before yesterday he received two summons in the amount of 90 dollars, with the notation that it must be paid by next Wednesday, otherwise his property will be seized. 500 dollars were already promised him at the beginning of February on a mortgage, but payment was always postponed, finally yesterday came the report that the debtor could not get the money, and he doesn't know what to do. There are actually several hundred dollars of other debts which must be paid at the latest by May, but for a couple of weeks his brother-in-law, Mr. Meier, who arrived on the 5th of this month, would lend him about a hundred dollars. He doesn't have much right now either. Debt prosecution is something really to be feared here, because it is the law and the custom that the creditor simply sends the constable, or turns the matter over to an attorney, so for example last fall he was supposed to have paid six dollars for a newspaper, because he cancelled it, so three weeks ago they sent the constable from San Luis Obispo, the latter demanded 14 dollars for his trip, and now that makes altogether 20 dollars.

Since I can find no way out of this distressful situation, I turn to you, honorable doctor, to see whether you could not send us 2 to 3000 francs, so that we could pay the most urgent bills. I shall take care of the interest in the best way possible, and I also think we can give back the capital in not too long a time. With good will, hard work and by saving money, we shall not fail to repay you.

A lot of money has been earned quickly here, but when things get difficult and money is short, things go downhill all the faster. Mr. Wyss has given you approximate information about his economic circumstances, as well as his intentions regarding me, because I told him that I would do nothing without the knowledge of his honored family. His filial and brotherly duty require that, and he also agreed with that. This letter will by now be in your hands. My trip from New York here cost 270 francs. When I arrived here, I still had 50 dollars. I have of course already given them to Mr. Wyss.

I have already stopped him from drinking liquor, that is going pretty well right now. He works hard, and I hope that with seriousness and goodness I can put him back on his feet as a man. Of course, that requires a little effort and patience, but I shall stick to my resolution.

On September 15th the lease with the tavern expires, and I shall not rest until it is closed. Nor can I omit the observation that the blame for this awkward situation lies not only with Mr. Wyss but mainly with the irresponsible and dissolute house of his dead wife.

If you could see and hear everything as I do, then you would not be surprised by the present circumstances. As I already mentioned, Mr. Meier is here with his family. He has bought 120 acres of land a mile from us and must now still build a cabin. Until the latter is built, the Meiers eat with us and sleep in the old house up on the hill. He is a very active and thrifty man; his wife, who is from Schwamendingen, is likewise very active and decent. She was horrified by the previous manner of keeping house here, because although I had put so much in order, they still saw enough traces of the past to be convinced of the negligence of their dead sister-in-law. We already planted the garden at the beginning of February, the onions which I set out are already big, the snow peas which you gave me are also beautiful, only the chickens have scratched up a lot of them.

I must stop writing. It is already 10 o'clock. Yesterday and today I have done the wash with a cold and a toothache. The mail leaves tomorrow.

The children are healthy and happy. Mimi now goes to school again; however, I must always send her off, so that she does not arrive too late. I must still note that your letters have arrived today and the day before yesterday those of the professor, also the Bürkli newspaper.

Now, doctor, please excuse my shamelessness. I didn't know what else to do, because I shall have no rest day and night until everything is settled. Warm greetings to you and to your worthy family from your grateful
                                  Seline Streuli
The school house is only 3 minutes away from us.

"I ask you to acknowledge me as your daughter-in-law."

                                                   Adelaida, April 23rd, 1889
Honorable Dr.

Several weeks have already past since my last, unfortunately unpleasant, letter to you, and I planned to send another letter to you, yet a lot of constant work and recently much poor health and also mainly an overly occupied mind have prevented me from telling you what I now must say.

Of course I now come unexpectedly and too late with my request, and I can unfortunately no longer await your reply, for which you will kindly excuse me. Tomorrow Otto must go to San Luis Obispo on business, and I am supposed by all means to go along, in order to get married there, because we do not want to do it here with the justice of the peace. You may well find that the decision is hasty and rash, and that would be my opinion as well, if I were still in Zurich.

Now I must adapt myself to the American customs, which are completely different. Specifically, it is not acceptable here for women to serve in the household of a man, where there is no wife. Here in such cases people have male, and usually Chinese, help, or the man remarries, and even as soon as only one month after the wife's death. Already in the first four weeks of my stay here, one neighbor dared to tell Otto that he should marry me, that it did not look decent for me to be living in his home in this way, which made me quite angry when he told me that. Mrs. Meier also told me that she had been at Mr. Meier's for scarcely a week when someone had told him the same thing, and her husband had been a widower for only four months, she is 48 years old.

So in order to preserve my good name, I don't know what else to do except either to marry or to leave, and the latter option would not be pleasant, forcing me to travel around, and I don't want to look for another job. Were I to do the latter, the family would be soon ruined, and so I hope that I shall set everything right again. As a full-fledged wife I naturally have more power than as a housekeeper, and as such, according to the customs of this country, I am also permitted to energetically confront and make demands upon others, which is very often necessary here in the midst of this mostly common race. The disorder and negligence here have been exploited enough, and I have already often told him that that must stop and we must take better care of ourselves. Naturally I would have a more carefree and freer life if I only concentrated on my own interests, and I could plan for my old age, but Otto already said in the very first month I was here: he can give me no salary, and he will not let me leave. Of course, he could not have legally forced me to stay, and he had already promised me hundreds of times to give up drinking, but naturally a bad habit can not be discarded overnight, but, thank God, it is now already going much better, and he works pretty hard. Last week he had to promise me to close the tavern in the fall, also because of the children. Mimi likes to go there so much, when a couple of urchins incite her mischievousness. I have often fetched her from there, because naturally she learns nothing good. I am going tomorrow with a heavy heart, because I do see for a long time more trouble and careworn days before me, yet if God allows us to stay healthy, hopefully nicer times will come our way, and I ask you, honorable Dr., to acknowledge me as your daughter-in-law, and I shall do my best to make sure that your old age will no longer be difficult. Otto has already been waiting for two weeks for an answer from you and is becoming very impatient. Two weeks ago he borrowed 500 dollars from a Jew in San Luis Obispo, with which he can pay the most urgent bills, but 15% interest is really too high.

The day before yesterday he leased to an American 160 acres, which lie six miles away up on the mountain. He will sell it at the next opportunity, I am very glad, because we certainly have no use for it. Other people's cattle eat our fodder. Here in this neighborhood there are 160 acres for sale. He wants to buy them, which I shall not permit. We already have more than enough with our old land. There is still a lot of land to improve, and just yesterday I told him, you mustn't buy any more land here, I would rather sell it, because in these hills and mountains, one can only get by with difficulty if one does not have other sources of income. He must have another couple of hundred dollars by the end of May. I don't know yet how we shall pull that off.

Mr. Meier will move into his new house next week. Up until now they were still living with us. He is very strong and active and regrets having come here. Otto is now trying to get the post office for him again. We only own the store. We should really purchase again the most sellable items, in order to get rid of the old merchandise. We already have rather hot weather, the nights cool and from time to time there is still frost. People are hoping for a good year, because it has rained a lot this spring. There is a lot of fodder, if we only had more cattle. The garden vegetables are beautiful, although we do need some more rain. I can't plant beans well because it is too dry, and you cannot plant them earlier because of the frost.

The children are healthy and happy. Dear little Alice has really developed since I have been here, she chatters on and on and sings like a school girl. I have a lot to do with Mimi because of her disobedience and flighty nature. She doesn't want to do housework. If we only could send her to a better school, also to church, here they just don't have religious instruction.

It is my determination to return again to the dear old homeland, if we remain healthy, hoping that we shall find all, and especially you, honorable doctor, still healthy; I am always, especially in gloomy hours, homesick. That is ordained by God. Warm greetings to you and to your honorable family from your devoted

Seline Streuli

"I have the money bag in my hands."

Adelaida, May 9th, 1889

Dear Father!

I picked up yesterday at the post office your letter of April 16th containing 175 dollars, and it appeared to me to be an angel of good fortune, because in the next days we shall have the opportunity to put it to good use. Warm thanks many times over for your goodness, and I hope, if we get 400 more dollars, that we shall not have to plague you any more.

Although we certainly do still have enough debts, we can now defray the most necessary expenses; a few calculations and worries don't do any harm, because you cannot feel too comfortable, financially.

Do not yet send me my 270 francs, which I needed to come here from New York as well as the other 50 dollars. We shall now try to do it otherwise; I can always withdraw that from the bank, if I later find it necessary. I shall invest no more money in these hills and mountains. I am constantly determined to leave here at the first favorable opportunity, we must stay here in this place for only another year, and afterwards we can look around, but selling does not go so quickly, although we still have one of the most advantageous pieces of property in this region.

Concerning my relationship to Otto, I am sorry to have entered into matrimony without your kind permission, as I explained to you in my letter of April 23rd (which by now is already in your hands), and for all these enumerated reasons on the one hand and Otto's stubborn mind (to which one must yield) on the other, I ask you, good father, to excuse my conduct, because I made this decision neither out of thoughtlessness nor out of indifference.

I do understand your reasons for the temporary refusal of our project, but as far as his economic circumstances are concerned, it is really good if I help you to regulate him. I have the money bag in my hands and shall use it in the best way possible for our economic benefit and improvement. [...]
Otto and Seline

"A civil register does not exist here."

Adelaida, California, May 13th, 1889
Dear Father!

Seline received last week a registered letter with $425.—makes altogether $600--. I must confess that the way it reached me and the way I read your letters today pleased me little, but I would rather have nothing at all than to be blamed for all my debts and mistakes because of misunderstood or completely misconstrued circumstances.

I truly had little joy in life after I had put my three boys in the grave, but I have always cared for my family and worked for a living.—This now gives me the opportunity to get rid of the 15% debts, and then things will get better. [...]

As far as I myself am concerned, I believe that my name is still good and I have fulfilled my obligations the best I could. And the fact that the illness and death of four children, and finally of the mother, would set back any man can certainly not be questioned.

If I have retained anything however from my youth, it is the curse of a miserable apprenticeship!

A civil register does not exist here, and births and deaths are registered nowhere. There is also no German pastor living in San Luis right now, and after much running back and forth I have only the choice of making a certificate myself, having the local justice of the peace to certify it, and then having the county court and finally the consul to certify it.

The document is already prepared, but not yet properly certified, but it will follow as soon as possible.—So hoping not to be perceived by you as even worse, I remain your loving son
Otto

"Some obstinacy and stubbornness are still in his head."

In this letter of May 31st, 1859, which we reproduce in extracts, Seline describes the circumstances which she found in the household upon her arrival in California, and her corresponding measures of reorganization.

Adelaida, May 31ˢᵗ, 1889

Dear Father!

We have just received the registrations of the certificates of birth and death as well as our marriage certificate from the Swiss Consulate and I should like to enclose a few words along with them. You will have already gathered from my and Otto's letters that we did receive your postal transmissions of money, and once again I say to you a thousand sincere thanks for your kind help. I now once again can breathe somewhat easier and shall gladly give you the requested information about the uses to which the money has been put. As Otto already wrote you, we have paid off the 300-dollar interest-bearing (367½ dollars with interest) mortgage. I carried it myself on the 16ᵗʰ of this month to the post office in Paso Robles, whither I had ridden in our carriage with Mr. Meier, in order to buy various necessities, for which I also needed 14 dollars.

We sent 130 dollars yesterday to San Francisco, to buy only the most sellable groceries for our store. We had no more groceries at all, and in order to be able to sell them cheaply, we paid for them in cash. You see, we had to purchase something in order to restock our shelves and attract customers, in order to sell the still moderately stocked dry goods and drapery ware, and mainly because we plan to rent the store next spring (if the homestead is our own); so we do *not* want to stop right now. Something is always going on right now, and Otto says: in the hot summer months, when many business people and families are traveling by here on their way to the coast, we need lots of preserved fruits, fish and meat, also crackers, which are kept here in all stores and are much used; that then will produce cash.

As much as possible I shall deal with the problem of giving too much frivolous credit. Just yesterday evening I sent on his way a man who wanted to get tobacco without any money. He also still owes us 20 dollars. We still have about 40 dollars of the rest of the money. Of the 500 which Otto received in San Luis for the land which we have leased, and from this rent, we can cover the capital interest. Otto still wants to buy cattle for 50 to 150 dollars. Out of the last 500 dollars we have paid almost all one-, two- and three-year store debts with their 15 percent interest; we have also had to pay for taxes and newspapers, 35 more dollars for the doctor and one dollar for the County Clerk; and I must tell you that we are still over 200 dollars in debt. However, I am calculating that from still outstanding bills which we soon expect to collect, we will be able to pay. [...]

Otto was somewhat indignant about the fact that you addressed the money to me instead of to him, but I told him that for a long time it would have been more proper for him to give his father more information about his economic circumstances; in addition, I have already often discussed with him his duties as husband and father, as son and brother, and then he thinks about what I have said, he collects himself together, and things go back to normal; however, few days go by when I don't do this, and I must always do it with a good attitude. By getting angry I would accomplish nothing, because some obstinacy and stubbornness are still in his head, and you can't get rid of that so easily. He listens to me so much and doesn't do much without my consent, and so far he has not spent a cent without my knowledge.

I am still very eager to know what he has written you, whether he has offended you in any way in his writing, because you did not send the money to his address; should that be the case, I beg you not to blame him for it but rather to attribute it to his stubbornness. He had shown me every time the letters which he had written to you, but not the last one, probably out of fear that he would have to rewrite it. From your last letter to him I saw that you see pretty clearly into his business and his economic circumstances, and these admonitions have certainly done no harm, although he thought he was no longer a school boy and wanted to reproach me for having written too much to you. You write among other things that the post office was closed probably because of disorganization; that is true, and it is not a wonder, if you had seen the disorganization in it.

Most people now really want it back, since it closed down, because now the situation is for the most part inconvenient.

Otto had also told you that his deceased wife had a few hundred dollars of saved money, but as he himself told me, she did not have quite 300 dollars, and she had inherited the greatest part of that, specifically 1200 francs. After she lived here for a while, she had saved about 100 dollars in San Francisco, where she worked for another year before they married. When she was in Zurich, she worked with Leuthold in der Enge. Her brother, who is here, always supported her. When Otto had her come here to America, her brother gave her 600 francs for travel money and then deducted that sum from this 1200 franc inheritance.

Warm greetings from everyone, from your thankful
Seline

A Call for Help out of Deep Need.

The following letter is the document of a drama through which we can sense Otto's spiritual loneliness and injury after all the calamities of life.

Adelaida, August 9th, 1889

Dear Father!

Sorrow, anger and dismay drive me to write. For the past two months I have been so overwhelmed by these feelings that, full of desperation, I must finally ask, what should I do? This question has already preoccupied and tormented me many a day and night, so that I find it is high time to give vent to the emotions of my heart, because I am physically so drained that tears often come into my eyes when I look in the mirror.

From March to June things went rather well, so that I had hope of seeing our existence improved, especially when you, good father, so quickly came to our assistance when I requested it. On Whit-Monday Otto received the letter from his sister-in-law, the professor's wife, and that was a real curse for me. (I really ask you, dear father, not to take this expression wrong, and I ask you to keep this to yourself.) Immediately after receiving this letter, Otto went to the tavern and drank too much, and reproached me that I had been writing home too much. I then spent a night such as I have never spent in my entire life. (Since, however, many more.)

He is now so certain that I have no more support from your side and each time when he has drunk too much he holds up to me the fact that I am only a stepmother. In his drunkenness, he is very bad, even common, as I have never seen any other human being. It is now 2 o'clock in the afternoon; he is sitting in the tavern again, after he has already drunk too much this morning (and only schnaps). I fetched him home for lunch, tried to prevent him from going back to the tavern, but in vain, I suggested to him, like several times, he had to pay me my salary or I would leave, to which he each time gave me the answer: I must request this from the professor, always in the firm belief that I can no longer find a sympathetic ear with your family.

Further he tells me every time that he will not allow himself to be dominated by me. If it were not for the children, I (frankly) would not have stayed here two months. The fact that he did reimburse me for my travel expenses would have been no impediment to that decision, but because I felt sorry for the dear children and the crying Mimi often held me back when I threatened to leave, I decided to marry him in the hope that things would then perhaps go better and because I could not have and would not have wanted to stay as a mere housekeeper. My hope is always that I could speak to you about this orally, but often it seems to me that this is no longer permitted me and that a patch of earth has been prepared for me here to serve as my final resting place.

The day before yesterday we had finally put in order the sad, for years neglected, book keeping. Put all the credits in the journal and in the ledger; therefore I would no longer leave him in peace, I helped him with it and so we had 15 afternoons of work to do until it was all in order. I certainly did shudder at times going through these books, and a picture of the most frivolous and the saddest shopkeeping presented itself to my eyes.

Many calculations had no longer or not at all been verified since the beginning of the year 1885, which was obvious looking at the numbers; I often had to tell Otto, you were just anxious to move the merchandise, but not to get the money for it. I had written to you in the last letter that Otto would buy cattle for 50 dollars, but he failed to do that. I told him he should use these 50 dollars to pay off the 320 dollar interest bearing debt in Cambria, when two years ago he bought calves for 500 dollars, of which so many died last year. He had paid half at that time. Now he still owes 272 dollars. Recently in this reigion here and there cows have died but we, praise god, have so far been spared; this illness comes, it would appear, almost every year about this time, when everything is dry and withered and there is almost no more water.

Then you see the dead animals only after a couple of days, because they often run around over wide distances. They are eaten by the birds and dogs, and you get almost nothing of their hides. Furthermore, in San Luis we owe over 300 dollars in interest bearing debts, for over three years now, for groceries. Last week Otto paid off 15 dollars of it. There are also about 12 dollars of debts for seeds in San Francisco, 90 dollars in Cayucos for whisky, also for three years, because they had sold wine and liquor by the bottle here, before the tavern existed. This local tavern earns good money, but that was, as I said, the ruin of Otto.

The credits, which we have or had to add up, doubly exceed the debits (I have not yet exactly calculated everything together); however I think we'll hardly receive a third of them, and we shall have to spend that money mainly on products or cattle, but when?

So far no new debts have been incurred. We have paid beforehand for everything which we have ordered. Last week we sent 60 dollars to Cajuccos, and so we still have thirty left over. Not much is going on in the store. It is fine with me, if those who don't pay don't come, and there are many such. Whether I can manage to close down the tavern, I don't know. Otto had promised me in March to close it by September 15th, and now he comes and tells me that the contract had been written up for two years at the time of the land's purchase, but as far as he knows, the contract has not been attested by the County Clerk, and then it will be valid for a year; in the other case the bartender would naturally demand a shameless amount of compensation if we tried to make him leave early. In the next few days I shall get information about this from the justice of the peace, who has now rented the old house by the quicksilver mine for 2½ dollars per month. His wife is a teacher here.

I must say, I could not stand it any more for a whole year. If this tavern were not here, then things would be fine, and the tavern is also a very bad influence on the children. Dear little Alic has been able to drink wine, liquor and beer for a long time. When an unreasonable drunk gives her something to drink, when she runs over to the tavern or when her father himself has had too much to drink, I of course always pay attention, but I don't always see it.

Sunday, August 11th

In order to close my writing, I must say, to my anger, that Otto today has been sitting in the tavern since 11 o'clock and already has had too much. He had just sent Mimi after the new horse (they sometimes go a long way in the wild), there is a man here with a wagon and two horses, here in the tavern, and Otto wants to swap with him. Mimi had to go, but I told her she should not bring the horse home. It is now half past five in the evening; he is still there, if it were only already tomorrow.

On Friday evening he told the children (as he always does when he has too much) that I am only their stepmother, that is painful. Especially since I can say in good conscience that I have more than fulfilled my duties as such, that however in such circumstances a good education is doubly difficult, is certainly understandable, especially since one has no help at all from the schools. Mimi is now in her 5th year at school, and she has still not learned to add two and two. I go over it with her every day and have already drilled it into her; there is no religious instruction whatsoever. Mimi needs so very, very much a good education, but I have already had many concerns and worries about it, because any reasonable person must admit that any ordinary stepmother can not be unconcerned about a spoiled child, and if I had more help from the father in this respect, things would probably work out fine. He is however not too good with things like that, but rather too indifferent. He just lets things pass. I beg you, dear father, not to hold against me the fact that I am a stepmother, because I constantly strive to present the situation as I see it and as it is, and I can only say that I have to bear on my two shoulders more than seems possible to me.

How light is even the hardest work, when you do it with happiness and contentment, how much have I already wished to be able to live without worries and discontent, whether or not I am allotted that?

I finally once again close with the request to express to me frankly and impartially your opinion about this, because I do think that I can receive most easily good advice from you as an experienced doctor and father. My warmest greetings from your devoted

Seline

Adelaida, August 22nd, 1889

Dear Father!

Here I am again, but this time, to your relief, thank God, with a somewhat better report than the last one was. I am very sorry to have to trouble you with such unpleasant news, but I don't know what else to do except to turn to you, because I do know from experience that one finds the best advice and help only from one's parents.

Otto had spent two more days frivolously, and so as a result of that I became sick with annoyance and vexation and had to stay in bed for three days, and I am still now not completely in order but, thank God, am feeling better. Otto is now again in good shape and sober, may it be God's will that it will last a long time. I have now with great difficulty persuaded the authorities to close the local tavern, after I spoke with Mr. Gibons, the justice of the peace, who told me that according to the contract we could not make the man from Ticino leave, there was however another way to force him to leave, if Otto was in agreement, he would prove through a petition with a couple of signatures that this tavern was an annoyance to the neighborhood, and then he would have to go.

Last month Otto settled things amicably with the man from Ticino, only he had to give him another month so that he could use up his supplies. I had told Otto decisively that that must stop or I would leave, which I would have done, and Mr. Gibons had also told him that.

The Meiers also strongly support me, and I can only say about Mr. Meier that he is always strong and active. Otto is away today collecting credits for our store; yesterday I added everything up, and thus I received the sum of $1305; if we received only $500 of it, then I am pleased. We now have terrible heat, and I'll be glad when the month is over.

Hoping that my last letter has not disturbed you too much and that these lines will find you in the best of health, greets you quite warmly your grateful
Seline

Things Are Looking Up.

Adelaida, September 30th, 1889

Dear Father!

I finally get around to acknowledging the receipt of your letters, which arrived here on the 19th of this month. Above all my sincerest thanks for your friendly and kind acceptance of myself as a member of your family, for whose honor and well-being I shall strive to live and to work.

It is very comforting to know, when you are far from all your loved ones, that on worrisome and gloomy days you can still count on their help and support, especially when you still have the good fortune to have a truly concerned parent's heart, which, although elderly, still beats warmly for its children. Of course, you learn to really appreciate that only when you are dependent upon yourself, when you have lost good parents at an early age.

Thirteen years have past since I lost a good father, and although at the time I was no longer a child, I have already missed him so much and so painfully, and feel all the happier to call again a dear and good father my own. May God preserve him for a long time yet.

Further, I have to sincerely thank you for paying the rest of my traveling expenses. I neither expected nor requested that. Of course, we can certainly use the money, but, notwithstanding that, I shall request no more money from outside, because (although we do still have enough to worry about) if Otto will help me to earn and to save money, as I have always been used to doing, we can already work our way out of this, so that we'll have things easier in a few years; if that were not possible, then that would be a detriment and a waste of what you spent. I likewise thank you for your good admonitions concerning the children. In this regard I shall also do my best to raise them to the well being and honor of your and the entire family. They are, thank God, always rather healthy and happy, and especially the dear little one has already sometimes brought me with her naïve chatter distraction and comfort in gloomy hours.

October 3rd, finally finishing my letter.

From your letter to Otto I unfortunately had to infer that he had treated you with ungratefulness, which I had indeed suspected. I ask that you might forgive his ingratitude and stubbornness, while I hope that he himself might still come to the true realization of his mistakes, in order to ask for forgiveness from his dear father, who just means to do well by his children. To be sure, he has not shown me your letter to him, but I did read it anyway, which he does not yet know. I thank you again for the good advice that you gave him in it, as well as for your blessing.

May it be God's will that he will not remain without blessings. These last couple of weeks things have gone so smoothly, and now the tavern is supposed to be closed within about ten days, which is certainly a great relief for me. [...]

Last Monday the small city of Cambria completely burned down, as a result of carelessness, because ashes which had not been completely extinguished were kept in a place which was not fireproof; with this heat and dryness these wooden cabins were naturally in a few hours at the mercy of the flames. They are already building again. [...]

Seline

Things are indeed improving. The worst is over. Seline's efforts seem slowly to bear fruit. In the letter of December 8th, 1889, she writes, for example:

We are all healthy and happy. Otto is forgetting, I believe, his bad habit of drinking. He works rather hard. The tavern has been closed since October 20th, and now we continue to live in peace. Naturally, all the hard work is now much easier on me, and thus, I hope, everything will eventually again go back to normal, which is certainly very necessary, because we always have enough to worry about.

Seline's letters contain many details about the daily life in Adelaida. They explain among other things how naturally people performed many jobs and fulfilled many duties, which in our day only specialized workers would perform. Following are a few extracts:

Concerning the Slaughtering of the House Animals.

Two weeks ago we slaughtered a four-year old cow, we sold what we could for 6 cents a pound, we have kept over a 100 pounds, we have salted it, and Otto has made a temporary structure for smoking meat in the machine house of the quicksilver mine. We have also made a lot of the beef into sausages, and I said, if only we could send a real piece of it to the Steinhof, it is very good meat. In the summer the butcher had offered 16 dollars for it, and so we found it was more advantageous to slaughter it ourselves. Now we have sold it for 15 dollars and still have a lot of meat. The cattle prices are presently rather low.

At the end of October we also slaughtered a pig, which we had to take in payment of a debt, we also sold some of it, I had then used the intestines and made blood sausages in the Zurich manner (people here don't know how to do this). I was of course a little afraid that they would not turn out well but they luckily turned out so fine that I must make them again the next time we slaughter a pig. I had learned that back home, when I would sometimes help out the butcher, when we slaughtered one of our cattle.

Preparations for Christmas.

Adelaida, December 8th, 1889

This year I really have a merrier and more pleasant Christmas than last year, when I was on the trip. On Christmas Eve here in the local school house is held a Christmas party, where a beautiful Christmas tree is erected. The evening before last, at the suggestion of Mr. Gibon and another neighbor, there gathered together here five men who organized the committee, in addition naturally also a number of women were chosen for the decoration and trimming of the tree. (Among them also myself with my Züridütsch.) The children are now already excited about it, old and young, adults and youngsters are given presents. Each family must give a contribution. When the party is over, there is a dance in our old house near the quicksilver mine. Dancing is always the main part of any party here. (Without dancing no party.) For the children I have ordered for each of them a plush cap, through my brother in Zurich. They arrived on Friday, also a woolen hood for Otto, when he goes out of the house, his head in a warm hood, then he receives as well a woolen jacket. We have another one of those in the store, and then I have begun for him another small scarf. Mimi was supposed to make it for her dear father, but her enthusiasm is already gone after she has done just a few needles, and I shall have to now make it myself.

For the children there is also naturally candy and a couple of games. Then, instead of at Christmas, we make for them another small tree for New Year's Eve, so that they will then have a little more joy. Dear little Alice wants to have another doll, she wants to be its little mother, she said yesterday. She is rather healthy and merry and has grown about a head in height this year. She chatters the whole day and is always active. Her favorite work is washing, otherwise she jumps after her dear father, and when he harnesses the wagon, then she cannot be kept in the house. I always have the same problem with Mimi, she does not want to sit down one moment, and I must urge her again and again to drive home a horse or the cow. On the horse, you don't have to tell her twice. I confess, it must be that way, and she wastes less time than her father, but I must then admonish her that she is a girl and not a boy and therefore also must learn to do housework. She is already so really American.

Knitting Stockings.

1890

In September I had begun a pair of stockings for her and told her she must finish them by Christmas, otherwise the Christ Child would certainly not come to see her; notwithstanding that, she has never voluntarily done this work; now, because she couldn't go to school because of a lot of rainy weather, she has half finished the stockings, but now we have run out of yarn, and I cannot get similar yarn here, because the former yarn was sent from Zurich. Mimi said it was from her aunts there. I am enclosing a pattern for you and ask you to send me some more if you can find any similar to it. I have of course found many strands of different yarn, all from Switzerland, also some wool, but a lot of it had been chewed or otherwise damaged by the mice, and I had to throw it away. If I had only brought along with me a real bundle of yarn, for myself I only need it for mending, and I still have that. But for Otto and the children here mending and knitting is not a custom, and one can find no real yarn here; wool even less and it is very expensive. Here everyone buys the ready-made stockings in the stores, which are bad and miserably manufactured. Otto also used to have such socks, but no longer owns even a single pair, and he was very happy about the ones which niece Alma had knitted for him. I have also made two pairs for him, which please him better than the knitted ones.

How You Make Your Own Mattresses.

Last week I made a mattress myself. We had bought hair. We still had ticking, and because mattresses here are badly manufactured and contain bad materials, I made one myelf. We had also plucked our geese in the summer, someone gave me a blanket which I finished the week before last, and so now we have a good warm bed, and I must not freeze again like last winter. Otto also likes is a lot; I also made a better one for the children. So I always have something else to improve and to fix, now it will soon be better, and we feel rather well. Otto is, thank God, always rather healthy and has a good appetite, and I only have to take care that I can satisfy it. Yet for this winter we have now taken care of pretty much everything, also, since it has turned cooler, I, thank God, am healthy and have a good appetite, and thus the work is going better.

Well I would almost have forgotten the most important thing, that we are expecting a little baby boy in the spring (April), which certainly bothers me a little given the local circumstances, where one in an emergency must fetch the doctor from so far away, and I am also no longer twenty years old.

Concerning the Garden Work.

Otto had usually taken care of the garden, and he was rather a little proud of it, whenever someone said to him, he had the most beautiful garden. I naturally have enough to do, taking care of the house and the yard, there is always here a lot to wash, especially in rainy weather, every week I have a load of washing, and after this naturally each time a lot of mending to do.

Concerning the Condition of Women in America.

People elsewhere say that women in America do not have to work so much, but be that as it may, if one does not want to stand in dirt, if one wants to have one's clothes properly in order and wants to use them, one finds just as much work here, or even more than in other countries. Of course, here mending and knitting are not customary, and Mimi even said, when she had to learn knitting from me, here no one knits and her mother had also not done that. I told her then, you must knit your stockings yourself or go without them. At home women and girls run around usually with torn stockings, where there is a hole or a run, it is stitched with a pin for as long as it still covers; and when a button falls off, it is replaced with a pin, and finally when everything no longer stays together, it is just thrown away and new clothes are bought. Otherwise women here are very vain; whenever they go on a trip or even to a dance, then the most beautiful clothes must be worn, and if there were a dance every two weeks, for each one there must be a new little dress. Each woman wants to be the most beautiful, and even if she otherwise never has money, for this purpose another couple of dollars must be scratched together.

Concerning School and Speaking English.

Mimi learns rather well in school; she does not lack aptitude, but here very little at all is expected. What she now learns in school, they learn in Zürich already in the second and third grades, and also here they don't have the discipline like over there. There, regarding child education, so much is expected from pupils, and here one has no help at all on the part of the schools, so it is doubly hard for the parents. You ask me whether I understand English; I can understand most of it, but I cannot yet speak it much; at home we always speak our Züridütsch. I must now however practice a little on the long evenings, so that I learn something by spring; if I only had more time.

The Founding of a Cooperative.

Adelaida, Easter, 1890

Dear Father!

On Thursday my dear wife had a little girl. Both are now well, yet upon laying the child on its mother's breast, the child bit her and caused her pain, and it is probably better to raise the child on cow's milk.

The midwife thought that it would be better in 1 to 2 days, yet now on the fourth day it is still not better, there is only little and watery milk. The little one weighs 8½ pounds, is fat and strong. We have hired a female servant, because I milk 9 cows and so I need help with the milkware and the butter making. Mimi goes to school, and she and Alice are delighted by their little sister. The mother is expected to remain in bed for 10 to 14 more days. The weather is warm and dry after a very wet winter. Grass and fodder are good, while grain and hay are behind in their growth and need more rain, while elsewhere the hay is ready for cutting.

Cattle had a good winter. I lost none, but on the other hand two weeks ago we found dead a young mare, which was supposed to give birth to a foal. A fox or wildcat stole three geese which were laying eggs, and we also found dead six small pigs. Butter is very cheap, hardly ten cents (50 Rappen) a pound. Wheat hardly one cent a pound. Beef just four cents per pound; two cents per pound of live animal.

Thus the prospects this year also are not splendid. We have recently begun an organization here, the "Adelaida Farmers' League" for the purpose of better sales of our products, professional instruction and support and assistance in emergencies and illness. The meeting place is our old little house, and I am its secretary. So far we have 24 members and several new people have applied for membership. It will be a while before we have it in full operation, pushing their way in are many rascals who are only thinking about making profits.

The school is also not going right; I am still a trustee on the school board, but the other two trustees stick together and do anything they like, there is no money there, the roof lets the rain in everywhere, and there are other debts, and then I am supposed to beg for the money for the necessary repairs.

It is getting late, warm greetings to my sisters, and to Aunt Ryffel from my dear wife and children, your

Otto

The Wyss-Streuli family with Seline as mother of her first child. From left, Alice, b. 1886, Otto, Mimi, b. 1878, Seline with daughter Seline, b. 1890.

"Concerning farming, people in other countries have no concept of how it operates here."

Adelaida, June 11th, 1890

Dear Father!

[…] The earlier small post office, which used to stand alone, was attached in 1887 to the right of the store when the latter was enlarged, and connected to it by means of a door. There, after I had thoroughly cleaned it out, I built our bedroom. The children sleep in the back room of the store, separately, and behind this room is the kitchen. We don't really lack fresh air, because we are directly under the roof; like many farmers here, we have no ceiling. In the wintertime I often wish it were less airy, when the wind blows in through the walls and under the roof. When the rainy weather lasts a long time, it is sometimes a little damp in the house, and as far as cleanliness is concerned, I do my best to keep the place spotless. I make everything pretty much according to the Zurich style. Most farmers' houses are only one story, the ceilings, if they exist, consist of light cotton cloth and are fastened to the walls on all 4 sides of the living room under the roof. Such a one is also in our old little house up on the hill. Last summer, before Gibons moved there, we had taken it down and washed it, and thoroughly cleaned the whole house. That was no easy task. We needed garden rakes and shovels in the kitchen. The economy building is rather well built. It consists of the front room, where the tavern used to be located, a big middle room , where two beautiful bedrooms can be built (we have a bed there, because in the summer sometimes travelers spend the night, that costs a dollar with dinner and breakfast), at the back there is a small but nice kitchen, a good cellar, in which we now have the milk and butter business.

I must still give you information about our horse's accident, because Otto is always so brief in his letters. People in other countries have no concept of how farming operates here; everything known as cattle runs around loose year in year out on the ranches; cows calve without supervision, horses give birth to their foals in a similar way, only when their owners see that their time is near do the owners go check on their livestock every now and then. Each farmer must fence in his ranch, if he doesn't want other cattle grazing on his land. Some people have not kept their fences in proper condition for a long time, and in addition, some people have put up barbed wire fences, which every 8 to 10 feet apart are stapled to a post, yet from time to time they are still broken through by the cattle, when they jump over them, and so they must be mended again.

For vegetables, gardens and orchards people make fences of thick slabs of wood, in order to keep out two- and four-legged livestock. In this regard we still have a lot of improvements to make, and we cold really use a hundred dollars worth of wire in order to fence in everything the way it should be done. Eventually everything will be fixed right.

It now looks somewhat better around the house and the barn yards, we are always busy fixing one thing or another. So now to come back to our horse, I must tell you that we found it dead about 10 minutes away from here up on the hill. Two young wild sons of a neighbor, Mr. Marshall, whose horses run around on our land and who wanted to then drive them home, have been racing around all over our land, up and down hills, and they have been loitering about with their horses and our mare, from which in the next few days we got the colt. It was the second colt our mare had given birth to; the first time everything had gone fine. At that time Otto scolded the boys, and she must have given birth to the colt the next morning or perhaps even on the same day, because she came everyday to the house or to the barn, only from that day on we saw her no more. On the third day after this race I became worried, so we sent Mimi to have a look. She mounted the old horse, and then she saw the mare stretched out dead at some distance. She didn't go any closer and then came straight back home with the news. I almost cried, because we are very sorry about the good animal. The next morning Otto went up with two men in order to take a look into the matter, and the latter agreed that the colt had died even before the birth, and that was because the mare had been raced too much, her condition proved that, and so Otto could legally demand replacement damages. The men are willing to testify for him. [...]

Many greetings from Otto, the children and from your
Seline

Concerning the Butter Which is Shipped to San Francisco.

Adelaida, June 14th, 1890

Dear Sisters Hanneli and Emilie!

My warm thanks to you for your dear letters. I finally get around to answering them. My writing is going faster and faster. Special thanks for the yarn you sent. However, you did not send the bill for it. Mimi has not yet used it much. Starting next Wednesday there is vacation, the first term is over, and the second will begin only at the end of July or the beginning of August. Here the school year is always divided into two terms, and almost every time there is another teacher, which naturally is a disadvantage for the children. For that reason they are always at the same point in their lessons. Mimi told me last week that she had to learn the multiplication table. She was the only one in her class (except a 15-year-old boy), who could do it correctly, and she then told the teacher her mother had taught her. [...]

On Ascension Day I went with Alice to Cayucos. A man (a smith by profession), who wants to build a smithy here, drove us there, because both of us, Otto and I, could not leave the farm together, and he had a lot of work to do with the cattle, so he sent me. We had a case of butter to take along, in order to send it by steamer to San Francisco. In hot weather you can't ship it by railroad. Since I otherwise naturally never leave the house and since I had never been on the coast, I enjoyed the trip, only it was not quite perfect for me because of the little ones. However, father thought he could take care of everything with Mimi. For Alice it was naturally a big thrill. When we saw the sea, she was quite astonished and said that she had never seen so much water. We spent the night there, and on Friday morning we drove from there to Cambria, 15 miles away. Then we went a long stretch along the sea, and we were then happy to be back home at 4 o'clock in the afternoon with our loved ones.

I must now still tell you how butter is prepared here before it can be sold. I find it somewhat involved. It is all salted and made into rolls with a mould which we also had to buy. A roll weighs two pounds. Each piece is wrapped in extra light white cotton wrapping cloth. To ship it you have to have a few cases. We bought two, which each contain 32 rolls. In order to be able to store it for a long time, you pack it in little barrels and add salt water to it. Yesterday we made 40 more rolls, and also salted these, in order to keep it until it can be sold for better prices. For the last shipment we received only 12 cents per pound and also paid the freight cost. So we earned only 10 cents per pound. [...]

For the month of April I had hired a maid, because, with the dairy farm and all, Otto naturally could not have done everything alone. But on the 13th day after the birth of our child she got some rheumatism in her left leg, and then she went back home, and I had to do everything by myself again. It was probably a little too much work for her. Here you just cannot expect as much from an American woman as from a Swiss woman, and we also had to give her 15 dollars for the month. The midwives here only take care of the birth, afterwards they don't come back. That costs 10 dollars. [...]

Today we have plucked the geese. Altogether we still have five, and five have been eaten by wild animals. Last week a neighbor's wife told me that, of 80 turkeys which had sat beside one another on a bench overnight, she had only 26 left the following morning. Is that not annoying? Here not all farmers have chicken coops, and not everyone has a barn. So the chickens spend the night in the trees and the geese and turkeys sleep on the ground. I must also mention that the 4th of July is a holiday which is highly celebrated throughout the entire country, in commemoration of the declaration of the independence of the United States. This year the celebration will be held on our place for the inhabitants of about four school districts. Here all the festivals are held outdoors. A stand is set up, where lemonade, sweets and fruit are sold. Under the trees a long table is set up, an ox is slaughtered and roasted over an open fire. Each family brings along its own pastries, bread, sugar and everything necessary for the picnic. Every housewife wants to bake the best cake, and at night there is a dance.

Well, I must close again. It is twelve o'clock, and in the morning I must do the wash. Mimi has no school on Saturdays. The warmest greetings from
Otto, the children and Seline

There are still setbacks for Otto, especially with the consumption of alcohol. He is exploited by many. Seline complains in the letter of October 1st, 1890, "because he is so generous." Seline even considers leaving Otto with the children. This letter contains a description of the election process, as it was practiced at that time out in the country in the USA:

[…] This month take place the elections for all county officers, who are newly elected every three years, and this type of election, as it is practiced here, is a quite original and a noble event!—For a radius of about 20 miles, the elections take place on our property. First of all are elected the delegates who must go to San Francisco in order to draw up the list of candidates, Republicans and Democrats each for their respective parties. This election took place four weeks ago. As a delegate of the Democratic Party, Otto with three others had to go to San Luis three weeks ago. He could have become justice of the peace again. But he didn't want to do that, because that is no enjoyable office here. With each election new men come to power here, and these men then ride around in the county, make speeches in favor of their candidacy at each voting place and then they pay for a round of drinks for the voters. If they are seeking a well paying office, one of these politicians will pay at least 10 to 20 dollars.

Alice is very gifted and capable. To be sure, she does have some very tough and steady ideas in her head, but I think that the time has now come to break her of some of her notions, if only her father were more energetic. Too bad that both girls cannot be sent to better schools. The little one is likewise already lively, capable and already shows us her mischief, which of course now still only gives us pleasure. At the beginning of September she got serious diarrhea which lasted 14 days, and for a couple of days we were really afraid we were going to lose her. Now she is all right again. […]

People here don't understand winemaking, the people from Ticino, of whom there are very many in this region, buy each fall many grapes and make wine. Otherwise only beer and whisky are drunk here; (drinking liquor, "this beautiful custom") you do not find anywhere like in this region, and I have already said from time to time that one ought to be able to enforce here the Swiss Alcohol Law.

Otto is School President and is Sued in Court.

Adelaida, August 27th, 1891

Dear Father!

[.,.] Now I must share with you our new family event. To wit, on July 2nd I once again gave birth to a lively little girl, and her name is Marie Mathilde. We had hired no stranger during this period of my confinement. Mimi had vacation at that time, and so she had to do the housework as well as she could. We are all healthy and well, and things are going rather well with us.

The school has been operating again since the middle of July. Alice also attends it regularly now. She learns well. We now have a man as teacher, and he is really one of the best who has ever taught here. He is a boarder at our farm. Otto is now school president. In brief, I must share with you that the day before yesterday we received the deed on the purchased land (on which the quicksilver mine stands). It has now been three years since Otto bought it. The seller (a man from Ticino) had not long before also received the property rights (like us last year for our homestead). After Otto had bought it, jealous neighbors had lodged a protest in order to prevent his possession of the deed, giving as their motive that they were being swindled, because it was mineral land. Namely, these neighbors use a stretch of our land as a road, as the best and shortest way to reach their places. Further it is the best fodder land that we have, and their cattle had always used it. It has now been a year since we have learned of this litigation. Otto turned over the investigation to a lawyer at the Land Office in San Francisco. The latter received a report from Washington that as a result of protests the deed had been suspended. Then, through a document prepared by the lawyer in which he had to prove with the signatures of three witnesses that everything was in order, Otto had to certify that this protest was groundless. There was a lot of paperwork and it cost more than 30 dollars, but we have it now, and it is a great relief for me, because without this document the land does not have as much value for the owner, and he cannot manage it as he wishes. We don't yet have the deed for our homestead, but we shall receive it without delay. At present our region is plagued by cattle stealing. Namely, it is a couple of young louts who have been making a living for a long time by stealing cattle, and we do hope that they will be caught once and for all. There is almost no farmer around here who has not had one or several heads of cattle stolen.

Warm greetings from Otto and the dear children and from your
Seline

[…] December 4th. After a long interruption I can now finally continue my writing. During this period we have once again received an addition to our family, a little girl, and so writing is becoming more and more difficult for me. It is almost no longer possible to sit still for even just an hour. In your last letter you bring Otto's attention to the need to register the children in the civil register of Affoltern; I already talked about that with him last year, and he thought it would cost about the same amount of money for one or two children, but now that we have three, he is not so excited about the prospect of registering the children, because of the expense.

Right now we are always short of money, but I think that in the course of the next year it will be possible to take care of that. Last week we had 7 days and nights of almost uninterrupted storms and rain. It has now been fair for two days, but it is cold at night. People already generally feared that another dry winter would follow; this fear is now allayed. The cattle will soon receive a little green fodder, if continuously cold nights don't prevent it. By January we shall again have five to six freshly calved cows and then eventually more, and so next year we can begin earlier with butter making than last year, only it will also become cheaper again. Cattle are cheaper than ever.

Otto has been working for four weeks for the teacher Mr. Minesch for 1½ dollars per day. To be sure, he had more than enough work at home, we were even supposed to have help ourselves, but we must have provisions for the winter, and then he would like to buy another good new harrow for about 30 dollars; otherwise he would not be able to afford that, because at this season of the year, you have no income from farming. So he will keep on working until Christmas, and then he will start ploughing.

So I must once again close. At year's end I wish you all from the bottom of my heart happiness, good health and God's blessings and hope that these letters will find everyone in the best spirits.

Warm greetings from

Otto, the children and Seline

"My feet are like icicles."

Adelaida, October 30th, 1892

Dear Sisters Hanneli and Emilie!

Mathilde liked the best the little red skirt which I made for her a couple of weeks ago, but little Seline thought that hers was no less beautiful. We have to report another addition to our family, which we received on August 1st, namely a little girl, whose name is Johanna Pauline. The father really wanted to have a little Pauline, because there is no little Hans here. This time everything went rather well, except that since then I always have back pains, so that sometimes at night I can almost not lie down. On the fourth day I was up again. Father and the children are all healthy and happy. Mimi and Alice go to school, which next week will close until next spring. Alice speaks good English, and Seline is also beginning to speak English. She learns a lot from Alice, then sometimes she deserts me for the school, and I must usually look for her there when she is not to be found at home. Mathilde has been walking since last month. She already wants to mimic everything she hears. She is healthy and rather fat, a real Wyss kid. The little one is also happy and jolly, and the older children love her dearly.

Last spring, all three, Alice, Seline and Mathilde, had very strong whooping-cough. They had caught it in a neighbor's house, where they had gone one evening with their dear father. They were plagued by this painful cough for almost two months. Mathilde even longer, and we had a lot of trouble bringing the little one through it. She threatened at times to completely choke. I had a hard time, day and night. Mimi was in Oakland last winter. That is a big city near San Francisco. She went to school there and stayed with a widow for 12 dollars a month. There she had the opportunity to go to Sunday school and to church and to learn to play the piano for an hour every week. Mr. Minegg, our teacher, had paid for Mimi's room and board, because he thought he owed us some money, because Otto helped him with his land. We could not have paid that, and at first I did not at all agree that Mimi had to live with Americans, because she has already assimilated enough of the cursed and superficial American ways. On the other hand, I certainly knew that it would do her good to observe other people and better manners than are customary here in our area. She liked it there, but in the second month she wrote that she would rather be back at home. In school she learned a little more than here, but you just don't find Swiss schools here, and so the people from Ticino (of which there are many in California) almost all who can afford it send their children to school back home in Switzerland. Mimi was away from the end of January until Easter. Naturally, that is not long enough. She must still go away, in order to learn in another place what she will not learn here, as soon as our circumstances permit it somehow.

You ask whether the children here also have religious instruction? That can be found here nowhere in the countryside. In the schools it is by law forbidden, because there children of all nations and religions are in the same school. No Sunday school has been held in our school house for over three years, and there have been no more ministers here for a long time. I have never seen a German as long as I have been here. So we unfortunately never had the opportunity to have the children baptized. Alice is also not yet baptized. I hope that we perhaps will find the opportunity in San Luis. At present no German minister is there, and I shall not permit that to be done by an English minister. Baptism is not a custom in the English culture, but our children must be baptized, I will not have it. It has already bothered me a lot that one can find here no opportunity for religious purposes and activities, and I can unfortunately do too little in this regard with the children. With all the work I have to do, I must be content if I can keep them in good order from early in the morning until late at night, as far as health and good manners require it. It has now been a year since I have used a sewing machine. I sold my old one to a neighbor's wife for 7 dollars and in its place I bought a Singer machine for 10 dollars from a man whose wife had died. It is not new, but it is still in good condition, and so I can catch up on my sewing, which would no longer have been possible without this help, because to sew everything for 5 children gives you a lot to do, and I must steal time for this work.

Hanneli asks further whether we have a big house to clean? To answer this, as I would like, is impossible. I can only say that every week I would have liked to clean out a big house, as I had done back home, and then I could feel well. Here I have a cabin to clean up every day. Usually I have to sweep out each room more than once, and that work really never stops. Over there you have no concept of the thick dust in summer and the dirt in winter in the rainy season, and because our cabin stands quite near the main road, I naturally have to clean all the more. How hard you work in such an unorganized house, can only conceive the person who must do the work, because when the chickens and young pigs are always coming into the house, you can hold the broom in your hand the entire day; the work is never finished.

Official chimney sweeps do not exist here. I do the chimney myself every 5-6 weeks; to be sure, it is much more simply constructed than back home in Europe. You only have to clean the oven and the pipe which leads from the oven to the roof outside. The worst part is always the freezing in the winter; so right now I am sitting near the fire and I'm freezing despite my warm clothes. My feet are like icicles, because for writing I cannot stretch them out toward the fire. You can best imagine this contrivance, if you imagine you had a fire in a corner in your barn, where you could warm yourselves. [...]

The letter from Seline ends with news concerning the state of the cultivations.

Adelaida, August 9th, 1893

Dear Father!

We have received your letters from January and it pleases us immensely to note that everyone is healthy and happy in your home. It will naturally also interest you to know how things are with us, and so I can, especially as far as health is concerned, report with satisfaction that everyone is rather happy, especially the dear children, who have also all, thank God, come through the winter well. Mimi has been back in Oakland for two weeks and goes to school there. She is again staying with the same woman, with whom she can live without paying room and board. However, she must help her do housework. This lady has boarders. We have to pay all other costs ourselves. A couple of years ago Otto was of the opinion to send her abroad, but now his views have changed, and he thinks she will get by better in life by staying here. That is certainly the main thing for Mimi.

People in our area are not satisfied with this year's harvest. From the end of January until the end of March we had too much rain and then no more, so the spring was too dry and also too cold. Thus we had frost in March almost every night, still a lot until the middle of June. There is a lot of fruit, but no hay and no wheat. The latter is worth only 75 to 85 cents per hundredweight. They are working again in the old Sunderland quicksilver mine; they think they can operate it again. A private man, Ed Smith, who last year inherited a big fortune from his father, is now having it worked. If so much comes out of the mine that it pays to operate it, he will sell it to a company which manages the business, which would naturally be an advantage for our region. Otto has been going there for four weeks and works in the tunnel for 2 dollars a day. It is a mile from here. Besides that, he must still milk the cows in the evening, which doesn't yield much now. We don't milk in the morning. Next week we shall ship the last butter, and only in April could we send off the first shipment. At the end of May everything was all dry and withered, so this year we did not have many earnings, only a lot of work. [...]

 Many warm greetings

Otto and Seline and children

Adelaida, August 13th, 1893

Dear Sisters Emilie and Hanneli!

[...] You ask, dear Hanneli, whether you might not be the godmother of the little one. We shall gladly answer this question with yes and be warmly grateful for this service, if we could only soon manage to have them all baptized. As we found out from a German, there is in Creston, 14 miles from Paso Robles and about 30 miles from here, a Lutheran Reformed Church. There preaches every two weeks a German minister. In that region almost all the settlers are Germans. We are planning to go there, but we won't do it this year, because we await another girl by November. We are frightfully hot, our garden this year is in bad shape. The spring was too dry, and high water in the winter washed away the pipes which go over the brook. All the others were all stopped up, and Otto could not unscrew them from one another. The reservoir had already been bad for a long time. The water always runs out, we should make a new one. So I myself must carry up to the house every drop of water from the brook.

 I must close. It is time to cook again. Many greetings to Aunt Ryffel; she certainly has been having a bad time with her eyes. Many greetings also to both of you from us all.

Otto and Seline

A Healthy Little Boy—"Father's nicest Christmas present."

Adelaida, December 29th, 1893

Dear Father!

[...] On November 29th we were overjoyed by the arrival of a healthy strong little boy, who is father's nicest Christmas present, and his sisters find a lot of joy in their little brother. In general, everyone is healthy and happy. The dear children now also find joy in their Christmas tree. Mimi is still away and will not come back before March. Otto is working again now in the quicksilver mine, which, however, still offers nothing certain. For almost two months he did not have much work there. Now he will be there again for a few weeks. They are still occupied with the preparatory work, which will last a couple of months. Yet judging from the present prospects, they hope for a good success, which naturally would be a big advantage for our poor region, if such a business could be brought into operation. The times are presently bad; no salary, only high interest. Cattle is worth nothing, and as a result of that the prices of goods have gone down; many farmers are losing their homes. The wheat harvest in our area was not quite average, and the hundredweight is only 80 to 85 cents, which is far too little considering the high workers' salaries. There was a lot of fruit, but it was also all dirt-cheap. We have enough for our use.

Otto, Seline and Children

N.B. I still want to share with you a few things about our economic circumstances and for this purpose I am using a separate sheet of paper. We are presently in a rather critical situation. As you know, 4 years ago Otto bought from the Ticinese Rufino Petraita 89 acres of land along with the appertaining house. He had given the latter 300 dollars as a deposit, and for 600 dollars a mortgage was made on it, whereas elsewhere here in our region one cannot receive more than 3-4 dollars per acre. Thus Otto could not have received more than 300 dollars for this land, except the creditors, likewise men from Ticino, are in San Francisco, they have a big commercial business there, and Otto had procured from them store merchandise for a couple of hundred dollars which he owed them, so then that had to be added to the mortgage, which made the debt go up to 600 dollars, and that was supposed to be paid off in 4 years. Last October the time expired when this particular debt should have been paid, and since by then three years of interest had accumulated on it, it has now risen to an amount which would be almost impossible to pay off. If the creditors really wanted to insist on payment, I don't know how far it could still go. To be exact, it was never really convenient for Otto to pay the interest. Since we had significant expenses in order to receive the deed, we would not have disputed any court proceedings, and thus the creditors could have lost the entire mortgage. Otto looked for money in San Luis Obispo. Mr. Brunner, cashier in a bank there, to whom our situation was already known through Petraita, advised Otto that he should not pay more than 500-600 dollars, that he had at the time been somewhat swindled with this sum and he should let only himself, Brunner, take care of things. He would fight it out with the creditors and pay off the debt, and we would then settle with him privately. Should they take the matter to court, which would cause them significant costs, he would also take care of that, and we could still pay. Otto had already been looking for money in October, before he had spoken with Mr. Brunner about it. He had then written to San Francisco that he would pay 500 dollars now and 100 dollars next year and 100 dollars in two years. They would have to forgive the remainder of the debt. They accepted the offer with the stipulation that he had to give good security for the other 200 dollars. Two weeks later we received a letter in which they calculated that we would have to pay, with interest and compound interest, the sum of almost 800 dollars. To pay that would be almost impossible for us, and we would probably not do that, come what might. Undoubtedly someone has been working against us, and that is none other than

Petraita's brother-in-law, the former tavern keeper here, who is doing whatever he can against us, since we gave him notice the tavern would be closed. He is a dirty idler, with whom even his brother-in-law Petraita himself does not want to have anything to do. Otto then wrote in the last letter, after he had spoken with Mr. Brunner, that he could post no security and also could no longer receive the 500 dollars, which was promised him, which of course is not so. We would only very unwillingly lose this land, and I hope that things can somehow be worked out. I still have somewhat over 400 dollars (2000 francs) over there in Europe, which is guaranteed on my father's home, which went to my third oldest brother. In recent years my brother had been burdened twice with paying securities (altogether 3000 francs), and so he asked me to wait a little until he had again worked off his losses a little. Last week I received a letter that I would receive the money in a couple of months, about which we are naturally very happy. We must now borrow money on another piece of property which we had paid off three years ago out of your money, in addition to other old debts with high interest. I had planned to report in detail about our circumstances, but today's date (and a reproachful letter from my brother, which arrived yesterday) admonish me to close.

Seline

The little boy Hansli (Johannes) died already in October, 1894 and was buried on the nearby hillside beside Ottilie and her three dead children.

Adelaida, June 2nd, 1895

Dear Father!

[...] Last February a Cooperative Company was organized here for the construction of a tannery. I offered 3 acres of land free and any additional necessary land at $10.00 per acre, and now they have about 8 acres and 9 ditches, and one building is already constructed, and a tanner (a Swede) is already at work with 40 skins. Last week I set up the bark mill, and tomorrow we shall begin grinding bark with one horse and horse-gin. Most of the work is done by the company's stock holders themselves. There are about 100 of them—there are about 400 shares at $5.00 underwritten partly in money, but for a larger part in work, yet so far everything is progressing well, and in three to six months some leather will also be made. Brother-in-law Meier brought yesterday two loads of oak bark.

At present we are all well, also Polly the smallest is again in good health. About four weeks ago, as Alice was taking a pan of boiling milk from the oven, Polly ran into her and the milk spilled over her right cheek, shoulder, ear and some spilled down her front and back, some skin was gone on her neck and chin.—We immediately got some fresh lime, and we covered the wounds with linseed oil and lime water and wads of cotton, and it festered only a little. [...]

Mimi is still in Oakland and goes to school there, besides which she helps out in the house of a widow doing housework; she will be there another year or year and a half, until she completes Grammar School. After that she is supposed to go another year or two to Normal School, if she can do it, and could then be a school mistress or teacher with a salary of about $60.00 per month. [...]

Otto

Last Thursday May 30th was Grave Beautification Day, and we did not forget our own dead. Especially Hansli's grave was quite green and white with roses and evergreen, arranged by loving hands.

"I need elbow room in the wide country."

Adelaida, October 14th, 1895

Dear Father!

We are sending the photographs again together, under separate cover, and the certificates of baptism will follow, when the consular and other necessary attestations and everything connected with it are there.—We were so bold as to record you, dear father, with Emma, as the baptismal godparents for Seline, "the second tallest in the picture." Presumably we shall later be able to arrange for religious instruction or the preparation for confirmation with the same minister. With Mimi we have to some extent neglected it, and a Baptist Minister (Anabaptist) wrote me he wanted to make her into a Christian, which I however politely refused, because she is baptized Protestant. [...]

The tannery, situated at the lowest point where the brook leaves my land, about 10 minutes (half a mile) from the house, is progressing slowly.[67] The pits, walled with stone but really not thick enough, in spots less than a foot thick, and then smeared with cement, contained cracks and lost a lot of steeping water. Many skins of calf-and goat leather are finished and soon also bigger ones will be done, yet the price of skins has more than quadrupled and so they are less available.

The red bark of the evergreen or live oak is most often used. It contains much tannin. However, it gives the leather a somewhat dark color. Black oak easily turns into tannin, whereas the plentiful white oak has not yet been regularly tested. Skins with deer or stag fur are tanned with alum.

Shall I ever return home for good? I don't think so; maybe on a visit or something, and if times were better, we would soon lease the place and would be free for a year—but over there in Europe what would I do? Everything is too small, too crowded, no horse for riding and driving—"I need elbow room in the wide country."

---

[67] Otto reports about this project in detail in the letter of June 2nd, 1895.

Here many things have improved. One can now receive the attention of a regular doctor, M.D., who has his diploma, within 6 hours for a cost of 10 to 15 dollars. Ten years back it took 24 hours and 40 to 50 dollars; our roads are still bad, but 10 to 12 miles from here you are already on better highways.

You can always sell eggs and chickens in the growing Paso Robles for cash, and thus in 10 to 20 years it will get even better. Moreover, we don't really have it so bad. We have what we need, and if the prices for farm products, especially meat and butter, were better, one would also have money to make improvements.—Yes and there is just the question of water. Here in dry California it is irrigation water which makes everything grow, and then I could do a whole, whole lot in the way of improvements. Not to mention the brook, I should conduct the two big, respectively, big and small springs into a reservoir pond, at a vertical height of 100 feet above the houses, and from there conduct it downward via pipes. I would need something over 1000 feet and pipes less than one and a half inch thick are too small, in order, for example, to employ a large amount of water.

I now have the water in gutters, which are 4.5 inch wide boards nailed together in a V-shape, which run 450 feet from the house into a small wooden reservoir 4 x 6 feet and 4 feet deep, and from there in 1½ inch pipes through the garden and to the house, but the gutters are often broken 6 times a week. Cattle and pigs step on them and knock them apart, and the hotter the water and the less the water, all the more do they like to stamp around the wet spot.

The best plant for irrigation is Luzerne or Alfalfa, as it is called here. Some garden varieties grow until December and are from the beginning until the middle of April again a foot high.

A reservoir which could hold an entire week's worth of water should be about 20 feet in diameter and 8 to 10 feet deep. I have measured the water flow, seven gallons—or something over 28 liters per minute, but now in the driest sesason it is less. Besides irrigation, there could be developed with a small, or even better a bigger, thin overshot waterwheel, a form of energy which could be applied to making butter, cutting fodder, breaking grain, turning grindstones and for many other purposes, before the water were used for irrigation.—Besides building more barns and stables, building these water contrivances would be one of my first improvements. [...]

I must also thank you once again for maintaining my subscription to the "Bürkli" as a continually welcome and always gladly read old friend.[68] Actually no longer through the "Bürkli" but rather through the Friday paper, I keep so up to date on Swiss and Zurich politics and, upon a possible visit back home, I would be already acquainted with so much.

---

[68] Meant is the "Zurich Kalender" and the Friday newspaper of David Bürkli, which, regularly collected, were sent at regular intervals.

PS: Should you have a little publication about reservoir construction and aqueducts, I could really use it, because here there is no expert far and wide with whom you could speak or whom you could ask.

The answer to one question you will probably find in the lexicon: How long should limestone be burned in order to make usable lime?

In October, 1895 baptism is finally arranged for all the children in a German speaking Protestant Church, a day's journey—ten hours—from Adelaida. (letter of October 14ᵗʰ, 1895)

Adelaida, October 14ᵗʰ, 1895

Dear Aunt Ryffel!

It has now been nine years since you offered to be the godmother of the then new-born little child. We finally got around to doing that and have had all our little ones baptized in a Protestant German church about 30 miles, ten hours, or a day's journey, from here.

Susanna Alice—has thus recorded you and brother Oscar as godparents and as proxy we had a Mrs. Stennger, a Swiss-born woman from Gontenschwil, Aargau; and a Mr. Friedrich Hirt, a German, who has a rather nice little place there, not far from the church.—The church, or better put the school house, lies in a little valley, in the vicinity of which 12 or more German families have settled within a radius of up to 10 miles.

The minister, Mr. Klaus, a North German, also has 160 acres and big, near-grown children. The school was full, about 60 adults, and since St. Michael's Day was observed as a Holy Day of Repentance, supper was also served. German songs—less known to us—were sung to the music of a parlour-organ, or harmonium; we were also provided with books.—All the people stayed for the baptism, and the minister especially stressed that after the baptism, later in the lesson, the preparation for confirmation and the confirmation should follow. For Emilie (Mimi) he gave me a letter of introduction to a Protestant minister in Oakland, which I sent to her.

On the following day, on the way home, in Paso Robles, we wanted to have made for ourselves and for our distant loved ones the little picture of the already quite grown baptismal children, in commemoration of the baptism, and we think that it turned out fine. Your godchild is the tall Alice, the spitting image of her blessed mother. With her long, abundant hair loosened, the ear rings are well delineated, while the bright dress does not stand out well.—To her left is Seline, also good, she presses a little against the chair, her hand is uplifted and looks dark on her bright dress, she is an anxious good child. But the best is Mättie, to the right; during all four photos she always stood up straight, and her dress stands out very well. When she was quite small, everyone said that, with her curled hair, she was the most beautiful baby in the region.

And the little lively Polly, it was the hardest for her to be still, with her head a little low, she looks like a little "droopy-mouth," but the picture is still the way she is in real life, and also her little dress photographs well. [...]

Otto

The Meiers Have Converted.

Adelaida, December 15th, 1895

Dear Father!

Once again another year is approaching its end, and today's date admonishes me to write, in order to reach the dear old homeland on time with our best wishes, because it is so far away. We always have more to do than we like, especially when the weather is so fair. Last night, however, it began to rain and to storm. It seemed as though the wet season would demand its rights in force, but now it is 4 o'clock in the afternoon, on a Sunday, and it is clearing up, and the rainy weather seems to be over again for a while. The small amount of rain has done some good. People don't yet actually want too much, because the farmers are all busy with plowing. Otto has plowed from 10 to 12 acres and has partly sowed them and is not yet finished. He wants to do even more. Two weeks ago we had an older man from Valais, who came here looking for work. He would have liked to stay in order to rest a while, and Otto hired him for 50 cents per day. He stayed two weeks, then he left again. Now we have a 16-year-old boy for a while. He is the tanner's son. For the same pay and he works pretty well. Whatever is sowed before New Year is really always the best. Otto has been having back pains for some time, especially in the morning; in the afternoon it was always better again. He thought it was rheumatism. Now it is pretty good again. He must protect himself from colds.

The tanner and his wife are Swedes. The most decent and most orderly people whom we have had in the place. Things are progressing slowly with the tannery. The company does not have much money. Now rather much leather is finished, and they are talking about hiring a harness maker and shoemaker. I would very much welcome the latter, so that we could have our shoes and also the horse harnesses repaired without having to go 16 miles. We have again become friends with Mr. Meier and his family, after they made some friendly overtures to us. Since dear Hansli's death we have again been on friendly terms with Mr. Meier. We had never been in their house, until a couple of weeks ago I went up there, because Mrs. Meier also came to see us. The whole family had recently converted to the Methodist Church. A zealous, pious minister came here about two months ago and stayed for two days in Meier's house from Saturday until Monday. He then fully converted Mr. Meier and baptized his son and his wife in the local church. Since then Mr. Meier has been a zealous Apostle for the word of God, and we now also have Sunday school in our school house, which he and a previous neighbor of his in Missouri, who is also now here, direct. I am pleased that the children receive religious instruction. We also naturally go, may it bear good fruit with all, especially with the many small thieves there are around here. At year's end we wish you from the bottom of our hearts happiness, health and God's blessings and many greetings from Otto, the children and Seline Wyss.

Concerning Cattle Thieves and "Artful" Politicians.

Adelaida, January 26th, 1896

My dear Nephew!

It has been two years since I received your dear letter, and I did intend at that time to answer soon, but in general I write little any more.—Now it is storming and raining outside, already for the second week a warm wind is blowing, and grass is beginning to turn green and the fruit is coming as well. It will also be good if a better year comes, because the last two were bad, fodder and wheat growth were slight. Two years ago it was too dry, and last spring the late spring rains were lacking, so that here fodder—hay and fruit—brought only a very moderate yield, and in addition the prices for everything were so low.

In comparison with ten years ago, the prices of wheat, meat, butter, etc., have fallen by half, which has the result that people are well provided with all necessary provisions, but yet never have much cash on hand, which is really necessary, if one wants to improve his place or wants to construct better buildings, fences and implements. This rain washes onto my place in many spots two to four feet wide and one to two foot deep trenches into the beautifully sowed farmland, makes more work for harvesting; good soil is gone for good. If we had put the stones in the necessary places and used them to build a dam against backwater, that would have improved the entire field.

To be sure, many people are also happy when the rain washes away their dung heaps, so that they don't need to carry them away, quite especially when it is leased or cleared land, it is often sowed in this way, and the tenant delivers a quarter of the wheat or yield as his rent.

Coming back to your letter, here it is customary among the Germans only to use "Du" in talking to one another, and that also seems more practical, since the Englishman and American use the same word—you—for everyone.

So you have now been a student for two years, whereas your brother Hans has already acquired his Dr. M.D., for which I congratulate him sincerely, and his inaugural-dissertation on eczema is also interesting for the layman, and I thank him for it sincerely. You write, a friend of yours is going to the Zambesi, thus into darkest Africa. It should not surprise me if in a larger or smaller number of years the stream of emigrants would make its way to Africa instead of to America, especially in the German colonies; although one can learn English, it is natural that here the English or Irish immigrant has a big advantage over the German, and even if he is the biggest ignoramus, he still thinks himself much better and assumes he belongs to the great nation—like for example the French before 1870.

It is outright funny when you hear a native-born, educated, intelligent American expressing his opinion about the tense situation with England—"Yes, of course, America for Americans, foreigners have no business here."—"But it would really be a shame if two English-speaking nations should go to war with one another, when together they could beat the entire rest of the world."—"How on earth could you think such a thing—of course there won't be any war!"

Everybody here who plans to obtain any kind of public office gets involved in politics, and the more he is a lazy bum, a rogue, a swindler, or at least a debtor, all the more does he think himself qualified to hold public office, and he thinks that he has better prospects—he must simply be "cunning" and "artful."

Hopefully we'll have a rest from cattle thieves. Around a dozen from this area have recently been imprisoned (two have already received seven years in prison), and others have looked for a "healthier" climate. Last year four head of our cattle disappeared and a breeding hog with five piglets.

It is storming, lightening and thundering, and it has almost put out the fire in the hearth, temperature 55 degrees F or 13 degrees C, so pleasant for January.

Good night, Happy New Year for 96 and I shall see that I write to your dear father in the morning. Answer at your convenience, your uncle
Otto Wyss

In a letter of January 27th, 1896 to his brother, Otto describes the character and the development of the four youngest children and then takes up the issue of his wife:

And Mrs. Wyss, who earlier always wanted to sell and move elsewhere, is beginning to become resigned to life here. Her health is better than ever, she makes the clothes for the children, and there is otherwise always enough to do. I myself always have my hands full of work, but unfortunately I feel that last year was not so good. A year back something broke on the wagon, so that I, holding the reins tightly, was pulled down on the ground and dragged away. Since then I have had from time to time pains in my back in the kidney region, especially after I get cold or after I pick up or carry heavy items. In warm weather it is better. Warm greetings from your brother.

On January 30ᵗʰ, 1896 Otto tells his father about Sunday School and the makeshift worship services:

We have begun a Sunday school here. Brother-in-law Meier is the superintendent in reading in the Bible for smaller and bigger children and adults and the singing of Christian songs. We also sing German songs from time to time and have four church song books, and at Christmas Meier gave a German sermon and prayer—we are about six families who come regularly, and just as many who only come occasionally. Now and then a preacher comes, yet Meier is not unskillful in interpreting a Bible passage, and has certainly inherited something from his grandfather Pastor Locher, from whom he also got some practice, and a few notes help him regularly, also in English.

Otto Becomes a School Administrator.

Adelaida, June 7ᵗʰ, 1896

Dear Father!

[…] Very nearby the tannery is now operating with two or three men, a harness maker and shoemaker have likewise begun, but all together have very, very little money.—They now request that I should divide up a piece of land into building sites, and as soon as a dozen or more have promised to buy building sites, I can do something, but first I must of course be certain that I can afford the expenses and can receive a good price for the land.

They are working again in the neighboring quicksilver mine, yet up until now the seven to eight men are earning only a modest salary, but with good prospects for later on.

Last Friday the citizens of this school district chose me as a school administrator. One is elected each year for a period of three years, because there are three of them. There are 39 pupils, and if possible we shall push on for a Grammar School, somewhat like our Realschule—whereas up until now only a primary school was held.

Alice and Seline attend the latter, and the former sits in the same class with 15-year-old urchins who moreover are quite far behind.—Mattie and Polly, the two smallest, keep one another good company, mix their Züridütsch and English often in a funny way. Thus Mattie said yesterday to the little cat: "I have too putz your Nase!" Mimi writes that she is making progress in Oakland's Grammar School, with a lot of homework. She will be finished with it next December, and in 10–14 days we expect her here for five weeks of summer vacation. She writes often and is glad like anyone to be coming home for a week.

Our cattle are not very big, but they are all fat—nine cows, two bigger and three smaller beef cattle, three oxen, a very tame bull, nine calves, two work horses and five young colts of one to three years; four big pigs and 16 young ones of all sizes, for which I must build better stables this summer and fall, and am glad to now have the means at hand to do it. [...]

Otto

About Mimi much good is reported. She received her diploma from the Grammar School and now enters the Teacher Training College in San José, where she is supposed to earn part of her upkeep herself by helping out in a family.

From Switzerland arrives the sad news of the death of Aunt Ryffel. In her will the good Aunt thought about her relatives in America.

Adelaida, March 28th, 1897

Dear Father!

The day before yesterday came your dear letter with the contents of the will, which pleasantly surprised me. So my good Aunt still showed that she always meant well by me. For me myself it is such a big help, so that I can help Emilie (Mimi) somewhat more, the eldest, because her move to San José, to the Teaching College of California, fresh clothes, books and everything cost rather more than expected. On February 2nd she then had to take another acceptance exam, and of 11 applicants she was among the six who were accepted.

A week back she wrote to me that she had had to borrow money for 5½ dollars of books and she prayed that better times would come and she would not have to leave school, in order to seek other kinds of employment. For the vacation time, from the middle of June until the middle of August, she has already verified that she then could earn something.—Now she has a room together with another pupil, and they cook and keep house together. It cost her last month a little over $8.00—With the inheritance from blessed Aunt Ryffel she is thus now assured again of funds for a whole year or more. [...]

Warm greetings and much thanks from your distant

Otto

Adelaida, March 28th, 1897

Dear Sister Emilie!

The letter containing the check for $600.00, the inheritance from blessed Aunt Ryffel, arrived here last Friday and was for me an extremely joyful, welcome surprise. Yes, I shall think of Aunt Ryffel and also tell the children about her, especially Mimi, when I see her again. [...]

The children often had to complain this winter, and Seline complains often about stomach pains and then eats almost nothing for a couple of days. Last year she said once she had swallowed a little needle, and then Mama often thinks that is what is hurting her, but I don't believe so.—Mama was sick in September with peritonitis, and we had Dr. Steiner here, but after two weeks it was better again. Since New Year she is better and stronger. I myself had a good winter again. I find woolen underwear and good boots are necessary for me in the winter, because I can't stand wet feet and wet clothes.

We milk 11 cows and four more will soon come, yet I keep my hands soft with some tallow, so that I can do the garden work. Alice helps rather enthusiastically, is skilful in fetching cows, preferably on horseback. Recently the horse shied at something at neighbor Maghall's and threw her off. She hit her chin on a stone, which grazed her skin. The horse remained standing by her, and the people bandaged her face, and she brought the cattle home, and in a few days it was fine again. [...]

Otto

In the letter of December 21st, '97, which Seline writes to Otto's father, the topic is the family's state of health:

The ending year has not gone by at our house without trials and misfortune. In June Mattie was sick. Then at the beginning of August Polli came down with it. She had a heavy fever and then after five days she got diarrhea, so that we could do nothing more about it. Finally, when she was quite near death, father went to see the doctor in Paso Robles, who then gave her medicine which soon produced a good effect. After a week she could stand again, then however I came down with it. Very bad headaches and fever, pain in my joints, especially in my neck and down in my spine hurt me so that I could almost not lie down or sit, obviously worn out from taking care of Polli. So for six days I had strong fever and unquenchable thirst in the awful heat. The hottest days of the entire summer, which made the sickness almost unbearable. At times I had faintness and heart attacks, so that for three days I had little hope of recovery, and my concern for my loved ones still almost broke my heart. We had the doctor come, who said these attacks come mainly from the great heat. He gave me medicine, and after a couple of days I already felt a little better but was as weak as never before in my life. At the same time Seline was also sick, only not as seriously as Polli and I, but she also looked emaciated and weak. So we certainly had a regular hospital at our house. We are now again all healthy and well, for which I cannot thank God enough. My rheumatism is now also better, I think, I have sweated it out.

Another misfortune overtook us then on September 24th. At 3 o'clock in the morning one of our houses burned down. A man had a store in it since February. We had the cellar under it, where we kept all milking equipment as well as many supplies of fodder, dried fruit, meat and nearly a hundred pounds of preserved, salted butter beside other fat, fruit, etc. We could save nothing at all. It was already all blazing in bright flames inside when I first saw it. In half an hour everything was burned up. At this time of year, when everything is hot and dry and parched, a wood house easily burns to the ground. The store owner lived with his family in the old mine house. He had insured his store merchandise. We had insured nothing. The lack of wind that night was to be thanked for the fact that our own house and barn were spared. How the fire broke out, we don't know, but we think that mice got into the matches which he had kept in a tin can. In this way many fires have started here.

We have taken apart the old mine house and erected it now on the site of the fire, because we need the cellar for the milk. Naturally we have also had to have it repaired and restored. Of course it also requires new material, new shutters, and tomorrow Otto is going to Cayucos in order to pick up new windows. The house is now safely under cover and the money has run out. […]

"I wish I were on the way back home."

Adelaida, March 11th, 1898

Dear Sister Hanneli!

Your and Emma's letters came today and I always wish it were also not so far and I were on the way back home. I still hope for a more favorable change in my situation here and that the upcoming spring might have its effect again. […]

Yes, it has now been almost 25 years since I said farewell to you and dear father accompanied me to the railroad station. I only knew that the time of my return lay completely in the dark, but I never thought there would be such a great distance between us.—Now, certainly, it would be impossible for me to come home, and I regret on the one hand that you must often be alone there with our sisters, but I am still glad to hear that brother Oskar can often come to visit.

If at any time, one feels in such hours that one should stay closer to one another, but that is not now to be changed.—I now ask you to write as much as you can. Everything interests me, for example, that father still sleeps on the sofa in the room beside the pharmacy.

We have a ten-year-old boy here to raise; a somewhat older brother of his was taken in by a neighbor, and so my wife also wanted to take in an orphan. He is an intelligent boy, we have a three-month probationary period and will then see; his father died and there were six children. […]
                                    Otto

Adelaida, June 8th, 1898

Dear Sister Emilie!

These last months I was much, much in my thoughts back home on the Steinhof and was glad each time that a few lines reported something of my dear father's recovery. Here in California we have had during the last five or six years no really good year. The winter rains, even if sufficient, were cold and not favorable to the growth of our crops, and the April rains, which we must necessarily have for a good year, were sparse or did not come at all. In addition, I know for a fact that often in the eighties, that we had in January and February better fodder for cattle than the last years in March and even in April.

Shall we then have lean years like the Egyptians? It almost seems so. In the meantime we must just do the best we can. Many young people went away, some to Alaska, other, recently being recruited as soldiers. The war[69] had at first favored an increase in the price of groceries, which now however has gone back down. Fat and meat have fallen.

About us ourselves I can say that we had a good winter. The children all go to school with the exception of Polly, who still stays at home, but not much longer. Mimi also is having a hard year, because the way it is, I cannot help her much, and she will try to earn as much as she can during the vacation, but unfortunately it will not be a lot, and she will be disappointed again.—If you have something for her in your savings account and you could and would send it to her the next time, it would help her out a lot. She would have gladly come home, but with the dry year she cannot help us, and she also did not want to just take the exam and be a mere primary school teacher, and so she writes, she wants, if at all possible, to take the whole series of teacher training courses.

We have here a little boy, from an orphan care organization. We had first his younger brother George, now however the older Orlando Albert Padgett, still provisionally on probation. He is not awkward, but small and weak for his 14 years. Little Alice, not yet 12, is significantly stronger and bigger.

Well I shall close, so that the letters will go out tomorrow. Many greetings from us all to everyone at home. Your faithful brother

Otto

I am much plagued with headaches this spring.

Travel Plans.

Adelaida, September 4th, 1898

Dear Father!

It's September again, that month of the year which above all others brings back so many memories.—It begins with the birthday of my first-born, which at the moment makes the clearest imprint on my memory.—The 4th of September, today's date, was anno 1870 in Paris also a Sunday, and I still remember clearly how it was agitated the whole night and how much noise there was in the streets; before daybreak the old gray-beard Bardian, with whom I lived, was

---

[69] Meant is the war of the USA against Spain of 1898, whereby Puerto Rico and the Philippines came under American sovereignty. The USA thus became a world power.

up on his feet, and when I asked upon getting up what was going on, he then shared with me the following, while tears were streaming into his beard.—We are beaten—Sedan—beaten, the Emperor captured, the Empress has fled. The Deputies held council the whole night—Republic declared.—Afterwards, down below in the street there rolled through the Rue Faubourg St. Martin—horses, wagons, cannon and soldiers of all branches of the service, wounded, etc.—in short the ruins of the French army in the most deplorable state. Everywhere the imperial insignia, eagles, were taken down and the tricolor banner was raised.—Well enough of that.

About the dates 7th, 8th and 9th in 85 and 88 I don't want to speak any more, but I do hope that these lines will arrive by September 20th, your birthday, dear father, and thus bring my greetings and best wishes on your 85th birthday, dear father. I would have preferred to come myself, but if it is God's will, I shall be with you on your next birthday or before. My wife is not afraid to be alone for a long time, and there are several good, dependable acquaintances here, two Austrians, who each have their little place of 160 acres and who feel almost at home with us and often help us out. Plus the almost 12 year old Alice is big enough to catch and saddle the horses and to look after the cattle. Because of the dry spell our cattle is already somewhat reduced, and with regular prices we would get rid of even more in the spring, so that the smaller number would be easier kept together. […]

So, dear father, I hope next winter or spring to get away from here. With fewer cows to milk, the children will be able to take care of everything, and for this or that the two Austrians would be there. Also the old man, a neighbor named Dodd, an American, is happy, when he gets a couple of days of work.

I could put my time there to good use and get information about various things, which would come in handy later on.—How and what I would decide then, I cannot really say, but my wife is of the best hope that it would please me so much better there that I would only come back and would sell my property here.

You can sell to the German Mennonites who immigrate here, but that does not work so easily, and this dry year is a big hindrance. In general, the 80s and beginning of the 90s showed a significantly better rainfall than the last five years. […]

        Otto

                                           Adelaida, September 4th, 1898

Dear Sister Emilie!

[…] Mimi is now 20 years old and she will take 2½ more years before she is finished with her studies, but she can now help out in a family, for which she receives her room and board, and that means less costs for myself. The 30 dollars will nearly last her for next year, or until times are better.

Last week I traded 60 hundredweights of hay for three cows and a pig, and I am happy that I thus have more fodder and less cattle to feed. [...]

Yes, if we receive no rain until February like last winter, it would be a bad thing, but usually enough comes in October and November and we hope for the best.—The cows and cattle will probably be worth more in the spring, when the time comes to sell, that is usually in March and April—fat cattle always is.

We are much plagued with herds of horses (and also cattle in smaller number) which break in, jump over fences or come in and drink all our water, not to speak of our fodder. Often four to five such thirsty horses come, which empty the whole trough and drink an astonishing amount of water. Our water is really cool and pure; most people only have a hole with stinking water for the cattle.

There are rather many acorns, good for our pigs. Last week we had ten young ones from two mother pigs.—A lot of fruit is lost. The slight rainfall last winter and the heat makes it fall off, before it is ripe.

Praise God that we all enjoy good health this year, with best greetings from us all, your brother

Otto

Adelaida, September 4th, 1898

Dear Sister Hanneli!

I want to enclose a few more lines to you, although it is late and is becoming rather cool. We paid another visit to German people who have been here for a year and are building themselves a barn and house. They are practical Prussians who have already lived for 20 years in Nebraska, U.S., and to all appearances they are also dependable people.

As I already mentioned, unfortunately we have a dry year and so are being set back somewhat, but besides that, the fire of last fall and building the new house are the two other reasons why we always only spend money and can not make any. I could of course take out a mortgage and go ahead and construct the house and afterwards make the trip, but the interest rate is currently 10–12% and that would cause us hardship for several years; I have great respect from that. Therefore I prefer to postpone the construction of the house for a year, this fall only set in place the windows and doors, and as soon as enough rain has fallen and I have sowed my fields, and the prospects for grass growth and fodder are in order, I could get away for a while.

Now I would need at least a hundred dollars, $100.00, and as soon as I have it, without making any debts or waiting to sell cattle, I could then after enough rain, which should fall in October and November, get away for about 3 to 4 weeks.

I must see that the letter leaves on time. Many greetings

your brother Otto

Father's Death.

Adelaida, November, 1898

Dear Brother!

This afternoon at 2 o'clock I received your telegram which informed me of the departure from this life of our dear father.—So it could not be that I would see him again.—I was worried about him last spring, yet I hoped and hoped he would get well, but when our sister wrote about his shivering in the middle of the day, as well as about his being confined, I then feared for him. Unfortunately I could not have accelerated much my departure, because, first, the year of bad harvest and, against all expectation, not enough rain this fall up until now, keeps me here. [...]

You recently mentioned that I would not be able to chat much more with dear father and would find him changed. I would not have expected that to be otherwise, but quite certainly my presence would have pleased him, and I would have liked so much to give him joy once again. Last spring I tried to imagine how our sisters keep our dear father company and care for him, which certainly was no easy thing for them; you yourself could also devote entire hours to his care, but for myself it would have been nothing but duty and obligation to take on my part of the responsibility. To be sure, the first priority is and was for me to take care of my family here, and in a year like this one that is not at all easy. If we had had a good harvest, then I could have got away in August, filled the barn with hay and the house with provisions. The fire from last fall also makes itself felt because I had to buy so much again, like all equipment for butter making, etc.

Sunday morning.—Last evening I began to write and I have got up because I just couldn't sleep.—The telegram was received in San Luis at 11:24 AM on November 2nd, given to the post there, first came on the third to Paso Robles (which is also a telegraph station), on the fourth to Adelaida, and the postmaster—a Frenchman—did not have the kindness to send it on to me, until I, on Saturday, as usual dispatched my postal affairs. [...]

Otto occupies himself with the question of whether he should sell and back home take over the "Steinhof." He thereby comes to talk about the different ways of managing agriculture:

November 5th, 1898

[...] For myself that is the most unpleasant thing—should I become an apprentice boy again, because farming there or farming or ranching here are very, very different things. I would have to learn everything all over again, do like others and quite especially without horses. Here everything is done with horses, ploughing, sowing, harrowing, then cutting the harvest again, raking, etc. There is relatively little manure, and that is now as dry as dust and will soon be all gone, but unfortunately we do have the dry years, and the seven fat and the seven lean years of the Egyptians can be understood quite well by the Californian.

Otto then individually enumerates the good and the dry years. As possible buyers for his property, Mennonites are a possibility.

Last year a few German families from the state of Nebraska came here, and if it had been a good year, then this year more would have followed; as it is, however, no more came. It is mainly a sect of the Mennonites to which they belong, which wants to do no military service and which emigrated from Germany about 20 years ago, partly to Russia, and which now here has already built its own German church about eight miles from here. If these people settle this land, then the present thieving and unprogressive settlers will certainly eventually have to leave. Yet such years as this cause us to have a relapse, and it will take a half dozen good years to repair the damage. Thus the times here now would be very unfavorable for land sales. [70]

I think it is better to postpone the trip home, perhaps until the harvest, yet I do appreciate your invitation. Within ten days I shall learn more by letter, from Emilie and Hanna. I had letters just four days ago, which mentioned nothing about father's poor health, on the contrary. Well, nothing can be done about that. I often thought after the death of Aunt Ryffel that not much more time would be granted to dear father, and so on Friday you all gave his earthly remains to the depth of the earth, without me being able to be present.—Well he was a good father, may he rest in peace. [...]

Otto

P.S. My wife hopes and wishes very much to go back to Switzerland, and therefore quite agrees that I should come. An Austrian neighbor Nic Millas would sell his cattle and then probably stay here, he has five head.

In a letter of December 14th, 1898, Seline speaks in a very detailed manner about the family's material situation. It is a kind of statement of accounts concerning the donations given them by her father-in-law. Thereby is revealed simultaneously an insight into the circumstances of their home and life:

---

[70] Otto's statements concerning the Mennonites are exact: After the Mennonites, the Dutch branch of the Anabaptists, had settled in Prussia, a portion of them followed the invitation of Catherine the Great to emigrate to the Ukraine. Later (end of the 19th century) a portion of them, because of growing pressure from the Tsar to do military service, moved to Canada and farther on to the USA.

You will have received Otto's letters. I was unwell when he wrote to you. I had strong pains and coughs. Then I got a terrible headache (neuralgia), so that I had to stay in bed until noon every day for a week. Two weeks ago Polli was sick again with erysiplas. However, she is now well again and is jumping around. We did not have a doctor. Yesterday evening I had an accident, while I was throwing a block of wood into the hearth. It slipped out of my hands and fell on the toes of my right foot, which pained me a lot for a while. After I had prepared dinner and fed the calves and pigs, after dinner I checked on my foot, which still hurt me. The middle toes were blue and swollen as well as the ball of the foot. With our homemade ointment I smeared the wounded part, wrapped it up and went to bed.

This morning it was quite fine. I have been walking around the entire morning and have done my work. Now my foot is swollen up over the instep and hurts me a lot; I can hardly walk. It is 5 o'clock, time to cook, but I am not able to feed the cattle. I must leave that to father, who is still out ploughing and sowing and will not come home before night.

Seline and Mattie are bringing the water now. Alice has been in Creston since the beginning of this month.

December 19th. I finally get around to continuing, after I had walked around too much on the next day and really hurt my foot, I had to stay still for two days. Now it is better again. However, I shall have to hobble around for another few days before it is quite well. Last week we had for the first time a little rain, but not enough to make the fodder grow. Ten days ago we had a good cow to die, and yesterday another one, and how the rest of our cattle will do, no one knows. Last winter we already had to give every cent that we could raise for cattle fodder, and now we must already do that again since September, but we shall soon have no more means to get fodder any longer, no income at this time; also in the spring we shall be able to make only a little butter. Yes, these are hard times and the Governor has been asked for help. Food for people and cattle has already been handed over for a cheaper price in our neighboring Montere Cti. [Monterey County].[71] In Paso Robles, a farmer's meeting was called the day before yesterday for the same purposes for giving advice, in order also to help out the needy population in our county. Everyone talks of moving, of looking for a better area. Certainly, I too would like to leave this Egypt land; may the Lord lead me back to the dear old homeland.

However, that we could take over father's homeplace and could make a living off it without an additional source of income, I consider to be impossible according to our present circumstances; we can now at present sell nothing at all; should we wait a couple of years, we can perhaps get 2-3000 dollars, if things go well. We have 370 acres of land and no debts on it. Otto, with a neighbor, has rented a farm adjoining our land, 160 acres. They have now

---

[71] The State of California is divided into counties. Otto lived in San Luis Obispo County, to the north lay Monterey County and to the south Santa Barbara County.

sowed 60–70 acres. Otto has used 80 dollars for seeds and 10 dollars for hay from the travel money which he had. If there is now a good year, he can make something out of it, if the wheat, like now, brings a good price next year.

A thief who always steals our cattle had rented that farm last year, and to get the right-of-way, Otto has taken that over for a year. The owner of this property lives in San Luis.

I find it necessary to inform you about some further details of our circumstances. Since I have been here, dear father had sent us several hundred dollars, but no one should think that I have had much enjoyment from it nor that I have squandered it. With it we have paid nothing but debts, which I would not have helped to make in better times. For the same purpose I have unfortunately also given the last cent of my money here, and we have paid off several more hundred dollars out of our sparse income.

The 500 francs, which dear father had sent us in January two years ago, Mimi alone had used last year. Altogether, her expenses, since she has been away, come to over 200, I think almost 300 dollars. It is obvious that we can no longer afford to send any of the others to the city school. So many thousands of francs have been wasted here years ago, and yet despite that, never has there been any true house or any true barn on the property, which makes me angry the most of all, and I don't see any way at all that we could ever make such improvements.

Nothing, nothing at all, has been done to improve my comfort. We are still in the old cabin, only the frame of the new house has been constructed; since last winter nothing else has been done on it. I have already said so many winters: this is the last winter that I'll spend in this stable. Of course, I am still in it, but this will certainly be the last.

I have used with care for ten years my bake oven, which was in a rusted, miserable condition, like everything else when I arrived here, but now it is so torn up that I can almost no longer correctly bake the bread. My old sewing machine is also worn out, and I must sew by hand or run over to the neighbor, in order to finish long needle work more quickly.

My expenses for myself, since I have been here, are 6 dollars for work dresses and about 10–12 dollars for shoes. My three children, who jump around barefoot almost the whole year and at home wear dresses made of ticking, have not yet cost altogether 30 dollars since they have been in the world. Out of the chickens, for which I likewise have no suitable and well built place (the pigs eat half of the young ones every year), I could never make much money at all up to now, 20–30 dollars a year, besides what we need for ourselves from the spring until fall, the eggs are always cheap, 8–10 cents per dozen. Then we eat them ourselves.

December 26th. The holy Christmas is already past, without me finishing this letter, and, like every year, so this year great anger and annoyance have not been spared me. I have spent two Christmas holidays here in peace and pleasant company since I have been here. With God's help may this holiday bring me salvation in this world. It is here the custom to honor the sacred Christmas Day with the drinking of alcoholic beverages. Otto also usually finds the opportunity for that, if not in the tavern, then at the house of a Ticinese compatriot, whom I hate most. With a heavy heart I sometimes look back over these last ten years, to which through hard work I have sacrificed my last best energy, and nothing remains for me except the consciousness of the faithful fulfillment of duty and the prospect of hard times in my old age. I cannot conceal this fact: the question whether I should still stay here much longer has already preoccupied me for some time, especially in consideration of my three still little children, whom I would like to know were well cared for in the event of my death, because my health worries me a lot.

Man thinks, yet God rules, I think again in the firm confidence that all trials only serve to make us the best human beings possible.

At the end of the year we send all our best wishes for happiness and blessings, and may God let his grace flow over us all there and also here in the New Year. Many warm greetings from us all,

Your Seline Wyss

In the letter of January 13ʰ, 1899 to his sister Hanna, Otto explains the reasons why a return to Switzerland and taking charge of the Steinhof are no longer an option for him. The text underscores how small his father's agricultural operation was, which had to be managed beside his extensive medical practice. However, it also illuminates the social and psychological dilemma in which emigrants found themselves after so many years in the new homeland.

Adelaida, January 13th, 1899

Dear Sister Hanneli!

[…] For me the question of a return home is a question of existence—here I have in normal years a good income and in good years I make some profit, whereas in one such as '98 you of course lose money—it is that way now, but that is the only off year I have had in 22 years.

Of how much land does our home consist [Steinhof in Otelfingen]? As best I recall, approximately as follows:

In front of the house, garden and orchard together about	2 jucharts
Behind the house, the orchard in the stony acres	1½ jucharts
Down on the road, toward Büel	½ juchart
On the Würenloser Strässli, Dreizipfel	½ juchart
Meadows toward Ötlikon—in Aargau	2½ juchart
In addition some woodland, also in the Ct. of Aargau, how much I don't know	
Total	7 juchart

In good years that yields hay for one cow, but I shall calculate I could make enough for two cows with clover, etc. and some potato land.—But I don't see how I could meet the needs of my wife and myself from this.—Enlarge the garden and plant some more vegetables, but for larger shipments of vegetables, the freight charge to Zurich is already significant, and the trains do not always go direct.—In order to get by, I should have at least six to eight cows and hire some one for the haymaking season. Also a horse would be all the more necessary for me since I could no longer take care of everything with hand work and cows.

March 14th. It is raining, and your letter has just arrived, which you posted in Örlikon and I want to finish writing mine right away. As I told you, I can calculate how and what I want, it won't work.—Last year here and the winter this year brought so little rain that almost everybody wants to sell and move up north. Under such circumstances you can and could not sell here, except if you gave it away very cheap. There are no buyers, not even at ridiculously low prices. I am sure I would regret going back home to Europe, and I have also spoken with many Ticinese acquaintances who went back to Europe with their families, but came back here in a few years and explained they were no longer satisfied over there in Europe. That is exactly what I fear, that I would come home and could not buy and build this and that, in order to make it profitable, and then I would bitterly and discontentedly regret ever having sold my present little place and home for a ridiculously low price. No, it is better for me to stay here.—On the one hand we really have an often dry climate, but on the other hand we never suffer from cold and long winters, and with a better house and better stables for the cattle you can make yourself more comfortable and make the work more profitable.

So sell our homeplace, it is better so.—On the hill up there, where six of my loved ones sleep, will one day be a little resting place for me as well.—If possible, however, I shall come home someday for a visit.—I'll close for this evening, thank God it is raining. […]

Otto

Adelaida, February 14th, 1899

Dear Sisters Hanneli and Emilie!

We have all received your letters and little packages, on the 10th of this month also the funeral sermon. I have not shown the enclosed letter to Otto. I knew that he would go wild over it, because I have told you about his drinking problem. I have read the funeral sermon twice with the thought: Might all parents be aware of their duty to maintain a good reputation, which endures beyond the grave, to serve as a model for their children, to their honor and blessing.

Yesterday also arrived the third package "for everyone" which I always really like to read. I find much consolation and many recollections in it. The

Bürkli newspaper always comes regularly and naturally we like to read it, but we would not have expected for you to pay for it. You have a lot of trouble and expenses with us. My warm thanks for everything, if I could only pay you back somehow for your trouble and goodness.

At present Mimi gives me a lot to think about. A letter from her on the third of this month tells us that she, as usual, again ended a term in January, but with bad results. At the beginning of January she was still sick with measles and could not go to school for two weeks. She says she passed only her reading exam. All other subjects must be repeated. Mimi thinks, if only she could borrow 2-3000 dollars and rent another room, that she would have all her problems solved. She could then pay back the money when she becomes a teacher; she would be through in 2-2½ years. As long as she must pay for her food, she can only slowly progress and perhaps never pass her exams. There are those who study with borrowed money. Our teacher last year had done his studies that way. However, there are others who study 1-2 years and then they practice teach as primary school teachers; they then go back and study until they finish. To be sure, those who possess no state license have to first pass a pretest, which takes place in every county twice annually in January and June.

Those who can pass this test then receive a school position for two years, and then they must go back and take the test again. They are also more demanding now than earlier, because there will soon be enough teachers. I always thought Mimi should also do it this way. She always fears she couldn't do it, and wants to continue to study, and as long as her father can scrape together the money, he lets her, as always, have her own way. My opinion is: practice is better than study, and there will probably not be much more left over for her, because to borrow money for this purpose would be a dangerous thing for us to do. I have now already worked hard for ten years to pay off debts which I did not help to make, and now I am sick and tired of it. That is a thankless and annoying task. Naturally it would be an unfortunate thing for us if Mimi had to stop now, after she has already cost us three hundred dollars.

Father had written to her, what, I don't know, and I am expecting an answer from her, would like to see what she says. In general I consider the affair to be somewhat of a mistake, and I had sometimes brought father's attention to the fact that Mimi was not born to study. But each time I received only rudeness and curses, when I talked about this subject. I was only permitted to save and to work, so that he could spend the money in a really unpractical way. I shall also soon report about everything in greater detail. Now I do not have much time.

The children must soon go back to school, and I still have so much to sew. New Year's Day had brought us rain; on the 14th and 15th of January it rained again, and afterwards everything began to grow beautifully. At the beginning of February we had cold nights and warm days, and now we need rain once again; hopefully it will soon come. People are almost anxious about a dry year again.

There is not yet much fodder, but we have so far lost no more cattle, and I think and hope that there is no more danger of that. We can only use the skins of the dead cattle. The rest gives pig fodder. A cowhide brings 1½-2 dollars. In the direction of the coast, when otherwise at this season there is enough fodder, there is now almost even less than here. Cattle perish there in large numbers.

Seline Wyss

Adelaida, March 16th, 1899

Dear Sister Emilie!

Your dear letters all arrived, also the obituary and writings in memory of dear father are all nice and we like to read them. But the big question, do you all want to come home, is very difficult to answer and for a long time will remain an impossibility. I shall soon write more about it to brother Oskar and also take this opportunity to inform you that you would do better to sell and not to wait for us. If I had known 10 years ago, I could have sold my property much better, because the 80s were all good, with enough rainfall, whereas 1894 and 1898 are among the worst in the entire history of California, and for that reason California estates are little sought after by speculators and such who want to buy farms. [...]

In San Luis Obispo last week two banks and in Paso Robles one bank suspended their payments, and in such times you are then also happy that you have nothing in the bank, you will certainly agree.

[...] Alice is coming with the horse and wants to go to the post office, and so I shall close and write more soon. In conclusion much thanks for the trouble you have taken on our account and perhaps I shall come home someday to stay.

In the meantime greetings from us all with love your brother

Otto

A small sheet of paper with notes from Otto Wyss lies between the letters. In them Otto expresses reservations concerning Seline. She seems to have been clumsy in the store business, in that she often made mistakes in her accounts; she refused to milk cows and tolerated Mimi's cheerfulness poorly.

It has been eleven years since my wife came to California, and I want to consider what we have done in this time and have not done.

At first I planned to run the store business again, because that would have maintained the value of this land at a much higher level and made it easier to sell.—At that time I had to be away from home much more on business and so allowed my wife and Mimi to take care of the business. However, Mimi was often sent for the cattle or to the kitchen or for this or that, and I soon found that Mrs. Wyss did not know how to manage a business. Butter, eggs and this or that are always being paid for, and there you must just check the prices in the newspaper and as much as possible add them up quickly in your head, and she just could not do this. She always made mistakes in the account books which were to our detriment. Weighing something on the scales was always an uncertain thing with her, and to this day she has still not learned to weigh something precisely and exactly. When she weighed coffee or something else half a pound too much, she wanted to give a good weight. I came home in the evenings and saw what was written down, or I would say, for example, sugar is going down, and you have sold it for cash, oh I have sold dollars to X, is it not recorded?—but it was not, and so I quite often saw that smaller and bigger entries were forgotten and especially that we were losing money.

Once I came home and said,—what, you have given credit to Soberanes, the shabby Spaniard, for almost ten dollars worth of underclothes, shirts, handkerchiefs, pants, etc.? He measured 6 feet and could speak pretty good English—she thinks more of tall people than short guys and he had let her know that he had money but could not exchange it, etc.—naturally we never again saw horse nor rider.

So for better or worse I had to give up the store, and I can't even think of reapplying for the post office.—That's the way it is.

Then I began to milk cows, but when I had to go away for a day, I had to hire somebody to help out and—pay them well, often a dollar—Mrs. Wyss could of course have helped out, but there I put my foot down.—She did not come to California to milk cows. Now she helps by feeding the calves quite regularly, even when they only drink out of the bucket. She also often makes these last years two or three rolls (2½ pounds) of butter, as long as we milk only a few cows, she now skims almost all the milk..

She always treated Mimi as though she were her godmother, why?—Mimi is a Sunday child and always had a merry personality. When she hears a song twice, she then sings the same song at work. While washing and doing all kinds of things, she sang her songs.—She was called frivolous, and dear father and sister Emilie themselves had once in their letters made a contemptible remark about Mimi. Once I came home one winter evening around nine o'clock and found Mimi crying by the stable—her mother didn't want to let her in the house until she found the cows and she had looked as long as she could see, but now at night—there was no moonshine—she could no longer walk. There was a pretty rough scene in the house—because when I get angry, I am not nice. In short, things did not go well until I sent Mimi away to school in Oakland, and then I had to make some money when I had to send Mimi a few dollars for shoes, clothes and so forth, yet, praise God, she has remained a good child.

And again Otto comes back in the letters to the question of a return to Switzerland. Again and again he presents his reasons for a refusal. So in the letter of May 28th, 1899 to his brother:

Adelaida, May 28th, 1899

My Dear Brother!

The day before yesterday arrived your dear letter of the 9th, and I certainly know I should have already written long ago. I wanted to get information in order to present all the reasons why I could not come home, because on the one hand my wife always wanted to go back, and secondly I would have done such a thing for my dear sisters who had so faithfully cared for dear blessed father for many years; but—I just can't do it. The Steinhof with its memories is dear and valuable to me, but with the surrounding fields, it still represents quite a big amount of capital, more than I could receive for my 20 times bigger property here, and so I would be tormented by the interest. Aside from the fact that I would have to learn farming there all over again, I could not count on the assistance which I have here in terms of horses and machines which alleviate so much manual labor, and in general over there it would be too crowded for me.

Here I know I can get provisions and everything necessary for my family and at the end of the year, after a good harvest, even save some money, but I just don't know whether I could do that over there.—I know there would be more work for me, early and late, whereas here we never get up early, and whereas there is always something to do here, there is still less of the constantly hard work.

For the children the prospects of finding employment later on are also better here, because first of all there is more opportunity for the employment of women in many fields. Two-thirds to three-fourths of the school teachers are girls and women, and they are striving to get for women the same employment and the same jobs for the same pay.

Here on my farm I have enough space if I want to hunt, like hares and partridges, and I can forbid it to anyone else; over there in Europe the right to hunt belongs to the State, and I would have to buy this privilege with a hunting license.—Unfortunately dry seasons are perhaps somewhat more common here than over there, yet with irrigation and the construction of barns for hay and straw, most problems can still be taken care of, which however does take time. The fact that every now and then cattle are stolen or something elses goes wrong cannot be so quickly helped, but new and better people are always coming here, and as soon as the latter are in the majority, it will drive away the worse element.

January 2nd.—Today it has stormed the entire day, and tonight is still the same. I got wet feet, which I can't stand as well as I used to.

The Steinhof has also occupied my thoughts a lot. Naturally as long as dear father lived, he was best off on the Steinhof in the faithful care of our dear sister. But with his departure from this life it is quite lonely for our sisters, and it is only good if no fear plagues them. I often thought, can you then find no tenant who could live there, could cultivate the land, keep one or two cows and a couple of pigs etc, and also earn a daily salary. In the summer, he could easily receive 5 francs per day, and that would be as much as here. Such a man would fertilize the soil more in his own interest, stables and everything which is used looks better, but for buyers you must wait, especially when the times are not favorable. The war will also damage a bit the economy, there as well as here.

It was in the winter of 1884 when blessed Ottilie and I discussed together whether and under which circumstances we could travel home and eventually take over the Steinhof. Our store business and our post office went well, new people came into the neighborhood, cattle had a good price, and at that time we could have sold and kept four to five thousand dollars in our pocket. We agreed that, if we could take along 10,000 dollars, then educate our children in the schools over there, we could arrange the Steinhof to hold 7 to 8 cows and make and sell butter ourselves on commission. Naturally more meadow grass would have been necessary, as well as buying clover and other fodder.—Everything would first have to be moved out to make room for the cows and their product, in addition to a few pigs and chickens; secondly, Ottilie had more aptitude than Seline. We often read together; I read out loud, and then we would discuss what we had read on the long winter evenings.—We calculated that in this way we could make the Steinhof make a profit, quite especially through the utilization of the barn and stables, and we didn't need to work ourselves to the bone any more here in California, among the thieves and rogues of all nations, but rather in the beautiful homeland—because it is beautiful there like nowhere else on God's dear earth, But "man thinks ... " […]

Seline would like to go back home to Switzerland: "My wife is still not assimilated here," writes Otto, and he continues: "Young people take the region the way it is."

Adelaida, November 12th, 1899

Dear Sister Hanneli!

I must write to you separately because of money matters, because of the $100 which you sent me last year to pay for my return home. With the unexpectedly sudden death of dear blessed father, I spent it otherwise. $20 for taxes, $50 for wheat seed and the rest for hay for the cattle, which at that time was $20 per ton or 5 francs per 100 pounds.—Now with the wheat that should all be paid back, but Mrs. Wyss has hired a carpenter and absolutely wants to finish the new house.—I can't see that I could pay it back this year, but I would like to ask your permission to keep it longer and then to be allowed to use it for Mimi. I shall pay it back with 8 or 10% interest, if you so wish.

You see, this is the way it is: Mimi must still have money to finish her studies, altogether $200, and Mama, Mrs. Wyss, does not want to help her any more and will not let me help, plus there is business to take care of, as always. That makes it hard for me to raise money, and therefore I must ask you to help me out again with Mimi.—I thought of writing to Oscar, but since I already owe you anyhow, it will all go into one bill.

I ask you, if possible, to send me another 100 dollars for Mimi. I personally vouch for the fact that Mimi will pay it back in 2 to 3 years, after she can earn a salary.—Even so I shall later wish a declaration from you that I should spend the $110 with interest on Mimi.

Mrs. Wyss really is no business woman and in such matters is more than ordinarily ignorant. [...]

Otto

The Klau Gentlemen Come into the Picture.

Adelaida, August 6th, 1900

My Dear Brother!

It has already been a while, since the hundred dollars came right in the nick of time, and I was so happy about it, for Mimi.

I thank you most sincerely and shall see that it is paid back to you with interest as soon as Mimi earns something. She had recently written that she has been advanced into the upper, Senior Class, but that she is very poorly provided with clothes, underclothes, etc. and was happy that the summer vacation was coming, which lasts until the beginning of September.

For a long time Mrs. Wyss has begrudged every dollar, even every dime, which I have sent to Mimi, and quite especially for that reason I am thankful to you for the assistance.—We ourselves could certainly not complain if we did not have much cattle to sell. Three head brought 80 dollars, previously 90 dollars—also butter was 15–18 cents a pound; we still milk 14 cows.

Naturally the new house, furniture, painting, carpentry has cost a lot, and she still speaks about a new sewing machine, oven etc., it is almost never over. These past few days she gave $2.50 to a quack for salve to rub into her joints.

The world wants to be deceived, especially my wife. If some guy comes along with ammonia wash, camphor and turpentine and a couple of drops of sistoel and praises its worth in curing arthritis and rheumatism, she instantly buys some charesalbi [smear fat for wagon wheels] for $2.00 with a couple of drops of creosot for 50 cents, liquorice and vinegar for coughs—landamin and peppermint for cholic. I gladly buy her some ogodeloc and spirits of camphor, and that is the simplest and best remedy for Gsüchter [collective word for rheumatism, arthritis, etc.]. I know that from my blessed grandmother—and one knows what one has. [...]

Klau Mine, near Otto's farm. First called Manhattan, then Sunderland Mine.

The quicksilver mine, which was closed in anno 1877, that is, no longer worked, is finally again in operation. At the suggestion of others, I rented[72] it for three years, and it is going well, six to seven men work there, and the last two weeks around 350 dollars in silver were produced.—On our property are two others which are looking for quicksilver. They are digging a shaft, are 65 feet deep now and will deliver to us 10% of the product, everything at their own expense.

Then there are also 12 Chinese on our place, who make 400,000 bricks for a German company, Karl Klau Quicksilver Company.

An Adolf Klau has bought the neighboring quicksilver mine for 50,000 dollars, and they are making the bricks in order to build a big oven for the burning of quicksilver ore of great quantity.

The Klau gentlemen speak fluent German. One was with his wife in Zurich two years ago; she has already been here too.—They are Jews, but they do have money. We receive 40 dollars for the clay for the bricks, the Chinese buy our eggs and young chickens etc. So eventually will come a better market for everything people have to sell. Many of my neighbors ask when I shall take over the post office again and shall open a business, but with a Madame Wyss such a thing is totally out of the question. She has absolutely no use for a

[72] "Leased" is probably what is meant.

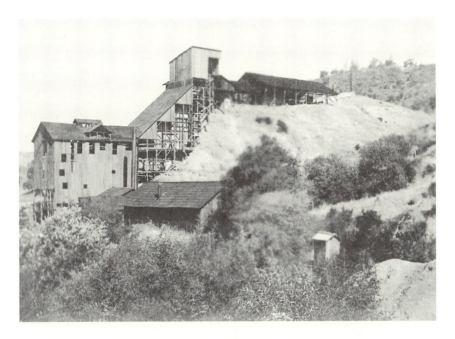

Detail of Klau Mine.

business and even less use for a post office, therefore I shall just let sleeping dogs lie. […]

Otto

"You would never regret a trip here."

Adelaida, October 30th, 1900

My Dear Sister Hanneli!

I have written to you so little, and yet since the departure from this life of our dear blessed sister Emilie, I have so often thought of you. I also wondered, what is going on now with sister Hanneli.

Even earlier, I had always thought that the big house back home is rather a burden, because it needs more and more repairs, and the upkeep is always more expensive than on a small house, all the more so when a young man cannot still partly take care of the repairs himself. When then brother Oskar announced the close of the sale of the house last spring, I was very happy, despite the fact that I had to tell myself it was now still the home of our youngest sister, our Hanneli.

At the time when you receive these lines, you will thus leave it, and I often ask myself if you have another home in mind. I must admit, at brother Oskar's house every space is filled, also another livelihood not so easily available.—At sister Emma's house it is also overfilled.

And at my house here in California, there is of course a lot of and enough space, and also a lot to do, but people here don't rush with anything. People take their time.—it is of course so far away, then you learn the language rather easily.—Should you decide to pay us a visit, you would have to extend it to a year, and then it is best to see whether and how you could fit into our life.

You will ask, what on earth could I do in California, and I well know that one feels best when one has his own independent livelihood.—Our old stone building stands empty; it only needs some groceries and dry goods to open up again.—The post office will definitely come back to our neighborhood within the year, because in the neighboring Klau mine a lot of work is done, 20-25 men now and if the great smelting furnace is built in six to eight months, up to 200 men are supposed to work there. That will give us again some lively times; money is also not lacking, because the price of quicksilver is still rising. 12 Chinamen have just finished baking 430,000 bricks on my place for the smelting furnace of the mine.

We thus expect and hope for better times ahead and if you could decide to make the big trip, you would also find in the children much joy and entertainment. Polly and Mattie would have no rest until Aunt rode after the cows on their horse Frank. Alice and Seline would sing with you and would chat with you in the purest Züridütsch. [...]

I believe, if you could decide to pay us a visit and went back home after a year, you would never regret the trip, but if the children and the area pleased you, perhaps you would make your home here with us and say yes there are good people everywhere, and people have more space, there are better sources of livelihood open, and where you find that, you often remain.

I hope and wish to pay another visit to the old homeland, but before Mimi comes back home from school, I cannot even think about it.

I close with greetings from us all, your faithful brother
                                            Otto

                                    Adelaida, March 6ᵗʰ, 1901
Dear Sister Hanneli!

I already received your card a week ago, and now I finally want to take some time again to write, in order to fulfill your request. We have all received the little package, for which I warmly thank you. I am very happy with the stocking wool. I had already used up my old wool this winter, and now I again have enough for next winter. I use it mainly for father and for myself. The children here don't use many wool stockings, because it is not so cold here, and they jump around almost always barefoot. The cotton material is quite beautiful, you get none such here.

We have sent Mimi her things. As far as I know, she goes to school. She has rented a room and cooks for herself.

The newspapers (for everyone) have all arrived, and it is every time a spiritual refreshment for me to read these in the couple of hours of rest on Sunday afternoon or at night. That you do feel homesick in your home sometimes I can certainly conceive, although you are now no longer alone in the house; but strangers are just not like your own family. You will not lack for work if you have another garden to take care of. But work is also the best pastime.

We now have plenty of work to do again; after a wet winter, the spring seems to be coming quite fast. It has been rather warm for a week. Otto finished plowing and sowing a couple of days ago, and he is now beginning to plant the garden. This year we shall again have enough water for the garden. We have 14 cows to milk and 19 calves to feed. The children can now help a lot.

This morning Mattie had an accident after she had milked a cow, and as she was bringing the pail full of milk into the house, she was pierced a little by the horn of another cow which had a calf last night. She fell down and dropped the pail full of milk (everything spilled). She cried, but recovered from the shock.—Last Monday she had begun school again, and so now the children must get up again earlier. Because I no longer can get up first, Alice usually makes the fire and sets out the morning meal, the oat meal on the oven, and then she helps with the milking, and Seline cooks until I come. Polli and Mattie must also help to feed the chickens and to milk. Over the winter father has left the fire in the morning as long as there was vacation.

It has been going better again for a few weeks; the Lord always gives me much patience and strength, in order to keep quiet. If only my limbs were better. Last week I again had much pain in my arms, as soon as it is better, then I exert myself too much again, so I never get over it. This week it is better again, but this morning I have made butter, and now my right arm hurts me again, as I am writing these lines. I have medicine to take for rheumatism; it is good, but naturally if one does not take good care of oneself, the medicine cannot help much. Last month I turned 49, and am still not over the bad time.

In our region it is always pretty lively. The big quicksilver mine is not yet in operation; they are still building it; there are many workers and construction people there. A store is also there now.

In our old mine things went slowly for a while; the continuing rainy weather hindered the work, but now they are back at work. The times are now pretty good here; all businesses are doing well, and the farmers also have prospects for a better year again. The cattle have a good price, better than in a long time. We have already sold a couple of cows and slaughter cattle for over 200 dollars.

Butter is already rather expensive, 15–18 cents per pound. Eggs 10 cents. Everything is beautifully green, and flowers bloom on the meadows, every day the children bring home a bouquet. I must close for now. Tomorrow I must go to Paso Robles with butter and bring home some things. I hope that these lines find you in good health, and I also await much news from you.

Many greetings from all and from your
Seline Wyss

Looking for Mussels at the Beach.

In the introduction Otto reports about the good accomplishments of his daughter as a pupil, about the successful harvests and then goes into the details about the completion of the new house:

July 17th, 1901

The house is finished, painted inside and out, the kitchen is whitewashed, carpets, floors, ceilings, in the living room and visitors' room carpets, but in the living room I don't like carpets, because there come the barefoot children and rub their feet in it, also chickens, cats and dogs (seldom) come inside and the carpet quickly gets and remains old and dirty. A well constructed and oiled wooden floor is much better—and cleaner.

I am building a new and bigger barn and shall have a dry roof over the heads of at least the cows which we milk. [...]

Since last year the old neighboring Santa Cruz Mine has been acquired and worked by a German Company—Karl Klau Q.S. Company.—That is not the Mahoney which lies near here, but rather the bigger one 20 minutes southwest of here. They have constructed many buildings, a big smelting furnace, etc., and are going deeper, where they then also find good ore. About 40 men work there, later probably more. I have leased the nearby mine, where I was earlier, and have given it to others, so that it will yield me a little profit. There is enough ore here, but it is not very rich, so that it only yields a little over the expenses.

Nevertheless the nearby mine shows that, if operated on a large scale, it can be made profitable. I now own all the most valuable adjacent land between both mines, and if a good price were offered me for the whole thing, I would then not think long about it and sell. Besides that, there arises another question: Should I take over the post office again? The superintendent of the Klau mine wanted to have a post office there, but it was refused him. The reason, there was no space, everything was too crowded. Now, however, the Germans who have come to this neighborhood would like to establish a post office in the vicinity, 4 miles or about 5½ kilometers from here, and I am thinking about applying again to be postmaster of the Adelaida Post Office.—I would have to and could rely on Alice to help me, because Mrs. Wyss is hated by so many people that I was told I must keep her away from the post office. It is strange, but when she has a prejudice against certain people, there is nothing good in them, whereas she is then friendly to others who do not in the slightest deserve her trust.—She seldom listens to reason.

The children seek to make a trip to the beach, before school begins again on August 5th.—So the plan is to go from here to Cambria on July 30th and stay at the beach until noon, then go fishing or hunting for clams or mussels, then go in the evening to a Ticinese acquaintance, where I shall buy calves and shall stay overnight. On the next day we shall drive about three hours to Morro Rock, along the sandy coast, set up a camp on the beach there and the next day we shall come back home with our two horses and Bernese buggy—that is what we plan to do.

I certainly feared that you would not be able to decide to pay us a short or longer visit.—If the circumstances here eventually permit me to partially or completely sell my property, my first trip would be a visit to Switzerland. [...]

Mimi could only help temporarily, and as she wrote me sometime back, she has been seeing young Mr. van Horn, who has been taking her out riding and has taken her on a visit to see his mother. So perhaps she will find in a few years her own home, here she was always a thorn in the eye of her stepmother. The people here knew the merry, singing child with the smiling face, who, always chattering, knew everybody everywhere, and next to her Mrs. Wyss was only perceived with scorn. You mustn't forget, it is certainly no different in Otelfingen, the old blessed smith, Meier, once said to me: you of course were born here, but your father is only a small farmer--, at the time I did not understand such things yet.

Here I belong to the oldest settlers, and recently in San Luis Dr. Norton presented me to others as the father of the Adelaida community.

It is now July 19th, and I shall stop writing so that the letter leaves on time. Recently a newspaper representative was here and took a photo of the house and family, and three copies have just arrived. I am pleased to be able to send one to you, and if I can receive more, then I'll send brother Oskar and sister Emma one each later. You will please show these to them. It shows our new house—on the other side of the street from the old. We had just finished that morning with milking the cow, Polly has a puppy, the others small kittens. Alice is holding the big cat, everyone in work clothes. Under the porch (veranda) sits Fred, the carpenter, who is working on the barn, in front of him, in the shade, the dog Mops. In the background the big evergreen live oak. The little barrels for the rainwater under the gutter, a couple of sunflowers, peppermint, blue lilacs in the foreground. [...]

Otto

Mimi is old enough to be dating men. Seline first thanks her relatives for the received things, among others for the "prize pictures" which will decorate the

*walls. Then—as usual—follows a report concerning the state of the cultivations
and the cattle raising.*

                                                      Adelaida, April 22nd, 1902

Dear Sister Hanneli!

[…] The children are all going to school, and besides that they must go after
the cattle and help do the milking. Alice helps me with washing. Seline can
also already help regularly, she is willing. Mimi has been engaged since last
summer, met a George van Horn; in German: (von Horn). I know nothing
further about him, only as she describes him, he has no defects. Mimi says he
has a house east of San José. His parents and his siblings are also there. He
always works with the farmers. Of course, she has never asked any of us if we
are pleased with her decision, not even her father, let alone her stepmother. She
had written a year ago that she thought she was old enough to date men. She
even made a remark about being an old maid, but she did not think of the fact
that she is too old to go to school. I think she has had a relationship with him
for a long time. When she was at home in the summer three years ago, she
always talked to me about marrying. She told me she would never marry
someone who drank; she had seen enough of that. I told her she was certainly
right, but as long as she was going to school, she had no business thinking
about marriage, or she should stop studying. Afterwards she stopped talking
about this topic.

   She still went to school until last March; then her eyes got so bad that the
optician told her she would have to have an operation if she did not stop
studying. And in February the teacher told her she was very behind in the
teaching of the English language, and she would have to study for at least a
year (that is, until next year in June) before she could take her exams. That has
finally worn her out, as well as her father. So, as far as I can tell from her last
letter, she has to pay the accounts and other things, over 50 dollars. She has
been going to see doctors for two years, dentists, opticians, and others. Last
summer on vacation she had diphtheria; that cost 52 dollars. In September she
again got an abscess on her right cheek, which the doctor had to cut out.

   She had now rented a room for a year and cooked for herself. To be sure,
it has unpleasantly upset her father that she had to give up her studies. He has
always thought that he could still force her to bear the name of teacher, and I
have always told him, Mimi will never be a teacher! When he wanted to send
her to Normal School, I told him, you can now have Mimi study, and then you
must also prepare her dowry. And that is what has happened, because I
certainly knew that in the choice of a husband she is not at all exact. She said
in the next to the last letter, her friends in San José have already told her for a
long time: you would do better to get a job and work, you will never be a
teacher, why are you trying that anyway, and Mrs. Colvards (at whose home
Mimi worked for food) always told her: you would do better to get a job and

work; you will never become a teacher. But she has never told us such things before. To be sure, she will again justify herself, because Mimi is never embarrassed to make excuses. She wrote in her last letter, she doesn't think that she has done anything wrong, because she now has as much education as any reasonable person needs. She could make herself useful in her surroundings. I don't personally see that such a lengthy education is necessary for poultry-farming, which is the occupation of most women around here (and Mimi also has this prospect). Now she complains she has had to work too hard beside the schoolwork. If you could give only the stepmother the blame for that, Mimi has now cost almost 1000 dollars. I think it would now be better if she had two-thirds of that in her pocket. [...]

Many warm greetings from us all. Your sister-in-law

Seline Wyss

A Wedding without the Stepmother.

In her letters Seline informs us of many human destinies, "faits divers," which are often tragic, for example, the destiny of the old Morton:

Adelaida, December 10th, 1902

Dear Sister Hanneli!

[...] At our house we never at all lack for changes, one way or another. Two weeks ago Otto had to go to San Luis to the hospital in order to visit the old Mr. Morton,[73] about whom I have already made mention in my letters. He is always knocking on our door. About four weeks ago he drove from here to the coast (Cayucos) with his young stallion. On the road the horse probably shied a little, and Morton was thrown out of the carriage and severely wounded in the head. He was picked up unconscious and taken to the County hospital. The hospital doctor informed us of the incident, and so Otto went there. Morton then wanted to come home with him, which naturally was not allowed to happen. That was all I needed, to take care of sick people besides my heavy amount of work. He is being cared for in the right place. Last week he then wanted to slit his throat with his pocket knife. He was found outside his house in a pool of blood, which is what the hospital director informed us. He is now better again. [...]

Then she comes to speak of Mimi's wedding, which she did not attend, which she really could not attend because both adults could not be absent for a long time from home. But Seline's letter also shows her deep ill-feelings:

---

[73] Morton Waterman, born 1827 in New Hampshire, married Martha Griffith in 1884 in Las Tablas.

Last Friday, the 5th, Otto again went to San José, in order to attend Mimi's wedding, so I am again alone with my three children. Alice has already been over at Mimi's for a long time. This wedding has already cost almost a year's worth of writing and preparation. Not to mention money, about which I am allowed to know nothing. In June Mimi had changed her job to a new job where she found the work less stressful and earned 25 dollars per month, with rich people. They have a Chinaman as cook. She stayed there until November 6th.

Since last winter she had always written about her upcoming wedding and had made plans for it. In the summer she wrote that Mrs. Edwards had invited her to get married and to have her wedding reception in her house. I certainly noticed what all this writing meant, but because I never had anything to say about her activities, but was only asked to work! I decisively resolved to mix myself up in no way in her wedding affairs. And for that reason I invited neither Mimi nor her bridegroom to celebrate the wedding here. That extremely angered her and angered even more her father, who has never yet denied her a single wish, and even if it should cost house and home.

If she had come uninvited, of course, I would not have sent her away, but she did not want to do that either. So then at the end of August, she had decided to marry in San José. Another reason why I was so stubborn in this matter is this: the last time she was at home, she had behaved rather falsely and rudely toward me. I shall not forget it so soon. [...]

Then the topic changes to Alice. Should she likewise go away to a higher school, as Mimi and her father plan? Seline opposes the idea; she fears that the girl could be "spoiled" away from home, and she temporarily still needs her help at home.

My nephews' wives all tell me I should not let Alice leave. She is now a nice child. If she leaves, she will just be spoiled. I then asked Alice whether she was planning to go to school. She said no, she wanted to stay at home and help out until her younger sisters were somewhat bigger, and then maybe next year take a six month business course, as many do here. I have nothing against that. Since June she has no longer gone to school here; a year ago Alice received the diploma for grammar school. Then she went to school for a year, but she can no longer go here.

Now I must come back once again to the slyly-made plans of father and Mimi. I sent Alice at the end of August to Breston on a visit; she had already been planning to go for a long time. She remained three weeks over there, and then father drafted another plan.

It then happened that a neighbor's daughter of the same age, Ida Goetschi, a German (she is two miles from here), went to San Francisco to see some relatives. She invited Alice to travel with her to San José, and since Alice had never been on the train, I said she should better go; she also agreed with that.

So they went with one another, on Sunday, October 13th, and on the previous day Alice spent almost the whole day crying. Miss Goetschi came back after two weeks, and she said, Alice had cried on the train; she had not wanted to go. In the first letter Alice wrote that Mimi and her bridegroom were different from one another. He didn't talk much, was tall, 6 feet, and slim and Mimi was short and fat and talked a lot. She says she thinks he is a good man. The mother is no longer living. The father had a homestead in San José but the bank took everything. I must then hear what else Alice says.

She has written everything. George is adding another kitchen onto the house and must put everything in good condition before the wedding. It is Wednesday today, and I have just received a letter from Alice, that father and she will arrive Thursday morning in Paso Robles, where they expect one of us with horses and a wagon in order to come home. So tomorrow I shall send a man there. He lives with his family in our old house. He works in the mine.

The old Morton died a week ago in the hospital. In the morning I'm going with father to Paso Robles to buy some necessities and something for Christmas. The children have already chopped down the tree yesterday. God willing.

Seline Wyss

"Things are looking better at Mimi's than expected."

San José, August 10th, 1903

Dear Sister Hanneli!

Two weeks have gone by since I sent you the card, and I did not get around to writing as long as I was in San Francisco. I got on the train on August 24th at half past eight in the morning in Paso Robles and then got off at half past two in San José, where Mimi picked me up. Alice had written her that I was going to the city, and then she asked me to visit her, which I now did. I naturally also was wondering how it looked in her home.

As far as her housekeeping is concerned, I am pretty content; it looks better than I would have expected. She keeps everything pretty clean and is, as far as I can tell, really thrifty with money. She lives happily with her husband. He is good-natured and active, and that is good. He must go to work every day, if they want to get ahead and save something. She finds that it costs a lot when you must buy everything. They have just the house here and a little garden and a shed where they put the little wagon. Mimi says that are planning to sell here. A man has offered them 700 dollars. They then want to buy something in the country where they can have chickens and cattle, and where George can still do something at home in rainy weather. He is pretty skillful in manual work. He has fixed everything up well in the house for Mimi, especially in the kitchen. I warned her by all means to watch what and where she bought, so that they would not lose the little that they still have.

Mimi is otherwise always in good spirits, fat, and an eternal chatterbox. When I left her for the city, she told me that she would be having a child in about two months. We were completely alone, Mimi and I, and so we also spoke about our relations at home. [...]

Now I must tell you something about San Francisco. On Sunday the 26th at 2 o'clock in the afternoon I got back on the train and arrived at 4 o'clock in the big city, where my friends were awaiting me. They were waiting at the nearer station (They live far outside the city). I however traveled into the city, and so I then had the pleasure to go to see people. Naturally I used the streetcar and with the help of a couple of requests for directions, I soon found my destination. Mrs. Johnson was amazed how I had found her so soon. San Francisco is becoming a mighty city, and there is a lot to see. The time passed quickly, but I went six days in a row to the dentist; that was no fun. I should have already taken care of this dental work long ago, but we are so far from Paso Robles, and now I wanted to take advantage of this opportunity in San Francisco. It has cost me less here, but still enough: 40 dollars. I still had only 4 bottom teeth and they had to be filled with gold filling. The other option, silver, is not durable, the doctor said. They and nine teeth are new. The dentist assured me that I would not have to have any more dental work done in my lifetime.

Because Mimi has a premature birth, Seline stays a while longer with her in order to help out. In this way there develops a certain closeness and understanding between both women.

[...] I was in San Francisco for almost two weeks and have still not seen everything interesting, but I was disgusted by all the noises and hustle and bustle of the city. A week ago on the afternoon of August 7th, I got on the train again, in order to be in San José by 4 o'clock, where I was expecting Mimi at the train station. However, she was not there. So I took a wagon to her house; it is two miles from the train station. When I got to the house, everything was closed up, and then a neighbor came and told me Mimi was sick in the sanitarium (private hospital). She had had a baby girl (premature birth). At that moment arrived Mimi's father-in-law and an hour later her husband arrived from work. He told me the child had been born 6 weeks too early. It is alive and is now pretty happy. It weighed 6 pounds after birth.

August 14th. On July 30th the child was born and Mimi says she doesn't know why it came too early. She has always been strong and healthy. On Wednesday night she received pains. She didn't know what it was. On Thursday morning her husband went to the doctor (Dr. Heines, a son-in-law of Edwards). When he came, he said she was having a premature birth, and that she would do better to go to the sanitarium. He feared it would give her a lot of difficulty and she had no one to care for her at home. So they harnessed the wagon and went to the hospital and at 1 o'clock the child was born. It had almost no skin and was then always washed with oil. That is a new method, and I think it is a good one. The child is now two weeks old, and it looks almost like a child carried for the full term of the pregnancy. Her husband took her home yesterday. She had good care in the sanitarium and is now again rather happy. On next Tuesday, the 18th of this month, I am going home. By then Mimi will again be able to do light housework. [...]

August 17th. Mimi told me she wished that father would break himself of his bad habit of drinking too much. Last winter, when he came to San José for her wedding, he had been pretty drunk. She had been really angry and ashamed. She thinks he is old enough to do the right thing.

A couple of hours ago, Mimi and I received letters from him. He says they will be happy when I come home. I think it is good for father that I have been away for a while. He will respect me and my work a little more when I go back. Alice and Seline have also written me I should come home again. Polly is homesick for Mama.

So tomorrow, in God's name, I shall start out on my trip home. The train leaves here at half past nine, and father and Polly will await me in Paso Robles at 2 o'clock, and so I am also happy to be back home again with my loved ones. If I could only take home with me the cooler air here. It is always so hot at home in Adelaida; father said in his letter, 100–106 degrees in the shade. It is a hot summer for us at home. Here, even if it is warm, every afternoon there comes a cool wind. It is a beautiful and fertile region here, beautiful palm trees and pretty flower gardens almost the entire year. But the land is expensive here in comparison with its use. Fruit trees are a main source of profit here. Many hundreds of miles of nothing but trees, all kinds.

Be many times greeted by Mimi and by your sister-in-law

Seline Wyss

Mimi says she also wants to write to you, if you could read English.

"I had many worries."

Adelaida, December 13th, 1903

Dear Sister Hanneli!

[...] I would have gladly come next summer, but I can't. I cannot think about coming home for good, and her family [Seline's] are of course all messed up, two in the mad house and an earlier admirer of hers in prison—or was in prison, because of forgery.

Now something else about my children. Mimi has a husband who does his work well and honorably, but he is not thrifty. They will scarcely make ends meet. They already have a 3½ month old little Alice; Mimi is completely full of maternal joy, but she wants to move to the country, because it costs too much in the city.—I'll write to you later about Mimi's story. Alice is again in Creston, in order to receive the confirmation instruction, and will afterwards go to a job with Germans in San Francisco. She would also like to have become a teacher, but I can't afford it. [...] Seline is a dear, good child, is really good in school like Mattie—Mathilde—is my mainstay, good with riding, herding cattle, and she helps of course best with milking. And Polly is almost the most difficult of the three, if also the youngest. She is weak in arithmetic and has seizures; all at once, she stares at something and hears nothing. I am really worried. We have consulted the doctor, but so far the medicines have done no good.

Tomorrow I go with Seline to Paso Robles to pick up Alice for two weeks of vacation. Best wishes at Christmas, as well as at New Year. I shall soon write to you again. With love and kisses,

your brother Otto

Concerning Illnesses and a Dramatic Accident.

Adelaida, March 27th, 1904

Dear Sister Hanneli!

[...] For today I would have liked to have gone to Creston, where Alice is being confirmed in the German church by a German minister—Jakob Gundlach. Unfortunately the roads are so bad, it has rained a lot these last weeks, and the horses are thin. In addition, there are eight cows to be milked, and they are still very scattered. Only next month can I fix the fence again and hold them together better.

For Alice I would have liked to have had a little book, such as one gives to candidates for confirmation, a Christian guide for life, something short, smaller. Perhaps you would send her something like that. I am still very thankful to you for all the things you have sent us, especially for the packages and Friday newspaper. Yet Alice is the only one of the children who can read and write German correctly, and should something change here, she could still write, and for that reason I would like to assist her in cultivating German.—She is also musically inclined and has had violin for four years, on which she plays many a self-taught song and on which she practices with her younger sisters.—She will stay in Creston until Easter and will then come home, in order, after a few weeks of temporary help here, to go to San Francisco, where a position was offered to her by well-off German people.—She would have liked to go to another school, but I can't afford that.

For the last two to three months my wife has been plagued with excema, a lengthy illness, of the type such as leprosy.—She earlier had dry scabs, oozing scabs, but with a few bottles of sassaparilla it gets better and better.

Now she drinks almost a liter of medicines and smears and salves herself and recently nearly poisoned herself to death with salves of excessively strong carbolic acid.

I myself had the worst winter I ever had.—In December I was coming back with Alice and Seline from Paso Robles. It was almost dark, and at a bad spot a holster hook in the horse harness fell out, and the young, somewhat nervous mare sprang sideways and turned over the light wagon. Alice was still able to jump out, while I myself fell under the wagon, which the horses dragged away until they got loose and ran home. A neighbor then took us home. The damage was luckily not too bad. Seline and I had minor scatches, but nothing was broken. In a week Seline was once again all right, while I myself, as a result of a cold, got rheumatism in my right arm and simultaneously in my left leg, especially in my knee. To be sure, I could still walk, but it still bothers me now when I stand up, for example when I'm milking. I still feel it in my shoulders and in the small finger of my right arm, despite the fact that I had a bottle for rubbing from Dr. Norton. When the warm weather comes, I'll take a few baths in Paso Robles. […]

The children, Seline and Mattie, are making good progress in school and help rather much to keep the kitchen in order, plus they help with the milking. Mattie is the smallest, somewhat shorter than the others, but the most active, my best help, and she rides horses as safely and well as you could wish.—Seline is more cautious, but a very good, devoted child. Polly is behind in school, especially in arithmetic, and she has seizures. At times she stands still, looks up and sweeps her eyes from side to side, and when you shake her and speak to her, she looks as though she is awakening from a deep sleep.—We already had medicine for her from two doctors, but it doesn't seem to help.

Little Hansli often made the same eyes, before the brain inflammation finally took him from us. I am much worried because of Polly. In short, I have a plagued existence, an ever complaining, dissatisfied wife, and I can scarcely work enough anymore. I wish so much that I was closer to you, but nothing can be done about that. Write soon again. Warm greetings and good Easter

Your distant brother Otto

Much Praise for Mimi.

Adelaida, January 1905

Dear Sister Hanneli!

I had such a happy and good Christmas that I want to tell you all about it.—Friday, two days before Christmas, I went to Paso Robles, to pick up Mimi, her husband George van Horn and the little one, Alice. They arrived, and we got back home safely, only on the way the little 16-month old Alice got thirsty, and I took her to the home of acquaintances, where she drank milk.

The next morning it rained and so we sat in the old house in front of the hearth fire and told stories, asked and answered questions and exchanged opinions and experiences.—So then I asked George how he is living with Emilie and if he is happy with her, because he always calls her by her completely full name. This is what he told me:

I knew that Emilie is good and sincere, but she is in every respect even better than I expected. When I come home after the day's work or after the week's work, everything is good and in order. The baby is always clean, my wash ready and mended. It I want to leave to go hunting or fishing at 3 or 4 o'clock in the morning, she always gets up and cooks my breakfast.—She does the shopping wisely, more cheaply than I ever could, including underwear or whatever. It is better than if I were to select it myself. […]

My four brothers, said George van Horn, are all married, but my father says he wants to stay with us, because I have the best wife.

And Emilie is so quiet and composed, no longer the singing, lively chatting child from the past, but always in a good mood, always with a pleasing word on her lips.—Old acquaintances say she is still Mimi. Too bad that we cannot have her here. […]

George van Horn went back home on January 3rd, after we had slaughtered a cow on December 31st and a pig on January 2nd. Emilie helped out two more weeks, especially with making sausages. I made about 300 pounds of sausages, salted meat, and I smoked it, so that we have a supply on hand. The little Alice is a good child and looks at one with her brown eyes so trustingly, so frankly, just like her father. Despite the fact that she came seven weeks too early, she is still healthy like, thank God, all those in our small family.

Otto

"Everything seems to you so big and so empty."

Adelaida, June 9th, 1905

My Dear Brother Oskar!

Just now have arrived the mournful tidings from your house, all the more surprising in that I have heard little from you for a long time. I only knew that your wife was less sick, whereas you yourself had to suffer more.

It makes me remember how nearly 17 years ago I felt so quite alone with two small girls after the death of my first wife Ottilie. Everything seems to you so big and so empty in these situations.

With my present wife, however, things are not going very well, i.e. her excema will soon be all right, but she is certainly not quite right in the head from time to time. Alice will be happy when she can find a job and work for other people. The times are not bad, but there is no hope for a woman like my wife who mainly only studies how she could deprive others of everything.

Polly continues to have her seizures, staring out into space, whereas Seline and Mattie are both hard working children.

I myself am pretty much over my rheumatism. A sprained food makes me limp around and I shall soon send more letters. The mail is coming. I assure you, I feel your irreplaceable loss. To you yourself and to your children, my best wishes from your brother

Otto Wyss

Strangers Are Lodged.

Adelaida, December 10th, 1905

My Dear Sister Hanneli!

[…] This week, on Friday after 11 o'clock came by an Alsatian Jew, an eyeglasses salesman. I gave him some meat, and my wife gave him soup and something to eat, and then she bought a pair of eyeglasses from him for 2 dollars (10 francs)—she didn't need them very much. Two years ago she bought a yellow (golden?) pair for 8 dollars, which is about 40 francs, and last year such a one made of nickel silver for 2½ or 3 dollars, and she still had both. At 12 o'clock we sat down to eat, the children came home from school, and then Mrs. Wyss began to look for her golden eyeglasses.—She found nothing, and she declared the German Jew has taken my eyeglasses.—First of all Mattie was sent after him, then Polly and finally Mrs. Wyss herself. At one o'clock the entire group came back, and the "Julien" declared he would not budge from the spot until the lost eyeglasses were found. I went to work, while my wife and the merchant inspected every pair of glasses in his bags, but they found nothing. Two hours later, after 3 o'clock, she found the missing eyeglasses in her chest of drawers.—The man then cooked enough meat for five lunches and stayed over night, always complaining about "such a woman." That night a gentleman and a woman came with a chaise and two horses and they stayed here, and they gladly paid 1½ dollars for four meals at 25 cents. And two beds at 25 cents. And then $1.00 for feeding 2 horses. My wife kept the 1½ dollars, and I myself kept $1.00 for feed. She likewise keeps the money from her sales of eggs, milk and butter, which comes to 5 dollars and more a month. I have nothing against that, if she would only then buy some feed for the chickens, but there everything must come out of the old man's pockets. When she takes $10 from me to go to Paso Robles, she makes more debts and then says, "Well, when one comes into a store and spends ten or fifteen, one feels respected."

Otto milking. Milking was always done outdoors.

Wyss family in front of their house, still extant. Left, Mr. Morton, then Otto and Seline and the three girls, Seline, Mattie, and Polly. Not shown are the daughters Mimi and Alice.

Commentary on Two Photographs.

Adelaida, March 18th, 1906

My Dear Sister Hanneli!

Ten days ago I mailed you a little package with sea shells, some little grains of sand, and a few pieces of quicksilver ore, etc. and hope that it has arrived all right. [...]

Alice collected the shells herself in Cambria and Carmel, where she stayed from the middle of January until February 20th with her sister Emilie in order to help out, because there was born a healthy boy Otto Benjamin van Horn. They are all healthy and happy, which makes me very, very happy. George van Horn works, which gives him a lot to do.

I want to add something in the way of explanation about the photograph. I am milking Bianchi (pronounced Biänggi), a good red cow. To the right is Chucli, to the left the big white headed Greta, behind her Dolly, Speik and Bossi or Patti, behind them can be seen a little higher up the back of the bull. To the left is hot water in the big wash cauldron and the two big water troughs as far as the tree on the right, which is a young oak which 25 years ago measured about 6 to 8 inches, now nearly two feet in diameter. On the other side of the 70-feet-wide road is the garden fence, behind this the old "log house," which I use as a wagon shed, to the right of the tree the gable of the new barn with cliffs in the background.

Now I want to describe another photograph which we had made about three years ago. My wife didn't want to let me have any and put them all to the side, but eventually I managed to get a few, which I shall send you in a few days. It shows our house, Selina, Polly and Mattie, each with a cat and then mama with Mops, the old sheep-dog, between us and to the left Mr. Morton, who used to live with us (dead for two years) and between him and us Bigelow (Pig), the young cow dog, excellent for herding cattle. In the front the front porch, to the left the kitchen with a window, two windows to the living room and the upper window in the childrens' room. I shall enclose a little plan of the house. Both sides of the house measure 24½ feet long by 28 feet wide, and the kitchen addition measures 16 feet by 12 feet. The house is completely big enough. It has only one stove and no fireplace; the chimney is only for the cooking oven. In the background the big, evergreen live oak, about 5 feet in diameter. To the right you can see the Chinese "Heaven's Tree," Ailanthus, big pinnate leaves on which hops spin their way up on hop poles. To the right of the entrance are three umbrella tress, which however are not visible. In the enclosed little drawing is shown the arrangement of the house, the living room with a little table in the middle, the spacious kitchen, from which you go up the stairs, where on the second floor there are two rooms. The children have a lot of room, the entire extent of the house. Upstairs are two big and one small bed, downstairs two more big beds.—I would have preferred to have more single beds, especially in the guest room, but my wife still has a taste for the old European customs in farm houses, the big beds for two and three.

About 20 steps down the stairs is the well and below it the brook in the cool shade of the live oak.

I am also enclosing another photo of some people known by Mr. Morton. It is a Swedish family. It shows a family on a wheat farm, with their horses, mainly strong work horses, the three boys and the mother with the youngest and the colt in the foreground. It is somewhat bigger and so hides from view to a certain extent the others. [...]

Otto

Otto verifies to his brother the arrival of inheritance money from his father's estate ("The amount far surpassed my expectations."—"My wife knows nothing about it, and it is better that she learns nothing about it"). Then he writes further concerning daily life on the farm:

[...] July 22nd. It is hot, 104° F = 40°C and sultry. My wife and children are at Sunday school, where there is singing, Bible reading, and sermons.

Alice has been in San Luis for a month, where she attends a business school for book keeping and business correspondence. The course lasts about six months, and somewhat longer if she wants to take courses in typewriting, and stenography. However, she will come back home after New Year, because then Seline and Mattie will go to Creston to the German School, in order to receive the instruction for the candidates for confirmation. I myself expect as usual to milk 16 to 20 cows, to sow sufficient wheat, barley and oats; to sell for hay about 12–15 head of cattle per year, mainly for slaughtering for the butcher, but also for milk cows. I have never tried to make cheese. I think it takes more time. However, I always have a good vegetable garden, and the children have this year an extraordinarily rich flower garden.

With the chickens my wife had little luck. Last year we found a skunk under the woodpile, which I shot with some buck shot. Then Mattie shot it with her small 22 carbine, and when we tore apart the pile, we found two more young ones, nearly grown, which the dog killed, because with the shouting he got all excited and wanted to help. We found a dozen and more of young chickens, and Mrs. Wyss declared: "No wonder I had no longer any small chicks!" There are also unusually many cayotes. I have only five pigs, but they are all fat, but it is too hot for slaughtering. [...]

Otto

So life in Adelaida goes on; it is no intimate cordial family gathering, but rather it crackles with domestic tensions. In this regard actual depressions can be detected in the letters, where the mutual mistrust becomes directly perceptible, as for example in Seline's long letter of July 25th, 1906:

Adelaida, July 25th, 1906

Most Worthy Brother-in-Law!

For weeks, indeed for a couple of months I have been overcome by uneasy, oppressive feelings, as if a heavy doom were hanging over our family, a heavy burden which will not fall from my shoulders. Father is always brooding about something, as if he had a guilty conscience. I can speak no reasonable word to him without him hurling the worst curses at me and calling me the worst names. He always looks for opportunities for quarrels, tries to see mistakes here and there, and he says he cannot talk with me unless he lets me have my say. He provokes me so and defies me, thinking that I will use vulgar and vile words with him before the children. But God always sends me the necessary patience so that I do not sin in this way.

Wyss family in front of their house. Left, daughter Alice, then Seline and Otto with children Seline, Mattie, and Polly.

A week ago, for example, as I was warning him about the dangers of drinking, there was once more a string of swear words, and when I reminded him again that he should not curse his own flesh and blood, he said like many times before that his father had paid the price for his cursing.

He cannot accuse me of any disorderliness or wastefulness, for which he always looks for some excuse, in a bad way. He keeps all his valuables, your letters and everything, in the old house over there, where his desk is, and when someone comes to pay something, he always takes the people there, so that I shall see and hear nothing. Sometimes he hides certain papers and then after a while he comes and swears, where has this or that gone, and wants to blame me for disorderliness. I am supposed to display my orderliness, I must never look for my things, neither letters nor papers nor photographs. But he comes and expects everything to be in place.

Seven years ago, when Mimi was home on vacation, father gave her, without my knowledge (I was not at home at the time) the photographs of his blessed father and mother. Mimi of course did not know his intention in doing that. The pictures were all in an album in the chest-of-drawers when I came here, and I had always also kept them beside my own things in the same place. A rather long time after that, when Mimi was away, the children wanted to look at the photos again, and then I noticed the old album was missing. I asked father about it. He claimed he knew nothing about it, and he told me I had probably given it to the children to tear up. Then three years ago, when I was over in San José, Mimi showed me her album, and then I saw there pictures of blessed father and mother, beside others. After my return home I told father that Mimi had said that father had given her the photographs. Then he went wild and called me a liar, although he knew before God that it was true.

Your big picture, which you sent a few years ago in the cardboard box, hangs in the living room. I had bought a frame for it. Now he accuses me of having lied to him about my money. He says I gave him a higher estimate of money than I had, and he believes brother has not sent everything. He knows that that is also an irresponsible lie. I had told him everything in a true and honorable manner, the pure truth, and my brother did send me everything, which I can prove through documents and letters.

But now he wants to deny me half of it, he, the father of my children. I still had over 52 dollars in my pocket when I arrived here, and I had loaned him that before we married. He paid debts with it, because at the time he was being pressured by his creditors almost every day. He now denies all that. I must also expressly tell you that he has never spent a cent of his father's money on me; I have also never wanted it. I was only glad that he paid debts with it. I knew nothing at all about the affairs of his inheritance since the death of his blessed father. I have never asked him about it, and he has never said anything about it.

If you or sister Hanneli have sent Otto any money, he has hidden it somewhere in some bank. He always defrays all expenses from our income. He has now sold again about 250 dollars worth of cattle. I don't see a cent of it; he puts this aside in the bank every year. I also have nothing from the butter money. I am only good for work. I don't think that it is my duty to allow myself to be enslaved much longer. I make no claim on his inheritance, but I certainly do have a right to have something of the money that I have helped to save with my own hard work and part of my own money from home.

Otto has now been using it for over 17 years.

I never would have had any problems with my stepchildren if their father had not always stirred them up against me, and he still does that in a sly way. They don't even know when they hurt me. Father always uses his two older children as a weapon against me, especially Mimi. Alice was otherwise always very attached to me.

Father always flatters my three girls and tries to attract them to himself if at all possible, but that can be no sincere love, otherwise he could not torment their mother so. All three of them are so honest and sincere and do everything for their father in order to keep peace. Just as I myself also daily make every effort to prevent any disputes, father always finds an opportunity for it. I almost never talk with him, in order to spare him the trouble of cursing.

I must also observe that I have never said anything offensive about or insulted either yourself or your sisters, just in case Otto should write that. I blame no one for my misfortune, and if Otto sometimes complains that his brother sent me here, I then tell him, if you were only half as good as your brother and sister, I would have no complaints.

Alice has been in San Luis in school for a month, for six months. She is taking a business course. Seline passed the grammar exam last month and she will now enter the ninth grade. She will soon be as big as I am. Mattie is short and fat. Polly is the heaviest of all, but because of her convulsions, she worries me a lot.

Oh how many thousands of times have I already wished that some of you could come here. If I had the money, I would come home, to tell you all this in person, but father will not let me go. My health is now pretty good, my legs are almost healed. But I am presently so thin that I can hardly stand up, just because of anger and vexation.

Now at the end of this letter it occurs to me that a couple of days ago we received the announcement of the engagement of your daughter, Alma, and I ask for forgiveness that I only now get back to you. I wish her from the bottom of my heart happiness and God's blessings, for a happy family life.

Now I want to close. I have written the accurate truth and ask you to recognize it as such. I have a clear conscience before God and man, and the heavenly father, to whom I appeal every day, will resolve everything for the best. Many greetings to you and your worthy family from your sister-in-law
Seline Wyss

Another Swiss Festival.

Adelaida, December 9th, 1906

My Dear Sister Hanneli!

[...] We seem to be having a regular earthquake year, because last Thursday night at 10:20 we were awakened by the shaking of the house. The children came downstairs, but luckily it was soon over, and after we were over our fright, we went back to bed.

In September there was a Swiss Festival in Cayucos. There, there are many people from Ticino, and so every couple of years a little festival is given in memory of the land of our birth, beautiful Switzerland. A few wagons with virgins and girls representing Helvetia, Columbia, Berna, etc., and smaller wagons representing the various cantons with their coats of arms, then music, dancing and speeches in Italian and English and then food—bread, cheese and roast beef, as much as could be brought under one roof. Three steers were roasted whole and consumed. Alice was also there from San Luis, with a young German—Herman Suderman. We went to the coast and collected a few more mussels, etc. and toward 5 o'clock we made our way home. Naturally, we spent the night only with acquaintances, at the home of Mrs. Haase, who with her mother lives on a place about 10 to 11 miles halfway between Cayucos and Adelaida.—Mr. Haase was in Alaska for about seven years, where he dug in the famous Klondyke gold mines and washed gold and had very beautiful pieces. I wanted to buy one for you, but he gave it to me as a present, so that I could send it to you, and so in a few days I shall send another small box and stick the little lump of gold in a shell, so that it won't get lost so easily. [...]

Otto

In front of the Klau school. The school stood below the mine. In back, Otto Wyss. Second girl, back row: Alice Wyss. Left of the right-side pillar is Mattie, to the right, Polly.

In the letter to his sister Hanneli from the summer of 1907 Otto recollects his youth on the Steinhof and his relationships with his sisters:

I always had to suffer from "criticism" when I came home from my apprenticeship or later. My elder sisters were so strict. Whenever I sang a little comrade's song, only Emilie and my dear Hanneli could laugh heartily, and also later, you, my dear sister, never scolded me like almost all the others, and therefore we belong together.

Mimi and her husband George van Horn move from San José and settle down with their three children in Adelaida. "You can imagine that I am happy about that." Thus Otto receives help from his son-in-law.

Why Adelaida is Called That, or Concerning the Importance of Having Your Own Post Office.

Klau Post Office, January 19th, 1908

My Dear Sister Hanneli!

It is foggy and rainy outside, and so I have sat down here in the post office, by a good hearth fire, in order to write about how things are going with us. The first and most important news is that Emilie with her husband George van Horn and their three children are here at our home and will stay here. He has already plowed and harrowed everything for me, while I myself have done the sowing, but this work is done, and we'll soon begin the milking and butter making. Mattie and Polly alone take care of five cows which we milk, and we shall first use the cream separator in two to three weeks when we have eight to ten fresh cows.

George and Emilie live in a little house which I bought from an earlier tenant. Then I had bought another, which George will tear down and rebuild on a 40-acre piece of land which borders our property to the east and which belongs to Alice. They will buy the 40 acres from Alice and make their home there. He calculates he will have the house built there and ready to move in within four to five weeks. They have good furniture, beds, etc., and since her marriage, five years ago, they have had no illness in their family, which is worth a small amount of capital.

He has built for me or for us both a little smoke house, out of sheet-iron, which he brought with him here, and we are currently smoking three pigs and shall also smoke in a few days a young cow. One of our cows broke a hip bone and can hardly walk, but otherwise it eats well. That happens from time to time with fallen animals when they are hit by bigger ones. [...]

Sunday afternoon.—Polly and Mattie are in the "flat" down there with Mimi. It is more entertaining there with the little ones. Mamá is reading and sleeping a little, and I want to tell you something about the post office.—When I came here in 1876, we had to pick up our mail in Paso Robles, 16 miles or about 20 kilometers, five hours, away. Then the superintendent of the local Almaden Mine and the superintendent of the neighboring Sunderland Mine got up petitions for the establishment of a post office. Our superintendent, van

Jeinsen, left it up to the workers to suggest a name and, since we were a rather cosmopolitan bunch, we suggested "Cosmo," whereas Mr. Sunderland suggested the name of his bride "Adelaida"; she was Adelaida Lane of Virginia. (Lane and van Horn come from Holland.) Mr. Sunderland became Postmaster (PM) on January 1st, 1877. In those days the mail came and returned twice a week, on the San Miguel-San Simeon route. When the mine ceased to be profitable, I had to leave my job there and became the postmaster's deputy, and in 1880 the local post office actually came on my property. North and south of here are located two big farms. The one, Ed Smith's, had over 2000 acres; the other, Wes Burnett's, had 8–10,000 acres. Both these gentlemen were speculators, and from 1882 to 88 they did everything they could to get the Adelaida Post Office moved to their own neighborhood, and so in 1889 it did move to Ed Smith's place and a year later to Dubost, a place between the two farms. Then in 1894 they wanted to have a post office west of here. That is "Gibbons," 6 or 7 miles from here. They also wanted to receive the mail twice a week, but there is not much there. Anno 1900, when Mr. Adolf Klau, a German Jew, with the assistance of others and "our people," they say the Rothschilds, bought the quicksilver mine, he also wanted to have his own post office for the new mine. He received permission for such, and this new post office was named "Klau."

The production of the Klau mine was pushed to the limit, big reduction furnaces were built, which burned 60-80 tons of ore, and for a while it was a profitable venture, producing 100 flasks per week. But the price fell from $55 to 45 and 34 dollars. The number of flasks and the production likewise fell, and so Mr. Klau sold the mine.

A greenhorn, Mr. Pearson of Boston, bought it and found, to his astonishment, that it made no profit. He has left, probably never to be seen again, and the postmaster position was again vacant.

We had, already in the past, found it convenient to see the mail coach from Paso Robles here, and it was so convenient to be able to ship butter, eggs, etc. directly from here, and so came some neighbors who wanted me to take over the local post office again. Two of these, Mr. Bagby and Mr. Kuhlman, promised me to put up the 2000 dollar collateral/security. (Another also offered to do it), and so I said yes, because Adelaida is now still three miles away.

When I gave my personal assurance that I myself would take care of the positon of Postmaster as much as possible, Klau was also declared a "Money Order Office," and so I can also write postal money orders for the entire United States. [...]

Sunday afternoon after 4.—The sun is shining beautifully and warmly, and I should finish the letter, must still feed and see after the cattle. A neighbor lost 12 head to an illness, so you really have to watch out.

My fingers are becoming stiff. Whenever I do the milking, I feel a little rheumatism, but otherwise I wish you could feel as good as I do. My appetite is good. I take my time chewing, but I still do have my own teeth; in the

mornings, when the day is breaking, that is now 6:30, I make a fire, warm up a little more coffee and take a sip. Then Mama and the children come and relieve me.—George does the more strenuous work, and he is happy here and says it is a good life, "you just find the wood and all you have to do is split it."
[…]
Otto

Travel Plans Become more Concrete.

Klau, January 24th, 1909

My Dear Sister Hanneli

I wanted to answer your dear lines at New Year, however, I didn't get around to it. Thank you so much for your friendly invitation, and I shall take advantage of it and be your guest as much as practical; although I don't need at all so much space and am happy in any corner or another. I doubt that my wife would come at the same time, but next year then for a longer time. In any event, I would look up many old friends, the schoolmates of the home communities, especially in Winterthur, Töss, Eglisau, and at Schleitheim on the border with Baden, and many more. I shall extend my stay to two, perhaps three months, but not more. If possible I shall try to leave here earlier than July. I still want to study practical water installations, also utilization of a small water wheel and turbine, and I am certain I can run my separator, electric light, etc. with it. I also wish to get information about burning lime and cement manufacture, and then much more. […]

Well some more about our Christmas.
On last Saturday Mama and Polly picked up Seline and Alice in Paso Robles, the following Monday I picked up Mattie from the coast, and on the day before Christmas they prepared the tree. Mama wanted to kill two chickens, because we had only four geese, but the old gander, a real cockfighter, tried to chase the bull out of his barley and bit into the bull, the bull broke his leg in two, and so we had to deliver him immediately to the kitchen. He made a good, big roast.
We had the tree on Christmas Eve, Thursday, and we sang many old school songs, church songs, etc., all in English, with Alicia and Mimi, because both have such confident voices, Mimi soprano, Alice alto, I bass. On Christmas Day I had to take Alice back to Paso Robles, because in San Luis she had to help sing in the German-Lutheran Church on Christmas night, and on the next morning she came back for a few more days.—Seline went on January 2nd to San Luis, back to school. A week later came a letter from Alice, that Seline had the fever and was in bed. She thought she had the measles. We wrote right away she should get Dr. Norton and then sent Polly to San Luis. However, it was only measles or light, red spots, and Seline was soon over it

and back in school. A week ago Polly came back home. With all that I had even more work, because come storm or rain, the cattle and the 25 calves and 9 or 10 horses must all be fed. […]
                                Otto

"I shall bring little luggage."

                                            Klau, February 7th, 1909
My Dear Sister Hanneli!

It has been stormy or rainy now for five full weeks, with hardly more than three or four days when the sun has come out again. In the newspaper you read about floods in the Sacramento Valley and about houses and almost entire villages which must be abandoned. Even in this county people near the coast had to leave their houses and drive their cattle up to higher ground. Yet even that will stop, because, as the poet says, "Let fog thicken as much as it might before the appearance of the sun, the sun awakens with its light the world to joy," and then there is much work sowing, harrowing, fencing, fixing, mending, and then the grass grows fast, and it is as though four or five cows only await beautiful weather to give birth to calves, and we have five already. So just a little sun, and we'll begin to milk.

We now send 1 gallon (4 liters) of milk every day to the mine and receive 10 cents, 50 Rappen per day. That is better than butter making but we make only just about as much, and we send it over with the mail, only on Sundays the children, Polly and Mattie, ride over and deliver it themselves. The cook there is a quite decent Japanese guy, and he often gives them "cookies," sweet baked goods. The "Jap" sent every month his salary to the Japanese Bank in San Francisco to Mr. Tokoshima, naturally via postal money order from here. He signs his name Tom Shiomi. […]

If you can think of anything that you would especially like from here, so please let me know, because I shall bring little luggage, and very few clothes except my workday suit, blue ticking pants and a jacket. I don't know whether you have engaged an extra room, because upstairs you really have no need for it since almost no one visits you. At any rate, don't go to any special expense on my account. […]

Alice is still working for the butcher Jakob Gingg, a born Appenzeller, who formerly was with me in the "Schweizerbund" singing group in San Francisco; recently two of his nephews came. Alice understands him well, "they don't know yet any English!" She does the book keeping there and lives with Seline in two rooms, for which they pay 12 dollars, about 60 francs, per month. Alice pays the rent to help Seline, and I understand that she can put nothing aside in the bank. Alice still takes piano lessons, while Seline is in the

Polytechnical School in San Luis. Back home they would call it agricultural school.

"Two traveling preachers are here."

Klau, March 26ᵗʰ, 1909

My Dear Sister!

I don't know whether I have written since you sent us the pretty pictures of the old well-known Otelfingen. And you can also see the telephone and telegraph poles.—We are just about to build the telephone line from Paso Robles to Adelaida and Klau also, but this week it has rained so much that the work was interrupted. [...]

Recently, in Paso Robles, I spoke with the agent about the ticket. I would take transportation from Paso Robles to Zurich, round trip, four months and probably on a German ship, but I'm not sure whether via Genoa. That makes a longer trip.—I shall take very little with me and shall travel as a worker, as I always was. With money you can always buy yourself extra privileges, for example, a bed in the train etc. [...]

There are two traveling preachers here, and this evening from 7 to 9 there is a worship service, then on Sunday from 11 until half past noon, then lunch, which most bring to church, and then at 2 o'clock until half past 3, a short sermon and more singing and praying. It is somewhat unpleasant. Here they always have new song books, so that only the two preachers sing and the people with very few books just follow along as well as they can.—One of the preachers is a Mr. Ducomune, a citizen of Neuchâtel, who still speaks good French but who came to America at the age of 12 or 14 with a big family. He preaches well, but his family and sisters are in Northern California and he will go back there to be with them. The other preacher is called Dreier, almost a German name. He speaks too fast, even when he preaches, so that you can barely follow him.—On Sunday evening they will pass around the hat, collect 5 to 10 dollars and then travel farther on. [...]

Otto

The Inspector Comes.

Klau, May 2ⁿᵈ, 1909

My Dear Sister Hanneli!

As you can see above, we have a new postal stamp and the rubber makes a better impression, especially the number of the date. [...]

It was convenient for me when last Monday a gentleman with a horse and carriage came riding by and said: "Are you postmaster Wyss?" and I replied, "That is I," whereupon he introduced himself as J. Warren, Post Office Inspector. He was friendly, and after I had taken care of the horse, he excused me for my milking, because he will inspect everything tomorrow. This is the first time since I took over the post office again that an inspector has come by.—At 5 in the morning we had Mimi helping us, and soon after 6:30 we were finished for breakfast, and afterwards from 7 until 11 o'clock all stamps, cards, envelopes, etc., were counted and recorded and money and everything balanced, including the money order department, which naturally is completely separate, and everything was correct to the last cent, and he was satisfied. He gave me a series of suggestions and instructions about how to do things here and there. He thought I should rent mailboxes and thus increase my income, and finally he advised me to keep my job at the post office, because, as matters now stood, I could no longer lose the job because of politics.

You see, if the inspector had come after I had left, the children would have behaved somewhat awkwardly. He said that I could appeal to him directly to take my vacation, and since everything is in order, I don't need to write to Washington.—Also good, and that saves me the trouble. [...]

I already have all your letters. For money, besides my round trip ticket, I shall take along $200—or more. It is just in case they could possibly request compensation for my lack of military service, although thanks to an absence of 37 years, perhaps no one will think to ask, but I must take into account the possibility.

The way everything is now, I cannot think of staying over there because, you see, if the children evenly divide everything after my death, each one will have about a hundred acres of land, each can have four cows, and two or three could milk the cows for seven months, more or less, then an employee can plow and sow, make the hay, etc., raise the calves, and they can sell about 20-25 head, when they are two to three years old, and lead a regular independent life.—They could also run a small store beside the post office and lease the land for 250 to 300 dollars per year.—George van Horn with his children would never be able to make it alone, and he himself is no business man. He is also not cut out to keep and raise horses, etc., and look, "what's not wood makes no whistle." [...]

Good-bye then until soon, dear, dear sister, and thank you for having always so faithfully stood by your brother, even during his apprenticeship. With kisses and love

your Otto

On June 26th Otto writes to his sister that the telephone now functions well, the children use it a lot, and on July 12th, 1909 he informs Hanneli of his definitive itinerary:

A Peter Stamper from Creston, 10 miles from Paso Robles, has two daughters and three boys, one of whom is married, and I have known him for 10 to 12 years. He is a good traveling companion, a German from Luxembourg, and he is coming on the trip with me; we have our tickets: Paso Robles—Zurich via New York—Hamburg, so we travel directly from Paso Robles to San Francisco—Omaha—Chicago—New York—Hamburg—Basel—Zurich and a different route back, if possible, Genoa—Naples—Gibraltar—New York—St. Louis Missouri—El Paso—Los Angeles—Paso Robles. We shall be ready to travel in a week, leaving New York on the 29th or 30th. Then via steamer, a new one with a third deck, on the morning of the 31st.

That is our present itinerary.—It is hot, a lot of work from 5 in the morning until 8 in the evening. [...]

"Off into the wavy sea."

Klau, July 16th, 1909

My Dear Sister Hanneli!

This morning I have transported the last hay and now hauled in some wood, and Monday and Tuesdsay I shall pack, and on Wednesday (July 21st) leave for Paso Robles, from where I shall send another card and shall leave on the same day.

Enclosed is a little bouquet which I picked yesterday and which is now dry.—This morning I killed a rattlesnake and will strip its skin and bring it with me. I have a few other animals and skins for Al. Güller in Hüttikon.—It is as hot as an oven 104–106° (F). My man, Fischer, patters around, but he has helped me tremendously with haying and transporting hay.—I just made a phone call; someone phoned who wanted to buy my blue mare—Lizzie; I won't sell my best horse. The mail will soon arrive. I must pack another cowhide. I don't have a regular passport, but instead identification documents, so that everywhere I can easily identify who I am.

In two weeks, I'll be in New York, ready to sail off into the wavy sea, on a three-deck ship.

Warm kisses and greetings from your ever loving brother
Otto

VIII

The Patriarch

Otto is now 63 years old and on a visit to the old homeland, which he left 37 years ago, when at that time, in 1872, his father accompanied him via Baden to Wildegg. He leaves his wife and children in California. He travels with the ship Cleveland in a cabin for four in eleven days from New York to Hamburg and from there in four days by train to Zurich.

In the old homeland, he visits Zurich, Otelfingen and additional places. He searches for the members of his family and old friends. His elder, widowed brother Oskar lives out in Wollishofen. The elder sister Emma Schmid-Wyss, who had seven children, lives in Höngg and the younger unmarried sister Hanneli lives at that time in Otelfingen.

In the course of the years in America, Otto had always dreamed of a visit back home in the old homeland, especially whenever a family member had died. A complete return home was also considered a few times. However, as the family grew, the daughters in California married, had children, his situation gradually improved and he grew older, he sensed that only a brief visit to Europe was possible.

Of the ten children whom Otto had with both wives, five girls remained alive, specifically: Emilie (Mimi), born on September 1ˢᵗ 1878, Alice Susanne, born on November 9 1886, Seline, born on April 3 1890, Marie Mathilde (Mattie), born on July 2ⁿᵈ 1891, and Pauline (Polly), born on August 1ˢᵗ 1892.

The second wife tried to bring order into the household. Otto was stubborn, they lived their separate lives, but stayed together.

Back in America life flies by comfortably. The younger daughters also marry and have children. Otto becomes a grandfather and great-grandfather.

The youngest, Polly, marries Eduard Dodd, who stays on the farm and later takes it over. Polly becomes the post mistress until she gives up the position.

Otto grows old, partly loses his memory. From this point in time, Seline, who since Otto's visit home had remained silent, begins writing again. After an accident Otto dies, and Seline further corresponds intensively for years.

The period from 1909 until 1935 is documented with many, many letters, which describe the rapidly changing life of the region, the growth of the family, daily life, weather, and the management of the farm. Only a small fraction of the extensive correspondence can here document this last portion of Otto's life.

Home visit in Otelfingen, in front of the old school, fall 1909. Jakob Otto Wyss (l.) and brother Johannes Oskar.

Zurich, Wollishofen, October 4th, 1909

My Dear Sister Hanneli!

When you wandered toward Regensdorf last Friday, I had another little meal and went, accompanied by Elise, to the streetcar in Höngg, but since all the cars were full and a crowd of people was standing there, I walked away, came to Wipkingen, then Aussersihl, and a nice man showed me the way to the tram stop, which took me to brother Oskar's house. On Saturday it rained, and I wrote a few cards. I want to go to Winterthur or Schaffhausen tomorrow or the day after tomorrow. Perhaps the middle of next week the harvest will begin, and since brother wishes it, I would help him with that and stay here until the beginning of the week after next, and help him supervise the harvest, however, not all of it, but just the end. Yesterday I was at Hans' house and sat beside Mr. Diener, and Hans gave me three cheers for my accomplishments in America.—With Mr. Diener I conversed well. Mr. Thomas was also there, not alone. I thought perhaps you would come tomorrow to Zurich and could await the arrival of the 9:30 train, and I would then come back with you. With kisses and love,

your brother Otto

Visiting Otelfingen, with brother and sisters, from left, Johanna Wyss, called Hanneli, Otto Wyss, Oskar Wyss, and Emma Schmid-Wyss.

"In the afternoon I was in the ladies' saloon."

On board the steamer Empress Auguste Victoria
November 10th, 1909
My Dear Nephew!

Today we have the first real storm, and I can't go for a walk, so I want to write you, even if my handwriting is a little crooked because the ship often rolls riskily on its side.—Yet my head is not dizzy. On Thursday, the 4th, we set sail at 12 o'clock, and at 1:30 the lunch bell was rung. There were 10 of us at our table, Peter Stamper, then a Pole with his brother, a Polish woman with a little girl, a German with his wife, and an English woman with her little daughter. Our table group was together for two days, then a few were missing. On Sunday it was beautiful and clear, and four of us had a photo made, which shows me with three traveling companions. We have on board about 450 passengers in the first class, somewhat more in the second class, and then 1800 in the steerage section, so that with the crew there are about 4,000 persons on board. We also have a 14-man orchestra, and whenever a foreign steamer comes by, the corresponding national anthem is played. The waves are splashing over the deck—shouts and yelling.

November 11th. Yesterday the sea was too rough, and so now I am writing more. Lunch was served on a table with a rim, so that the plates just fit on it, because otherwise everything would slide off. A few of us refused to let the rough sea spoil our appetite. We had herring à la Bismarck, i.e., with the bones removed and spiced with sour sauce, and we emptied the relish tray twice.

In the afternoon I was in the women's saloon, and there were three Württemberg mothers there, each with a little child, and since they were all seasick and felt bad, I watched their children for them.—In the evening they played music as usual in the dining room—except there were several rows of guests which were noticely cleared, and we had plenty of room. I slept well, despite the fact that a full wave hitting the ship made a noise like a cannon shot. The round portholes of the cabins were all hermetically sealed yesterday with a lid, because in a second-class cabin such a finger thick pane of glass had been broken by the waves and a lady wounded.—The second class passengers are mainly Germans, then Poles, Hungarians, Frenchmen, Englishmen, Swiss, and Russians.—In steerage are mainly Lithuanians, Russians, Poles, Hungarians, and a few Germans and a few Italians. They dance and make music and sing and fight for fun, but yesterday and today it is quiet, because now they must gasp for air. Once again my warm thanks for your kind hospitality during my stay and for driving me around. I send to Mr. Diener, to your wife and children, and to you yourself my best greetings,

your uncle Otto

On the return trip on the SS Empress Auguste, *from left, William Biedermann, New Jersey; Herman Leist, Los Angeles; Peter Stampe, San Luis Obispo; and Otto Wyss, Klau near Paso Robles.*

"The goose is eaten."

On January 16th, 1910 Otto writes to his sister Hanneli:

It is Sunday morning. There has been rain the last two days and even now, and I have just fed the pigs. An extra one is penned up for fattening; she has six young ones. Cows, calves, all my young cattle, horses are also here, in order to claim their hay, bran, and barley, because on Sunday it is a little later than usual, especially when it rains.—Breakfast over, for lunch we have a goose. Mimi, George and the three little ones will be with us for lunch. George has plowed for us, this week I have sowed about 6 acres, and George has harrowed it.—The goose has been eaten. We were all happy and had the laughter of the children. I also have a photograph which I can enclose, rather dark, but still not badly made. There is the tall George, Mimi so short beside him, a full head shorter, little Alice looks at you smiling, the little boy Otto looking somewhat sour and in the middle Aeggie with a regular positive "Wyss head." Naturally the dog is not missing either.

*Wedding announcement of daughter Alice
with Adolph Witkosky*

I have an iron stove here, the walls and ceiling made of canvas and whitewashed. It will soon be warm here—but there comes Mattie with the cows, but she says, "I still have to get a few," and she goes off again into the rain. In the meantime I was over there and had a sip of coffee. Mama had also got up. We have porridge, fried eggs and a few egg slices. Mama has cornflakes; it is a thin disc-shaped piece of grain like a cookie or something similar, quite good to eat and ready to go straight from the package onto the plate. A quarter of an hour later we are out milking.—From Oskar I hear that Alma was well delivered of a little girl. Then my brother writes me that you have asked him what you should do about the organ playing in Otelfingen, as they offer 50 francs less than in Regensdorf, you were right to refuse it. To be sure, last winter I thought more than once on Sunday morning, now certainly Hanneli, my Hanneli, must be on her way again to Regensdorf; that is however a little hard for Hanneli. But then she does receive joy playing the organ, and she knows people do listen to her and that gives people joy and creates a hallowed atmosphere to the honor and praise of the almighty Father. I am writing fast, and the pen is not good, now I'll take a horsefeather.—If the mail comes, I must shorten this.—Your dear card has just come, which expresses your concern about brother Oscar. I have a letter from nephew Oscar. He says, his father has pleurisy, and they have twice drained off water, and he hopes things will now go better. Hopefully no complications will come in the meantime. I am so glad that I visited you and him last year, because now I am busier this year. In June Mattie wishes to take a commercial course like Alice, and when Seline comes home for a short time, you never know how long; Seline, who is completing her studies this year at the Polytechnical School, is the first in her class, and is supposed to give the valedictory address. She is a little shy, but I hope she does give the speech and shall go there myself with Mama.—Alice has communicated to me in confidence that she has said yes to her Frankie and will also come home this summer.—Yesterday I sold two young horses. Alice is coming home to make her dowry, because at the beginning of August she wants to marry a Frank Witcosky, a Polish name. His father speaks German, he too. He buys cattle for butchers and takes them to them; he now earns 60 dollars a month with the butcher Gingg. On August 10th Mama and I went to Paso Robles and by train to San Luis, where we arrived at 4 o'clock. At 8 o'clock we went to the beautifully decorated church, where we found many white flowers, lilies of the valley, mainly the work of Selina and Mattie. Seline was the bridesmaid and Mattie arranged the flowers. Alice was dressed in white with a big veil, and was quite beautifully decked out in her bridal gown. The minister first delivered a short sermon in German, but he did the actual wedding in English; a few daughters sang, and at half past eight they were man and wife.—We had a banquet, we drank, we sang; turkeys and all kinds of good food were served. The next morning we left for home at 7 o'clock, and around 1 o'clock I was back home with Mama, Selina and Mattie.—Soon came the news that fire had broken out near a threshing-machine, and I hitched up the horse again and drove some men there to put out the fire. On the next day fire broke out in another place, and over 1000 acres, mainly pastureland, were burning. It is still hot, today 105° in the kitchen, as you can tell by my writing. It could be better.

And on October 20th, 1910, likewise to Hanneli:

We did not sleep the best last night, because little Otto always had to kick about with his feet, and we're no longer used to that sort of thing. Toward 11 o'clock Polly came home with the report that Mimi had a little baby boy, a big beautiful baby.—In the morning Mama and I went and found Mrs. White with Mimi, and she looked smiling inside and showed us her 9-pound baby boy with a round head and face, similar to her daughter Aeggie, who takes more after the Wyss side of the family. Alice and Otto have narrower faces and heads. What should he be called? His father has named him Loyd and Emilie Freddie, so it will be Loyd-Frederic.—In a week, on Tuesday, November 8th, will take place the elections for the state of California. As a rule I am present at these elections as a clerk, or recorder, and that is my job this time as well. There are two of us who have to register and count the votes, and they say my report was always correct, and then I fill out all titles, the date, if I have the time, because at night everything goes slower. Four years ago, it was past Wednesday night before we were finished. Two years ago at half past 10, for the presidential vote, there were many people and women who afterwards wanted to begin with dancing.

Daughters Alice (l.) and Seline.

Again to his "dearest Hanneli!" on June 21ˢᵗ, 1911:

We have the longest day today, and I am in the middle of the hay season. For the past two weeks I have spent most of my time on the mowing machine or on the horse rake, today on the latter, and the rough ground with many washed-out furrows makes it difficult to remain in your seat, and I must often hold myself as well as I can in order not to fall down.—Polly and Seline take care of the cows alone rather well, but the prices, which last year were 30 cents and over per pound, are now 22-24 cents, which means a full third less income. The costs are the same for shipping things, and instead of $300 and more we shall this year bring in only $200 or less. In addition, the mine is standing still. There is almost no milk to sell, and little goes through the post office, a third of the amount last year at this time.—But we are healthy and happy and have a good appetite. This year we must go to no wedding, but my daughter Alice Witkowsky is expecting the pains and joys of motherhood, may the former be alotted to her in more moderate measure, the latter in full measure. We had a good photo of Mattie. A friend of hers had made the photo; she speaks German and told her what a beautiful country Switzerland is and she must also visit it.—We are having hot weather, 100° and above day after day, and I still have a lot of hay to transport and little help. On July 4ᵗʰ Polly and Seline went to Paso Robles. There was a celebration there with many parades, music, speeches and in the evening fireworks, and the young people of course must see that. On Friday morning the telephone brought the news that Alice had been delivered of a happy little girl and everything was fine. Mimi went down two weeks ago with her two youngest to help out her sister Alice. They have 250-300 young chickens, and little Alice can help to take care of them. We still do our own milking, but I let my daughters take care of that.—I now still have to feed the postal horses here, which always make something else to take care of.—Mama has renovated the beds beautifully, but on hot nights a couple of small mammals still come to disturb our sleep, and then I am so tired on the next day with all the heat. With Alice everything went well. She wants to name her little daughter Evaline, and Alice is up again and is cheerful. Mattie had an accident when she was climbing up to the hayloft; she broke a tile of the ladder, and she fell down and sprained her foot, so that she had to stay at home in bed for two weeks. Now after three weeks she limps to work in the office and is brought home for lunch and in the evenings by horse and wagon. Her boss sends her her paycheck every Saturday—and he is a good old soul, writes Mattie, and you can see that she is valued at work.—

On November 12th, 1911:

Yesterday another Ticinese man came to pick up his mail; he brought a bottle of new wine for us to sample; so we chatted, and I didn't get back around to writing. This morning it is cold again. The neighbor, to whom I gave a rifle and cartridges for hunting, brought me this morning a big hare and two partridges—for our part, I must now skin the hare. I go hunting very little any more, near the barn, garden or field I shoot a couple of partridges or wild doves. There are no longer as many rabbits as earlier. My neighbor's wife often goes hunting and is a good shot. [...]

Polly and Mattie

Klau, January 16th, 1912

My Dear Sister Hanneli!

[…] At Christmas we had a good turkey and a lot of company, Alice with baby Evaline, her husband, Polly, Mattie from San Luis, Van Horn and Mimi and a friend Hobson and four children and a couple of neighbors' children, and in the evening by the tree two or three who would like to become my sons-in-law, plus neighbors with six girls and boys. We sang, played, danced. Also the jig or Irish dance and the Negro dance were performed. Only at half past ten did some guests begin to harness their horses and drive home.

Voting Rights for Women Come—"The World Progresses."

Klau, January 21st, 1912

My Dear Brother!

[…] At Christmas we had a lot of company for turkey and chicken—a festive meal—Emilie van Horn, her husband and four children, his brother-in-law Hobson, Alice and her husband and Baby Evaline, Polly, Mattie and Seline and a couple of neighbors. Singing and music and dancing around the Christmas tree, because the Christmas tree at the Wyss house always dominates the house.—Today we had as the rearguard seven neighbors' children for lunch, because there was no room for them at Christmas, and they were delighted by the music of the gramophone, after they had feasted on roast pork, sausage, cake, cooked prunes, etc.—With the new law which also gives voting rights to women—the world progresses—I receive more time-consuming work. Specifically, I have been Deputy County Clerk for many years, and every two years all voters must be newly registered, and we have in our Las Tablas voting district about 75-85 voters; earlier it was over 100, but it was reduced in order to make the Paso Robles voting district bigger. So far 40-50 had to register, because the post master in Adelaida registered as well, and so that went by, without wasting much time. I receive 10 cents per name. But now, in order to register the women, I calculate it will take much more time, because there there will be endless questions, and then to get their correct age will be another difficult issue.—In a few days comes another questionnaire from the Agricultural Department in Washington, because for the past 15 years I have been a corresponding citizen. I am supposed to know how things stand with the crops, pastureland, cattle, horses, prices etc. Inquiries are made concerning everything, even brooks, rivers, springs, wells and their depth. There is no pay for this job, but the results of the survey, and books published by the government, are sent to me free.

"Short of breath"

On April 24ᵗʰ, 1912, in a long letter to Hanneli:

It is half past eight, and we are finished with the cows and milking. I usually milk three, Seline and Polly four each, and I rotate the centrifuge ¼ hour to 20 minutes, which wears me out and makes me gasp, so that I must sit down awhile. In general, for the past year after each exertion I am short of breath, and that means: "You are getting older!"—[…] Yes, and so now you will move out of the Steinhof, and I would like to tell you again, sell what you don't need of the furniture, and in the attic are still so many old things which are only a burden for you. Away with all that!—It always has seemed to me, you should find an apartment later on in Regensdorf and then stay there.—Who plays now in the church in Otelfingen?—My wife is now going back to San Luis and wants to stay with Alice, because she has a good bathtub, with warm and cold water. I shall buy a bathtub myself and install it here in our house, because for the past six weeks she has been talking about taking longer baths. Will then her legs be all right?? Yes, I have an expensive wife! She has bought a tub of clay for $10–, then herbs, pills for so much more.—The mail is coming—now by automobile—yes, the world is making progress even here! Farewell with kisses and love,

your brother Otto

Seline and Alice

On June 13th, 1912:

I now have so little time for writing, and in the evening I am dead tired because I am in the middle of the hay harvest. I thought I had a man to help me, but he didn't come. So then last week I sat for two days on the mowing machine and cut five acres on the hillside, after which I gathered the cut hay with the horse rake, and now I am finished with making haystacks. [...]

My wife still has her more or less bad legs. She seldom gets up before 11 o'clock and now uses the natural cure system. She drinks pure California olive oil and eats only twice a day, drinks almost only water, lemonade, and buttermilk. Earlier she had had shipped to her from Chicago a dozen cases of Farnis Alpine herbal blood-invigorating healing oil, etc., and for me that always means pay, pay. It was that way from the beginning. She brought her bad legs with her, but back then it was called only wet scabs or something like that. In the afternoons she feeds the chickens and geese and gathers the eggs, from which, as her private property, she always sells whatever she can. [...]

"So I thus have a third son-in-law."

Otto, on September 27th, 1912, to Sister Hanneli:

Polly got married the day before yesterday, to a John Eduard Dodd, who used to work here.—He will stay here and will take over all work on the farm, and I think that is the best that I could do, because this way I must not always pay out salaries, and then half the work is not being done. He works well, is always early and strong and milks well and gets along well with the horses. All these are important matters on any farm. He has been going with Polly more or less for the past two years.

She herself is the biggest and strongest of my children, stronger in her hands than even I.—They are now in Los Angeles on their honeymoon, in order to see for themselves the miraculously developing Southland.—So I thus have a third son-in-law with my Polly, who is now called Mistress John Edward Dodd. He is 27 years old and a born Californian. His parents live in Cambria and came here from Kentucky in the middle of the 70's. His parents don't have much; a half brother is married, then there are two younger brothers, about 22 and 18, and a sister of about 16. He doesn't drink, also smokes a pipe, and is a good hunter and marksman. I am not worried about this marriage, and I hope I have done well.

On November 10th to brother Oskar:

Earlier I was usually the first to make the fire in the morning. Now it's Ed and soon Polly, and only when I hear the coffee mill, do I get up to come to breakfast. We have determined everything in writing for five years. We share everything. Each family receives half the farm's income, and we also share the house. For her wedding I gave Polly a three-year-old, tame mare. She will soon also ride it.

A Respectable Property.

Klau, February 7th, 1913

My Dear Brother!

We have rainy weather, and I want to use it to write to you and to make you a little better acquainted with my property, and so I have made a little map of my Bueno Vista or Klau Rancho. I have marked the brook in blue, also the springs with a blue ring. The Preimtion is the first piece of property, for which, at the time of blessed father's 70th birthday (IX, 1883), I went to San Francisco with two witnesses and signed the papers and made the payment of 2½ dollars per acre. I had there a cabin, a little house, because I had to live there for a certain time.—I could only receive the first papers for my homestead when, with the election of the Democratic President Cleveland[74] anno '84, the land reserved for the railroad was given back to the settlers, because the time to build the railroad had already expired several years earlier. So I became, and then remained, a Democrat.—I have leased the Duncan McNee land for 25 years. I know the man. He has a lot of land, was earlier in the U.S. Land Office in San Francisco, and has acquired a lot of land. He does not want to sell it. I pay 1 franc 20 per acre = $16 a year, it comes cheaper than interest and taxes, and in case he dies, I would have the prerogative to buy it, and since he is now going on eighty, I must always be ready, because you see, the brook comes in there and has over a 20 foot fall until it comes out down below in my land. I bought the 89 acres around the Buena Vista Mine from the Ticinese Ruffino Pedraita, because it was located directly across from me and has a splendid spring high up.—It made me sweat in the 90's, with the low prices for cattle and butter, to bring together the necessary interest, and with the 18, 19 or 20 cows to do all the other work and to make the butter and to get up at two or three in the morning in all kinds of weather, to work and to pack the butter, then to milk and then to drive to Paso Robles and back again and to milk again, that was a lot of work. [...] Half of the Buena Vista Mine is bushes and stone, the other half I use for grazing land. It is now again being worked a little.—The outlying land has two or three locations, and one has beautiful quicksilver stones, ore with a lot of iron in it, and is harder to burn, to reduce. Then I had the opportunity to buy the rough land cheaply, 116 acres at $4 per acre, so we are

---

[74] Stephen Grover Cleveland, President of the USA from 1885-89, fought against the corruption in his own party.

Polly on an ostrich, Los Angeles.

fencing it in along the ridge in a nearly straight line.—Now something more about the "Bell" land, which I have sketched for you. The 116 acres have no spring, but near the property line are cliffs, and if the spring on the Bell land has good water after plentiful rainfall in the winter, it too will always have water. There is nothing or little to plow, the upper part has beautiful pastureland, and I would also buy those 80 acres, if it for once were offered for less than $10 per acre. The main road, which is not marked in red, which is maintained by the County, follows the brook more or less, with two bridges on my land. The bridges are now well made and are kept in good condition. You can see, drawn in on the line between the brook and the road, the house which I built in 1899–1900. It is comfortable in the summer, but in the winter a bit chilly. My wife wanted no fireplace, because she always burned her slippers and shoes, when she tried to warm her feet. So there we have fire only in the kitchen, and that room is pretty big. Across the road is our old house, where I had the store with the post office in a corner, two rooms out back as an addition with a porch, a terrace out back beside the barnyard, where we milk. A little farther up, the old barn, which holds 12–15 tons of hay, is becoming dilapidated. Then there is the old little house, where we lived in the beginning years; it has a good fireplace and two beds for possible workers or overnight guests. On the other side of the bridge, 200 paces from here, is the school house, above that the newer bigger barn, which can hold 25 tons of hay. I use

it mainly only for young and old horses. On Alice's 40 acres is a low, big house, which George built. [...]
                                     Otto Wyss

"Everyone is only out to make money for himself."

                                                    Klau, July 2nd, 1913
My Dear Sister Hanneli!

I have just concluded my money order calculations, written out the report, and several entries are done in red with this ink, and the pen also works well, and so I am writing to you with it. A week ago my wife again went to San Luis and Los Angeles to see Doctor Schulz. I have a letter from her, saying she needs 25 dollars, and I should send her 50 more dollars. The doctor has said that last year she was not there long enough and that the disease is now breaking out also on her head. Recently both her ears began to drip and she has blemishes on her head, and also four bumps are growing again. She had three bumps on her head when she came here, she then had them cut out, and they healed. After a while they came back, and so she again went to see Dr. Glass in Paso Robles, who operated again. Then she always massaged her head, especially the bumps, but she had them again. She was able to hide them pretty well with a wig. The doctor requires 25 dollars for 11 days of care, or 11 francs per day, and she has room and board with a Miss MacDonald. Yes, that makes indeed for an expensive wife!—Selina visits her when she can. She is now working as a nurse in the hospital and has little free time.—We feed two postal horses for 12 dollars per month, besides which the post brings things, cream, canned goods, etc. for us free from and to Paso Robles. In addition, it delivers barley or oats for the horses. [...]

The telephone is a beautiful thing, but now comes again a bill for $8—since January/February—The difficulties with Japan, that Japanese should be able to buy and own no land in California, has good grounds, because racial mixing, like with the Negroes in the South, is certainly not desirable. [...]

Remain healthy and happy. I am okay when my wife is in Los Angeles. I'll be glad though when she comes back home, and with kisses and love your faithful brother
                                     Otto

                                                    New Year's Eve, 1913

We have Mattie here visiting with us since Christmas, but every evening she is at Polly's and Ed's in the old little house up on the hill and comes down only at 10 or 11 o'clock with a lantern, and by that time we are already asleep, because we usually go to bed at 9 o'clock. Outside it has been storming and raining for a week, and the last three days without stopping, slowly but steadily. My wife or Mama is sitting beside me reading. We speak little. And tomorrow Mattie goes back to San Luis, in order to go back to her job on the 2nd. I had hoped she would come down at least one evening and suggest we could sing a couple of songs, as we used to do in earlier years, but no, they don't think about how they could give us "old people" a little joy. Ed does not sing. He has never learned. He also seldom goes when a preacher comes and we have prayer, sermons, and singing. Usually 30-75 people come to the nearby school house, but he has no time. Everyone is only out to make money for himself and to get through life the best he can.

Otto in the garden.

"Happy is he who forgets what cannot be changed."

On February 8th, 1914, to Sister Hanneli:

It's Sunday again, and in the days from January 12-25 we had the biggest rains which I have seen here. Polly lives with her Eddie in her own house and is happy when I help her, because I can tell you, it is no fun when everything is cold and wet in the morning, to make a good fire for bath water in the cauldron outside, because Madame wants to bathe, to get the spots she missed with her herbal bath. We have now slaughtered the third pig. It made 220 pounds of meat, clear for sale, and I heard Mama say the day before yesterday, as we were releasing the fat drippings, that she was glad that there was not more, she had all pots and pitchers and a pail full of lard. Slaughtering is what she does best. Earlier she even made black puddings, because her brother Ruedi always went to help people slaughter their animals and then brought home scraps of meat to make into sausage. It is very good that she has experience in this area. She can thus manage things like the butcher himself. She has just now taken another sitting bath and is peeling the flakes off her legs. Her ears and head still look bad, and she still has them bandaged up. I have peace and quiet, because happy is he who forgets what cannot be changed. [...]

Mattie milking the cow Fanny.

The Automobile Begins to Replace the Horse.

Klau, February 21st, 1914

My Dear Brother!

Yesterday arrived right on time your dear letter with a check, and I extend to you my deepest thanks for your kind concern. I still have this and that to do, especially mending the roof, because the raging tornado has broken off many shingles, so that I have sent for 200 new ones and must think about reshingling the various roofs during the coming year. I shall have to decide whether I want to buy, for part of the repairs at least, galvanized sheet iron, because in case of fire in the hot summer it would be a much greater danger the way it is now. Last summer some school boys made a little fire on the way home on my land on the hill ¼ mile from the school. There was a north wind which chased the flames up to the summit of the hill, and soon came 20-30 men we had phoned for help, so that we quickly could control it. Still a watch of four to five men remained there. [...]—Horses are becoming too cheap. Autos and gasoline tractors are replacing them in many places; I sold a horse for 75 dollars, which four years ago would have brought me 150 dollars. Cattle bring good prices and with the prospect of much good fodder, nearly 1000 head were bought in Mexico and arrived here last week. I hope that they bring no sickness with them. I recently reread your instructions concerning castration and shall follow them closely. I always have clean rainwater in bottles, which I keep also for the washing of the eyes especially of horses, when it is necessary. Our spring water is all hard, limish. [...]

On March 13th, 1914, to Sister Hanneli:

[...] My daughter Seline will receive two weeks vacation and will then come home. Otherwise she seems to be content. Caretakers and nurses such as herself are not permitted to work more than eight hours, according to a new law. Ours work 10 and 12 and 14 hours; naturally I don't mean myself right now, but rather when I was younger and had to do all the work.—The day before yesterday there was an eclipse of the moon from 7-9 in the evening, precisely the best time to observe it, or early in the morning. Yesterday came your dear card with the pretty bouquet, well made; thank you very much [...]

Polly—New Post Mistress.

April 3rd. My quarterly postmaster report is ready to be mailed. The next one will perhaps be signed by my daughter Polly as Post Mistress, because she has been appointed and recommended as my successor by a post office inspector who was here. He said it was no sign of any complaint against me or any mistake I had made, just that it is the policy that between 65-70 post masters are retired. –Naturally, I shall do most of the work as usual as assistant post master, except that upon arrival of the mail Polly will then open the mailbag and sort the mail, and I shall sort the packages and newspapers. The parcels help out a lot. Since they use ⅓ more stamps, that means so much more income for us.

Recently at a school election to renew the three school administrators, Mimi was unanimously elected by eight or nine votes, and then had to accept as well the position as clerk, who has to do all the paperwork, keep all the purchases in order, and that can give George some work now and then.

On June 7th, 1914, to Brother Oskar:

The day before yesterday I was in Paso Robles in order to sign the papers for Polly's position as post mistress and to put up collateral for 500 dollars. A Mat.

Claus, whose father was previously a pastor in Creston and who in his day baptized Polly, Mattie, and Selina, was the other guarantor. [...] The recently built centrifugal house has a cement floor, on which the centrifuge stands, and is quite clean, with openings on all four sides covered with wire netting against flies. I myself made the roof this week, because I am always my own carpenter, but the work went slower than earlier, because, especially on the scaffold, you must be careful. So it will soon be finished. When the inspector comes to inspect the dairy, he will not have so much to find fault with. I have read with interest about the dedication of the University of Zurich in the Bürkli newspaper, and now the agricultural exhibition in Bern is in full swing, about which it will also report a lot, and that leads my thoughts back to my old homeland and, in my imagination, I visit nephew Fritz Schmid with you, like five years ago. Peter Stamper, who made the trip to Europe with me, suddenly died last week; heart disease was the cause of death. [...] My wife feels better, and her legs are almost healed; she still takes herbal baths and Fornis medicine. [...]

July 4th. We chatted with our daughter Seline rather much yesterday evening. She is a nurse now. She explained well that the hospital can accept up to 160 sick people, and is almost always full. The costs are 15 dollars per week in the open room and 25 dollars for your own private room. The first year she had more usual illnesses and children; the second year she was there she had operations, etc., and in the third year she was in the maternity ward, in the birth institute. Sick people come all the time. Those who die are as a rule picked up after dark. Polly and Ed are still as good as during their honeymoon, and the big strong Polly also helps Mama with washing and everything. She is always cheerful and in high spirits, and if she almost completely turns over the post office to me, she claims little more than her stamps.—Her husband Ed is always finished early with his work and milking the cows, and he is also never behind in his other work. In that respect, George Van Horn is different; he is always a little behind. [...]

The Shadow of the World War.

Klau, August 14th, 1914

My Dear Sister Hanneli!

The war and nothing but war news in the newspapers always upsets me. I cannot think clearly at all and write even less; yet we recently had Selina here for 10 days and also Mattie a couple of days and we all had a pleasant happy Sunday together, as the enclosed photos will give you an idea. [...]

We are ordered to send as little postal weight as possible to Europe, because English, German, and French steamers cannot accept mail, because of the risk, and so usually newspapers and packages are sent back to the sender. I can just not write anything decent, and the thermometer indicates 104°F or 40°C, so I shall promise you, when cooler weather comes, to chat pleasantly with you.

Otto and Seline with grandchild.

The Van Horn family

On January 10ᵗʰ, 1915 to the wife of his nephew, Ida Wyss-Diener:

Most Honored Mrs. Wyss!

With the ugly war in Europe, the uncle in California must think quite often about his sister and brothers and nephews and great-nephews in dear old Zurich. The fact that your husband and the father of your children must also go to the border in order to fulfill his duty for the dear fatherland, leaves you alone with the children, and you have much more trouble and work and concerns to watch over them all. I hope that Switzerland will no longer be threatened and pulled into the conflict, because war these days is quite gruesome and lethal.—I still am delighted with the hours which I spent in your house, the beautiful walk to Fluntern, also in the company of your father, and wish I could do it again. It would be my deepest wish that an offer of peace would come soon.

"My wife takes sit-down baths."

February 3ʳᵈ. My dear brother! A good fire in the fireplace warms us, because the sun does not, although wind and rain have stopped. Ed and Polly went fishing and just brought us a 9½-pound fine salmon. They make a good meal.—A German, Dody, is going by right now with a four-horse wagon. He says he has to pick up freight in Paso Robles. With good roads he could pick it up with two horses, but with bad ones even four have enough work to do. The last six or eight years almost no gravel has been put down, and so the red clay is almost impassable.—Then I have a good little picture of the family Van Horn, which I have enclosed for you, quite obviously a farm family showing the wagon full of children and Emilie and George on each side and the two dogs. If George were somewhat more industrious and used the farm's advantages better, he could make a lot of profit, but he doesn't even have a pig to which to feed the fallen apples and they just rot where they lie. The teacher will come next Monday, but with these bad roads she will probably receive board at Polly's house nearby and stay in a guest room with us, which brings Mama $5 a month. Polly's husband Ed must still learn when cows calve and must see to it that the placenta is fully removed. On the second day after birth you have to go in with your hand and clean it out. Since then a neighbor has helped us out for 2 dollars, because now I can no longer do it myself like earlier, because of my rheumatism.—My wife takes sit-down baths, Turkish baths and every Sunday a complete bath. For that purpose she cooks oat-straw, absinthe, fern roots, and other ingredients, and always uses Furnis blood purifier, which I have shipped here from Chicago in dozens of cases.

February 28ᵗʰ. And in San Francisco, the world fair has begun with the usual pomp and splendor.—I am also sending you a newspaper.—I still don't know whether I shall go there, because without a good friend as guide I would not mix well with the crowd. It is March 31ˢᵗ, a cold day, rain with hail and every now and then some sun.

Newspaper Article: "The German Kaiser a real Prince of Peace."

Klau, March 9ᵗʰ, 1915

My Dear Brother!

Your letter of February 15ᵗʰ has just arrived, in which you tell me about the Bethanienheim, and I am glad that you are once again recovering. The first letter from Oskar[75] frightened me, because I feared you could not survive the operation, but an operation today seems not as dangerous by far as it was 20 years ago. To be sure, I believe that here there would be more to risk, because medical people here are not yet so well prepared. [...] The Bethanienheim is, as I understand it, a private hospital of the company, and Oskar is the chief of staff there. Nurses are thus trained there in a similar way to Seline in Los Angeles; for example, she was in the maternity ward. Now she is in the operating room, and at the beginning two years ago the workday was 9–10 hours, whereas now it is only 8 hours, and the farm workers also want to implement that policy, which however has as a consequence that threshing for grain will come much higher.—Our newspapers also bring surprising news. Thus an English paper brings German news written in Gothic letters: "The German Kaiser is a true and real Prince of Peace."—"No Intentions for World Dominion" and historical interviews. Underneath it is translated into English. But there is nowhere yet any prospect of an imminent peace. Unfortunately.—Polly works well together with her Ed. He is now plowing for corn. In the meantime, when she is alone, I help to milk four or five cows, but my left hand is no longer strong. Every day I also prune trees, so one to two hours is long enough to stand on the ladder. [...]

"35 years ago I also had a little boy."

Klau, August 1ˢᵗ, 1915

My Dear Brother!

It is Sunday afternoon, 100°F and more, but now here comes a little breeze which makes the heat more bearable. It is Polly's birthday, the 22ⁿᵈ. She lives well with her husband, and he has made out a life insurance policy for Polly for

---

[75] Karl Max Oscar Wyss 1874 – 1956 was the second oldest son of brother Oskar Wyss and the chief of staff at the Bethanian Hospital in Zurich.

Otto and Seline with daughter Seline, working as a nurse.

$1500, just in case, so that she would be properly cared for in the event of his death. She expects in November a new citizen, may the child come safely and stay healthy. Then I have a little picture which brings back my memories, 35 years ago in 1880. I then also had a little boy of my own (the first one). I had sowed wheat, about 6 acres, and it was the time of year when it was ripe. A threshing machine for such a small harvest costs too much, so I made a board box on the old wagon which I had bought, mowed with the scythe in the morning until 10 o'clock, and in the afternoon and evening made haystacks with a wide fork and transported it to the barn, where I had smoothed out a level round spot, about 50 feet in diameter, with a yellow clay floor. I laid the wheat around in there and drove with two horses and wagons around up there in 110°F heat and threshed it out. I had borrowed a windmill, and my wife also helped a lot, so that we filled 35 140-pound sacks. We had chickens and pigs, so that nothing was lost, and no salaries. Naturally the years have changed everything. We now have the railroad, a mill in Paso Robles, but they accept nothing for grinding. The wheat is bought, and the meal is sold at a fixed price, only barley or oats is ground for the horses. This year then is a good wheat harvest, and the prices are good. Yes, and today six years ago I was on the steamer crossing the Atlantic which was taking me back home over the sea, back to the old homeland where I was so cordially received again. Yes it pleases me that I went back home at that time, because at present you could not undertake any such journey. [...] Yes the ugly war, and I am also glad that I am far away from it. People are saying that the local quicksilver mines are supposed to be worked again. People need it for ammunition, ignition caps, etc.—All the better then, because that would help the post office and bring everyone more pay. [...]

August 12th. A card has probably already announced to you the arrival of a 7th child of Emilie. He is supposed to be named Oscar Bernhard, and everything is fine. Mattie rides over every morning to see her with the soon to be three-year old Frank Witkosky behind her on the horse. He could fall off, couldn't he! He is a pert little boy, never yells except when he shouts with joy, and he wants to be everywhere and help. The mail now comes early by car. We now also have here more autos than horses and wagons. An Englishman, Mr. Sutton, brings it. There are many Englishmen here who do not desire American citizenship; the Swedes are also of the same opinion. [...]

Otto Wyss with grandchild.

"On a shaky ladder the highest branches make you dizzy."

December 5th

[...] Now I must answer your dear letter, thanking you for your best wishes on my birthday and name day. Yes I am now in my 70's and must admit that I get tired doing any kind of work. I myself have picked the good produce of the apple and pear trees, but only gradually, a little each day, because after one or two hours on the ladder I stopped again, and on the shaky ladder the highest branches made me dizzy.—Yes the letters now come completely open, opened once, then taped back up, and then opened again. Yes and the ugly war, you describe it quite correctly, and I always say, thank God that dear Switzerland remains and hopefully will remain spared.—Unfortunately there is still no end in sight. [...]

Seline and Otto with grandchildren Dodd.

Klau, January 28th, 1916

My Dearest Sister Hanneli!

The neighbor has borrowed my black ink and has not yet brought it back, so I'm using this (red) ink, and it flows well out of the pen. The storm wind yesterday broke about a dozen branches from the old five to six foot thick oak tree below the house, so we'll have much less shade next summer, and the probably 150 to 200-year-old tree will eventually die. The same thing also happens with the fir trees; when you plow near them, they die out, old stone-pines with long needles, with pine cones on them which are full of small nuts and which we later use to smoke our meat. [...] I'm writing here in the post office beside the fire in the fireplace, and it has just begun to snow again. On Christmas Day I went with my wife to Emilie van Horn's. We found the little ones in a merry state around the tree. George explained how, with his work on the threshing machine and on the hay press, he had again paid the rent of $100 for the upcoming year and how he had had a very good yield with the Egyptian corn he had planted, and he will plant 10 acres this year. The roast goose was also not missing at our Christmas meal, and Mimi and all the little ones sang "Merry merry Christmas," etc. [...]

Because of the War the Mine is Worked Again.

February 11th. [...] From the hill below you can hear the explosions of the blasting operations, because two men are working there in the old Buena Vista Mine and are finding really good ore. The nearby Klau Mine is sold to four men in the County, for $20,000—or 100,000 francs, to two American and two Ticinese gentlemen. They will soon begin to work, and that also will bring business to the post office. Thanks to the American ammunition manufacturing, quicksilver has risen five or six times in price, and three mines in the neighborhood are again producing quicksilver. [...]

Klau, California, February 27th, 1916

My Dear Brother!

This week came "Switzerland, Wake Up" 1914/15, and was looked at by dozens with great interest, quite especially by me and the family, then also by some local Ticinese people and by a Swede who stayed here a few days. The pictures are very good, and so many show how our soldiers make many useful and good things, and hopefully these serve their purpose of keeping foreign troops out of dear Switzerland. [...]

Otto Wyss in the garden

"Chüechli for the Herrenfasnacht."

On March 5ᵗʰ, 1916, to Sister Hanneli:

The first Sunday in March we have Herrenfasnacht, and Mama has made some "Chüechli," but she wants to make more for "d'Burefasnacht."[76] It is now your birthday, and I can ask no one whether it is the 23ʳᵈ, as I believe, so on your 58ᵗʰ birthday, I wish you the best of health and the resolve to take everything which comes your way with the best attitude possible. Whoever can do that spares himself much anger. [...]

St. Valentine's Day.

Klau, February 14ᵗʰ, 1917

My Dearest Sister Hanneli!

Now a few lines, because today is St. Valentine's Day, on which every boy sends a pretty little card to his sweetheart. Yesterday and this morning, I have sold around 50 such cards. Today there is beautiful rain, which makes the grass grow for the 12 cows which we milk, soon to be six. Ed and Polly are taking care of that this year. Everything is really fine, only Polly's little boy pulled down a coffee pot full of hot coffee from the stove and burned his face and his little right arm. He had blisters, but he is improving fast. [...]

The Boys Must Go Off to War.

Klau, September 16ᵗʰ, 1917

My Dear Brother!

We are having a rather hot Sunday, 108°F = 42°C. It is the afternoon, and there is not a breath of air. The main topic of conversation these days is naturally the conscription of our youth.[77] A former neighbor, Joe Tartaglia, who now for several years has leased a dairy near Cambria with 45 cows, has three boys in the military school, and two from here are in San Francisco, and our former postman is in the aviation corps in Texas. Two others are excused for the time being; as the youngest they are still needed on the farm. Frank Witkosky is still excused as the provider for a wife and four, soon five children; in addition, as a cattle merchant he is of course excused in order to provide supplies for the

---

[76] The days after Ash Wednesday.
[77] On April 4ᵗʰ, 1917 the USA had declared war on Germany, on December 7ᵗʰ, 1917, followed the declaration of war against Austria-Hungary.

army. Polly's husband is already 32. His youngest brother Alonzo has a wife and child and was called up, but he will probably get out of it.—Some unexpected news came from Selina, that her boy friend, William Sonntag, who has a good job with Bell Telephone Company, wants to marry her in the second week of October, and they will visit us. Selina has a good job, and she said during her visit that she often earns $5 per day. [...]

The Dodd-Wyss family with children, from left, Eroll, Shirley, Jane, James, and Raymond.

On December 15th, 1917 to my "Dear Good Brother!":

The narration of your trips has pleased me so much, and in my imagination I have again seen the Hochwacht on the Lägern, the castle, and Boppelsen. I have also read out loud everything in your letter to Mattie and Selina. They said they could understand it so much better than if they were to read it themselves. Selina came to visit us with her husband right after the wedding. Her husband, William Sonntag, is a strong, broad shouldered man, who is 6 feet tall. He explained that his father, a born Berliner with a good education, emigrated to America and first held a position as a book-keeper in Missouri, married there a Mrs. Reel, after a few more years moved to Texas, where he had a good position there as a teller in a bank, and where William had been born, had grown up and his father had died. When telephone lines were built there, he found work and has always worked as a lineman installing and maintaining such phone lines, and so has a position making 4½ dollars per day. He once broke his left arm, which is still not right, and hopes that will free him from military service. Selina now only wants to be a housewife and only seldom works as a nurse.—And scarcely was Selina settled in her new home that Mattie came to Los Angeles with a Mr. Smalling, whom she presented as her bridegroom, and asked Selina and her husband to be witnesses, and they were married.—Well, Mr. Smalling is a widower with boys of 6, 9, 12, 14 and 16. The eldest works for the railroad in San Luis. Last Sunday Mama herself wanted to go to San Miguel, and so we hitched up our old Billy to the light buggy, but he trotted slowly and about two miles from San Miguel there came a freight train puffing its black smoke, and our Billy spooked and pulled back, but Mama jumped out of the buggy and held him by the bridle bit and calmed him down with soothing words, until the train had gone by, and in half an hour we were being warmly welcomed at Mattie's house. He has a nice little house with land and a garden, a chicken coop/yard, and two to three dozen hens, windmill and water reservoir, electric light. He has a steady job with the Salinas Valley Lumber Company, sells construction wood and barley for horse feed.

Brother Oskar is Dead.

Klau, Cal. June 22nd, 1918

My Dear Nephew Hans!

It has already been two weeks since I received your letter and three days later the sad news that my own dear brother has left us and has gone over to a better life in the hereafter. It wrang my heart and the temperature at the time was 100°F, so I couldn't write. Nine years ago he had taken me up to Enzenbühl and showed me the grave of his Caroline and beside it, the spot where he would one day rest, and where he does indeed rest now; he also showed me the two graves of little Alice and Margritli, and now he is with them, as our beautiful Christian faith teaches us.—I thank you for writing to me, when you saw that he was getting worse, because I knew that I lost my brother and the best friend and advisor whom I had, and I cried and cried. […]

On August 11th, 1918 again to Nephew Hans:

[…] Tomorrow Polly and her husband, Ed. Dodd, want to go with the two boys Errol and Raymond to the coast, in order to cool off there in the salt water. Polly made herself a green swimsuit, embroidered with black borders. It goes down to her knees and shows very well her full figure. She is two inches taller than me.—I remember happily the day nine years ago when I went for a walk back home with Mr. Diener and your wife, and Mr. Diener's remarks about building and houses etc., and I said to myself, I could learn something there. Then I had a nice drive in your car and I admired the changes and revolutions in the hustle and bustle of the city, and then down in the Hard Valley we almost flew when there was a good road.—Upon my departure from Switzerland I said, should anyting happen to my brother and he is called away from this life, would you take over my small inheritance from my blessed father and administer it. At that time you promised me that you would; so I fervently hope and expect that you will do so; it is in your hands. [...]

And on October 20th, 1918 again to his "Dear Only Sister Hanneli!":

Now we are the last two of the once so happy brood of 7 children on the Steinhof in Otelfingen. Dear brother has had to endure so many pains in the last years and went to his well-deserved rest and now lies beside his dear wife Caroline. And dear sister Emma has unexpectedly quickly followed him. Nephew Hans has written me how she gradually fell asleep with her weak heart, without pain, and went to her eternal rest. Yes, I am sorry that we are so far from one another, because it would be a consolation for us if we could chat together again, be together again. [...]

Flu is Also Raging in America.

Klau, California, January 8th, 1919

My Dear only Sister Hanneli!

I am still alone, i.e., my wife is still at Mattie's, because it appears the newborn baby boy does not accept his mother's milk well. I cook for myself except at lunch. I am so sorry that the flu has made you weaker, and then it is easier to catch such a catarrh, and you can't get rid of it. Here too we had to wear handkerchiefs over our mouths and noses for about 20 days at the beginning of November, but no one became really sick, whereas in Paso Robles nearly 20 people died, especially several women with many children.—While I'm thinking about it, don't write Postmaster after my name anymore, because my daughter Polly Dodd is now the real postmaster, and I sign my letters pr. O. Wyss Ass. P.M., but just my name and Klau, California, USA is the best way to address mail here. I arranged it so that Polly learns really well all the details of post office management so that the post office will remain here, even when I am no longer here. I am also enclosing for you a good picture of our President[78] and believe that by next spring a definite peace treaty will be negotiated.—May God grant that! [...]

---

[78] Woodrow Wilson (1856–1924), President from 1913–1921.

"Nothing is as precious as the memories which we have."

On January 19th, 1919, again to Hanneli:

It is Sunday evening and I want to chat with you a little again. We had planned to go to Mattie's and Mama's, i.e., I with Polly and Ed in Ed's car to San Miguel, and then from there to Paso Robles to see Emily with her eight children, but it looked so much like rain that Ed said he didn't dare to make the trip, because on the way home, if it rains, the wheels would slide, and he could get stuck. And just now comes a beautiful warm rain, which we need. The last 14 days we had hard frost to minus 8°R. I am enclosing my letter to my wife and her answer, and a card which she sent me at Christmas. The caption, translated, means: "Nothing is as precious as the memories which we have. And since I know you are really good at telling stories which never grow old. I love to sit beside you and listen while you tell stories—about all the other Christmases which you remember so well." It should actually rime, but I am not a poet. [...]

On May 17th, 1919, again to "My Dear True Sister Hanneli!":

[...] Emily is still in Paso Robles with her 8 children. The two older ones go to high school, something like our Sekundarschule, and they are all better, because for a long time they had whooping cough. Her husband works in Santa Barbara, about 80 miles farther south in bean fields, and seeks to acquire a little place of his own of a couple acres land. Mattie is still in San Miguel, and her little boy, who had a break in his diaphragm, is again healthy. She has her own car and recently drove alone—together with her little boy—to see her husband in the oil fields, where he works, and then she came back with him. [...] Now Ed. Dodd wants to have a new house, and the old house, which I first built on the place 43 years ago, is dilapidated, so I went with Ed to Paso Robles, where we bought sawed lumber for a house of 20 x 30 feet. The lumber cost $250.—and the house well over $300.—

On all Sides New Generations of Offspring.

On September 19th to "My Dearly Loved Only Sister!":

[...] Last Sunday a week ago Ed was on the phone before day break, and by 6 o'clock in the morning Dr. Dresser was here, and two hours later Polly was delivered of an 8½ pound healthy little girl. He brought Mrs. Weidenbach as an experienced caregiver, and Polly was happy to have her. Dr. Dresser's bill was $40.—(about 200 francs) and the nurse received $2.50 per day. Thank God Polly and Baby are healthy. Polly gives her breast feeding, and she will probably be named Pauline. They are now happy to be in the new house. Ed milks only three cows once a day, and the pastureland is short, so he feeds them alfalfa. But the brook is dry, as I have never yet seen it, and the spring also gives little water for the garden, but of course there still is cauliflower, cabbage, turnips, and beans.—Alice is also expecting an addition to her family in San Luis, and I would like to pay her a visit there this fall.—Emily has bought a house and little place near Paso Robles and was involved in the Camp Meeting. She also especially helps out with singing, because she has a confident voice and leads the other singers. October 3rd. We received the news from Alice that she had given birth to an 11¼ pound healthy baby boy, who is supposed to be named Leonhard Charles, and everyone is healthy. So she has three little boys and three girls. [...]

Seline in the garden.

Seline Begins to Write Again.

Klau, December 4th, 1921

Dear Sister-in-Law!

[...]You will certainly have received my card, and yesterday your letter of November 16th arrived here, for which we sincerely thank you. Dear father said, I must write to Hanneli, when I admonished him, but he cannot do it, so I must take care of that, although writing is no longer my favorite work. My memory is becoming poor, but poor father has almost none left. You will have seen that in his last letters. It always pleases him when letters come, and he can still read everything, but he forgets it right away again. Since last New Year he has written neither letters nor cards. He no longer knows his own age. On his last birthday, he thought he was 78. Then I said no, he was 75 years old, isn't that right? In February I shall also be 70, I can still do my necessary work, but if I walk too much, I have pain again in my legs. Otherwise everything is going as usual. Ed and Polly take care of the ranch. They have four children. The youngest is eight months old. James is his name, and the eldest is 6 years old and now goes to school. Raimond is 4 years old, and Gorrli, the girl, is 2 years old. So Polly has enough to do. She gave up the post office last February; it costs more to keep than it brings in. The post office is now in the mine over there. The week before last, on Thanksgiving Day, Alice and Mattie were also here with their families. Alice has six children. The youngest is two years old. Things are going well for them; her husband runs a butcher shop and cattle business with three other partners. Mattie has been living the past two years in Templeton, 16 miles from here, where her husband is a freight agent and has to take care of the grain warehouse. She has a little boy three years old. At harvest time she helps her husband with the book keeping.—In September Seline was here on a visit. She has a good salary in Los Angeles, and she works in a doctor's office for 100 dollars a month.—Everyone is doing fine. Only Mimi is always behind. She has eight children, and they live in Paso Robles. Her eldest daughter is now out of school, is 18 years old and earns 12 dollars a week. [...]

Concerning Homesickness in old Age.

Seline writes on October 7th, 1923, to her Sister-in-Law:

You can't get father to write any more. I personally would be glad if he could take care of this task himself, but his memory is fading more and more. Nonetheless, he said yesterday he still had a good memory, when I asked him something which he could not answer. He sometimes has attacks of homesickness. A couple of days ago he went over to Polly and asked whether his sister was not there. You must pay us a visit. If traveling were not so expensive, I would come back to the old homeland for a visit myself, but I don't want to travel alone any more. Our daughter Mattie had on August 10th a premature birth, a little boy who lived only 10 hours. She is now healthy again. Selina came and took care of her. Her husband fetched me when she went to bed. On the fourth day I went back home, because I cannot leave father alone any more, even if Polly does take care of him. He is otherwise quite healthy, always has a good appetite and complains about nothing. His favorite work is still splitting a little wood for the kitchen; he no longer wants to do anything else. Sometimes he gets it into his head that he wants to go to Otelfingen, but then I tell him he must now certainly give up that plan. [...]

We are almost halfway between Paso Robles and the coast. Cajuccos 18 miles, Cambria 20 miles. Paso Robles is the nearest city where we usually do business, 15 miles. San Luis Obispo, our county seat, is 40 miles. There lives our second oldest daughter Alice. She wrote two weeks ago that they have not yet had any frost this fall. There it is warmer in winter and cooler in summer, because it is only 3-4 miles from the sea. There oranges and lemons grow in the gardens. In January and February people here already begin to plant their gardens. The narcissus and violets are by then already in bloom. We can get vegetables out of the garden the entire winter; late cauliflower begins to grow right only after the first rain. We are, as I believe dear father once said, about 2000 feet above sea level. Two years ago father had entered his 78th year in good physical health, if only his memory were better. Every winter thousands of immigrants from the east come here to Southern California, especially to Los Angeles, where every corner is full of people. The city now has over two million inhabitants. There are also oil fields there. [...]

Foot and Mouth Disease.

June 10th, 1924. For the past ten days it has been cooler, but always rather windy, which dries everything out rather much. People fear a hot summer. In addition, here in California at the end of March the foot and mouth disease broke out among out cattle, and as a result several thousand head of cattle had to be slaughtered, which nearly ruined many a farmer. Thank God it did not come to our county. The government has ordered strict measures; at every county border a creosote bath[79] has been set up, and the automobiles and other vehicles had to drive through it. The occupants must get out and also wade through it, and then they are also fumigated. [...]

Dear father helps me a little with the garden and splits the wood, but always too small. I had an accident with my left hand. Three weeks ago I tried to open a jar of preserved fruit, and then the top of the jar broke off, and a piece of glass made a deep cut about an inch long between the thumb and the index finger of my left hand, with which I was holding the glass, while I was trying to pry open the lid with a knife in my right hand. It bled a lot. Polli bound my hand, and the wound is now healing, but I shall still feel it for several weeks. I cannot yet use the hand for all work. The cut is deep, down to the knuckle. The two older boys of Polly wash my dishes and help out with small jobs; they now have vacation. I don't know whether I can take care of the garden next year. In the last three months I have lost the last of my three brothers; Gottfried

---

[79] Creosote is a distillate of beechwood tar, here used for disinfection.

in January and the two elder ones in April, then there is only one more sister alive over there. She will soon be 80 years old. [...]

October 21st, 1924. At the end of July and August we had building to do. We had to half-way tear down our house in order to escape the danger that it would fall down. It made a lot of extra work for me, and I had to be glad that my daughter came to help me. The house is now only one story, just room enough and furnished enough for us two so that we shall not freeze in winter. I am happy that it is done right and no longer wobbles. At the end of this month the Klau Post Office will cease to exist, so you must address all postal matters to Adelaida again like previously; the mine is no longer worked. It has been standing still for three months, the post master is leaving, and we don't want it any more. [...]

Otto's Last Letter.

Adelaida, California, November 25th, 1924

My Dear Sister Hanneli!

Here I am in California and am sending you these lines so that you and my loved ones will hear something from me again, and it would please me if I should soon receive an answer from you.—I am enclosing a card from Felix Tartaglia. As you can see, he is a corporal in the US Army.—We have also improved our house, and it is now warmer inside. We still have cold nights, but at midday still warm sun. It is only cold at the beginning of the night.—The oak trees have abundant acorns, and the pigs are really fat.—It will please me to hear something from Otelfingen again and especially that everyone is fine and happy. Here no one complains much. With best greetings to all who ask about me,

your brother Otto Wyss

Adelaida, November 28th, 1924

Dear Sister-in-Law!

A couple of days ago father requested paper, pen, and ink. He said he wanted to write to his sister. Naturally I immediately gave him everything. Polly was here, and we were doing the wash. We then showed him how he should begin, and so he wrote the enclosed brief letter. It was Tuesday morning. I have not got around earlier to writing, and so I want to do it now so that we can send off everything. A photograph has come into his hands, and he wants to send it to you, although I told him you don't even know this young man in the photo, but he insisted, and so I want to send along this picture. It is the oldest son of Mr. Tartaglia, who went home to Ticino four years ago. […]

February 8th, 1925. The holidays have gone by peacefully for us. We also had a Christmas tree for the children. Father received his plug of tobacco from Seline and felt slippers from Alice; we have received the thoughtfulness of all. But the best is still to come. On January 4th father became the great grandfather of a brown boy, who, as Mimi says, was born two months too early. He is alive. It was a hard birth; the doctor had to intervene with an operation. The mother is now again all right. They are still over there in San Mateo. At the beginning of next month Polly is also expecting another child. I hope that everything goes well. So there will again be more work, which sometimes almost frightens me. Otherwise everyone is well. Only my legs are now again irritated, and so I must or I should take better care of myself. You don't know what you have when you have healthy limbs. Eight days ago I entered my 74th year. I would not have believed ten years ago that I would become so old. […]

"No one has any concept of how many cars there are here in America."

March 23rd, 1925. On March 9th Polly was blessed with a baby girl, and I am glad, as is she, that it is not a boy again. Jane Ethelin is the new baby's name (Jane = Hanna). We have a year of lamentations before us, already the third winter without enough rain. In the southeastern and western part of the state everything is withered and dry, the cattle is starving, the hay is used up, and most people have no money to buy feed. The big stores are letting go part of their employees, and so there are rather many unemployed; also on the little ranches no one is being hired. The last ten years we had good salaries and good harvests and, if many people had understood the importance of saving money, the distress would not be so great, but people just live from one day to another, only from today until tomorrow in many places, and then, when bad times come, as is always the case in certain periods, then begin the howling and the moaning, and so many do not think of the fact that they themselves are to blame for their misery. If there is a single dollar left in the money jar, it goes for a car or some other sport. No one over there in Europe has any concept of how many cars there are here in America, especially in California. […]

Father is always healthy and does what he likes. He thought he ought to see about getting work in a machinery business, but he can no longer even hammer a nail without me showing him how.

Otto's Slow Dying.

Dear Sister-in-Law!

Several weeks ago I sent off a letter to you, and now unfortunately I must once again take pen in hand to inform you of the tragic event which has overtaken your dear brother and our dear father. On last Friday at half past eleven, dear father took as usual a roll of newspapers and told me he had to see someone over there, and then said bye, I'll be right back. I didn't want him to go out alone and told him I would soon have lunch prepared and he must stay, but it didn't help. He ran up the road. I called Polly, and then she ran after him and brought him back home. Then he went back down the road, with me right behind him, and I had difficulty bringing him home. He then ran around the house, and I prepared lunch, and a couple of minutes later I heard him moaning and calling for me. I ran down the steps, and a couple of steps below the house he was standing bent over on his hands and feet, and said he couldn't stand up. He had fallen down.

I tried to raise him up, but he moaned a lot. He couldn't walk. His left leg was hurting, and then I helped him to sit down on the doorstep to the bath house and told him I would call Polly and Ed to help me bring him into the house. They came right away and carried him into the house, and we were afraid he had broken his left leg. However, he said no, and we bedded him on the couch and Polly and Ed ate their dinner, and I also gave father something to eat, and then he said, "Oh, I am so glad that someone looks after me." He was pale and his left upper leg was swollen up toward the hip and we could see nothing of a break. After a while, after I had washed the dishes and wanted to see after him, he was sitting on a chair which stood near the bed, and then I told him he should have lain still. Otherwise his leg would not get better. We rubbed in some self-prepared ointment which father also always used for wounded cattle. He was tired, so we assumed it was not broken, so we didn't call the doctor.

But on the next day we had no rest. The leg was so badly swollen, and I told Polly she should call the doctor, and at two o'clock he was there on Saturday. He said it was a break, but could not determine where it was and said we should bring him to his office. He would have to uses the x-ray beams in order to determine how and where the break was located. Within an hour the ambulance was there. Father moaned a lot when they picked him up, and he made it fine to Paso Robles. A second doctor helped with the examination, and they found the upper hip joint broken and a piece of bone broken off. The doctor said he would do nothing for a couple of days. As soon as the swelling went down, he would apply a plaster cast on Wednesday. He would never be able to walk again without crutches. The doctor thought it was better to wait, because sometimes pneumonia sets in in such cases with old people, and that would be his end. He now has fever every day. We are now at Mattie's house.

It is only 6 miles from Paso Robles and so nearer the doctor. Also, this way it costs less, and Mattie is good for helping out and has more time than Polly. The worst part is, father understands no one any more and doesn't know how to give a correct answer. […]

He always pushes back the covers at night. Mattie and I have not slept much the last two nights. Mattie has now driven to Paso Robles to buy several things, including a slip cover for the mattress, because father sometimes wets the bed. I myself am not well today, and just now had to go outside and throw up. I also have a cold, but hopefully that will soon get better. I shall soon report again how things are going. […]

Seline describes the difficult care of the demanding patient, who "just no longer has any mind," but is always cared for.

On September 28ᵗʰ, 1926 Seline writes to her nephew (Dr. med. H.O. Wyss) and thanks him for his advice:

[…] For the past three weeks dear father has been a little sore from lying around, and last week the doctor gave us another medication to rub in, and then I made another salve of bacon and mustard plant, such as our old midwife back home had given us when my dear mother had to lie in bed so long, and it did help him. Father's wounds are now better. If I don't wipe him right away when he must urinate, he just lets it run on the bed, but we never let him lie wet. It is the same way with his bowel movements. He does everything in bed, and we have to do the wash every morning. He is an impatient patient. He receives good care. Mattie is like a nurse and her husband is also good. He is big and strong and can easily lift father. We don't think that father will ever again be able to walk, and the doctor says that even with crutches, he still can no longer think clearly. Otherwise he lacks for nothing. He is only bored and plays with the bedding, tears one sheet after another. I then give him a strong wool blanket, which he cannot tear. Three days ago I bought a folding chair, and Mr. Smalling brought it here from Paso Robles. It costs 4½ dollars. The day before yesterday we set him in this chair in a lying position, in order to cool off his back, on the proch in the sun. It pleased him for a couple of hours. […]

On October 8ᵗʰ to her Sister-in-Law:

[…] A neighbor's wife helps out Mattie when I am away. We must wash father sometimes three to four times a day and tidy up his room, and each time that requires two people. You must hold his hands. As soon as you touch his legs, he moans so. His back is better. He now sits in his deck-chair every afternoon. […]

On October 11th, Seline again describes Otto's condition in a detailed manner, his pains, his hygiene, and how he is cared for:

December 2nd. The year is already again approaching its end, and with our dear patient the procedure remains the same. He sits or lies beside me in his deck chair. He has no pains, if you leave his hurt leg alone. It has been swollen for a couple of weeks and has three open wounds, one inside his knee and one inside the calf on his shin bone, and another down on his ankle. It seems to me as though all impurities musts come draining out there. We must prevent his back from being chafed or sore. He can still read, but only for a few minutes, then he puts away his reading material. He always eats his meals regularly and still has strong nerves. Last week it rained a lot again. The earth has been well-softened and now it is also dark again, there is still more. The grass is growing, and at the higher elevations it is quite green. [...]

Otto Wyss in old age.

Templeton, New Year Morning, 1927

Dear Sister-in-Law

Your dear brother, our dear husband and father, seems with the New Year to want to pass over to a better homeland. The last two weeks his health has really declined. The doctor was here ten days ago and said, father has held out longer than he at first believed possible, and the New Year will soon bring him a solution to his problems. Yesterday father still ate his food correctly, but now he lies peacefully in his bed and doesn't care about food, and I shall not bother him. Perhaps he'll be better at noon. He is quite blue around his eyes. For the past week his other leg has also been swollen, and on his hips he has big wounds and on his right shoulder and below on his back from lying so much. We are doing everything to ease his last hours. I hope and pray that the Lord will soon free him. […] Mattie and her husband have been a great help to me. Mr. Smalling is coming tomorrow and is bringing Seline with him, because she wants to see her father again. Polly was up the day before yesterday to say her farewells. Mimi's oldest daughter, Alice, has again received an addition to her family, a little girl. Alice from San Luis will probably come for a visit on Sunday morning. She is getting fatter and fatter. We have rather cold nights now, and I am glad that I can heat father's room for him. We can only leave the side doors open. […]

I wish you and all in the family a blessed and happy New Year and many greetings from your sister-in-law Selina.

By the time these lines reach you, dear father will have already gone to his eternal rest.

"Now I am always missing something."

Templeton, January 5th, 1927

Dear Sister-in-Law!

It is now Wednesday at half past one, and yesterday precisely at this time we arrived home with the corpse of our dear father, in order to lay him to rest in our small cemetery beside his dear predecessors on the road to Paradise. He died on Sunday evening 15 minutes after 5 o'clock, January 2nd. Unexpectedly quickly he slumbered over without pain to his Lord, where there is no trouble and no sadness.

Seline arrived here Sunday morning with the 5 o'clock train with Mr. Smalling. She was still early enough to greet father, who was still conscious, and then to close his eyes. We then had the undertaker come, from whom, as is the custom here, you buy the coffin. He brought the hearse. I gave him the clothing, among which the last white shirt which father took home when he made his last visit to you 20 years ago, an heirloom from his blessed father. Yesterday at 11 o'clock, we went to the Lutheran-Protestant German Church in Paso Robles, where the German pastor Heusser held the funeral service. The small church was half full, the piano was played and a couple of beautiful songs sung, and then at 12 o'clock we accompanied dear father on his last trip to our old home, where our neighbors and friends were waiting for us. The pastor and his wife also came, and on the gravesite, before the coffin was sunk into the earth, the pastor held another short sermon on the text from the 14th chapter of St. John, verses 1 to 4. It was the most beautiful funeral sermon I have ever heard here, which others also said, and Mattie and her husband were very pleased. The coffin was decorated with flowers which now lie on the grave.

It was a splendid winter day yesterday. Spendid sunshine accompanied us, and to my contentment Polli and Ed had fenced in the cemetery with a good new beautiful fence, which was already my year long wish. Our daughters were all there, except for Mimi, who unfortunately because of the quarantine could not come: she sent a beautiful wreath. Her son Otto was there. Alice and her husband Francis were there. I have come back home with Mattie. We have a lot of wash and cleaning to do. Seline is also here and must go home again on Sunday. At her wish I shall go with her, because I don't like to let her travel alone in her condition. It is an 8-hour trip, and she has her little girl with her and luggage. Today there is cold air and a little sunshine.

Dear father has taken good care of me. He himself wrote the will about five years ago. Only Polly was present as a witness, and the document decrees that the children will receive their portion of the inheritance only after my death. We are talking about 160 acres of land. Polly will receive the place with 240 acres, and they have bought 90 acres from me and paid for them. What I gave her was in my own name. Polly is a proxy administrator; according to the local law she must now go before a court in San Luis in order to have the will certified. […]

I shall gladly turn all that over to Polly, because not only my memory but also my hearing have noticeably declined. In the fall I gave Mattie 200 dollars, so that she could build a porch in order to make room for father and me. Her sisters agreed to it. So everyone has received something except Seline. She says she can wait. Alice has 40 acres near our house, which her father turned over to her about 20 years ago. We have always used it and paid taxes on it. I don't know what else father decided with her about this. She will receive her portion after my death, and she received 600 dollars long ago, besides the land. Mattie and her husband took care of the funeral. He had a splendid coffin for 150 dollars. Mattie said she could not have accepted one any cheaper; included in the price is the trip from Paso Robles and the burial. May the Lord bless his soul. Now I always lack something to do, it seems to me that I have nothing more to do. Polly and Ed say it is as though everything has died since dear father departed this life. He was always running up and down the county, and back and forth, but the last couple of years he ran around too much. Now our Father in Heaven will make everything good again. I ask you to inform the family Schmid in Höngg of the death. I still have more than a half dozen letters to write. The next one is to Dr. Hans Wyss and siblings. Now I must ask you not to completely forget us in the distant future, but please do give us a sign of life. Our daughters are always interested in news from the old homeland. The warmest greetings and blessings for the newly begun New Year from Selina and Mattie and everyone here and from your sister-in-law

Selina Wyss.

"Each week we bring a bouquet of flowers to the grave."

July 8th, 1927. For the past few weeks I have been postponing my writing from one day to the next, and now, since it is too hot for me to work, I want to again give a sign of life from us. It is commercial harvest time. We can be content with the yield. There is not as much fruit as last year, but yet there is enough, and because there is moisture in the earth, the fruit is also bigger. Milking is now again almost finished. Ed and Polly have milked 18 cows, and the two older boys are also now helping. Next month they will milk four to five more. Thank God, they are all healthy; my feet are bothering me again. […]

Mattie has bought a small gravestone in San Luis for 10 dollars, which Cousin Dr. Oscar Wyss has sent us. They brought it on May 30th, National Grave Decoration Day. Mr. Smalling set it in place. Next winter we want to set out a couple of more trees on the cemetery hill. Flowers don't grow well up there, and it is too strenuous to take the water up there. Every week we bring a bouquet of flowers to the grave. […]

We recently also had a wedding in the family. Otto Van Horn, Mimi's oldest son, married on the 14th of this month a daughter here in Mattie's neighborhood in Templeton. She works there in a store. They are ten children of a poor widow. Her father was killed two years ago in a car accident. I think she is a good daughter. My grandson Otto is 21 and his wife as well. […]

In My Old Age Still on a Warship.

May 22nd, 1928. I have received your card from Comano and thank you warmly for it. I want to get out of my lazy habit of not writing and give you a brief update on our lives. There has not been much news in our family. At the beginning of March I came back home again, and since then I have been back in my old peaceful nest. Polli and the grandchildren have fixed up my house and keep me good company. Polli has much work. They milk 20 cows, and Ed is now harvesting hay. Alice has rheumatism in her legs, so that sometimes she can hardly walk. She is now in those years of life where there are all kinds of pains for women and especially for meat eaters like her. Mattie also has much work. They have built a big chicken coop and have about 1200 chickens, almost all young ones, which are now two months old. Her husband is still plagued from time to time with his stomach problems, and it will also probably never again completely stop. I want to enclose a few photographs of Selina's family. They are pretty good. Selina, her husband and two children, and their doll sitting on the chair. The older one is called Mary Mattilda and the younger one Margarit Emma. However, they call her Patzi, because she was born on Patricia Day. In March she was a year old. On New Year's Day, Mr. Smalling wanted to visit his second oldest son, who is in the navy, on the big warship New Mexico. They were stationed for a few months in Los Angeles harbor.

They wanted me to come along, and so I let myself be talked into it. It is about 15 miles to the San Pedro harbor. We had to climb into a motor boat. We had to travel about 3 miles before we reached the big warship, where we had to climb up a rather long staircase. It seemed to me like a big hotel. However, we had only an hour, in order to be back on land before nightfall. I was in a lounge, and on the first deck are the big guns. There were three more such colossuses in the harbor. I would not have believed that in my old age I would have come on such a warship. The sea was calm. Otherwise I would not have gone. I am beginning to tremble and must close. [...]

August 27th, 1928. Dear Cousin! I received your card on the 16th of this month, and I thank you for it sincerely. The same mail brought me the announcement of death of your unfortunate nephew Karl Thomas,[80] whose tragic death we all deeply regret. Of course, he could not be buried at home. Polly's oldest son Errol, about a year ago, had dislocated his upper hip bone upon falling out of bed, which momentarily hurt him. However, he did not want to go to the doctor. It was not broken, he said, but afterwards it continued to hurt him, and on New Year they took Errol to Paso Robles to Dr. Bänker, who said the hip bone was dislocated, and he reset it and recommended caution. But Errol is a lively, fine-boned boy. In October he will be 13 years old. He is not at all big for his age. So he had dislocated his hip for the third time, and for the past couple of months he has begun to limp. Last month they took him to San Luis and had him examined with x-rays, whereby it was determined that the upper leg bone was somewhat strained and it was feared that atrophy of the bones could set in. Polly and Ed then went with Errol to a specialist in San Francisco, who recommended to try a plaster cast for the present.. We had feared an operation would be necessary, but hopefully everything will heal up. [...]

August 13th, 1930. Last Sunday we had a family party at my daughter Mattie's house in Templeton. Alice and Frank Witcosky were celebrating their 20th wedding anniversary and at the same time the farewell party for Smalling's son. All our daughters with their families were there, including Selina from Los Angeles, and so it was a merry family gathering. A couple of friends of Alice were also there from San Luis. We had a picnic in front of the house, where tables were set up. Eveli, Alice's daughter, and her husband were also there, about thirty people altogether. The families are all healthy and happy, only Frank and Alice are no longer completely content. He has too much competition in his business, but you just have to take things like that as they come. The two younger daughters of Emilie also have boy friends. [...]

---

[80] Karl O.T. Thomas (1907–1928) was the oldest son of Alma Thomas Wyss, the youngest daughter of Professor Oskar Wyss-Kienast. Karl was killed in a mountain accident.

The Trip to the Chinese Doctor.

February 4th, 1931. I have been at Mattie's in Templeton for the past three weeks, and am again writing with bandaged hands. My health is declining more and more. It seems to me that everything I eat breaks out on my skin. However, I eat mainly green vegetables and fruit only. Two weeks ago Mattie went with me to San Luis to a Chinese doctor. They cure only with herbs. This doctor gave me herbs for two weeks. Each morning I must drink a cup of tea and also wash off the sore spots with this tea. My back and breast are also sore, as well as my neck and head. It is now somewhat better. That is certainly the last remedy I shall try. No one knows what I have already suffered for thirty years with this plague. The last six months were the worst, and I look like a prisoner with my bandaged hands. My 80th birthday was on last Sunday, and I hope that I must not complete my 80th year, if I don't get better and I don't receive relief from my suffering. Children and grandchildren are thank God healthy, and all have work. [...]

Unemployment.

October 13th, 1932. Dear Cousin! Your letter arrived two weeks ago and I thank you for it. I am always glad when news comes here from Europe. You plan, so it seems, to stay in the canton of Ticino, if you don't actually become Italian. According to the news reports, it looks as if Europe is arming again for a new war. Hopefully it will not break out. We all had enough of the last one. Among you all in dear old Switzerland, it must now also be bad, many unemployed people. Here in America unemployment is increasing more and more, but there are thank God enough provisions in the country for the population. In our family, at present everyone is working, only George Van Horn has been at home for several weeks, but will soon receive work again. [...]

General Strike.

July 16th, 1934. Last Sunday Agnes was here with her two youngest sons and her oldest daughter with family (Alice). They had to leave the city of San Francisco, in order not to starve, because of the general strike. The strikers allow no groceries to enter the city, and so the people can buy no bread and meat or anything else. They fear revolution. Alice and her husband and the children will stay with their mother in Paso Robles until the strike is over. The poor people, who cannot flee the city, are now in a sad situation. If a motor lorry comes into the city, it has to turn right back around, or is overturned. It is restless everywhere in the country, no peace. Here at home we don't notice much. Alice Witcosky's oldest son will also soon marry. [...]

"Weddings are popping up all over the place."

October 25ᵗʰ, 1934. Last Saturday Agnes, who has been here two days, had to leave again in order to begin her work in the evening. She got work in King City. Through a car accident four people were hurt, which happens here in this country daily, and now that drinking is allowed again, people are getting used to these mutilations. The lady by whom Agnes was employed is now again so well-established that she can manage without her help. Agnes told me she would have liked it better in Switzerland, but everything is so expensive there. Railroads and groceries. She said that in Ticino, where they live, it is beautiful, but she is happiest in California. In several days I'll go to Templeton to Mattie's to spend the coldest season. I don't think that I can go to Los Angeles. Last month Agnes's third oldest brother got married. His name is Morris, and in August Alice's oldest boy got married in the Catholic church. Weddings are popping up all over the place. […]

Seline's Last Letter.

Adelaida, May 22ⁿᵈ, 1935

Dear Cousin and Family!

I have received your letter and cards, today the one from the 7ᵗʰ of this month. Thanks for the news from over there. I am always pleased to receive news. The card for Polly has also arrived today. I am especially pleased that your dear wife and daughter Margarith are doing well, and hope that they can enjoy the best health at this beautiful season of the year, when everything is turning green and is blooming. There is a locust tree near the house, now in full bloom. Its white blossoms hang down like grapes and look in at the window, a splendid sight to see. The children are again looking forward to the upcoming vacation. Next week, Jimmy told me yesterday, he is graduating from grammar school, then next term he can go to high school in Paso Robles with his brother Raymond and his sister Shirly. Raymond will be finished next year. The youngest child Janice is entering the fifth grade. She is now the only one of Polly's children who attends the elementary school here. How time does fly. Mattie's son Bernard will also be beginning his last year of high school this summer, and must now help his father during the vacation in the office and warehouse. Emilie's second youngest son Oskar will also be graduating from high school in two weeks and is looking for work, a job. As soon as school is out, Emily wants to move to King City, where her youngest daughter lives. She must give up her laundry business, she says, because she is getting rheumatism in her arms. Three weeks ago Agnes was also here on a visit. She has a job in an army hospital where her husband is in the military. Emily still has only the two youngest who are not married. Oskar says he will soon get a job. The middle son and the youngest daughter of Alice, Margarith, are also graduating from high school. So only the youngest, Leonard, still remains at home.

As I have gathered from the newspapers, you have also had a revolution in Ticino. People always fear war, but then I say they certainly have no money for war. They still have enough debts from the last war. Let's hope for the best. The Klau mine is being worked again, not on a big scale, but there are about half a dozen men at work there. Polly sells milk and eggs in the mines, and Ed and the boys, wood. Things are going fine for me, as well as I can expect, but I can no longer do anything in the garden. My legs no longer want to carry me, and my arms and hands are also not better, so I must be content if I can still help myself. With warm greetings to you and to your loved ones from us all,
                    your old aunt Seline Wyss

Funeral Notice

DIED

Sept. 25th, 1935
In Templeton, California

Seline S. Wyss

A Native of Zurich, Switzerland
Aged 83 years, 7 months, 24 days

Beloved mother, of Mrs. Seline Sonntag of Los Angeles; Mrs. Matilda Smalling of Templeton; Mrs. Pauline Dodd of Adelaida; Mrs. Emelie Van Horn of King City; Mrs. Alice Witcosky of San Luis Obispo.

Funeral services will be held Saturday, Sept. 28th, 1935, at 10 a. m., at the Paso Robles Lutheran Church, with Rev. Theo. F. Haeuser officiating, under direction of Kuehl Funeral Home.

Friends and relatives respectfully invited.

Funeral notice of Seline Wyss.

Index